Greenhill Books

Allied Submarine Attacks
of World War Two

This book is published under the auspices of the
Bibliothek für Zeitgeschichte (Library of Contemporary History), Stuttgart

Allied Submarine Attacks of World War Two

European Theatre of Operations 1939–1945

Jürgen Rohwer

with special assistance from Miss J. S. Kay and I. N. Venkov

GREENHILL BOOKS, LONDON

Greenhill Books

Allied Submarine Attacks of World War Two
First published 1997 by Greenhill Books, Park House, 1 Russell Gardens,
London NW11 9NN

British Library Cataloguing in Publication Data
Rohwer, Jurgen
Allied submarine attacks of World War Two : European theatre of
operations, 1939–1945
1.World War, 1939–1945 – Naval operations – Submarine
I.Title
940.5'451

ISBN 1-85367-274-2

Edited and designed by Roger Chesneau
Printed and bound in Great Britain by Butler & Tanner, Frome, Somerset

Contents

Preface

The *Bibliothek für Zeitgeschichte* (Library of Contemporary History) was founded in 1915 as the *Weltkriegsbücherei* (World War Library) with the object of collecting together all printed material relating to the Great War. After the war the library was commissioned to expand its coverage to include the period before and after the war, and finally the entire twentieth century, and to compile a complete inventory of its stock. Each year since 1921 it has published the *Bücherschau der Weltkriegsbücherei*, listing its new acquisitions of international literature relating to political developments and conflicts since about 1900; in 1934 this was expanded to include the *Bibliographische Vierteljahreshefte der Weltkriegsbücherei*, containing bibliographic reviews on specific topics of contemporary history.

With the destruction of the library building during an air raid in 1944 the publication of these listings was interrupted after 24 volumes of the *Bücherschau* and 40 of the *Vierteljahreshefte*. The library resumed its work as the *Bibliothek für Zeitgeschichte* after the return in 1949 of about 75 per cent of the book collection, which had in the meantime been transferred to the United States. In 1953 the *Bücherschau* was started again; it was renamed *Jahresbibliographie* in 1960. The most recent volume, No 66, covers the acquisition year 1994. Special bibliographies were resumed in 1962 with the *Schriften der Bibliothek für Zeitgeschichte*, which now runs to more than 30 volumes.

To complement its predominantly bibliographical publications, the library began in 1968 to edit a *Chronology of the War at Sea* for the Second World War, which has already appeared in two updated and revised English-language editions, in 1972–74 and 1992, the latter published by Greenhill Books and the United States Naval Institute. Also appearing in 1968 was *Submarine Successes of the Axis Powers in the Second World War*, republished in a revised English-language edition in 1983 by the US Naval Institute. The intention was to list all successes reported by German, Italian, Japanese, Finnish and Romanian submarines during the Second World War and compare these reports with the recorded losses and damage to Allied and neutral ships. The present title is a companion volume recording the attacks made by all Allied submarines in the European Theatre on Axis or neutral shipping.

It is hoped that this work will be a valuable and reliable tool for checking facts based on scarce source material that have hitherto been unavailable in one volume.

Jürgen Rohwer
Stuttgart, March 1996

Introduction & Acknowledgements

Since the end of the Second World War I have been trying to collect data about the fates, and especially the losses, of German warships, U-boats, auxiliaries and merchant ships. The data was at first compiled using information from the Hamburg 'Navy House', the Headquarters of the German Minesweeping Administration, and the Allied office responsible for notifying relatives of the deaths of personnel who had died in combat. From 1946 to 1948 I contacted groups of German former naval officers who worked in Bremerhaven for the US Naval History Division and in Brunsbüttel for the Historical Section of the British Admiralty on the history of German naval operations. Most helpful during this time were Commander Claus Henning von Grumbkow at the 'Navy House', Vice-Admiral Friedrich Ruge at Bremerhaven, Captain Günter Hessler at Brunsbüttel and Lieutenant-Commander Werner Techand in the Allied office. In addition I made contact with Ludwig Dinklage, who had saved from his office at the end of the war data concerning German merchant ships.

While it was possible, with the documentary materials they provided, to compare in most cases the attack reports made by German ships and U-boats with the Allied losses, a similar comparison of the German losses with Allied attack reports initially proved more difficult. Moreover, because on the Axis side not only German but also Italian and many former enemy and neutral ships were lost or damaged, it was necessary to obtain the published lists of the losses from these countries which appeared from the late 1940s to the mid 1950s. Very helpful in this connection were the directors of the Italian *Ufficio Storico della Marina Militare*, *Ammiraglio di Squadra* Giuseppe Fioravanzo and his successors *Ammiraglio di Squadra* Aldo Cocchia, *Contrammiraglio* Vittorio Tognelli and *Contrammiraglio* Alberto Donato. For the Finnish losses I obtained many details from Lieutenant-Commander Erkki Ainamo, for Swedish losses from

Commander Karl-Erik Westerlund, for Norwegian losses from *Orlogskaptein* E. A. Steen and for French losses from *Capitaine de Vaisseau* Claude Huan. Also of great assistance were L. L. von Münching, who provided me not only with details of Dutch losses but also with volumes of the *Weekly Naval Notes*, a secret British wartime publication containing many reports of British submarine attacks; and, later, Paul Scarceriaux, the editor of the journal *The Belgian Shiplover*. Last but not least, I obtained a great deal of information from my Swiss friend Jürg Meister.

Thus I began in the mid-1950s to collect data about Allied submarine attacks to compare them with the losses and damage reports on the Axis side. In order to obtain more information I began an intensive exchange of correspondence with the Allied naval historical organisations. In Great Britain assistance came from the members of the Naval Historical Branch, Rear-Admiral R. M. Bellairs, Commander M. G. Saunders, Lieutenant-Commanders P. K. Kemp, H. C. Beaumont and J. D. Lawson; and especially Rear-Admiral P. N. Buckley (himself a submariner), who provided me with a copy of a list of British submarine successes as assessed after the war. It was also important to obtain details of the other Allied navies which employed submarines in the European Theatre. Data for French submarines came from *Médicin en Chef* Hervé Cras of the *Service Historique de la Marine* in Paris, for Norwegian submarines from *Orlogskaptein* Steen and for Dutch submarines from L. L. von Münching.

Soviet submarines were more of a problem. Some details could be established from German radio intelligence sources made available by the mentioned Bremerhaven group. Some information was forthcoming when, in a short period of *glasnost* in the early 1960s, several memoirs of Soviet submariners appeared, and I also benefited from correspondence in 1962–63 with the then head of the Historical Section of the Soviet

Navy, Captain 1st Class V. I. Achkasov. I originally intended to include details of the submarine war against Japanese shipping in the Pacific and Indian Oceans and obtained from my good contacts in Japan, especially Rear-Admiral Sakamoto of the Office of History of the Japanese Self-Defense Forces, a copy of the important volume *The Imperial Japanese Navy in World War II*, prepared by the Military History Section of the US Far East Command and containing detailed listings of all Japanese losses and damage, to compare this with the well-known list published by the US Joint Army-Navy Assessment Committee on Japanese naval and merchant shipping losses. As a result of long correspondence with the members of the Historical Division of the US Navy—Rear-Admiral Ernest M. Eller and especially Captain F. Kent Loomis—and later with Dr Dean Allard, Bernard Cavalcante and Kathleen Lloyd, it was possible to correct many mistakes contained in these lists. However, when I learned about the work of John D. Alden on *US Submarine Attacks During World War II*, a companion volume to my *Axis Submarine Successes*, I was glad to abandon this part of my project—which in any case had been put to one side from the mid-1960s because of pressure of work and also because it remained difficult to obtain the necessary British and Soviet data. Some effort was continued in respect of Soviet submarines because of the many articles and publications I was preparing about the Soviet Navy, based, for the Soviet side, on publications by Soviet authors like Captain 1st Class Professor V. I. Dmitriev and a number of submariners.

Many discrepancies remained in our publications, hindering progress on the companion work for Allied submarines in the European Theatre. This changed suddenly after 1990 when, at a meeting of the International Commission of Military History in Madrid, personal contact was made with the Head of Archives of the Soviet General Staff, Colonel Igor Venkov, and his assistant, Major Oleg Starkov. In 1993 Colonel Venkov provided me with copies of the three volumes of the *History of Soviet Submarine Operations*, prepared by a team under Vice-Admiral G. I. Shchedrin in 1969–70 and containing a complete list of all torpedo attacks with very detailed information. In addition, since 1991 the journal *Morskoj Sbornik* has published a monthly chronology with many details concerning submarine operations. It was now possible to compare losses and damage in the Arctic, the Baltic and the Black Sea more precisely with the German and other sources. Work on *Allied Submarine Attacks* could resume.

Now it was necessary to obtain details of British submarine activities, which up to this time were also inaccessible to the private individual. Fortunately my long-standing contact with the Naval Historical Section and its head, David J. Brown, and with the great expert Robert Coppock, helped me to get in touch with HMS *Dolphin*, the Submarine Museum at Gosport. There Gus Britton was able to provide me with copies of the official history of British (and Allied) submarines in home waters and the Mediterranean. Because the information provided was not as comprehensive as that found in the Soviet sources, I was asked to get in touch with Miss J. S. Kay in London, who had for many years worked on British submarine operations. Such was her generosity that it was at last possible to complete the listings for British submarines; the details in this book are to a great extent based on her findings.

Data for the Allied submarines working under British authority were checked with *Captaine de Vaisseau* Claude Huan for the French submarines, with *Dozent Dr habil* J. W. Dyskant for the Polish, with Dr. P. C. van Royan for the Dutch, with Professor Olav Riste for the Norwegian, with Major-General Photios Marmigidis for the Greek and with John D. Alden for the US submarines operating in the Bay of Biscay. For Soviet submarine operations, additional assistance has come from correspondence with experts in Soviet naval history Ralph Erikson in Phoenix, Arizona, *Capitaine de Vaisseau* Claude Huan in Paris and Jürg Meister in Montpellier. From the former Soviet side I was provided with much additional information by Professor A. V. Basov in Moscow, Professor V. I. Dmitriev in St Petersburg, M. E. Morozov in Moscow, A. Ovcharenko in Kiev and I. V. Ustimenko in Mikhailinskii, Belorus. Questions about Swedish and Finnish losses were answered by Lieutenant-Colonel Stellan Bojerud of Stockholm and Commodore Erik Wihtol of Helsinki.

I know that a book such as this is never without error or omission, and I therefore ask all readers who find discrepancies to send me a note so that changes can be made. I thank all those mentioned, and those unmentioned experts and ship enthusiasts who have helped me to complete this work. Lastly, I thank my patient publisher Lionel Leventhal.

Prof. Dr Jürgen Rohwer
Am Sonnenhang 49
D-71384 Weinstadt
Germany

Explanatory Notes

In order to present the maximum amount of data in the minimum amount of space, the tables that follow have been grouped in five parts according to the main theatres of Allied submarine operations in Europe: the Arctic; British Home Waters from the Lofoten Islands to the Biscay; the Baltic; the Black Sea; and the Mediterranean. Finally, one page is given over to Soviet operations in the Pacific in the last weeks of the war, which John D. Alden was unable to include in his volume.

Each part starts with a report on the sources consulted. The entries are arranged chronologically by date and time, provided the time of the start of the attack is known. Each table contains columns at the top, numbered from 1 to 17. In the columns the data are presented in abbreviated form as follows.

Column 1

Date and time of the start of the attack or first shot, according to the submarine's report. The two numbers preceding the slash specify the date of the month mentioned above; the four numbers following the slash give the time according to the 24-hour clock as reported by the submarine.

Column 2

Nationality of the submarine. Abbreviations used are as follows:

am	=	American
br	=	British
fr	=	French
gr	=	Greek
nl	=	Dutch
nw	=	Norwegian
pl	=	Polish
sj	=	Soviet

Column 3

Number or name of the submarine. In 1942 new British submarines had only 'P' numbers, but they received names in 1943. The boats' final names are generally given, although in the Notes and the Index both the 'P' numbers and names are quoted.

Column 4

Family name of the commanding officer. The initials of the first names and the ranks are, where known, given in the Index.

Column 5

Target designated by the submarine. Warships, together with their estimated standard displacements in long tons, are shown in italics:

BB	=	Battleship
CA	=	Heavy Cruiser
CL	=	Light Cruiser
CM	=	Minelaying Cruiser
DD	=	Destroyer
DL	=	Destroyer Leader
LC	=	Landing Craft
PC	=	Submarine-Chaser
PE	=	Corvette
PF	=	Frigate
PG	=	Gunboat
PM	=	Ocean Minesweeper
PR	=	Coastal or Motor Minesweeper

PS	=	Sloop
PT	=	Motor Torpedo Boat
SS	=	Submarine
TB	=	Torpedoboat

Auxiliary ships, together with their estimated sizes in gross registered tons (grt), all begin with the letter 'A' and are shown in roman type:

ACL	=	Armed Merchant Cruiser
ACM	=	Auxiliary Minelayer
AD	=	Destroyer Depot Ship
AG	=	Special Ship
AH	=	Hospital Ship
AK	=	Naval Transport
AM	=	Depot Ship for Motor Minesweepers
AMS	=	Depot Ship for Motor Minesweepers
AMX	=	Mine Counter Measures Ship
AN	=	Netlayer
AO	=	Naval Oiler
APC	=	Auxiliary Anti/Submarine Vessel or Auxiliary Patrol Vessel
APG	=	Auxiliary Gunboat
APM	=	Auxiliary Minesweeper
APY	=	Patrol Yacht
AR	=	Repair Ship
ARS	=	Salvage Vessel
AS	=	Submarine Depot Ship
IX	=	Unclassified auxiliary vessel

Merchant ships, together with their estimated sizes in gross registered tons (grt), all begin with a hyphen (-) and are shown in roman type:

-Bg	=	Barge
-D	=	Steamer
-Dc	=	Coastal lSteamer
-Df	=	Steam Trawler
-Dock	=	Floating Dock
-DP	=	Steam Liner (Passenger)

-DT	=	Steam Tanker
-M	=	Motorship
-Mbt	=	Motorboat
-Mf	=	Motor Trawler
-MP	=	Motorship Liner (Passenger ship)
-MT	=	Motor Tanker
-S	=	Sailing Vessel
-T	=	Tanker
-TBg	=	Tug with Towed Barge
-Tg	=	Tug
-Y	=	Yacht

A dash (–) in Column 5 indicates that the submarine was lost before it could report an attack.

Column 6

In italics, standard tonnage in long tons; in roman type, gross registered tons (grt). The symbol '...' indicates that the tonnage or grt is not known.

Column 7

Reported result of the attack:

+	=	sunk
+?	=	probably sunk
=	=	damaged
=§	=	damaged beyond repair
=?	=	probably damaged
/	=	missed
/?	=	assumed missed
?	=	result of attack questionable
P	=	taken as a prize

Column 8

Weapon used by the submarine:

1-T	=	number of torpedoes fired
-T	=	torpedoes, but number unknown
TA	=	torpedo and artillery/gunfire

A	=	artillery/gunfire
50M	=	number of mines laid
M	=	mines laid, but number unknown
LM	=	limpet mines attached
Psc	=	taken as a prize and scuttled
S	=	demolition charge
Sc	=	scuttled
P	=	prize crew embarked
R	=	ramming

nw	=	Norwegian
pa	=	Panamanian
pt	=	Portuguese
ru	=	Romanian
sj	=	Soviet
sp	=	Spanish
sw	=	Swedish
sz	=	Swiss
tu	=	Turkish
un	=	Hungarian

Column 9

Position of attack according to the submarine report, if known, with latitude/longitude or otherwise quoting the nearest landmark, if possible with the distance from it in nautical miles and the direction.

Column 10

Date/time as reported by the attacked ship. An entry reading, for example, 20.10.M shows the date when the ship was hit by a mine laid on the date given in Column 1.

Column 11

Nationality of the attacked ship. Abbreviations used are as follows:

be	=	Belgian
br	=	British
bu	=	Bulgarian
ca	=	Canadian
da	=	Danish
dt	=	German
es	=	Estonian
fi	=	Finnish
fr	=	French
it	=	Italian
jg	=	Yugoslavian
jp	=	Japanese
le	=	Latvian
nl	=	Dutch

Column 12

Type of ship attacked. For the abbreviations used, see Column 5.

Column 13

Name of the ship attacked. Warship names are shown in italics, auxiliaries and merchant ships in roman type. Names within parentheses indicate ships attacked but not hit; their size is included if known. Data given within square brackets relate to ships which have sometimes erroneously been considered to have been lost to submarine attack; details of the actual fates of these ships are given in the footnotes. Names accompanied by an asterix (*) are former names of attacked ships.

Column 14

The standard tonnage of the attacked ship is quoted in italics, gross registered tonnage in roman type. A dash (–) indicates that the ship was missed and undamaged.

Column 15

Result of the attack. See Column 7.

Column 16

Position of the attack as reported by the attacked ship, as described in Column 9.

Column 17

Number reference given for the Notes below.

I. Arctic

This chapter contains only the attacks that took place in the operational area of the Soviet Northern Fleet north and east of the Lofoten Islands. The few attacks made by British submarines in this area are also included. The sources used are as follows.

Soviet

'Velikaya Otechestvennaya, Den' za dnem. Iz khroniki boevykh dejstvij VMF v Ijunya 1941–Mae 1945 gg', in *Morskoj sbornik*, 6/1991–5/1995.

Khronika Velikoj Otechestvennoj vojny Sovetskogo Soyuza na Severnom morskom teatro. Edited by NKVMF SSSR, Ministerstvo Vooruzhennykh Sil SSSR, Voenno-Morskoe ministerstvo Soyuza SSR/Morskoj generalnyj shtab. Vols 1–8. Moskva: Voenizdat, 1945–50. This material was not accessible before the period of *glasnost*.

Boevaya deyatel'nost' podvodnykh lodok Voenno-Morskogo Flota SSSR v Velikuyu Otechestvennuyu vojnu 1941–45 gg. Edited by G. I. Shchedrin et al. Vol. I: *Podvodnye lodki Severnom flota . . .* Moskva: Voenizdat, 1969. Not accessible before the period of *glasnost*.

Dmitriev, V. I. *Atakujut podvodniki*. Moskva: Voenizdat, 1964.

Huan, Claude: *La marine soviétique en guerre*. Vol. I: Arctique. Paris: Economica, 1991

The several monographs, memoirs, articles and 'epic' stories published prior to 1988 provided some information but have been rendered obsolete by more recent publications and are therefore not mentioned.

Additional information was received via correspondence with the following experts: Professor V. I. Dmitriev, St Petersburg; Rolf Erikson, Phoenix, USA; *Capitaine de Vaisseau* Claude Huan, Paris; and A. Ovcharenko, Kiev, Ukraine

British

Naval Staff History, Second World War. Submarines. Vol. I: Operations in Home, Northern and Atlantic Waters (Including the Operations of Allied Submarines). London: Historical Section, Admiralty, 1953. Not accessible prior to 1990.

Correspondence with Gus Britton, HMS Dolphin, Gosport; and Miss J. S. Kay, London.

German

Kriegstagebuch der Seekriegsleitung 1939–1945. Edited by Werner Rahn, Gerhard Schreiber and Hansgeorg Maierhöfer. Herford/Hamburg: Mittler & Sohn, Vols 22–66, 1990–96.

Kriegstagebuch Admiral Polarküste 1941–1945. Original in Bundesarchiv/Militärarchiv, Freiburg.

For shipping losses on the German side the following sources were used:

Gröner, Erich. *Die deutschen Kriegsschiffe 1815–1945*. Continued and edited by Dieter Jung and Martin Maas. Vols 1–8/2 and Index. München/Bonn: Bernard & Graefe, 1982–94.

Dinklage, Ludwig, and Witthöft, H. J. *Die deutsche Handelsflotte 1939–1945*. Vols 1–2. Göttingen: Musterschmidt, 1970–71. (Studien und Dokumente zur Geschichte des Zweiten Weltkrieges, Bd.5a/b.)

Krigsforliste Norske Skip, 3 September 1939–8 Mai 1945. Edited by Sjoefartskontoret. Oslo: Groendal & Sons, 1949.

1	2	3	4	5	6	7	8	9	10	11	12	13	14	15	16	17
JUNE 1941																
27/1806	sj	SC-401	Moiseyev	APC	500	/	1-T	Bukten/Vardö								
JULY 1941																
07/	sj	M-174	Yegorov, N. E.	-D		/?	-T	Vardö	07/				–	/	70°21N/31°10E	1
14/12..	sj	SC-401	Moiseyev	-D		/	1-T	Vardö								
14/1628	sj	SC-402	Stolbov	-D	6000	+	2-T	Honningsvaag	14/1545	dt	-D	(Hanau/5892)	–	/	70°57N/25°50E	2
15/0510	sj	SC-401	Moiseyev	APM		+	2-T	Kibergsneset	15/	dt	APC	(UJ177, UJ178)	–	/	70°03N/30°10E	3
AUGUST 1941																
10/0007	sj	K-2	Utkin	APM		/	A	Tanafjord								4
10/2045	sj	K-2	Utkin	-D		/	2TA	Tanafjord	10/	nw	-D	(Stanja/1845)	–	/	Kongsfjord	5
13/07..	sj	K-2	Utkin	-D	5000	+?	2TA	Gamvik	13/	dt	-D	(Hansa/276)	–	/	70°57N/27°10E	6
13/1337	sj	K-2	Utkin	APM		/	1-T	Gamvik								7
13/1416	sj	K-2	Utkin	APM		=	A	Tanafjord								8
17/0730	br	TIGRIS	Bone	-D	6000	+	-T	70°58N/26°48E	17/	nw	-D	Haakon Jarl	1492	+	71°03N/26°43E	
19/0930	br	TRIDENT	Sladen	-D	5000	=	-TA	71°01N/24°34E	19/	dt	-D	Levante	4769	=	Lopphavet	9
19/2300	sj	D-3	Konstantinovich	-D		/	1-T	Persfjord								10
21/1345	sj	M-172	Fisanovich	-D	8000	+	1-T	Liinahamaari	21/1300	dt	-D	(Monsun/6950)	–	/	Liinahamaari	11
22/1500	br	TRIDENT	Sladen	-D	3030	+	-T	70°12N/21°05E	22/1500	dt	-D	Ostpreussen	3030	+	Kvaenangenfjord	
23/1400	sj	M-172	Fisanovich	APY	1500	+	1-T	N Liinahamaari	22/2300	dt	AH	(A.v.Humboldt/686)	–	/	69°45N/31°30E	12
23/							1-T		*23/1110*	*dt*	*SS*	*(U752)*	–	/	*70°27N/30°30E*	
27/1218	sj	SC-402	Stolbov	-D		/	2-T	Nordkyn								
29/0606	sj	SC-402	Stolbov	-Tg		/	1-T	Laksefjord								
30/1714	br	TRIDENT	Sladen	-D	3000	+	2-T	70°27N/21°55E	30/1715	dt	-D	Donau II	2931	+	70°35N/21°45E	
30/1715	br	TRIDENT	Sladen	-D	1500	?	2-T	70°27N/21°55E	30/1715	dt	-D	Bahia Laura	8561	+	70°35N/21°45E	
31/1528	sj	SC-402	Stolbov	-T		/	2-T	Kjoellefjord	*31/*	*dt*	*DD*	(*Hans Lody*, convoy)	–	/	Polarkste	13

(1) Submerged submarine observed.
(2) One torpedo detonated against the harbour pier, one torpedo beached.
(3) One torpedo passed ahead. 36 depth charges dropped.
(4) *K-21* fired 8 × 100mm shells. The ship hid in a fjord.
(5) No torpedo was observed. The ship was not hit by gunfire.
(6) A torpedo was observed but missed. No hits by gunfire.
(7) Attack continued with gunfire but no hit achieved.

(8) 15 × 100mm shells fired.
(9) Torpedo missed; shell hits on bridge and funnel.
(10) Attack not observed.
(11) One torpedo detonated at the pier ahead of the ship.
(12) One torpedo detonated against the shore.
(13) One torpedo observed but no hit.

1	2	3	4	5	6	7	8	9	10	11	12	13	14	15	16	17

SEPTEMBER 1941

1	2	3	4	5	6	7	8	9	10	11	12	13	14	15	16	17
03/0759	sj	SC-422	Malyshev, A. K.	-D		/	1-T	Vardö								
03/									03/1456	dt	*SS*	*(U451)*	–	/	*35m N Kildin*	*1*
03/1932	sj	SC-422	Malyshev, A. K.	-D		/	1-T	Vardö								
05/18..	sj	SC-422	Malyshev, A. K.	APM		/	1-T	Omgang								
05/1922	sj	SC-422	Malyshev, A. K.	-D		/	1-T	Omgang								
10/0808	sj	K-2	Utkin				18M	Vardö								2
12/									12/0039	dt	APC	*(NT 05/Togo/Otra)*	–	/	N Vardö	3
12/0845	sj	SC-422	Malyshev, A. K.	-D	6000	+	3-T	Tanafjord	12/0730	nw	-D	Ottar Jarl	1459	+	70°57N/29°00E	
12/1034	sj	K-2	Utkin	-D	6000	+	26A	76°36N/30°43E	12/0945	nw	-D	(Lofoten/1571)	–	/	NW Vardö	4
12/1331	sj	SC-422	Malyshev, A. K.	-D		/	1-T	Tanafjord								
12/1715	sj	SC-422	Malyshev, A. K.	-D		+	3-T	Tanafjord	12/1735	nw	-D	(Tanahorn/336)	–	/	Tanafjord	5
13/1110	br	TIGRIS	Bone	-D	2000	+	-T	70°50N/23°57E	13/1110	nw	-D	Richard With	905	+	70°50N/23°57E	
13/	sj	M-171	Starikov	-D		+	2-T	Liinahamaari								6
14/1740	sj	M-172	Fisanovich	-D	3000	+	1-T	Bokfjord	14/1720	nw	-D	(Ornulf/80)	–	/	Varangerfjord	7
15/	sj	K-2	Utkin	-Df		?	A		15/0730	nw	-Df	(...)	–	/	NW Vardö	
15/	br	TIGRIS	Bone	-D		/	4-T	Lopphavet	15/	dt	-D	(Bessheim/1774)	–	/	Lopphavet	
17/1236	br	TIGRIS	Bone	-D	3000	=	4-T	10m SW Loppa	17/	dt	-D	(Convoy *R 152*)	–	/	70°21N/21°10E	8
23/	br	TRIDENT?	Sladen						23/	dt	-D	(Weser/999)	–	/	70°21N/21°30E	9
26/1125	sj	D-3	Konstantinovich	-D	2000	+	2-T	Kongsfjord								10
26/1736	sj	M-174	Yegorov, N. E.	-D	5000	+	2-T	Liinahamaari	26/1635	dt	-D	(Aldebaran/7896)	–	/	Liinahamaari	11
27/0200	br	TRIDENT	Sladen	-D	1000	+	-T	Rolvsoy-Sound	26/2348	dt	APC	UJ1201/F.D.33	527	+	AC 7279	
27/1230	sj	D-3	Konstantinovich	-T	1500	+	3-T	Gamvik/Tanafj.	27/							12
30/1001	br	TRIDENT	Sladen	-D	4000	+	3-T	71°03N/24°34E	30/	dt	AH	(Birka/1000)	–	/	AC 7286	13
30/1355	sj	D-3	Konstantinovich	-D	3200	+	3-T	Tanafjord								14

(1) One torpedo missed.

(2) No losses or damage on this barrage.

(3) Two torpedoes observed.

(4) 26 × 100m shells fired, four shots observed, no hits. German Ar 196 aircraft dropped depth charges.

(5) Torpedo attack reported.

(6) Attack reported in memoirs of CO but not observed.

(7) One torpedo passed behind the vessel. The claimed Norwegian steamer *Renöy*/287 in fact survived the war.

(8) Torpedoes observed but all missed.

(9) Torpedo attack reported but no hits.

(10) The attack made by *D-3* was not observed.

(11) Two torpedoes detonated at the pier. *Aldebaran*/7896, *Mimona*/1147 and *Ch. Sending*/3076 were not hit.

(12) There was one unescorted tanker westbound. No attack reported.

(13) The torpedoes missed the ship.

(14) There were two unescorted transports eastbound but no attack was reported.

1	2	3	4	5	6	7	8	9	10	11	12	13	14	15	16	17
OCTOBER 1941																
02/1402	sj	M-171	Starikov	-D	6000	+	2-T	Liinahamaari	02/	nw	-D	(Mimona/1147)	–	/	Liinahamaari	1
02/1402	sj	M-171	Starikov	-D	3000	+	"	Liinahamaari	02/	nw	-D	(Ch. Sending/3076)	–	/	Liinahamaari	1
03/0737	sj	M-176	Bondarevich	-D	5000	+	2-T	Lille Ekkeroy								2
08/0937	sj	M-175	Melkadze	-D	5000	+	1-T	Havingsberg								2
11/	br	TIGRIS	Bone	-D	2000	=?	4-T	North Cape	11/	dt	-D	(Konvoi-Ost)	–	/		3
11/	br	TIGRIS	Bone	-D	2000	=?	"	North Cape	11/	dt	-D	(Konvoi-Ost)	–	/		3
11/	br	TIGRIS	Bone	-D	2000	=?	"	North Cape	11/	dt	-D	(Konvoi-Ost)	–	/		3
11/1425	sj	D-3	Konstantinovich	-D	5000	+	3-T	Kongsfjord								2
14/1021	br	TIGRIS	Bone	-D	5000	+	3-T	71°05N/27°10E	14/	dt	-D	(Mimona, Tugela)	–	/	71°03N/27°10E	4
14/1021	br	TIGRIS	Bone	-D	3000	+	3-T	71°05N/27°10E	14/	nw	-D	(Havbris)	–	/	71°03N/27°10E	4
17/1628	sj	SC-402	Stolbov	-D	4000	+	4-T	70°20N/22°30E	17/1035	nw	-D	Vesteraalen	682	+	Soroy/Nufsfjord	
27/	sj	K-1	Avgustinovich				6-M	Mageroy-Sund	08.11.M	dt	-D	Flottbek	1930	+	70°56N/25°43E	
29/	sj	K-1	Avgustinovich				7-M	Breisund								5
29/	sj	K-23	Potapov				20M	Kirkenes	05.11.M	*dt*	*PM*	*M22*	*685*	*=*	*Bokfjord–Einfjord*	6
									15.02.M	nw	-D	Birk	3664	+	Kirkenes	6
NOVEMBER 1941																
02/1326	sj	SC-421	Lunin	-D	4000	+	2-T	70°20N/20°30E	02/	dt	-D	(João Pessoa/3023)	–	/	Lopphavet	7
03/0825	br	TRIDENT	Sladen	-D	4000	+	-T	70°58N/26°58E	03/0930	dt	APC	UJ1213 (Rau IV)	354	+	71°03N/26°10E	7
03/0825	br	TRIDENT	Sladen	-D	2000	=	"	70°58N/26°58E	03/0930	dt	-D	(Altkirch/4713)	–	/	71°03N/26°10E	7
07/0321	br	TRIDENT	Sladen	-D	2000	+	3-T	71°06N/26°57E	07/	dt	AM	(MRS 3/Bali, 1428)	–	/		8
09/1653	sj	SC-421	Lunin	-D	10000	+	2-T	Bergsfjord	09/	dt	-D	(Weissenburg/6281)	–	/	Lopphavet	9
09/19..	sj	K-21	Zhukov	-D		/	2-T	Hammerfest								10

(1) Two torpedoes hit only the shore. The APC *Togo* dropped D/Cs.
(2) Attacks not observed.
(3) Three hits claimed but not observed.
(4) *Tigris* reported three ships hit but there were three explosions on the rocks.
(5) *K-1* claimed that the steamer *Androméda*/658, estimated at 6,000t, hit a mine. The ship was stranded in a storm on 23.11.41.

(6) Six other mines were swept on 11.11.41.
(7) *SC-421* claimed *UJ1213*, but the attack missed *João Pessoa*. *UJ1213* was sunk by *Trident*.
(8) *Flottbek*/1930 was in fact sunk on 8.11.41 on a mine laid by *K-1*.
(9) *Weissenburg* was missed aft by one torpedo.
(10) Attack not observed.

1	2	3	4	5	6	7	8	9	10	11	12	13	14	15	16	17
NOVEMBER 1941 *continued*																
10/	sj	K-21	Zhukov				10M	70°51N/24°20E								1
10/1242	sj	SC-421	Lunin	-D	4000	+	2-T	70°09N/21°12E	10/1150	dt	-D	(Weissenburg/6281)	–	/	70°49N/21°12E	2
11/	sj	K-21	Zhukov				10M	Hammerfest	21.11.M	dt	-D	Bessheim	1774	+	70°39N/23°38E	
									09.07.M	dt	APC	UJ1110/F.D.6	510	+	70°39N/23°38E	
12/1420	sj	K-21	Zhukov	-D	4000	+	3-T	70°43N/24°04E 1	2/1336	dt	APC	(V6109/Nordwind)	–	/	Kvaloy	3
12/1429	sj	K-21	Zhukov	-D	5000	=	2-T	Kvaloy					–	/		3
15/1519	sj	M-171	Starikov	-T	8000	+	2-T	Kirkenes								4
18/1045	br	SEALION	Colvin	-T		+	A	71°00N/27°01E	18/1045	nw	-T	Vesco	331	+	70°57N/26°50E	
19/	sj	K-23	Potapov				6-M	Bergsfjorden								
19/	sj	K-23	Potapov				5-M	Okolo/Sillen								
20/	sj	K-23	Potapov				5-M	Frakfjord								
20/	sj	K-23	Potapov				4-M	Kvaenangenfjord								
22/0120	br	SEAWOLF	Raikes	-D	1774	+	-T	3.5m Syltefjord					–	/		5
23/	sj	K-3	Malofeyev				10M	Reinoysund	30.01.M	nw	-D	Ingoy	327	+	Maasoy	
23/	sj	K-3	Malofeyev				10M	Mageroysund	09.07.M	dt	APC	UJ1110/F.D.6	527	+	73°39N/23°38E	
24/0030	br	SEAWOLF	Raikes	-D	4000	=	-T	70°30N/30°30E	24/	dt	-D	(Asuncion,Grazi-ella,Wendingen)	–	/	Syltefjord	6
24/0030	br	SEAWOLF	Raikes	-D	4000	+?	"	70°30N/30°30E					–	/	Syltefjord	6
26/0544	sj	K-23	Potapov	APM	800	+	15A	70°25N/22°00E	26/	nw	-Df	(Start/...)	–	/	Lopphavet	7
28/1402	sj	D-3	Bibeyev	-D	6000	+	3-T	70°54N/26°15E	28/1344	dt	APM	(Convoy)	–	/		8

(1) The claim of the German steamer *Rigel*/3828 for this barrage was untrue: the ship was sunk on 27.11.44 in an RAF attack off Bodö. The barrage was swept without loss.

(2) *Weissenburg* was missed by one torpedo aft.

(3) Two torpedoes missed.

(4) One hit reported. Attack not observed.

(5) *Bessheim* was in fact sunk the day before on a mine laid by *K-21*.

(6) *Bahia* was damaged and beached on 7.12.41 at Varberg, and salvaged and sunk on 22.4.44 off Lister by the Norwegian submarine *Ula*.

(7) 15 × 100mm shells fired, 12 shots observed. *Start* was not damaged, but seven crewmen were wounded by splinters.

(8) Eastbound convoy with two APMs did not observe the attack.

1	2	3	4	5	6	7	8	9	10	11	12	13	14	15	16	17
DECEMBER 1941																
03/1328	sj	K-3	Malofeyev	-D	6000	+	4-T	70°48N/24°00E	03/1230	dt	-D	(Altkirch/4713)	–	/	70°51N/23°50E	1
03/1507	sj	K-3	Malofeyev	APC		+	39A	70°54N/23°46E	03/1430	dt	APC	UJ1708/Faröer	470	+	S Rolvsoy	1
03/1514	sj	K-3	Malofeyev	APC		+	"	S Rolvsoy	03/1507	dt	APC	(UJ1403, UJ1413)	–	/	S Rolvsoy	1
05/1253	sj	D-3	Bibeyev	-D	8000	+	4-T	70°59N/26°36E	05/	dt	-D	(Leuna/6856 et al)	–	/	Kongsfjord	2
05/1340	sj	M-171	Starikov	-T	4000	+	2-T	70°30N/30°58E	05/	dt	-D	(Convoy)	–	/		3
05/1435	br	SEALION	Colvin	-D	638	+	-T	71°07N/27°54E	05/	nw	-D	Island	638	+	Mehavn/Tanafjord	
06/1358	sj	D-3	Bibeyev	-D	10000	+	3-T	Laksfjord	06/1305	dt	-M	(Moshill/2959 ea)	–	/		4
09/	sj	K-22	Kotelnikov				12M	Rolvsoy								5
09/	sj	K-22	Kotelnikov				8M	Sommelsund								
09/0855	sj	K-22	Kotelnikov	-D	5000	+	1TA	Rolvsoysund	09/0730	nw	-Df	(Veidingen/200)	–	/	Reinoy/Ullsfjord	6
11/0855	sj	K-22	Kotelnikov	-D	350	+	A	Kvaloy	11/1400	nw	-Df	...	...	+	N Mylingen	7
11/15..	sj	K-22	Kotelnikov	-TBg	400	+	A	Kvaloy	11/1400	nw	-Df	...	...	+	N Mylingen	7
13/1356	sj	SC-421	Lunin	-D	5000	+	4-T	70°30N/30°55E	13/	nw	-D	(Mimona/1147)	–	/	Persfjord	8
16/	sj	K-1	Avgustinovich				5M	Ullsfjord	26.12.M	nw	-D	Kong Ring	1994	+	Ullsfjord	9
16/	sj	K-1	Avgustinovich				7M	Vannsund	26.12.M	nw	-D	Inger Nielsen	1862	+	Ullsfjord	9
17/	sj	K-1	Avgustinovich				4M	Kogsund	26.12.M	nw	-D	Kong Dag	1862	=	Ullsfjord	9
17/	sj	K-1	Avgustinovich				4M	Lyngenfjord								9

(1) *K-3*, with the divisional commander, Captain 2nd Class Gadzhiev, on board, made an unsuccessful submerged attack against *Altkirch*, and when attacked by the A/S vessels surfaced and sank *UJ1708* in a gun duel with 39 × 100mm and 47 × 45mm shells, but the two other ships were not hit. The German ships had only a light AA armament against the 2 × 100mm and 2 × 45mm guns of *K-3*.

(2) An eastbound convoy with the steamers *Leuna* and *Feodosia*/3075 and two APMs did not observe the attack.

(3) Attack not observed.

(4) The Norwegian motor vessel *Abraham Lincoln*/5740 was at the time in New York. The attack missed the steamers *Moshill* and *Ringar*/5013 with two escorts and was not observed.

(5) The German steamer *Steinbek*/2185 was in fact sunk in error by the German *U134* in AC 8148 on 9.12.41.

(6) The torpedo missed. Of 23 × 45mm shells fired, ten were observed, but missed.

(7) *K-22* claimed one tug, one barge and one small motor boat sunk with 20 × 100mm and 54 × 45mm shells. According to German reports, one barge and two unidentified Norwegian fishing vessels were sunk.

(8) No torpedo observed.

(9) It is unclear on which of the four minefields the losses and damage occurred.

1	2	3	4	5	6	7	8	9	10	11	12	13	14	15	16	17

DECEMBER 1941 *continued*

1	2	3	4	5	6	7	8	9	10	11	12	13	14	15	16	17
18/1919	sj	SC-403	Kovalenko, S. I.	-D		=	4-T	Porsangerfjord								1
18/1927	sj	SC-403	Kovalenko, S. I.	APC		=	2-T	Porsangerfjord								1
18/2321	sj	SC-404	Ivanov, V. A.	-D		?		N Norway								2
21/1354	sj	M-174	Yegorov, N. E.	-D	7000	+	1-T	70°04N/30°32E	21/1306	dt	-D	Emshörn	4301	+	Varangerfjord	
22/1808	sj	SC-403	Kovalenko, S. I.	-D	10000	+	2-T	70°50N/26°00E	22/	nw	-D	(Ingoy/327)	–	/	Honningsvaag	3
22/1808	sj	SC-403	Kovalenko, S. I.	APC		+	"	70°50N/26°00E								3
28/1228	sj	K-1	Avgustinovich	-D	4000	+	2-T	70°23N/22°26E								4
29/1937	sj	SC-404	Ivanov, V. A.	-D	5000	+	2-T	71°06N/28°39E	29/	dt	APM	(M1505, M1503)	–	/	Tanafjord	5
29/2003	sj	SC-401	Moiseyev	-D	3000	+	4-T	Bosfjord								6

JANUARY 1942

1	2	3	4	5	6	7	8	9	10	11	12	13	14	15	16	17
06/	sj	K-23	Potapov				11M	Porsangerfjord	30.01.M	nw	-D	Ingoy	327	+	71°06N/25°00	
07/0038	sj	SC-401	Moiseyev	-D	8000	+	3-T	Helnes								7
07/	sj	K-23	Potapov				9M	Porsangerfjord								
10/1523	sj	S-102	Gorodnichii	-D	2000	+	2-T	70°30N/30°55E					–	/		8
12/	sj	K-21	Zhukov	-Mbt		+	A	Lopphavet								9
13/0858	sj	K-21	Zhukov	-D	4000	+	2-T	70°50N/23°50E	13/	dt	-D	(Fechenheim/8116)	–	/	S Rolvsoy	10
14/1039	sj	S-102	Gorodnichii	-D	8000	+	4-T	70°37N/30°32E	14/0940	dt	-D	Türkheim/ *Fagervik	1904	+	70°33N/30°50E	11
14/1039	sj	S-102	Gorodnichii	-D	5000	+	"	70°37N/30°32E								11

(1) Attack not observed.
(2) Attack not observed.
(3) Claimed double success, but two torpedoes detonated on the rocks.
(4) One ship, one escort reported; no German observation.
(5) Two torpedoes missed, eight D/Cs dropped.
(6) Attack not observed.
(7) The claimed German APC *V5103/Blitz*, ex *Poseidon/223* was not sunk. *Blitz* was really *V5101* and survived the war; *V5103/Taifun/Isflora/149* was sunk on 9.8.42 off Lervik in a collision.

(8) The German steamer *Walter Ohlrogge/1994* was in fact sunk on 21.1.42 off Sogvaar in South Norway by mine. Attack on westbound convoy not observed.
(9) Attack not reported.
(10) Convoy with *Fechenheim*, Norwegian steamer *Tyrifjord/3080* and four escorts observed surface-running torpedoes, which were evaded; the escorts dropped ten D/Cs.
(11) Convoy with two ships and three escorts. Submarine heard two detonations, but only *Türkheim*, ex Swedish *Fagervik*, was sunk.

1	2	3	4	5	6	7	8	9	10	11	12	13	14	15	16	17
JANUARY 1942 *continued*																
17/1130	sj						?	70°58N/26°35E	17/	dt	-D	(Convoy)	–	/	Nordkyn	1
18/1302	sj	SC-422	Malyshev, A. K.	-D	800	+	2-T	70°04N/28°25E								2
19/1131	sj	K-23	Potapov	-D	4000	+	2TA	70°59N/26°43E	19/1100	nw	-D	Soroy	506	+	Svaerholt	3
19/1503	sj	K-22	Kotelnikov	-D	3000	+	3-T	70°49N/29°20E	19/	nw	-D	Mimona (wreck)	1147	=	Berlevaag	4
19/1514	sj	K-22	Kotelnikov	-D	3000	/	3TA	70°49N/29°20E				"				4
19/1525	sj	K-22	Kotelnikov	APC	700	+	31A	70°49N/29°20E	19/1550	nw	-Df	Vaaland	106	+	Berlevaag	4
19/1546	sj	K-22	Kotelnikov	-D	5000	=	"	70°49N/29°20E								4
21/1853	sj	K-21	Zhukov	-Tg		+	A	71°09N/24°35E	21/2200	nw	-Df	...	...	+	NW Ingoy	5
21/1853	sj	K-21	Zhukov	-Df		+	"	71°09N/24°35E								5
22/	sj	K-22	Kotelnikov	*SS*		?	A	*Helnes*								6
23/1111	sj	SC-422	Malyshev, A. K.	-D	8000	+	3-T	71°11N/27°40E	23/	dt	-D	(España/7465)	–	/	Nordkyn	7
26/15..	sj	SC-422	Malyshev, A. K.	-Mbt		+	S	71°09N/24°35E	26/1345	nw	-Df	...	...	+	S Slettnes	8
26/2030	sj	SC-421	Lunin	-D	8000	+	4-T	71°00N/27°05E	26/	dt	-D	(N. Schiaffino/4974)	–	/	North Cape	9
26/2219	sj	SC-422	Malyshev, A. K.	-D	4000	/	/	Tanafjord								10
27/0528	sj	M-171	Starikov	-D	4000	+	2-T	70°36N/30°35E	27/				–	/		10
27/1030	sj	SC-422	Malyshev, A. K.	-D	6000	+	2-T	71°01N/28°25E	27/	dt	APC	(UJ1706, UJ1707)	–	/	Nordkyn	11

(1) Eastbound convoy. One explosion reported.

(2) Unescorted coastal transport, westbound. No attack observed.

(3) Two torpedoes missed, then the submarine attacked with gunfire: 31 × 100mm shells were fired and the ship was set ablaze.

(4) The claimed German *Mimona*/1147 was beached on 11.1.42 and became a total loss. *K-22* first fired three, then one, and then two torpedoes, which missed, and then attacked with gunfire, causing the wreck to blaze. Then a gun attack was made on a patrol vessel and the Norwegian trawler *Vaaland* was hit and set on fire, followed by an attack with gunfire against an unidentified ship. 50 × 100mm shells were fired in all.

(5) An unidentified Norwegian fishing vessel was sunk by 2 × 100mm shells.

(6) *K-22* reported attacking a U-boat with gunfire but this was not reported by German sources.

(7) Convoy with *España*, *Hedwig*/1288, *Karin*/1453 and four escorts observed one torpedo that missed.

(8) One unidentified Norwegian fishing vessel was sunk by charges after a gun attack with 2 × 45mm shells. The crew were taken prisoner.

(9) Convoy with *Nicoline Schiaffino*, *Lumme*/1730, the hospital ship *Fasan*/1075 and three escorts observed four torpedoes that missed.

(10) Surface night attack by *SC-422* against eastbound convoy frustrated; three D/Cs. On radio report *M-171* came into contact but torpedoes missed the unidentified ships.

(11) The APCs *UJ1706*, *UJ1707* and *V6111/Franke/Larwood* evaded one surface-running torpedo.

1	2	3	4	5	6	7	8	9	10	11	12	13	14	15	16	17
FEBRUARY 1942																
01/1247	sj	SC-421	Lunin	-D	10000	+	2-T	70°55N/26°05E	01/	dt	CM	(*Brummer*, M1501)	–	/	Laksfjord	1
05/1402	sj	SC-421	Lunin	-D	6000	+	3-T	70°54N/26°02E	05/1309	dt	-D	Konsul Schulte	2975	+	Porsangerfjord	
05/									*05/1609*	*dt*	*DD*	*(Theodor Riedel)*	–	/	*Polar coast*	
06/1634	sj	S-101	Vekke	-D	5000	+	2-T	70°47N/29°25E	06/	nw	-D	Mimona (wreck)	(1147	+)	Berlevaag	2
15/	sj	K-1	Avgustinovich				13M	Tanafjord								
18/	sj	SC-403	Kovalenko, S. I.			/	?	71°00N/26°20E	18/2340	dt	CM	(*Brummer*, M1503)	–	/	70°57N/26°10E	3
19/	sj	SC-402	Stolbov	-D		/	2-T	Porsangerfjord	19/	dt	-D	(Oldendorf/1953)	–	/	70°33N/30°50E	4
27/1230	sj	SC-402	Stolbov	-D	8000	+	2-T	Svaerholtklubb	27/1412	dt	APC	NM01/Vandale	392	+	Svaerholtkl.	
27/1507	sj	SC-402	Stolbov	-D	6000	+	2-T	Svaerholtklubb						–	/		5
MARCH 1942																
03/1735	sj	SC-402	Stolbov	APM		?	1-T	Porsangerfjord	03/1625	dt	APC	(UJ1105, UJ1102)	–	/	Laksfjord	6
14/1340	sj	D-3	Bibeyev	APC	800	+	2-T	Tanafjord	14/1238	dt	APM	(M1504)	–	/	NE Sletnes	7
16/1512	sj	M-173	Terekhin	-D	3500	+	1-T	Varangerfjord									8
18/	br	SEAWOLF	Raikes	SS		/	-T	Arctic									
20/1319	sj	M-171	Starikov	APM		+	1-T	70°09N/30°40E									9
22/0745	sj	M-171	Starikov	*SS*		=	*1-T*	*70°5N/30°40E*									9

(1) Unit with minelayer *Brummer/Olav Tryggvason*, *M1501* and *M1502* reported three torpedoes that missed.

(2) *Mimona* was beached on 10.1.42 and damaged by *K-22* on 19.1.42. The torpedo fired by *S-101* hit the wreck.

(3) The attack was frustrated by *M1503*, which lightly rammed *SC403* and captured the CO, but the submarine returned, damaged, to base.

(4) Convoy with *Oldendorf*, *Inger Johanne/1202*, *UJ1205* and *UJ1214* observed a torpedo which missed, and the UJs dropped D/Cs.

(5) The claimed APC *V6117/Cherusker* was sunk on 6.12.42 by a mine laid by *K-1*.

(6) The UJs observed one torpedo ahead and dropped 16 D/Cs. The submarine was damaged and escorted home by *K-21*.

(7) *D-3* attacked a unit with the minelayers *Brummer* and *Cobra* and four escorts. *M1504* evaded one torpedo. 22 D/Cs were dropped.

(8) The claimed German steamer *Utlandshörn/2643* sank on a TKA-laid mine at 69°41´N/31°27´E on 16.3.42. The loss of the Finnish steamer *Petsamo/4596* did not occur at this time and place.

(9) *M-171* reported one or two explosions but these were not observed.

1	2	3	4	5	6	7	8	9	10	11	12	13	14	15	16	17
MARCH 1942 *continued*																
26/	sj	M-176	Bondarevich	-D	10000	+	2-T	Komagsnes								1
28/1538	sj	SC-421	Vidyayev	-D	5000	+	4-T	Laksfjord	28/1432	dt	-M	(Moshill/2959)	–	/	Laksfjord	2
29/0650	sj	M-171	Starikov	SS		=?	2-T	70°12N/31°15E								3
31/1003	sj	K-21	Lunin	-D	7000	+	6-T	Syltefjord	31/	dt	-D	(Admiral Karl Hering)	–	/	Syltefjord	4
31/1202	sj	SC-404	Ivanov, V. A.	-D	5500	+	2-T	Tanafjord	31/	dt	-D	(Admiral Karl Hering/1436)	–	/	Syltefjord	5
APRIL 1942																
01/1351	sj	M-176	Bondarevich	-D	3500	+	1-T	Sturskaer					–	/		6
01/1827	sj	SC-404	Ivanov, V. A	-D	10500	+	3-T	Makkaur	01/1823	dt	-D	Michael/Kangars	2723	+	70°45N/30°10E	6
03/1351	sj	M-176	Bondarevich	-D	5000	+	1-T	Komagsnes								7
03/1923	sj	K-22	Kotelnikov	APC	800	+	2-T	71°32N/27°52E	03/1845	dt	APM	(M1505)	–	/	Sletnes	8
03/1940	sj	K-22	Kotelnikov	-D	8000	+	1-T	71°32N/27°52E					–	/		8
06/	sj	K-1	Avgustinovich				10M	Kvaenangenfjord	08.04.M	dt	-D	Kurzesee	734	+	70°06N/21°00E	9
07/1647	sj	M-173	Terekhin	-D	7000	+	2-T	Persfjord					–	/		10
08/	sj	K-1	Avgustinovich				10M	Kvaenangenfjord	23.05.M	dt	-D	Asuncion	2454	+	70°17N/21°21E	9
09/	sj	M-174	Yegorov, N. E.	-D		+	-T	Kirkenes	09/	dt	-D	(Dollart/534)	–	/	Kirkenes	11
10/1415	sj	M-176	Bondarevich	-D	8000	+	2-T	Varangerfjord	10/1643							12

(1) Attack not observed.

(2) Eastbound convoy with *Moshill*, *Georg L. M. Russ*/2980 and three escorts observed four torpedoes that missed.

(3) *M171* reported one small explosion; no German observation.

(4) Westbound convoy with *Admiral Karl Hering*, *Almora*/2522, *Oleum*/475 and four escorts observed two torpedoes that missed. *K-21* reported three explosions.

(5) The same convoy as in Note 4. *UJ1104* observed one torpedo that missed sinking ahead of the convoy.

(6) The claimed *Kangars* is the same ship as *Michael*, which was sunk by *SC-404*.

(7) This attack is possibly the same as that on 1.4.42. Not observed.

(8) *K-22* reported one transport and one of three minesweepers sunk: these were actually the APMs *M1505* and *M1506*. *M1508* evaded three torpedoes and attacked the submarine with guns and 34 D/Cs.

(9) It is not known for certain on what barrage laid by *K-1* the two ships sank.

(10) Attack not observed.

(11) Convoy with *Dollart* and *Feiestein*/461 and two escorts. Torpedoes not observed.

(12) Westbound convoy. Attack not observed.

1	2	3	4	5	6	7	8	9	10	11	12	13	14	15	16	17
APRIL 1942 *continued*																
12/0949	sj	M-172	Fisanovich	-D	8000	+	2-T	Sturskaer	12/	dt	-D	(Convoy)	–	/		1
14/0727	sj	M-173	Terekhin	-T	10000	+	2-T	Sturskaer	14/	dt	-D	(Convoy)	–	/		2
15/0857	sj	M-172	Fisanovich	-D	4000	+	1-T	Lille Ekkeroy	15/0813	dt	-D	(Oleum/475)	–	/	Ekkeroy	3
15/	sj	K-2	Utkin				20M	Vardö	29.11.M	dt	-D	Akka	2646	=	Varangerfjord	
19/	sj	SC-401	Moiseyev	-D	4000	+	-T	Tanafjord	19/	dt	-D	(Forbach/7999)	–	/	Tanafjord	4
20/0638	sj	M-172	Fisanovich	-T	5000	+	1-T	Kibergsneset	*20/0545*	*dt*	*PM*	*(M251)*	–	/	*S Vardö*	5
20/1455	sj	M-171	Starikov	-D	6000	+	2-T	Harbaken	20/1400	dt	-D	(Petropolis/4845)	–	/	Syltefjord	6
22/0933	sj	M-173	Terekhin	-D	12000	+	2-T	Syltefjord	22/0815	dt	-D	Blankenese	3236	+	70°32N/30°47E	7
23/	sj	SC-401	Moiseyev	–			T	Tanafjord	23/0556	nw	-D	Stensaas	1359	+	71°04N/28°20E	8
23/	sj	SC-401	Moiseyev	–			3-T	Tanafjord	23/1014	dt	APC	(UJ1110)	–	/	N Vardö	9
26/0549	sj	M-176	Bondarevich	-D	10000	+	2-T	Varangerfjord					–	/		10
29/1950	sj	M-171	Starikov	-D	9000	+	2-T	Varangerfjord	29/1830	dt	-D	Curityba	4969	=	70°07N/30°34E	
MAY 1942																
02/1738	sj	K-2	Utkin	-D	6000	+	4-T	Tanafjord								11
02/2115	sj	D-3	Bibeyev	-D	6000	=	2-T	Harbaken	02/1644	dt	-D	(Iris/3232)	–	/	E Kjolnes LT	12
11/0722	sj	M-172	Fisanovich	-D	12000	+	2-T	Salknes	11/	dt	-D	(Hartmut/2713)	–	/	Varangerfjord	13

(1) Eastbound convoy with one merchant ship and two escorts. No German observation.

(2) Westbound convoy with two ships and two escorts. No German observation.

(3) Eastbound convoy with *Oleum*, *Nogat*/1337, *Lowas*/1891 and three escorts. One torpedo missed *UJ1109*; 22 D/Cs dropped.

(4) Radio report on 23 April. Convoy with *Forbach* and two escorts. *M251* observed one torpedo which missed; 13 D/Cs dropped.

(5) *M172* reported two hits. Eastbound convoy. Torpedo observed aft of *M251*; 14 D/Cs dropped. The claimed *Ange Schiaffino* was the same ship as *Blankenese* (see 22 April entry).

(6) Eastbound convoy with *Petropolis* and three escorts. One torpedo observed which missed.

(7) *Blankenese* (ex *Ange Schiaffino*).

(8) *SC-401* reported two attacks on 23 April by radio.

(9) The attack was made by *SC-401*. *UJ1110* reported three torpedoes which missed. *SC-401* may have been sunk in error by two Soviet MTBs on 25.4.42.

(10) Attack not observed.

(11) Attack not observed.

(12) Convoy with *Iris*, *Algol*/976 and three escorts. Three torpedoes missed, 56 D/Cs dropped.

(13) Convoy with *Hartmut*, *Skjerstad*/593 and four escorts. Torpedoes not observed.

1	2	3	4	5	6	7	8	9	10	11	12	13	14	15	16	17
MAY 1942 *continued*																
12/1030	sj	K-23	Potapov	-D	6000	+	4-T	Oksefjord	12/0922	dt	-D	(K. Leonhardt/6115)	–	/	Nordkyn	1
12/1030	sj	K-23	Potapov	APC		+	A	Oksefjord								1
12/1030	sj	K-23	Potapov	APC		+	A	Oksefjord								1
14/0659	sj	M-176	Bondarevich	-D	8000	+	2-T	Varangerfjord					–	/		2
14/0659	sj	M-176	Bondarevich	*TB*		=	2-T	*Varangerfjord*								2
15/2240	sj	M-172	Fisanovich	-D	6000	+	1-T	Varangerfjord	15/2250	dt	AH	(Birka/1000)	–	/	Varangerfjord	3
16/1223	sj	D-3	Bibeyev	-D	9000	+	3-T	Bosfjord					–	/		4
16/	sj	M-172	Fisanovich	-D	6000	+	1-T	Syltefjord					–	/		4
17/1445	sj	D-3	Bibeyev	-D	11000	=	3-T	Makkaur	17/1346	nw	-D	(Hallingdal/3180)	–	/	Syltefjord	5
19/	sj	M-176	Bondarevich	-D		+	2-T	Makkaur	19/1145	dt	AH	(Birka/1000)	–	/	Makkaur	6
23/1734	sj	M-171	Starikov	-D	11000	+	2-T	Varangerfjord	23/1641	nw	-D	(Vardö/860)	–	/	Varangerfjord	7
25/0639	sj	S-101	Vekke	-D		/	1-T	Tanafjord	25/0946	dt	AH	(Meteor/3715)	–	/	Tanafjord	8
27/1951	sj	M-176	Bondarevich	*SS*		+	2-T	*Varangerfjord*	27/2150	dt	APC		–	/	Varangerfjord	9
JUNE 1942																
02/0958	sj	SC-402	Stolbov	-D	15000	+	2-T	Harbaken	02/	dt	-D	(Leuna/6856)	–	/	Vardö	10
08/1852	sj	SC-403	Shuiskii	-D	7000	+	4-T	Varangerfjord					–	/		11
11/0559	sj	SC-403	Shuiskii	-D	8000	=	4-T	Varangerfjord					–	/		12
19/1416	sj	M-171	Starikov	-D	4000	=	2-T	N Kirkenes					–	/		12

(1) *K-23*, with Captain 2nd Class Gadzhiev on board, attacked an eastbound convoy with *Karl Leonhardt* and *Emsland*/5170 and six escorts. Four torpedoes missed. *UJ1109*, *UJ1101* and *UJ1110* dropped 93 D/Cs and followed as the submarine tried to escape surfaced, and reported the attack by radio. Submarine was forced to dive by A/C and sunk. Soviet sources claim two APCs sunk but this is incorrect.

(2) Attack not observed.

(3) Convoy with *Birka* and *Gerdmoor*/761 and five escorts. One torpedo missed ahead, 136 D/Cs dropped and surfaced submarine attacked with 38 shells but escaped.

(4) Attack not observed.

(5) Ship with five escorts. One torpedo observed by *UJ1106*.

(6) *Birka* with four escorts. Two torpedoes observed missing; 13 D/Cs dropped by *V6106*.

(7) Ship with three escorts. Two torpedoes observed, 166 D/Cs dropped by *V6106* etc.

(8) Ship with four escorts. One torpedo observed missing, 80 D/Cs dropped by *V5903* etc.

(9) Torpedoes not observed.

(10) Westbound convoy with *Leuna*, *Gerdmoor*/761, *Tijuca*/5980 and six escorts; three torpedoes missed.

(11) Attack not observed.

(12) Attack not observed.

1	2	3	4	5	6	7	8	9	10	11	12	13	14	15	16	17
JULY 1942																
05/1801	sj	K-21	Lunin	BB		=	4-T	Ingoy/Rolvsoy	05/1702	dt	BB	(Tirpitz/42343)	–	/	Ingoy	1
22/2248	sj	SC-402	Stolbov	-D	8000	+	4-T	Vardö	22/2152	dt	-D	(Pompeji/2816)	–	/	S Vardö	2
25/0725	sj	SC-402	Stolbov	SS		/	3-T	Varangerfjord					–	/		3
AUGUST 1942																
04/									04/	dt	-D	(Convoy)	–	/	Varangerfjord	
06/	sj	K-1	Avgustinovich					19M Porsangerfjord	12.09.M	dt	-D	Robert Bornhofen	6643	+	70°43N/25°58E	4
08/1607	sj	SC-403	Shuiskii	-D	8000	+	4-T	Varangerfjord	08/1540	dt	-D	(Thorland/5208)	–	/	E Vardö	5
11/0857	sj	SC-403	Shuiskii	-D	10000	+	4-T	N Kirkenes	11/0800	dt	-D	(Santos/5943)	–	/	Kiberg/Vardö	6
16/	sj	K-21	Lunin					20M Sillen/Lopphavet								
19/2213	sj	K-21	Lunin	CM		+	4-T	70°27N/21°39E	19/	dt	-D	(Sèvres/5089)	–	/	Lopphavet	7
19/2213	sj	K-21	Lunin	APC		+	"	70°27N/21°39E					–	/		7
19/2239	sj	K-21	Lunin	APC		+	4-T	70°27N/21°39E					–	/		7
23/0748	sj	SC-422	Vidyayev	-D	4000	+	4-T	Kibergsneset					–	/		8
24/1748	sj	SC-422	Vidyayev	-D	8000	+	4-T	70°12N/30°51E	24/1725	dt	-D	(Irmtr. Cords/2843)	–	/	70°08N/30°49E	9

(1) *K-21* reported two detonations after 2min 15sec and assumed a hit on *Tirpitz* and possibly on a destroyer. In fact the attack was not observed by the German task force and became known only after the interception of *K-21*'s radio signal.

(2) *Pompeji* was escorted by five vessels. *M31*, *M154* and *R56* reported two misses and dropped 22 D/Cs.

(3) Attack not observed.

(4) *Robert Bornhofen* was employed from 10.39 to 11.41 as *Sperrbrecher III* and *Sperrbrecher C* and on 7.42 again became a merantile transport. The claim that *Sperrbrecher 14* was sunk is erroneous: this ship was the former *Bockenheim* and served 1940–44 in the Bay of Biscay.

(5) *Thorland* was escorted by three vessels. *V5909* observed two torpedoes which missed and dropped eight D/Cs.

(6) Convoy with *Santos*, *Rauenthaler*/3727 and seven escorts. Three torpedoes observed, all of which missed. *UJ1104* and *UJ1108* dropped 110 D/Cs and presumed the submarine sunk, but in fact the latter returned to base.

(7) *Sèvres* and the two escorts did not observe the four torpedoes (which missed).

(8) *SC-421* reported a convoy of three ships and two escorts and heard three detonations. No observation in German sources.

(9) Convoy with *Irmtraud Cords*, *Ortelsburg*/1309, *Lysaker*/909 and seven escorts. Two torpedoes observed, which missed. *UJ1101*, *UJ1108* and *UJ1112* dropped 179 D/Cs and assumed that the submarine had been destroyed, but see 28.8.42.

1	2	3	4	5	6	7	8	9	10	11	12	13	14	15	16	17
AUGUST 1942 *continued*																
28/	sj	SC-422	Vidyayev	-D	6000	+	4-T	Kibergsneset	28/	nl	-D	(Kerkplein/3580)	–	/	Kibergsneset	1
SEPTEMBER 1942																
13/1105	sj	SC-422	Vidyayev	APC	1600	+	2-T	Porsangerfjord	13/1028	dt	APC	(V6108)	–	/	Porsangerfjord	2
15/1107	sj	SC-422	Vidyayev	APC	600	+	2-T	71°44N/26°30E	15/1028	dt	APC	(UJ1103)	–	/	N Svaerholt	3
20/	br	P614?	Beckley						20/1622	*dt*	*SS*	*(U408)*	–	/	AB 1376	4
22/1220	sj	SC-404	Ivanov, V. A.	-D	5500	+	2-T	Varangerfjord	22/1125	dt	AH	(A.v.Humboldt/586)	–	/	S Kiberg	5
22/	sj	SC-422	Vidyayev	-D		?	-T	71°44N/26°30E								
OCTOBER 1942																
19/	sj	K-2?	Utkin	-D		+	-T	Syltefjord					–	/		6
25/	sj	SC-403	Shuiskii	APC		+	-T	Nordkyn	25/0942	dt	APC	(V6106)	–	/	71°04N/27°10E	7
27/	sj	L-22	Afonin				20M	Nordkyn								
28/1104	sj	SC-403	Shuiskii	APM		+	2-T	70°06N/30°37E					–	/		8
31/	sj	L-20	Tamman				20M	Kongsfjord								
NOVEMBER 1942																
03/	sj	L-22	Afonin				20M	Syltefjord	14.11.M	dt	APC	Schiff 18/Alteland	419	+	69°56N/30°00E	
07/1746	sj	L-22	Afonin	APM		/	4-T	Syltefjord								9
09/	sj	SC-422	Vidyayev	-D		+	2-T									9
09/	sj	K-1	Avgustinovich				20M	Porsangerfjord	06.12.M	dt	APC	V6116/Ubier	350	+	70°56N/26°02E	
09/	sj	K-1	Avgustinovich						06.12.M	dt	APC	V6117/Cherusker	304	+	70°56N/25°47E	

(1) Convoy with *Kerkplein*, *Tijuca*/5980 and three escorts; four torpedoes missed.
(2) Two torpedoes missed *V6108* and *V6110*.
(3) This attack possibly also missed the aircraft depot ship *Karl Meyer*.
(4) Possible British attack during operation QP.14.
(5) Convoy with *Alexander von Humboldt*, *Stadt Emden*/5180 and six escorts; two torpedoes missed, *V5906* dropped 17 D/Cs.

(6) The claimed Norwegian steamer *Nordland*/725 was sunk on 19.10.42 in Saltenfjord, Norway, on a mine laid by the French submarine *Rubis*.
(7) Three escorts observed one torpedo explode on the rocks. *V6106* and *V5909* dropped 55 D/Cs and assumed that they had damaged the submarine.
(8) Attack not observed.
(9) Attack not observed.

1	2	3	4	5	6	7	8	9	10	11	12	13	14	15	16	17

NOVEMBER 1942 *continued*

1	2	3	4	5	6	7	8	9	10	11	12	13	14	15	16	17
27/	sj	L-20	Tamman				20M	Helnes								

DECEMBER 1942

1	2	3	4	5	6	7	8	9	10	11	12	13	14	15	16	17
04/	sj	K-1	Avgustinovich				20M	Hammerfest								
04/0331	sj	SC-404	Ivanov, V. A.	-D		/	2-T	Porsangerfjord								1
04/1223	sj	SC-404	Ivanov, V. A.	-D	8000	+	2-T	Porsangerfjord								1
13/2051	sj	M-171	Starikov	-D		+	2-T	Varangerfjord								1
14/1251	sj	SC-403	Shuiskii	-D	7000	+	4-T	Lille Ekkery	14/1109	dt	-D	(Dessau/5933)	–	/	Kiberg/Vadso	2
15/	sj	K-1	Avgustinovich				20M	Rolvsoysund								
20/	sj	L-22	Afonin				20M	Bosfjord	14.04.M	dt	-Tg	Pasvik	237	+	69°55N/30°00E	
29/	sj	L-20	Tamman													3

JANUARY 1943

1	2	3	4	5	6	7	8	9	10	11	12	13	14	15	16	17
01/0325	sj	L-20	Tamman	-D	10000	+	6-T	Kongsfjord	01/0415	dt	-D	Muansa	5408	+	70°53N/29°27E	
05/0836	sj	M-171	Starikov	-D	12000	=	2-T	Syltefjord					–	/		4
12/									12/2000	dt		(Convoy)	–	/	Off Petsamo	5
17/1922	sj	SC-404	Ivanov, V. A.	-D	10000	=	4-T	Laksfjord	17/	dt	-D	(Rotenfels/7584)	–	/	Laksfjord	6
21/	sj	L-20	Tamman				20M	Kongsfjord								
22/2145	sj	SC-404	Ivanov, V. A	-D	14000	+	4-T	Nordkyn	22/1945	dt	-D	(Mülheim-Ruhr/ 5350)	–	/	Nordkyn	7
23/0420	sj	M-172	Fisanovich	*DD*		+	*2-T*	*Syltefjord*					–	/		*8*
23/0843	sj	SC-402	Kautskii	-D	6000	+	4-T	Varangerfjord	23/	dt	-D	(H. Schulte/5056)	–	/	Varangerfjord	8

(1) Attack not observed.
(2) Convoy with *Dessau, Weilheim*/5455, *Poseidon*/3910, *Utviken*/3502 and three escorts. Two torpedoes missed; *V6109* dropped six D/Cs.
(3) *V5905/Nordriff*/320 was accidentally stranded on 29.12.42 in 70°21´N/21°50´E.
(4) Attack not observed.
(5) *R173* reported one torpedo missing.

(6) Convoy *Rotenfels, Inger Johanne*/1202 and three escorts. Four torpedoes missed but were not observed.
(7) Convoy with *Mülheim-Ruhr, Schwaben*/7773, *Bahia*/4117, *Schillinghörn*/2973 and four escorts. One torpedo observed, which missed; *V5910* dropped five D/Cs.
(8) Convoy with *Henriette Schulte, Itauri*/6338, *Aludra*/4930, *Poseidon*/3910 and four escorts. Neither attack observed.

1	2	3	4	5	6	7	8	9	10	11	12	13	14	15	16	17
JANUARY 1943 *continued*																
29/0256	sj	M-171	Starikov	-D	12000	+	2-T	Persfjord	29/0105	dt	-D	Ilona Siemers	3245	=	70°33N/30°50E	
FEBRUARY 1943																
01/0543	sj	M-172	Fisanovich	-D	10000	+	2-T	Syltefjord	01/0540	dt	APC	V6115/Ostwind	560	+	70°15N/31°01E	1
01/	sj	SC-402	Kautskii	APC		+	-T	Batsfjord	01/0810	dt	APC	V5909/Coronel	541	+	70°42N/30°15E	1
01/1245	sj	L-20	Tamman	-D	12000	+	6-T	Porsangerfjord	01/1047	dt	-D	Othmarschen	7077	+	71°07N/27°30E	2
01/1245	sj	L-20	Tamman	APC		+	"	Porsangerfjord					–	/		
02/1254	sj	SC-402	Kautskii	-D	8000	+	4-T	Varangerfjord	02/1058	dt	-D	(H. Fritzen/4818)	–	/	S Kiberg	3
05/1248	sj	L-20	Tamman	*DD*		+	6-T	*Porsangerfjord*	*05/1105*	*dt*	*CM*	*(Brummer)*	–	/	Nordkyn	4
05/2309	sj	K-3	Malofeyev	-D	8000	+	4-T	Kongsfjord	05/2113	dt	APC	UJ1108/Elbe	462	+	70°53N/29°20E	
06/	sj	K-22	Kotelnikov	–	–		3-T		06/0755	dt	CM	(Brummer)	–	/	30m N Kongsfjord	5
06/							3-T		06/1048	dt	CM	(Brummer)	–	/	W Nordkyn	5
12/1257	sj	K-3	Malofeyev	-D	10000	+	6-T	Batsfjord	12/1105	dt	-D	Fechenheim	8116	=	Batsfjord/Kongs-fjord	6
12/1430	sj	K-21	Lunin	4 Mbt		+	A	Lopphavet	12/	ne	-Mbt	... (?)	...	+?	Lopphavet	7
12/1430	sj	K-21	Lunin	Mbt		=	"	Lopphavet								7
16/1550	sj	M-119	Kolosov	-D		/	2-T	Kiberg	16/1505	dt	-D	(Sturzsee/708)	–	/	Kiberg	
18/	sj	K-21	Lunin				20M	Lyngenfjord	22.04.M	dt	-D	Duna	1926	+	Lyngenfjord	8
18/1558	sj	M-171	Starikov	APC		+	2-T	Syltefjord					–	/		9

(1) The times in Soviet and German documents do not correspond, so it is not entirely clear which ship was sunk by which submarine. There is also a report that the attack against *V6115* was made by *SC-403*.

(2) *Othmarschen* was the French steamer *Ville de Metz*. The APC claimed, *V5905/Nordriff/320*, was sunk on 29.12.42 by stranding in a storm in 70°21´N/21°50´E.

(3) Convoy with *H. Fritzen*, *Tripp/364* and six escorts. *SC-402* reported two detonations and one torpedo surface-runner. *V5910* dropped five D/Cs.

(4) Minelaying force with *Brummer*, destroyers *Theodor Riedel* and *Z31*, minesweepers *M361* and *M381*, and *UJ1102* and *UJ1104*. Two torpedoes evaded by *Brummer*; escorts dropped two D/Cs.

(5) The same minelaying force as in Note 4 was, on its return, attacked twice without suffering hits. At least the first attack was probably made by *K-22*, which was lost on a mine on 7.2.43 and did not report its attack(s).

(6) *Fechenheim* was beached, salvaged on 16.3.43, towed to Germany on 23.1.44 and sunk with explosives on 16.3.46.

(7) The crew of the last motor boat were taken prisoner

(8) Ship escorted by *NKi05*. One torpedo hit the rocks, the submarine was fired on by a coastal battery and *NKi05* dropped 49 D/Cs.

(8) It is possible that the ship was lost on a German defensive mine barrage.

(9) Attack not reported.

1	2	3	4	5	6	7	8	9	10	11	12	13	14	15	16	17
FEBRUARY 1943 *continued*																
20/0218	sj	K-21	Lunin	APC, 5Mb		+	4-T	Bogenbay					–?			1
20/1515	sj	SC-422	Vidyayev	-D	10000	+	4-T	Kjolnes/Tana	21/	dt	-D	(Convoy)	–	/	Kjolnes	2
21/0957	sj	M-119	Kolosov	-D	8000	=	2-T	Kiberg	21/0820	dt	AM	(Bali)	–	/	S Kiberg	3
25/0821	sj	M-172	Fisanovich	*TB*		+	*2-T*	*Varangerfjord*					–	/		4
26/1211	sj	M-171	Starikov	-D		/	2-T	Varangerfjord	26/1927	dt	APC	(Guschi II)	–	/	S Kiberg	5
27/1540	sj	SC-422	Vidyayev	APC	800	+	4-T	Tanafjord	27/	dt	-D	(Banco/461)	–	/	Berlevaag	6
MARCH 1943																
04/1435	sj	M-119	Kolosov	-D	6000	+	2-T	Varangerfjord					–	/		7
11/1440	sj	M-174	Sukhoruchenko	APC		=	2-T	Varangerfjord					–	/		7
16/1757	sj	M-122	Shipin	-D	8000	+	2-T	70°12N/30°51E	16/1544	dt	-D	Johannisberger	4533	=§	69°58N/31°03E	8
17/	sj	K-3	Malofeyev	–	–		6-T		17/0725	dt	-D	(Roter Sand/4221)	–	/	Nordkyn	9
20/1429	sj	SC-402	Kautskii	-D	6000	+	3-T	Syltefjord								7
21/1218	sj	M-119	Kolosov	-D	7000	+	2-T	Varangerfjord								10
21/	sj	K-3	Malofeyev	–	–		6-T		21/1752	dt	-D	(H.Fritzen/4818)	–	/	71°12N/27°41E	9
22/1154	sj	S-101	Yegorov. P. I.	-D	7000	+	4-T	Kongsfjord	22/1000	dt	-D	(Drau/5141)	–	/	Batsfjord/Tana	11

(1) *K-21* reported one APC and five motor boats destroyed, but these were not confirmed.

(2) Convoy with nine vessels, the mine clearance ship *Bali*, two tugs, eight escorts and one aircraft. Three torpedoes were observed, but these missed.

(3) *Bali* evaded a surface-running torpedo.

(4) *M-172* reported two detonations; no German report.

(5) *M-171* reported a miss; *Guschi II* reported two torpedoes that missed (27.2.42).

(6) Convoy with *Banco*, *Hartmut*/2713 and two escorts. Two torpedoes missed, one of them a surface-runner.

(7) Attack not observed.

(8) *Johannisberger*, ex French *Lyon*, was beached but became a total loss.

(9) Attack not reported by *K-3*, which was lost. First attack against eastbound convoy with six ships, eight escorts and aircraft; five torpedoes (one on surface) missed. D/Cs dropped by *V5902* etc. Second attack against convoy with three ships, eight escorts and one aircraft; four torpedoes observed missing, one exploding against the rocks. *K-3* was sunk by D/Cs from *UJ1102*, *UJ1106* and *UJ1111*.

(10) *M-119* reported two hits; no reports in German sources.

(11) Convoy with hospital ship *Fasan*, *Drau* and *Bahia*/4117, six escorts and one aircraft. Two torpedoes were evaded; *V6109* dropped D/Cs.

1	2	3	4	5	6	7	8	9	10	11	12	13	14	15	16	17
MARCH 1943 *continued*																
28/	sj	S-101	Yegorov. P. I.	-D		+	3-T	Porsangerfjord	28/0652	dt	-D	(Convoy)	–	/	16m NW Nordkyn	1
29/0655	sj	M-122	Shipin	-D	6000	+	2-T	Kibergsnes	29/	dt	-D	(Kyphissia/2964)	–	/	Vardö	1
29/1124	sj	S-55	Sushkin	-D	8000	+	4-T	70°43N/30°17E	29/	dt	-D	(Kyphissia/2964)	–	/		1
29/1124	sj	S-55	Sushkin	-D	3000	+	"	70°43N/30°17E					–	/		1
29/1159	sj	S-101	Yegorov. P. I.	-D	8000	+	4-T	Kongsfjord	29/1058	dt	-D	Ajax	2297	+	70°49N/29°30E	1
APRIL 1943																
05/1427	sj	M-171	Kovalenko, G. D.	-D	2500	+	2-T	Varangerfjord	05/	dt	-D	(Oldenburg/8537)	–	/	Kibergsneset	2
09/1443	sj	K-21	Lunin	*DD*		+	6-T	*70°34N/21°38E*	*09/*	*dt*	*CM*	*(Brummer)*	–	/	*Batsfjord*	3
10/1511	sj	S-56	Shchedrin	-D	8000	+	2-T	Tanafjord	10/	dt	-D	(Convoy)	–	/	Sletnes	4
12/	sj	K-21	Lunin	4 Mbt		+	A	Lopphavet	12/1400	nw	-Df	...	...	+	Svendsgrunn	5
14/1346	sj	S-56	Shchedrin	-D	6000	+	2-T	Kongsfjord	14/1250	dt	-D	(Convoy)	–	/	Kongsfjord	6
16/0616	sj	M-104	Lukjanov	-D	12000	+	2-T	Varangerfjord	16/0515	dt	-D	(Giselau/....)	–	/	Kiberg	7
17/1557	sj	M-122	Shipin	AG	1500	+	2-T	Varangerfjord	17/1514	dt	-D	(Giselau/....)	–	/	Kiberg	8
18/0815	sj	M-172	Fisanovich	-D	12000	+	2-T	Varangerfjord	18/	dt	-D	(A. Binder/3515)	–	/	Kiberg	9

(1) Convoy with nine ships and seven escorts. Three torpedoes missed (one on the surface); *V6109* dropped 19 D/Cs. Convoy reinforced by five minesweepers, attacked again on 29.3.43 at 1058 when *Ajax*/2297 was sunk. However, from the time sequence and the positions of the attacks on 29.3.43, *Ajax* was not sunk by *S-55* as claimed but by *S-101*. *M-122* and *S-55* attacked the convoy with *Kyphissia*/2964, *Liselotte Essberger*/1593 and five escorts going west; *M322* dropped 28 D/Cs. The German steamer *Bahia Castillo*/8580, claimed by *S-101*, was not in one of these convoys and was not damaged on this day.

(2) Attack without periscope from depth of 17 metres. Convoy with *Oldenburg* and five escorts. Torpedoes not observed.

(3) Minelayer *Brummer* with five escorts. Two torpedoes observed missing; six D/Cs dropped.

(4) Convoy with seven ships and 11 escorts. Submarine observed by aircraft. Two torpedoes missed. UJ dropped 28 D/Cs.

(5) *K-21* reported four motor boats, one sunk and two damaged; German sources report one Norwegian fishing vessel sunk.

(6) Westbound convoy with 10 transports and 10 escorts. Launching of torpedoes observed, one passing the steamer *Detlef* at 10 metres. 11 D/Cs dropped.

(7) Convoy with seven ships and four escorts. One torpedo exploded at the end of its run.

(8) Two escorts evaded two torpedoes.

(9) Convoy with four ships and six escorts. Two torpedoes missed; 54 D/Cs dropped.

1	2	3	4	5	6	7	8	9	10	11	12	13	14	15	16	17
APRIL 1943 *continued*																
19/1710	sj	SC-422	Vidyayev	-D	14000	+	4-T	Bosfjord	19/1628	dt	-D	(Markobrunner/8140)	–	/	Makkaur	1
20/1001	sj	M-105	Khrulev	-D	7000	+	2-T	Varangerfjord	20/	dt	-D	(Convoy)	–	/	Varangerfjord	2
23/1125	sj	SC-404	Makarenkov	APM		=	4-T	Varangerfjord					–	/		3
24/1051	sj	L-22	Afonin	-D	8000	+	6-T	Lopphavet					–	/		3
25/1125	sj	SC-404	Makarenkov	APM		+	4-T	Varangerfjord								
25/1156	sj	S-101	Yegorov. P. I.	-D	7000	+	4-T	70°55N/29°30E	25/1130	dt	-D	(Convoy)	–	/	Kongsfjord	4
29/1744	sj	S-55	Sushkin	-D	10000	+	4-T	Tanafjord	29/1647	dt	-D	Sturzsee	708	+	Sletnes	5
29/1744	sj	S-55	Sushkin	-D	10000	+	"	Tanafjord					–	/		5
MAY 1943																
01/1813	sj	M-119	Kolosov	-D	10000	+	2-T	Bosfjord					–	/		6
04/	sj	S-51	Kucherenko	-D	10000	+	-T						–	/		6
06/	sj	L-22	Afonin				20M	Syltefjord	01.06.M	dt	AH	Birka II	1000	+	70°25N/21°40E	7
07/2326	sj	M-172	Fisanovich	-D	12000	+	2-T	Varangerfjord	06/night	dt	AH	(Fasan/1075)	–	/	Vardö/Kiberg	8
13/0830	sj	S-51	Kucherenko	-D	10000	+	4-T	Tanafjord	13/0730	dt	-D	(Africana/5868 ea)	–	/	Mehamn/Nordkyn	9
13/0830	sj	S-51	Kucherenko	APC		=	"	Tanafjord					–	/		
17/0545	sj	S-56	Shchedrin	-T	6000	+	4-T	70°45N/29°27E	17/0455	dt	-DT	Eurostadt	1118	+	70°48N/29°34	10
17/0545	sj	S-56	Shchedrin	-D	5000	+	"	70°45N/29°27E	17/0455	dt	-D	Wartheland	5096	=	70°49N/29°34E	10
31/0559	sj	SC-422	Vidyayev	-D	6000	+	4-T	Syltefjord	31/0503	dt	-D	(Convoy)	–	/	70°46N/30°04E	11

(1) Convoy of 10 ships with four escorts. Four torpedoes exploded on rocks.

(2) Same convoy as before, reinforced by three minesweepers. No torpedoes observed.

(3) Attack not observed.

(4) Convoy with four ships and seven escorts, one aircraft. Four torpedoes observed behind the ships; two turned and exploded. Nine D/Cs.

(5) Westbound convoy with two ships and six escorts. *S-55* reported three detonations and assumed two ships sunk, but only *Sturzsee* was hit and sank. Escorts dropped 90 D/Cs.

(6) Attack not observed.

(7) *L-22* was assigned two mine successes on this barrage.

(8) Ship and five escorts going south. Two torpedoes observed, which missed; 11 D/Cs dropped.

(9) Attack without using periscope from 20 metres' depth. Convoy with four ships, one landing barge (F), one tug and seven escorts. *S-51* reported one transport sunk and one escort damaged. Two torpedoes were observed and evaded. 11 D/Cs were dropped by *V6109*.

(10) The convoy had eight escorts. *Wartheland*, ex Norwegian steamer *Skjelbred*, was hit by a torpedo which did not explode.

(11) Convoy of four ships with five escorts. Two detonations on the rocks, one surface-runner.

1	2	3	4	5	6	7	8	9	10	11	12	13	14	15	16	17
JUNE 1943																
13/0043	sj	S-101	Yegorov, P. I.	APC	800	+	4-T	Kongsfjord	12/2343	dt	-D	(Convoy)	–	/	Kongsfjord	1
13/0043	sj	S-101	Yegorov, P. I.	-D	3200	=	"	Kongsfjord					–	/		1
14/1933	sj	S-101	Yegorov, P. I.	-D	3200	/	2-T	Kongsfjord								2
19/1035	sj	S-101	Yegorov, P. I.	-D	5000	+	2-T	Kongsfjord	19/0935	dt	APC	(V6108)	–	/	Batsfjord	3
22/	sj	L-15	Komarov, V. I.				20M	Soroy								
22/1533	sj	S-101	Yegorov, P. I.	-D	7000	+	4-T	Kongsfjord					–	/		2
23/1034	sj	S101	Yegorov, P. I.	-D	7000	+	2-T	Kongsfjord	23/0832	dt	-D	(Convoy)	–	/	Vardö	4
23/1533	sj	S-51	Kucherenko	-D	7000	+	4-T	Tanafjord	23/	dt	-D	(Convoy)	–	/		5
23/1533	sj	S-51	Kucherenko	-D	4000	+	"	Tanafjord					–	/		5
27/0630	sj	S-51	Kucherenko	-D	5000	+	4-T	Tanafjord					–	/		6
27/0630	sj	S-51	Kucherenko	APM		+	"	Tanafjord					–	/		6
28/1612	sj	S-54	Bratishko	-D		/	4-T	Kongsfjord	28/1445	dt	APC	(UJ1206)	–	/	Tanahorn	7
29/	sj	M-105	Khrulev	-D	7000	=	2-T	Harbaken	29/0202	dt	-D	(Convoy)	–	/	Persfjord	8
JULY 1943																
04/									04/1010	dt	SS	(U586)	–	/	75°39N/17°10E	9
04/	sj	SC-422?	Vidyayev					Vardö	04/2305	dt	APC	(NKi08, NKi09)	–	/	Vardö	10
05/	sj	M-106?	Samarin					Vardö	05/0610	dt	APC	(UJ12..)	–	/	N Vardö	10
14/	sj	SC-422	Vidyayev	-D		+	-T						–	/		11

(1) Convoy with two ships and two escorts. *S-101* reported one escort sunk and one transport damaged. Two torpedoes which missed were observed.

(2) Attack not observed.

(3) Eastbound convoy, no hits.

(4) Westbound convoy with *M35* observed torpedoes which missed.

(5) *S-51* reported two transports and one minesweeper sunk, with three detonations. No German report.

(6) No report for 27.6.43, but possibly same attack as that by *S-54* on 28.6.43 (?).

(7) UJ group with *UJ1206* reported three detonations on the rocks.

(8) Convoy with six transports, 10 escorts and one aircraft. Two surface-running torpedoes missed.

(9) Three torpedoes missed.

(10) One torpedo missed in each attack. The first attack is assumed to be that made by *SC-422*, which did not return. In the second attack four UJs dropped 73 D/Cs and *UJ1217* sank *M-106* by ramming.

(11) Claimed as the 11th and last victory of *SC-422*.

1	2	3	4	5	6	7	8	9	10	11	12	13	14	15	16	17
JULY 1943 *continued*																
17/0238	sj	S-56	Shchedrin	APC		+	4-T	Tanafjord	*17/0135*	*dt*	*PM*	*M346*	*551*	+	*Makkaur*	1
17/0238	sj	S-56	Shchedrin	-D	7000	=	"	Tanafjord								
17/2054	sj	SC-403	Shuiskii	APM		+	3-T	Kongsfjord	17/2015	dt	-D	(Convoy)	–	/	Kongsfjord	2
18/							4-T		18/2015	dt	-D	(Convoy)	–	/	Batsfjord	3
19/1908	sj	S-56	Shchedrin	APC		+	2-T	Tanafjord	19/1832	dt	APC	NKi09/Alane	466	+	Gamvik	4
19/1928	sj	S-56	Shchedrin	-D	5000	+	4-T	Tanafjord					–	/		4
20/1516	sj	SC-403	Shuiskii	-D	6000	+	4-T	Kongsfjord	20/1430	dt	-D	(Convoy)	–	/	Kongsfjord	5
AUGUST 1943																
07/									07/1531	dt	-D	(Convoy)	–	/	Syltefjord	6
15/	sj	L-15	Komarov, V. I.				20M	Altafjord	26.04.M	dt	APC	NH24/KFK...	105	+	71°01N/24°00E	
18/0509	sj	S-102	Gorodnichii	-D	6000	+	2-T	Tanafjord					–	/		7
18/0708	sj	L-15	Komarov, V. I.	APM		+	3-T	70°48N/29°26E	18/	dt	-D	(Convoy)		/	Syltefjord	8
18/0708	sj	L-15	Komarov, V. I.	APM		+	"	70°48N/29°26E					–	/		8
25/	sj	L-22	Afonin				20M	Honningsvaag	28.12.M	dt	-PM	R64	125	+	Honningsvaag	
26/	sj	S-102	Gorodnichii	-D		+	2-T	Tanafjord					–	/		9
28/1030	sj	S-101	Yegorov. P. I.	SS		+	3-T	76°49N/69°42E	28/0950	dt	SS	U639	769	+	Karasee, missing	
30/	sj	L-20	Tamman				20M	Persfjord								

(1) A minelaying group comprising *Brummer*, *Ostmark* and four minesweepers, with one aircraft, was laying a mine barrage when *M346* was hit and sunk. *Ostmark*, claimed as sunk, narrowly evaded three torpedoes.

(2) Convoy with five ships, eight escorts and two aircraft. Three torpedoes observed at 5,000 metres' distance by one of the aircraft, which dropped bombs, detonating one and turning the other two away.

(3) Convoy with *V6103* observed four torpedoes which missed.

(4) The claimed sinking, besides *NKi09*, of *V1121* did not take place: such a vessel did not exist.

(5) Convoy with three ships, one landing barge, one tug and 10 escorts, with two aircraft. Four torpedoes missed, one exploding on the shore.

(6) Two torpedoes missed.

(7) *S-102* reported two hits and the transport sunk, but there was no German report.

(8) Convoy with nine transports and 17 escorts, with two aircraft. Two torpedoes observed, one on the surface; five D/Cs dropped. *L-15* reported three hits and two APMs sunk.

(9) Convoy with five transports, the minelayer *Roland*, 17 escorts and three aircraft. Two torpedoes evaded.

1	2	3	4	5	6	7	8	9	10	11	12	13	14	15	16	17
SEPTEMBER 1943																
01/1350	sj	L-22	Afonin	-D	7000	=	6-T	Syltefjord	01/1253	dt	-D	Rüdesheimer	2036	=	Persfjord	1
01/1350	sj	L-22	Afonin	-D	6000	=	"	Syltefjord					–	/		1
03/0520	sj	S-51	Kucherenko	APC		+	4-T	Kongsfjord	03/0437	dt	APC	UJ1202/	464	+	70°47N/29°35E	
												F. Dankworth				
03/1043	sj	L-20	Tamman	-D	3000	+	3-T	Porsangerfjord	03/1025	dt	-D	(Convoy)	–	/	Nordkyn	2
05/1053	sj	S-51	Kucherenko	-D	2000	+	2-T	Kongsfjord					–	/		3
08/1220	sj	S-51	Kucherenko	-D	6000	+	4-T	Kongsfjord	08/1135	dt	-D	(Convoy)	–	/	Tanahorn	4
11/1128	sj	M-107	Kofanov	-D	7000	+	2-T	Syltefjord	11/1519	dt	APC	UJ1217/Star 22	303	+	70°38N/30°26E	
14/1237	sj	SC-404	Makarenkov	-D	8000	+	4-T	Varangerfjord	14/1154	dt	-D	(Convoy)	–	/	Nr Kiberg	5
20/1311	sj	SC-404	Makarenkov	-D	6000	+	3-T	Varangerfjord	20/				–	/		6
20/1331	sj	M-104	Lukyanov	-D		/	2-T	Syltefjord	20/				–	/		7
22/	br	X6	Cameron	BB		=	LM	Altafjord	22/	dt	BB	Tirpitz	42343	=	Altafjord	8
22/	br	X7	Plaice	BB		=	LM	Altafjord	22/	dt	BB	Tirpitz	42343	=	Altafjord	8
OCTOBER 1943																
04/0115	sj	M-105	Khrulev	-D	8000	+	2-T	Varangerfjord	04/0507	dt	APC	UJ1214/Rau V (?)	354	+?	70°25N/31°03E	9
04/													–	/		10

(1) *L-22* reported two hits and two ships damaged. The convoy of five ships and 15 escorts, with one aircraft, observed three torpedoes, one of which hit *Rüdesheimer*, which was beached but later towed away to Germany. This attack is also credited to *M-104* (Lukyanov) off Persfjord.

(2) *L-20* reported two hits and one ship sunk. The UJ group, with *UJ1209* at a convoy, observed two torpedoes that missed.

(3) *S-51* reported two hits, but these were not observed on the German side.

(4) *S-51* attacked without periscope from a depth of 19 metres and reported two hits. The westbound convoy with *V6104* observed five (?) torpedoes that missed.

(5) *SC-404* reported an acoustic attack with two detonations. The convoy with *R121* and two escorts evaded three torpedoes, which detonated on the shore.

(6) *SC-404* attacked without periscope from a depth of 22 metres and reported one tube runner and two detonations. There was no German observation.

(7) Attack not observed.

(8) The two midget submarines were towed to the scene of the operation by fleet submarines. They dropped mines below the battleship, which was heavily damaged.

(9) *UJ1214* was escorting one ship to the west, close to the coast, and it is assumed that she hit a mine. The time difference makes this more probable than an attack by *M-105*.

(10) The sinking of the Norwegian steamer *St Svithun* /1376 was claimed as a submarine success. She was beached at 1838 following a British air attack off Stadlandet.

1	2	3	4	5	6	7	8	9	10	11	12	13	14	15	16	17
OCTOBER 1943 *continued*																
09/1743	sj	M-107	Kofanov	-D		/	2-T	Varangerfjord					–	/		1
12/0859	sj	S-55	Sushkin	-D	8000	+	4-T	Porsangerfjord	12/0748	dt	-D	Ammerland	5381	+	70°59N/26°26E	
12/0859	sj	S-55	Sushkin	-D	4000	=	4-T	Porsangerfjord								
13/	sj	M-119	Kolosov	-D	2000	+	2-T	Korneset	13/0710	dt	-D	(Convoy)	–	/	Batsfjord/Syltefjord	2
16/	sj	M-171	Kovalenko, G. D.	-D	10000	+	2-T	Makkaur	16/	dt	APC		–	/	Makkaur	3
26/	sj	SC-403	Shuiskii	-D		+	-T	Svaerholthavet	26/	dt	-D	(Convoy)	–	/	Svaerholt	4
26/1708	sj	S-101	Trofimov, E. N.	APM		+	4-T	Tanafjord					–	/		5
26/1708	sj	S-101	Trofimov, E. N.	APM		+	4-T	Tanafjord					–	/		5
NOVEMBER 1943																
19/1157	sj	M-119	Kolosov	-D	2000	+	2-T	Syltefjord					–	/		6
22/1325	sj	L-15	Komarov, V. I.	*CM*		+	*6-T*	*Porsangerfjord*	22/	dt	-D	(Convoy)		/		7
23/1447	sj	S-15	Madisson	APM		+	4-T	Laksfjord					–	/		8
24/0547	sj	L-15	Komarov, V. I.	APM		+	3-T	Porsangerfjord	23/	dt	APM		–	/		8
DECEMBER 1943																
08/							-T		08/1020	dt	-D	(Convoy)	–	/	71°03N/28°30E	9

(1) Attack not observed.

(2) Eastbound convoy, with 11 ships, the minesweeper depot ship *Bali*, 15 escorts and two aircraft, observed two torpedoes which missed. It is possible that this attack was made by *M-172* (Kunets) which went missing on this day.

(3) There were two escorts. No torpedoes observed.

(4) Convoy with seven transports, two tugs and 15 escorts. Submarine broached after firing and was pursued for 10hrs; 12 D/Cs were dropped. *SC-403* was probably lost after this attack.

(5) *S-101* reported two torpedoes each against two minesweepers, which were assumed sunk. No German report.

6) Attack not observed.

(7) *L-15* reported an attack on a minelayer, escorted by a destroyer and two patrol vessels, and one hit on the minelayer. The two westbound German convoys in the area did not observe this attack.

(8) Attack not observed.

(9) Eastbound convoy with *UJ1209* reported one torpedo that missed.

1	2	3	4	5	6	7	8	9	10	11	12	13	14	15	16	17
JANUARY 1944																
	sj	L-22	Afonin				20M	Tromsö								1
19/2144	sj	M-201	Balin	-D	6000	+	2-T	70°52N/29°11E	19/	dt	-D	(Wreck Natal)	–	/	Makkaur	2
19/2144	sj	M-201	Balin	-D	6000	?	2-T	70°52N/29°11E					–	/		2
20/2245	sj	S-56	Shchedrin	-D		/	2-T	Tanafjord	20/	dt	-D	(Convoy W.103)	–	/	Sletnes	3
20/2335	sj	S-102	Gorodnichii	-D		+	4-T	Laksfjord	20/	dt	-D	(Convoy W.103)	–		Sletnes	3
23/	sj	S-56	Shchedrin					E Nordkyn	23/1820	dt	-D	(Convoy)	–	/	Tanafjord	4
28/	sj	M-105	Khrulev	-D		+	2-T	Vardö	28/	dt	APC	(NKi03/Havbryn)	–	/	Vardö	5
28/	sj	M-108	Judovich	-D		?	-T						–	/		6
28/1603	sj	S-56	Shchedrin	-D	10000	+	2-T	71°07N/28°17E	28/1401	dt	-D	Henriette Schulte	5056	+	70°08N/28°14E	
31/1140	sj	M-105	Khrulev	-D	5000	=	2-T	Makkaur	31/1155	dt	-D	(Wreck Natal)	–	/	Makkaur	7
FEBRUARY 1944																
03/1032	sj	M-108	Judovich	-D	5000	+	2-T	Syltefjord (?)	03/0830	dt	-D	(Wreck Natal)	3172	=	Makkaur	8
MARCH 1944																
03/2259	sj	M-119	Kolosov	-D	5000	+	2-T	70°43N/30°16E	03/	dt	-D	(Convoy W.109)	–	/	Vardö	9
04/0416	sj	S-56	Shchedrin	-D	6000	+	2-T	71°04N/28°34E	04/	dt	-D	(Convoy W.109)	–	/	Omgang	9

(1) There was a report about a minelaying operation by *L-22* off Tromsö in early 1944 but the date is not clear.

(2) The German steamer *Dessau*/5933 was stranded during a storm at 1645 on 7.1.44 near Makkaur. *M201* reported a first attack with two torpedoes that missed and a second with two torpedoes on an anchored ship, which was hit; four torpedoes ran ashore east of the wreck of *Natal*.

(3) The attacks on Convoy West 103 comprising 11 transports and 16 escorts were not observed. It was later claimed that *S-102* had sunk the minelayer *Skagerrak*/1281, but this ship was sunk at 1135 10m south-west of Egersund in an RAF air attack.

(4) *S-56* tried to attack two escorts but was forced to abandon the attempt when *NKi10* and *UJ1206* opened fire.

(5) Attack against *NKi03* not observed.

(6) Attack not observed.

(7) One torpedo detonated before hitting the beached wreck of *Natal*.

(8) The wreck of *Natal* was hit by one torpedo.

(9) The convoy had three transports and eight escorts. *M-119* was attacked by *UJ1219* and *UJ1207* with six D/Cs. *S-56* attacked without using a periscope from a depth of 25 metres and reported that one torpedo failed to launch and one hit after 45sec, but *UJ1220* observed the wake and dropped D/Cs.

1	2	3	4	5	6	7	8	9	10	11	12	13	14	15	16	17
MARCH 1944 *continued*																
10/1918	sj	M-104	Lukyanov	Mbt		+	2-T	70°44N/30°08E	10/1725	dt	-D	(Wreck Natal)	–	/	Makkaur	1
15/									15/	dt		APC (UJ12..)	–	/	Porsangerfjord	2
17/1146	sj	M-105	Khrulev	-D	4000	+	2-T	Syltefjord	17/0945	dt	-D	(Convoy E.110)	–	/	Syltefjord	3
31/0236	sj	M-119	Kolosov	APC		+	2-T	Syltefjord	01/	dt	-T	(Unkas/499)	–	/		4
APRIL 1944																
07/1136	sj	M-107	Kofanov	APC		/	2-T	Kongsfjord					–	/		5
18/1457	sj	M-105	Khrulev	-D		/	2-T	Syltefjord					–	/		6
MAY 1944																
26/0345	sj	M-201	Balin	APC		+	4-T	Kongsfjord	26/0030	dt	-D	(Convoy E.120	–	/	Syltefjord	7
26/0345	sj	M-201	Balin	-D		=	"	Kongsfjord					–	/		7
26/0439	sj	S-15	Vasilev	-D	4000	+	4-T	Syltefjord	26/0349	dt	-D	(Convoy E.120)	–	/	Syltefjord	7
26/0439	sj	S-15	Vasilev	APC		=	"	Syltefjord					–	/		7

(1) The claim that *M-104* destroyed the transport *Riga*/655, stranded on 29.2.44 near Kirkenes, or sank an APC guarding an anchored ship off the Syltefjord is untrue: the attack was made off Makkaur on the wreck of *Natal*.

(2) A UJ of the 12th Flotilla reported a submarine torpedo. No Soviet report.

(3) The convoy, comprising five transports and 13 escorts, observed one torpedo passing under the steamer *Sèvre*/5089, the other behind the ship. The escorts with *K3* etc. dropped 18 D/Cs. This attack was first attributed to *M-201* (Balin).

(4) *Unkas*, with two escorts, did not observe the attack.

(5) The attack on six escorts was unsuccessful and was not observed.

(6) The attack on an convoy with six transports and 12 escorts was reported by *M-105* but was unsuccessful. No German observation.

(7) Convoy, with eight transports and 21 escorts, was reported by aircraft. Four submarines were ordered to attack. *M-201* reported two explosions, but the torpedoes passed aft of the ships. Three UJs attacked the submarine. The claimed *UJ1764*/*KFK216* was sunk on a mine laid by the French submarine *Rubis* on 17.10.44 at 0206 in 58°22´N/05°59´E. *S-15* reported four explosions, was attacked by escorts with 30 D/Cs, broke surface but escaped damaged. The Norwegian steamer *Solviken*/3502, claimed later, was in fact sunk at 2123 on 25.5.44 by a Soviet airborne torpedo in 70°59´N/28°38´E.

1	2	3	4	5	6	7	8	9	10	11	12	13	14	15	16	17
MAY 1944 *continued*																
29/1427	sj	S-103	Nechayev	APC		+	4-T	Laksfjord	29/	dt	APC	(UJ1209)	–	/	Laksfjord	1
29/1427	sj	S-103	Nechayev	APM		+	"	Laksfjord					–	/		1
29/1427	sj	S-103	Nechayev	APM		+	"	Laksfjord								
JUNE 1944																
16/0937	sj	M-201	Balin	-D		?	2-T	Syltefjord (?)	16/	dt	-D	Wreck Natal	3172	=	Makkaur	2
20/	sj	M-200	Gladkov	-D		+	-T	Syltefjord	20/	dt	-D	(Convoy W.)	–	/	70°25N/31°30E	3
20/1627	sj	S-104	Turayev	-D	8000	+	4-T	70°00N/28°39E	20/1527	dt	-D	(Convoy W.)	–	/	70°09N/22°30E	3
20/1627	sj	S-104	Turayev	APC		+	"	70°00N/28°39E	20/1527	dt	APC	UJ1209/KUJ21	542	+	71°06N/27°47E	3
20/1627	sj	S-104	Turayev	APM		+	"	70°00N/28°39E	20/1527				–	/		3
20/	sj	M-201	Balin	-D		?	-T						–	/		3
JULY 1944																
	sj	L-15	Komarov, V. I.					20M Rolvsy								
13/0911	sj	S-14	Kalanin	APM		=	4-T	Bosfjord	13/	dt	-D	(Convoy)	–	/	Makkaur	4
15/0613	sj	S-56	Shchedrin	*DD*		+	*4-T*	*Kongsfjord*	15/	dt	-D	(Convoy E.124)	–	/	Harbaken	5
15/0613	sj	S-56	Shchedrin	-D		=	"	Kongsfjord					–	/		5
15/0727	sj	M-200	Gladkov	-D	5000	+	2-T	Persfjord	15/0627	dt	-D	(Convoy E.124)	–	/	Persfjord	5
AUGUST 1944																
11/	sj	L-20	Alekseyev, E. N.					20M Batsfjord								

(1) *S-103* attacked *UJ1209*, *UJ1211* and *UJ1219* and claimed two vessels sunk. The torpedoes were not observed.

(2) One torpedo exploded against the wreck of *Natal*.

(3) Westbound convoy with five small transports and 11 escorts. In the first attack torpedoes were not observed but 33 D/Cs were dropped. In the second *S-104* reported three hits; *UJ1209* was hit by two torpedoes, two detonating at the end of their run. A D/C attack was made by UJs. The third attack was not observed.

(4) Convoy with *R. L. M. Russ*/1448 and two escorts. Torpedoes not observed.

(5) *S-56* claimed one destroyer and one transport sunk. The convoy comprised 10 transports and 21 escorts. Two torpedoes passed astern, there was one surface-runner and D/Cs were dropped. In the second attack, by *M-200*, torpedoes were not observed, although *V6110* had a sonar contact.

1	2	3	4	5	6	7	8	9	10	11	12	13	14	15	16	17
AUGUST 1944 *continued*																
15/0526	sj	L-15	Komarov, V. I.	*DD*		/	6-T	*Laksfjord*					–	/		1
19/0049	sj	M-201	Balin	-D	10000	+	2-T	Persfjord	18/2325	dt	APC	V6112/Friese (?)	452	+	70°N/30°59E	2
23/	sj	S-15	Vasilev	-T		+	-T	Makkaur	23/	dt	-T	(Gretchen/255)	–	/	Makkaur	3
23/1111	sj	S-103	Nechayev	-TBg		/	2-T	Makkaur								
23/1223	sj	S-103	Nechayev	-T	3000	+	3-T	Syltefjord	23/	dt	-T	(Gretchen/255)	–	/	Makkaur	3
24/0646	sj	S-15	Vasilev	-D	7000	=	4-T	Tanafjord	24/0550	dt	-D	Dessau	5933	=	Nordkyn	4
28/1339	sj	S-103	Nechayev	-D	700	+	4-T	Kongsfjord	28/1238	dt	-D	(Convoy W.128)	–	/	Harbaken	5
28/1339	sj	S-103	Nechayev	APC		+	"	Kongsfjord								
SEPTEMBER 1944																
03/	sj	L-15 (?)	Komarov (?)					Kara Sea	03/1435	dt	SS	(U739)	–	/	74°21N/82°30E	6
24/1925	sj	S-56	Shchedrin	-D	4000	+	4-T	Laksfjord	24/-	dt	-D	(Convoy W.134)	–	/	Nordkyn	7
26/1347	sj	S-56	Shchedrin	*PM*		/	2-T	*Laksfjord*	26/1315	dt	*PM*	(M31)	–	/	*NE Nordkyn*	8
26/	sj	S-56	Shchedrin	*PM*		+	2-T	*Laksfjord*					–	/		8
OCTOBER 1944																
10/1057	sj	S-51	Kolosov	-D	8000	+	4-T	Porsangerfjord	10/	dt	-D	(Convoy E.136)	–	/	Laksfjord	9
10/1057	sj	S-51	Kolosov	*DD*		+	"	*Porsangerfjord*					–	/		9

(1) Attack not observed.

(2) Convoy E.128 with six transports and 18 escorts. *V6112/Friese*, the former British trawler *Bradman*, was possibly sunk later in an attack by Soviet TKAs, as was the German steamer *Colmar*, claimed in some sources also by *M-201*.

(3) Attack made with ET-80 torpedoes. *Gretchen*, with three escorts, evaded first two, then three torpedoes. *NKi08/Ruhr/*325 (actually the Norwegian trawler *Rotges/*382), claimed by *S-103*, was not hit and survived the war as *V6701*.

(4) Attack made with ET-80 torpedoes. Convoy W.127 with *M25*. *Dessau* received one torpedo hit and was towed to Mehamn. D/Cs dropped.

(5) Convoy with three transports and seven escorts. Three torpedoes evaded, one surface-runner. *K3* etc. dropped D/Cs.

(6) *U739* reported evading four torpedoes. According to German sigint, *L-15* was in the Kara Sea on 17.8.

(7) Convoy with the steamer *Gothia/*1972 and four escorts evaded three torpedoes.

(8) *S-56* fired first two torpedoes which detonated against the coast, and then two more, one of which exploded and was assumed a hit. In fact, all the torpedoes missed.

(9) *S-51* attacked with ET-80 torpedoes, reported two hits and assumed one transport and one destroyer sunk. Convoy E.136 had three transports and 10 escorts. The torpedoes were not observed.

1	2	3	4	5	6	7	8	9	10	11	12	13	14	15	16	17
OCTOBER 1944 *continued*																
11/1035	sj	V-2	Shchekin	APC	600	+	4-T	Laksfjord	11/	dt	-D	(Convoy E.136)	–	/	71°09N/27°30E	1
11/1035	sj	V-2	Shchekin	APM		=	"	Laksfjord					–	/		1
12/0726	sj	M-171	Kovalenko, G. D.	APC	600	=	2-T	Syltefjord	12/	dt	-D	(Convoy W.135)	–	/	70°39N/30°30E	2
12/1317	sj	S-104	Turayev	-D	7000	+	4-T	Tanafjord	12/1120	dt	-D	Lumme	1730	+	70°55N/29°07E	3
12/1317	sj	S-104	Turayev	APC	800	+	"	Tanafjord					–	/		3
12/1716	sj	V-2	Shchekin	-D	3000	=	4-T	Laksfjord	12/1520	dt	APC	UJ1220/KUJ8	542	+	71°09N/27°57E	3
12/1716	sj	V-2	Shchekin	APM	600	=	"	Laksfjord					–	/		3
15/0050	sj	S-104	Turayev	-D	5000	+	3-T	Tanafjord	15/	dt	-D	(Convoy E.137)	–	/	Berlevaag	4
15/0103	sj	S-104	Turayev	-D	5000	+	1-T	Berlevag								4
16/1327	sj	S-14	Kalanin, V. P.	APM	600	+	4-T	Laksfjord	16/1136	dt	-D	(Convoy E.138)	–	/	Porsangerfjord	5
16/1327	sj	S-14	Kalanin, V. P.	APM	600	+	"	Laksfjord					–	/		5
16/2032	sj	M-171	Kovalenko, G. D.	-D	8000	+	2-T	Syltefjord	16/	dt	-D	(Convoy E.137)	–	/	Persfjord	6
18/0106	sj	V-4	Iosseliani	-T	3000	+	5-T	Porsangerfjord	18/	dt	AM	(Paris/1753)	–	/	Nordkyn	7
20/0446	sj	V-4	Iosseliani	-D	10000	+	2-T	Porsangerfjord	20/0247	dt	APC	UJ1219/KUJ1	542	+	71°06N/27°47E	8
20/0446	sj	V-4	Iosseliani	-D	8000	+	"	Porsangerfjord					–	/		8
20/0914	sj	S-14	Kalanin, V. P.	-D	3000	+	4-T	Laksfjord	20/	dt	-D	(Convoy W.138)	–	/	Nordkyn	9
23/	sj	L-20	Alekseyev, E. N.				17M	Soroy Sund	27.11.M	dt	-D	Adolf Binder	3515	=	Svaerholt	

(1) *V-2* reported three hits. Convoy E.136 (as in 10.10.44 entry) saw one torpedo explode on the coast. The claimed *V6517/KFK120* was in fact in Hammerfest on this day and survived the war as *V6530*.

(2) *M-171* reported one possible hit. Convoy W.136, with two transports and 20 escorts, evaded two torpedoes; the escorts dropped D/Cs.

(3) *S-104* reported two hits and assumed one transport and one escort sunk. The claimed escort *UJ1220/KUJ8* was sunk 4hrs later by *V-2*, which at first claimed two hits and assumed one transport and one minesweeper damaged.

(4) *S-104* made two attacks against the same target and reported one ship sunk. Convoy E.137 had four transports and 20 escorts. Torpedoes not observed.

(5) *S-14* reported hits on two ships and assumed two minesweepers sunk. Convoy E.138, with two transports and 17 escorts, reported two torpedoes evaded. *K3* etc dropped D/Cs.

(6) *M-171* reported one transport sunk. Same convoy as in Note 4; torpedoes not observed.

(7) *V-4* reported three attacks, with three, one and one torpedo: one torpedo failed to launch, but the last hit a tanker. In fact the minesweeper depot ship *Paris* evaded four torpedoes.

(8) *V-4* reported two ships sunk. *UJ1219* was hit by two torpedoes.

(9) *S-14* reported one ship sunk. Convoy W.138, with two transports and 17 escorts, did not observe the torpedoes.

1	2	3	4	5	6	7	8	9	10	11	12	13	14	15	16	17
OCTOBER 1944 *continued*																
									24.11.M	dt	APC	NKi-05/Sperber	178	+	70°46N/29°52E	1
24/	sj	S-102	Gorodnichii	-D		?			24/0950	dt	-D	(Convoy)	–	/	Kongsfjord	2
									30/2338	*dt*	*DD*	*(Z31, Z33)*	–	/	*Vardö*	3
31/0808	sj	S-101	Zinovyev	*DD*		=	*1-T*	*Laksfjord*	31/	dt	APC	(UJ1207/UJ1222)	–	/	Nordkyn	4
31/1515	sj	S-101	Zinovyev	APM		+	2-T	Laksfjord	31/	dt	APC	(UJ1222)	–	/	Nordkyn	5
NOVEMBER 1944																
01/	sj	V-2	Shchekin	-D		+	A	Kelsnerung	01/	nw	-Df	Stortind	169	+	Billefjord	
29/	sj	L-15	Komarov, V. I.				-T	Svaerholt								6

(1) *NKi05/Sperber/Jarnbaden* was hit by a mine at 2025 on 24.10.44 and sunk by gunfire from *M3221* on 25.11.44.

(2) Among the escort, *K3* observed a torpedo which missed.

(3) The two German destroyers reported torpedoes which missed.

(4) *S-101* reported a destroyer damaged by an ET-80 torpedo. The two German UJs evaded three torpedoes.

(5) *S-101* reported one minesweeper sunk with two ET-80 torpedoes. Two more torpedoes failed to launch. *UJ1222* reported one torpedo evaded and dropped D/Cs.

(6) The claimed German steamer *Adolf Binder* was probably damaged by a mine.

II. Norway, North Sea and Biscay

This section lists attacks by British, Polish, Dutch, Free French, US and Norwegian submarines off the coast of Norway south of the Lofoten Islands, in the Skagerrak and Kattegat, in the North Sea, the English Channel and the Bay of Biscay and in the Atlantic Ocean on German vessels and vessels under German control. The sources used were as follows.

British

Naval Staff History, Second World War. Submarines. Vol. I: Operations in Home, Northern and Atlantic Waters (Including the Operations of Allied Submarines). London: Historical Section, Admiralty,1953 (not accessible prior to 1990).

Correspondence with Rear-Admiral P. N. Buckley, London; Gus Britton, HMS *Dolphin*, Gosport; and Miss J. S. Kay, London.

Polish

Correspondence with *Dozent Dr habil.* J. W. Dyskant, Warsaw.

Dutch

Correspondence with Dr P. C. van Royen, Institute for Maritime History, The Hague.

French

Huan, Claude. *Les sous-marins Français 1918–1945*. Paris: Marines Edition, 1995.

US

Correspondence with John D. Alden, Pleasantville, USA.

Norwegian

Correspondence with Prof. Dr Olav Riste, Institut for Forsvarsstudier, Oslo.

German

Kriegstagebuch der Seekriegsleitung 1939–1945. Edited by Werner Rahn, Gerhard Schreiber and Hansgeorg Maierhöfer. Herford/Hamburg: Mittler & Sohn. Vols1–66, 1988–96.

For shipping losses on the German side the following sources were used:

Gröner, Erich. *Die deutschen Kriegsschiffe 1815–1945*. Continued and edited by Dieter Jung and Martin Maas. Vols1–8/2 and Index. München/Bonn: Bernard & Graefe, 1982–94.

Dinklage, Ludwig, and Witthöft, H. J. *Die deutsche Handelsflotte 1939–1945*. Vols1–2. Göttingen: Musterschmidt, 1970–71. (Studien und Dokumente zur Geschichte des Zweiten Weltkrieges, Bd.5a/b.)

Krigsforliste Norske Skip, 3 September 1939–8 Mai 1945. Edited by Sjoefartskontoret. Oslo: Groendal & Sons, 1949.

Correspondence with *Capitaine de Vaisseau* Claude Huan, Paris; Jürg Meister, Montpellier, France; L. L. van Münching, Amsterdam; and Paul Scarceriaux, Antwerp.

1	2	3	4	5	6	7	8	9	10	11	12	13	14	15	16	17
SEPTEMBER 1939																
09/1923	br	URSULA	Phillips	SS		/	5-T	53°52N/06°05E	09/1925	dt	SS	(U35)	–	/	53°57N/06°35E	1
09/1923	br	URSULA	Phillips	SS		/	3-T	53°52N/06°05E	09/1950	dt	SS	(U21)	–	/	53°57N/06°35E	1
10/2100	br	TRITON	Steel	SS		+	2-T	Obrestad	10/	br	SS	Oxley	1354	+	Off Norway	2
11/									11/18	dt	SS	(U4)	–	/	Horns Reef	3
14/0043	br	STURGEON	Gregory	SS		/	3-T	56°22N/01°28E	14/	br	SS	(Swordfish)	–	/		4
17/1210	br	SEAHORSE	Massey-Dawson	SS		/	4-T	56°42N/00°52E	17/	dt	SS	(U36)	–	/	North Sea	5
29/1154	fr	PONCELET	de Saussine	-D		P	–	38°05N/30°40W	29/	dt	-D	Chemnitz	5522	P	Off W Africa	6
30/									30/	dt	SS	(U10)	–	/	15m N Kinnaird	7
30/0220	br	H34	Collett	SS		/	2-T	15m N Kinnaird	30/2245	dt	SS	(U3)	–	/	57°45N/08°00E	8
OCTOBER 1939																
01/0105	fr	REDOUTABLE	Cosleau	-D		–	A	32°40N/13°23W	01/	br	-D	(Egba/6681)	–	/		9
06/0105	br	SEAWOLF	Studholme	CL		/	2-T	57°39N/09°28E	06/	dt	CL	(Nürnberg/Falke)	–	/		
14/1452	br	STURGEON	Gregory	SS		=	3-T	57°49N/09°59E	15/0020	dt	SS	(U23)	–	/	58°03N/10°00E	10
NOVEMBER 1939																
05/	br	L27	Cowell	SS		/	-T	Utvaer								
06/0943	br	SEALION	Bryant	SS		/	6-T	55°10N/02°11E	06/0940	dt	SS	(U21)	–	/	59°21N/03°24E	11
20/1555	br	STURGEON	Gregory	APC		+	4-T	54°33N/06°27E	20/1700	dt	APC	V209/*Gauleiter Telschow	428	+	54°32N/05°10E	12
DECEMBER 1939																
04/1330	br	SALMON	Bickford	SS		+	-T	57°00N/05°20E	04/	dt	SS	U36	754	+		13

(1) *U35* reported two torpedoes and *U21* evaded three, but there was only one attack and a near miss ten minutes later.

(2) *Oxley* was outside the patrol line and was torpedoed in error.

(3) *U4* reported a failed attack.

(4) *Swordfish* was attacked in error but narrowly evaded the torpedoes.

(5) *U36* was surprised while searching a Danish steamer, but the torpedoes missed.

(6) *Chemnitz* was taken as a prize and became the French *Saint Bernard*. She was returned after the German-French armistice.

(7) *U10* reported two torpedoes which missed.

(8) *U3* was surprised while searching a steamer, but the torpedoes missed.

(9) *Redoutable* stopped the British ship, assuming her to be a German blockade-runner, but the latter, which had fired back, was released after establishing her identity.

(10) *Sturgeon* regarded the attack as successful but *U23* reported two torpedoes which missed.

(11) *U21* reported an underwater explosion 500 metres distant.

(12) First British submarine success in WWII.

(13) One torpedo was a surface-runner, but bad sighting conditions covered this.

1	2	3	4	5	6	7	8	9	10	11	12	13	14	15	16	17
DECEMBER 1939 continued																
12/0930	br	SALMON	Bickford	-DP		/	A	57°02N/05°52E	12/	dt	-DP	(Bremen/51731)	–	/		1
13/1036	br	SALMON	Bickford	CL	6000	=	6-T	56°47N/04°00E	13/	dt	CL	Leipzig	6310	=	130mW Jutland	1
13/1036	br	SALMON	Bickford	CL	5000	=	"	56°47N/04°00E	13/	dt	CL	Nürnberg	6980	=	130mW Jutland	1
14/1131	br	URSULA	Phillips	CL	6000	=	4-T	54°08N/07°55E	14/1230	dt	PF	F9	825	+	54°00N/08°00E	2
14/1131	br	URSULA	Phillips	PC	200	+	"	54°08N/07°55E	14/							2
29/	fr	FRESNEL	Daussy	-D			A	Canaries area	29/	br	-D	(Patriot)	–	/		3
JANUARY 1940																
07/1100	br	UNDINE	Jackson	APC		/	1-T	10m W Heligo-land	07/	dt	APM	(M1201, 1204, 1207)	–	/	Heligoland Bight	4
09/0930	br	STARFISH	Turner, T. A.	DD		–	4-T	55°00N/07°10E	09/	dt	PM	(M7)	–	/	Heligoland Bight	5
16/0700	fr	PASCAL	Chuinaud	-D		–	A		16/	br	-D	(Highland Princess)	–	/		3
17/0250	br	TRIBUNE	Balston	SS		=?	6-T	57°50N/11°00E								6
21/	br	TRIBUNE	Balston	SS		?	-T	57°46N/11°00E								6
FEBRUARY 1940																
12/1815	fr	ACHERON	Alliou	-D		–	A	34°25N/18°08W	12/	br	-D	(Somme/5265)	–	/		3
19/0957	br	SUNFISH	Slaughter	SS		/	4-T	54°28N/07°11E	19/	dt	SS	(U14)	–	/		
23/0200	br	SALMON	Bickford	-Df	P	P		10m E Smith's Knoll	23/	be	-Mf	Helene	145	P	Harwich	7
23/	fr	PROTÉE	Garreau (?)	-D		–	A	32°10N/11°00W		fr	-DT	(Aragaz/5009)	–	/		3
25/0752	br	NARWHAL	Burch	SS		+	–	58°40N/00°10W	25/	dt	SS	U63	291	(+)		8
28/2009	br	TRITON	Pizey	-D		/	A	Kristiansand	28/	dt	-D	(Wangoni)	–	/		9

(1) *Salmon* had first tried to stop the German liner *Bremen*, returning from Murmansk, but the ship disregarded the signal and escaped. Then the group with the cruisers, sent out to cover the return of destroyers after a minelaying operation, was attacked. *Nürnberg* was damaged, as was *Leipzig*. The latter became a training ship following repairs in December 1940.

(2) *Ursula* attacked the same force on the next day, assuming the cruiser and an escort hit. *Leipzig* was not hit, but *F9* observed the attack, interposed herself in the torpedo tracks in order to protect the cruiser, was hit and sank.

(3) The French submarines stopped the British vessels, assuming them to be German blockade-runners, but released them.

(4) *Undine*'s torpedo missed one of two trawlers closely astern and was then forced to surface by D/C attacks from the three auxiliary minesweepers and had to be scuttled.

(5) *Starfish* tried to attack a vessel assumed to be a destroyer, but because of a mistake in drill her torpedoes were not fired. The submarine was forced to surface and had to be scuttled when the German minesweeper *M7* tried to board her.

(6) *Tribune* missed a large U-boat. Second attack unclear.

(7) *Helene* was taken as a prize.

(8) *Narwhal* only sighted *U63*; the sinking was accomplished by the destroyers *Escort*, *Inglefield* and *Imogen*.

(9) *Wangoni* disobeyed the order to stop and escaped.

1	2	3	4	5	6	7	8	9	10	11	12	13	14	15	16	17
MARCH 1940																
21/1421	fr	ORPHÉE	Meynier	SS		/	2-T	57°N/05°E	21/	dt	SS	(U51)	–	/		1
21/2146	br	URSULA	Phillips	-D	4947	+	A-T	57°48N/10°53E	21/	dt	-D	Heddernheim	4947	+	Skagerrak	2
23/2330	br	TRUANT	Hutchinson	-D	2189	+	A2T	56°42N/08°04E	24/	dt	-D	Edmund Hugo Stinnes 4	2189	+	Off Jylland	2
APRIL 1940																
04/0413	br	NARWHAL	Burch				50M	57°37N/06°35E	13.04.M	dt	-Df	Deutschland	432	=	E Cape Skagen	3
05/0848	br	UNITY	Brown	SS		/	-T	56°03N/06°35E	05/	dt	SS	(U2)	–	/		4
08/1100	pl	ORZEL	Grudzinski	-D		+	2-T	58°08N/08°29E	08/12..	dt	-D	Rio de Janeiro	5261	+	Off Lillesand	5
08/1215	br	TRIDENT	Seale	-T	8000	+	A1	58°54N/10°21E	08/1330	dt	-MT	Posidonia/*Ossag III	8036	+	48°57N/10°25E	6
08/1758	br	TRITON	Pizey	BB		/	10-T	Off Skagen	08/1900	dt	CA	(Lützow/Blücher)	–	/	Off Skagen	7
09/1604	br	THISTLE	Haselfoot	SS		/	6-T	59°00N/05°10E	09/	dt	SS	(U4)	–	/		8
09/1700	br	SUNFISH	Slaughter	-D		+	2-T	58°13N/11°13E	09/1500	dt	-D	Amasis	7129	+	58°14N/11°14E	9
09/1856	br	TRUANT	Hutchinson	CL	6000	+	10T	58°04N/08°40E	09/2136	dt	CL	Karlsruhe	6730	+	57°55N/08°14E	10
09/	br	TRIAD (?)	Oddie				-T	Kattegat	09/1225	dt	-D	(Kreta/2359)	–	/	59°02N/10°30E	11

(1) *U51* reported torpedoes which missed.

(2) The German steamer *Ostpreussen* was observed by *Truant* aground off Hirtshals and had to be left. The two other German ships were stopped according to prize rules but they tried to escape and were sunk.

(3) The German trawler *Emden*/709grt, claimed by the Admiralty as foundering on this barrage, survived the war. The trawler *Deutschland* was only damaged.

(4) *Unity* missed a small U-boat.

(5) There were three attacks, at 1200, 1205 and 1315, with one torpedo each; the last hit and sank the ship. *Rio de Janeiro* was a troop transport for Operation 'Weserübung' and surviving soldiers in uniform gave the secret away.

(6) *Posidonia* transported fuel for the *Luftwaffe*. The ship was salvaged in June and became the tanker *Stedingen*.

(7) *Triton* assumed her quarry to be the battleship *Gneisenau* and fired 10 torpedoes against the German task group bound for Oslofjord but in fact missed *Lützow*, *Blücher* and *Emden*.

(8) *Thistle* first attacked *U4* and was then sunk by her.

(9) *Amasis* was a returning blockade-runner, the first ship to be sunk following the 'sink on sight' order.

(10) *Karlsruhe* was damaged and later sunk by torpedoes from the escorting torpedo boat *Jaguar*.

(11) *Kreta* reported an attack but was not hit. Swedish reports led to British claims about her sinking by *Sunfish*.

1	2	3	4	5	6	7	8	9	10	11	12	13	14	15	16	17
APRIL 1940 *continued*																
10/0620	br	TARPON	Caldwell	-D		/	2-T	56°43N/06°33E	10/	dt	APC	(Schiff 40)	–	/		
10/1150	br	SUNFISH	Slaughter	-D		/	1-T	3m Maseskär Lt	10/	dt	-D	(Hanau)	–	/		1
10/1520	br	SUNFISH	Slaughter	-D	3000	/	2-T	Maseskär Lt		dt	APC	(7. Vp-Flotilla)	–	/		1
10/1726	br	TRITON	Pizey	-D		+	6-T	57°50N/11°23E	10/1845	dt	-D	Friedenau	5219	+	57°27N/10°46E	
10/1726	br	TRITON	Pizey	-D		+	"	57°50N/11°23E	10/1845	dt	-D	Wigbert	3648	+	57°27N/10°46E	
10/1726	br	TRITON	Pizey				"	57°50N/11°23E	10/1820	dt	APC	V1507/*Rau 6	354	+	57°50N/11°22E	
10/1822	pl	ORZEL	Grudzinski	APC		+	2-T	Skagerrak	10/	dt	APC	(V705)	–	/		2
10/1845	br	TRIDENT	Seale	-D		/	2-T	58°38N/10°32E	10/	dt	-D	(Wandsbek)	–	/	58°36N/10°58E	3
10/2000	br	SUNFISH	Slaughter	-D		+	-T	58°11N/11°17E	10/2105	dt	-D	Antares	2593	+	58°03N/11°00E	1
11/0034	br	SPEARFISH	Forbes	CA		=	6-T	6m N Skagen	*11/0200*	dt	CA	*Lützow*	*11700*	=	57°50N/11°00E	4
11/0055	br	TRIAD	Oddie	-D	4000	+	2-T	58°30N/10°35E	11/night	dt	-D	Ionia	3102	+	Qu. 4129	5
11/1648	br	SEALION	Bryant	-D	3000	+	-T	56°30N/11°30E	11/eveng	dt	-D	August Leonhardt	2593	+	56°29N/11°43E	
11/2145	br	SEVERN	Taylor	-D	6000	/	2-T	Off Kristiansund								
12/0340	br	SNAPPER	King	-T		+	2TA	58°53N/10°43E	12/	dt	-MT	Moonsund	322	+	Off Larvik	6
12/0415	br	SUNFISH	Slaughter	-D	4000	/	1-T	Maseskär								
12/2130	br	STERLET	Haward	-D		/	-T	57°47N/09°39E								7
13/	br	NARWHAL	Burch				50M	57°26N/10°45E	13.04.M	dt	APC	(V302/*Bremen/408)	–	/	E Cape Skagen	8
									14.04.M	dt	APM	M1101/*Fock und Hubert	518	=§	E Cape Skagen	8
									23.04.M	dt	APM	M1302/*Schwaben	436	+	57°28N/10°46E	8

(1) *Sunfish* made two unsuccessful attacks on 10.4.40 and then sank *Antares,* which lost 500 men as a result. The unsuccessful attacks might also have been directed at *Antares*.

(2) *Orzel* fired two torpedoes at a patrol vessel, with unknown results.

(3) *Trident* missed *Wandsbek*.

(4) *Spearfish* claimed *Admiral Scheer* but in fact hit *Lützow* aft with one torpedo and removed her rudder. The ship was towed with great difficulty to Kiel and became operational again only in 1941.

(5) *Ionia* sank on 12.04.40.

(6) *Snapper* missed with two torpedoes and sank the small tanker with gunfire, taking six POWs, two of whom died.

(7) In her last signal *Sterlet* reported an unsuccessful attack on a convoy.

(8) The Admiralty claimed the German trawlers *V302/Bremen* and *M1703* on this minefield, but both ships survived the war. The claimed *Marion*, of c3,000t, could not be identified. The fourth patrol vessel to be claimed as sunk in this field, *UJB* (ex *Treff*), was actually sunk by *Tetrarch* on 23.4.40. *M1101* was beached on 15.4.40 and was a total loss.

1	2	3	4	5	6	7	8	9	10	11	12	13	14	15	16	17
APRIL 1940 *continued*																
13/1222	br	SUNFISH	Slaughter	-D	3000	+	2-T	58°01N/11°27E	13/1325	dt	APC	Schiff 40/*Schürbeck	2448	=	58°01N/11°20E	1
13/1628	br	NARWHAL	Burch				50M	57°26N/10°45E	21.04.M	dt	-D	Togo	5042	=		
13/2158	br	NARWHAL	Burch	-D		/	6-T	Aalbeck Bay								
14/0140	br	SNAPPER	King	-D		/	1-T	58°00N/11°00E	14/	(dt	APC	Schiff 35) (?)	–	/		
14/1400	br	SNAPPER	King	-D	7500	=	5-T	57°59N/10°51E	14/1516	dt	-M	Florida	6150	+	58°10N/10°59E	2
14/1800	br	TRIAD	Oddie	-D		/	2-T	Oslofjord									3
14/1945	br	SUNFISH	Slaughter	-D	6000	+	2-T	57°50N/11°15E	14/2130	dt	APC	Schiff 35/*Oldenburg	2312	+	57°42N/10°54E	2
14/2200	br	STERLET	Haward	*PS*	2400	+	4-T	*58°42N/10°00E*	*14/2335*	*dt*	*PS*	*Brummer*	2410	+	*58°40N/09°56E*	
15/0345	br	SNAPPER	King	-D	7000	=	4-T	57°55N/10°53E	15/0459	dt	APM	M1701/*H.M. Behrens I	525	+	Qu. 4186	4
15/0345	br	SNAPPER	King	-D	500	=	"	57°55N/10°53E	15/0459	dt	APM	M1702/*Carsten Janssen	472	+	Qu. 4186	4
15/1418	br	SHARK	Buckley	-D		/	5-T	57°55N/10°08E	*15/1525*	*dt*	AS	(*Saar*/Angelburg)	–	/	Qu. 4427	5
16/2140	br	PORPOISE	Roberts	*SS*		/	6-T	58°18N/05°47E	*16/*	*dt*	*SS*	(*U3*)	–	/		6
17/0342	br	TAKU	Van der Byl	*DD*		/	4-T	*Stavanger*	*17/*	*br*	*DD*	(*Ashanti*)	–	/		7
18/0100	br	SEAWOLF	Studholme	-D		=	A	Skagerrak									8
18/	br	SEAWOLF	Studholme	-D	5874	+	6-T	58°09N/10°32E	18/0205	dt	-D	Hamm	5874	+	Qu. 4432 r.M.	8

(1) *Sunfish* reported that she had driven a southbound merchant ship ashore. This must have been *Schiff 40*, which was towed into Frederikshavn and repaired.

(2) *Florida* was claimed for *Sunfish* but it seems more probable that she was sunk by *Snapper*, which reported a large ship damaged. *Sunfish* actually sank *Schiff 35*.

(3) *Triad* carried out several abortive attacks between 11.4.40 and 17.4.40.

(4) *Snapper* reported a large ship torpedoed and an escort sunk.

(5) The submarine depot ship *Saar* evaded torpedoes, which must have been fired by *Shark*.

(6) *Porpoise* was credited with the sinking of *U1*, but the attack actually missed *U3*; *U1* had probably been lost already, on or around 6.4.40, on a British mine in approximately 54°06´N/04°24´E.

(7) *Taku* was notified about five German destroyers, but had no knowledge of British destroyers in the area and missed *Ashanti*.

(8) *Seawolf* reported one steamer damaged by gunfire. Possibly it was *Hamm*, torpedoed the next day and sinking while under tow.

1	2	3	4	5	6	7	8	9	10	11	12	13	14	15	16	17
APRIL 1940 *continued*																
19/1530	br	TRIAD	Oddie	-D	4400	+	4-T	58°18N/10°48E	19/	dt	AD	*(Tsingtau/Nautilus)*	–	/		*1*
20/0930	br	TRIAD	Oddie	-D		/	6-T	58°15N/10°15E	20/	dt	-D	(Convoy)	–	/		
20/1318	br	SWORDFISH	Cowell	-D		/	6-T	58°48N/10°19E	20/	dt	-D	(Santos/5943)	–	/		
21/1421	fr	ORPHÉE	Meynier	SS		+	2-T	*57°N/05°E*	*21/*	dt	SS	(U51)	–	/	*North Sea*	2
22/0725	fr	SFAX	Groix	-DP		/	2-T	58°30N/05°30E	22/	dt	-M	(Palime ?)	–	/		3
23/	br	TETRARCH	Mills	-Df		P	–	70m S The Naze	23/	d	-Df					4
23/	br	TETRARCH	Mills	-Df		+	A	70m S The Naze	23/	d	-Df		...	+		4
23/1830	br	TETRARCH	Mills	-D	Large	/	2-T	58°21N/10°24E	23/	dt	-D	(Wolfram ?)	–	/		4
23/2222	br	TETRARCH	Mills	APC		+	2-T	58°21N/10°24E	23/	dt	APC	UJB/*Treff V	330	+	Qu. 4189 l.m.o.	4
25/0545	br	TRIDENT	Sladen	-D		/	2-T	57°30N/06°10E	25/	dt	-M	(Palime, Pelikan)	–	/		
MAY 1940																
01/9727	br	NARWHAL	Burch				50M	57°30N/10°43E	01.05.M	sw	-D	Haga	1296	+	Skagerrak	5
									03.05.M	dt	APM	M1102/*H.A.W. Müller	460	=		5
01/1825	br	NARWHAL	Burch	-D	8500	=	6-T	57°05N/11°35E	01/2035	dt	-D	Bahia Castillo	8580	=§	Qu. 4468 r.u.	6
01/1825	br	NARWHAL	Burch	-D	6000	+	"	57°05N/11°35E	01/2035	dt	-D	Buenos Aires	6097	+	Qu. 4468	6
02/0930	br	TRIDENT	Sladen	-D	5000	=	3TA	Björn Fjord	02/	dt	-M	Cläre Hugo Stinnes	5295	=	Björn Fjord	7
04/0451	br	SEVERN	Taylor	-D	1786	+	1-T	57°57N/06°13E	04/	sw	-D	Monark (dt Prize)	1786	+	SW Norway	8
04/0859	br	SEAL	Lonsdale				50M	57°33N/11°35E	04.05.M	sw	-D	Aimy	200	+	Off Vinga	9
									06.05.M	dt	-D	Vogesen	4241	+	Off Vinga	9
									28.05.M	sw	-D	Torsten	1206	+	4m S Vinga	9
									05.06.M	sw	-D	Skandia	1248	+	Off Vinga	9

(1) *Triad* reported a steamer sunk after two torpedo hits.

(2) *U51* reported torpedoes which missed.

(3) *Sfax* missed a liner.

(4) *Tetrarch* captured two Danish fishing vessels, sinking one and taking the other as a prize to Leith. She then attacked a large ship with three escorts, but was hunted for 42hrs, and, surfacing, was surrounded by A/S vessels of the 5th UJ Group. She fired two torpedoes, one of which sank *UJB*. This loss was at first attributed to a mine laid by *Narwhal* on 13.4.40

(5) Four ships are sometimes claimed for this field, but probably all the successes on the three fields laid by *Narwhal* are included (see 3.4.40 and 13.4.40). Probably *Haga* was lost and *M1102* slightly damaged in this field.

(6) Both ships were first taken in tow, but only *Bahia Castillo* reached harbour, later to be broken up; *Buenos Aires* sank after 3hrs.

(7) The first torpedoes ran under the ship, which was then attacked with 70 rounds of gunfire, forcing her to beach herself; then there was a final torpedo hit. *C. H. Stinnes* was later towed into harbour and repaired (see 6.8.40).

(8) *Monark* was a German prize and was sunk according to prize rules.

(9) It is probable that the four ships struck mines in the field laid by *Seal*.

1	2	3	4	5	6	7	8	9	10	11	12	13	14	15	16	17
MAY 1940 *continued*																
06/1400	br	SEALION	Bryant	-D		=	3-T	19m SW Vaderob.	06/	dt	-D	(Moltkefels)	–	/		1
06/1525	br	SNAPPER	King	-D		/	2-T	56°30N/06°24E	06/1629	dt	ACL	(Schiff 21/Widder)	–	/	55°35N/07°16E	1
06/	br								06/	dt	-Tg	(Tow *Seal*)	–	/	Frederikshavn	2
08/1736	br	TAKU	Van der Byl	-D	3000	+	10-T	56°45N/06°12E	*08/1845*	*dt*	*TB*	*Möwe*	842	=	Qu.3848	3
10/0735	fr	RUBIS	Cabanier				32M	58°21N/06°01E	26.05.M	nw	-Tg	Vansö	54	+	Egersund	4
									07.07.M	nw	-D	Almora	2433	=		4
									24.07.M	nw	-D	Kem	1706	=§	58°22N/06°02E	4
									28.07.M	nw	-D	Argo	412	+	2m Skarvy	4
									17.10.44	dt	APC	UJ1764 (KFK 216?)	110	+	58°21N/06°00E	4
11/2357	fr	AMAZONE	Richard	SS		/	2-T	*52°55N/04°28E*	*11/*	*dt*	*SS*	*(U7 or Shark)*	–	/		5
11/1701	br	NARWHAL	Burch				50M	62°58N/06°48E	30.05.M	dt	APC	V1109/*Antares	291	+	Off Molde	6
13/1345	br	CLYDE	Ingram	-D		/	A	Stadlandet	13/1240	dt	ACL	(Schiff 21/Widder)	–	/	60°21N/04°24E	7
15/1045	br	PORPOISE	Roberts				50M	61°40N/04°55E								8
20/0056	fr	ANTIOPE	Balastre	SS		/	3-T	*53°23N/03°44E*	*20/*	*fr*	*SS*	*(La Sibylle)*	–	/		9
20/0333	br	SPEARFISH	Forbes	-Df		+	A	55°00N/03°00E	20/	da	-Df	S.130	...	+		10
20/0450	br	SPEARFISH	Forbes	-Df		+	A	55°00N/03°00E	20/	da	-Df	S.175	...	+		10
23/1202	br	TETRARCH	Mills	-Df		+	S	56°55N/06°50E	23/	da	-Df	Terieven	...	+		10
23/1330	br	TETRARCH	Mills	-Df		P	P	56°59N/06°58E	23/	da	-Df	Emmanuel	...	P		10
23/1430	br	TRUANT	Haggard	-D		/	-T	71°12N/26°50E	23/	dt	-D	(Alster, br prize)	–	/	N Norway	11
23/1730	br	TETRARCH	Mills	-Df		P	P	57°00N/07°00E	23/	da	-Df	Jens Hvas	...	P		10
27/0435	fr	RUBIS	Cabanier				32M	59°28N/05°12E	28.05.M	nw	-S	Blamannen	174	+	Bleivik	12
									31.05.M	nw	-D	Jadarland	938	+	Sletten/Haugesund	12
									.10.M	nw	-D	Öyulf	173	+	Haugesund	12

(1) The two attacks are probably the same.

(2) *Seal* was damaged and surrendered to a German aircraft and patrol vessels; she was attacked while under tow to Frederikshavn, but the torpedoes missed.

(3) *Möwe*, escorting a convoy, lost her rudder and screws but was towed in and repaired.

(4) *Kem* was claimed by *Snapper* in error on 24.06.40 (q.v.); the ship was raised and repaired. The Norwegian sailing vessel *Cito* is sometimes claimed but was lost on a German mine off the Sognefjord. The loss of *UJ1764* after so long a period is doubtful.

(5) Both *U7* and *Shark* reported torpedoes that missed.

(6) The Admiralty claimed *Blamannen* for this barrage, but it was later established that the ship sank on the *Rubis* barrage of 27 May.

(7) *Schiff 21* tried to evade the gun attack but fired back and forced *Clyde* to dive.

(8) No success known.

(9) *Antiope* attacked *La Sybille* in error but the torpedoes missed.

(10) *Spearfish* and *Tetrarch* searched Danish fishing vessels, sank the first three after saving the crews and took the last to to Leith.

(11) *Truant* missed *Alster*/8514grt, taken as a prize by HMS *Icarus* and escorted by HMT *Ullswater. Preussen*, sometimes claimed, was in fact in the Mediterranean at the time.

(12) *Blamannen* was also claimed for the British *Narwhal* (see Note 6). The Norwegian steamer *Kyvig*/763, sometimes claimed, was sunk on 26.10.40 by RAF aircraft off the Sognefjord. The barrage was partly swept by the 5th R-Flotilla on 2.6.40.

1	2	3	4	5	6	7	8	9	10	11	12	13	14	15	16	17
JUNE 1940																
03/1937	br	NARWHAL	Burch				50M	58°46N/05°25E	*05.06.M*	*dt*	*PM*	*M11*	*682*	+	*Feiesteio1*	*1*
									05.06.M	dt	-D	Palime	2863	=§	Jaederensrev	1
									28.09.M	dt	-D	Clara L. M. Russ	1600	=	Off Jaeren	1
09/2210	fr	RUBIS	Cabanier				32M	60°36N/04°55E	10.06.M	nw	-D	Sverre Sigurdsson	1081	+	Hjeltefjord	2
12/2119	br	NARWHAL	Burch				50M	59°26N/05°10E	16.08.M	nw	-D	Jaederen	908	+		3
									16.08.M	dt	APC	NB15/Biene	178	=		3
									26.08.M	nw	-Df	Arild	128	+	Osterfjord	3
									13.10.M	dt	APM	Gnom 7	50	+		3
									13.10.M	dt	APM	Kobold 1	50	+		3
									13.10.M	dt	APM	Kobold 3	50	+		3
14/1448	br	PORPOISE	Roberts				50M	63°30N/08°12E	*18.06.M*	*dt*	*PM*	*M5*	*682*	+	*63°30N/08°09E*	
16/0508	br	TETRARCH	Mills	-T	8000	+	-T	58°12N/06°13E	16/	dt	-MT	Samland	5978	+	SW Lista	4
20/0029	pl	WILK	Karnicki	*SS*			*R*	*56°50N/03°37E*		*nl*	*SS*	*O-13*	*568*	+		5
20/1630	br	SALMON	Bickford	-D		/	2-T	58°18N/05°40E								
20/2209	br	CLYDE	Ingram	*BB*	26000	=	6-T	64°43N/09°32E	*20/*	*dt*	*BB*	*Gneisenau*	*32200*	=	*63°43N/09°32E*	*6*
21/1810	br	H44	Norman, E. D.	-D	3000	+	2-T	12m Dutch coast	21/	d	-D	Alfa	844	+	Off Texel	
22/0136	br	TRIBUNE	Balston	-D	7000	/	-T									
23/0332	br	TRIDENT	Sladen	-T		/	4-T	64°21N/09°12E	23/	dt	AO	(Dithmarschen)	–	/		
25/1535	br	SNAPPER	King	-D		+	3-T	58°54N/05°05E	25/1520	dt	APC	V1107/*Portland	286	+	S Stavanger	7
25/1604	br	SNAPPER	King	-D		/	3-T	58°54N/05°05E								7
26/0300	fr	RUBIS	Cabanier				32M	62°28N/05°20E								8

(1) *Palime* was beached after striking a mine; *Clara L. M. Russ* was damaged.

(2) Six mines were swept on 12.6.40, 19 more on 14.6.40. The Norwegian tug *Draugen*/184 sank on a German mine on 15.7.40 off Salhus, north of Bergen; *Snorre I* sank on 20.11.40 at Kjkkelvik off Bergen on a mine, probably German.

(3) The positions of the last five losses are not known for certain.

(4) *Samland* sank after two hits.

(5) The rammed submarine was very probably the Dutch *O-13*, which went missing at this time in the area.

(6) *Gneisenau* received one hit in the bow and had to cancel an Arctic operation and return to Trondheim.

(7) The Norwegian steamer *Kem*/1706 was assigned because of an error in the date (June/July); the ship was actually sunk on a mine laid by *Rubis* (see previous page, Note 4).

(8) The German patrol vessel *UJD/Treff VIII*/356, sometimes claimed, in fact sank on 6.7.40 farther east in 63°16´N/07°30´E on a mine but was salvaged. The Norwegian trawler *Draugen*/184 was sunk on another minefield.

1	2	3	4	5	6	7	8	9	10	11	12	13	14	15	16	17
JULY 1940																
03/1748	br	SNAPPER	King	-D	1400	+	-T	58°18N/05°13E	03/	nw	-D	*Cygnus*	1334	+	58°13N/05°06E	1
03/1748	br	SNAPPER	King	-D		=	"	58°18N/05°13E								1
03/1550	br	SEALION	Bryant	-D		/	6-T	Skudesnes								2
04/	br	NARWHAL	Burch				50M	63°15N/07°34E	06.07.M	dt	APC	UJD/*Treff VIII	356	+	63°15N/07°39E	2
07/	br	SNAPPER	King	-D		=	-T	Jaeren					–	/		4
07/	br	SNAPPER	King	-D		=	"	Jaeren								4
08/	br	SEALION	Bryant	-D(wr)		/	1-T	Obrestad	08/	dt	-D	(Palime wreck 2863§)		/		5
16/2230	br	CLYDE	Ingram	-Df	15	+	A	62°18N/04°19E	16/	nw	-Df	*S.F.52*	15	+	62°13N/04°15E	
18/0737	br	H31	Wanklyn	APC		+	1-T	53°29N/05°03E	18/0855	dt	APC	UJ126/*Steiermark	422	+	53°28N/05°01E	
26/	br	THAMES (?)	Dunkerley						26/1550	dt	TB	*Luchs*	922	+	*60°N/04°E*	6
27/ ?	br	NARWHAL	Burch				M?	63°16N/07°13E								7
28/	br	SWORDFISH	Cowell	-Y		+	A	55°33N/01°31E	28/	nw	-Y	*Maski*	...	+		8
29/	br	THAMES (?)	Dunkerley						29/2233	dt	SS	(U62)	–	/	*58°21N/04°24E*	7
AUGUST 1940																
01/1615	nl	O-21	Van Dulm	*SS*		/	-T	*North Sea*	01/	dt	SS	(U62?)	–	/		9
02/1620	nl	O-22	Ort	*SS*		/	-T	*North Sea*	02/	dt	SS	(U37 or U38)	–	/		9
04/1515	br	SEALION	Bryant	-D	3300	+	-T	58°17N/08°38E	04/	nw	-D	*Torun*	3318	+	Homborsund	10
06/1700	br	SEALION	Bryant	-D		/	4-T	Kristiansand	06/1513	dt	-D	(Cläre Hugo Stinnes)	–	/	57°51N/07°24E	10
19/	br	CACHALOT	Luce				50M	47°03N/04°21E								
20/0116	br	CACHALOT	Luce	*SS*		+	-T	47°06N/04°51E	20/	dt	SS	*U51*	753	+	*Biscay*	11

(1) *Snapper* reported two ships hit, one of them sunk. German A/S vessels hunted first *Snapper* and then *Sealion* for 45hrs.

(2) *Sealion* fired six torpedoes, all of which missed.

(3) *UJD* was also attributed to *Rubis'* minefield of 26.6.40 but *Narwhal's* was closer to the position in which the ship sank.

(4) *Snapper* claimed two ships damaged.

(5) *Sealion* missed a wrecked steamer, probably *Sigurd* or *Palime*.

(6) There are claims that the British submarine *Swordfish* fired a spread against the battleship *Gneisenau*, returning for repairs to Germany escorted by the cruiser *Nürnberg*, four destroyers and five torpedo boats. *Luchs* was hit, broke in two parts and sank. However, the attack may have been that carried out by the lost *Thames* on *U62*, or it may have been made by an FAA *Swordfish*.

(7) It is unclear whether *Narwhal* completed her minelaying before being lost.

(8) The yacht was used by four Norwegians to escape. They were picked up by the submarine and the yacht was sunk.

(9) The U-boat attacked on 1.8.40 was probably not the claimed *U60*, which departed for a patrol only on 4.8.40, but the returning *U62*. The second attack was probably directed against either *U37* or *U38*, which were departing for an Atlantic patrol from the North Sea.

(10) *Torun's* loss was at first attributed to a mine. *C. H. Stinnes*, damaged by *Trident* (see 2.5.40), was missed by four torpedoes. *Sealion* was rammed by *UJ123* and damaged.

(11) *U51* was damaged on 16.8.40 by Sunderland 'H/210' 170m NW of Tory Island.

1	2	3	4	5	6	7	8	9	10	11	12	13	14	15	16	17
SEPTEMBER 1940																
01/	br	TIGRIS	Bone	-Df	600	+	A	Biscay	01/	fr	-Df	Sancte Michael	168	+	Off Brest	1
01/0150	br	TUNA	Cavenagh-Mainwaring	SS		/	-T	*56°09N/02°15E*								
02/2234	br	TIGRIS	Bone	SS		/	-T	*47°29N/04°04W*	02/	dt	SS	*(U58)*	–	/		*1*
02/2300	br	STURGEON	Gregory	-D	10000	+	2-T	*57°50N/10 46E*	02/	dt	-D	Pionier	3624	+	57°58N/10°45E	2
03/	br	TRUANT	Haggard	-D	5781	+	Psc	*47°00N/10°43W*	03/	nw	-M	Tropic Sea	5781	+	46°50N/11°50W	3
06/0640	br	TRIBUNE	Balston	SS		+	-T	*57°58N/08°13W*								4
10/1348	br	STURGEON	Gregory	SS		+	-T	*Skagerrak*	510/	dt	SS	*(U43)*	–	/		
16/0448	br	H49	Langley	-D		=	2-T	*53°16N/04°42E*								5
22/	br	TUNA	Cavenagh-Mainwaring	-D	7230	+	3-T	*45°19N/01°20W*	22/1340	nw	-M	Tirranna	7230	+	18m N Culebra	6
24/	br	TUNA	Cavenagh-Mainwaring	-D		+	-T	Off Royan	24/0542	dt	AV	Ostmark	1280	+	47°01N/03°02W	7
24/	br	CACHALOT	Luce	SS		+?	-T	*46°58N/05°56W*								
OCTOBER 1940																
01/	br	H49	Langley	-D		/	-T	Dutch coast								
01/0947	br	SWORDFISH	Cowell	TB		+	-T	*49°48N/01°24E*	01/1050	dt	TB	*(Falke, Kondor)*	–	/		8
05/0716	br	TIGRIS	Bone	SS		+?	-T	Biscay	05/	it	SS	*(Otaria)*	–	/		
08/dawn	br	TRIDENT	Sladen	SS		=	A	*47°28N/03°25E*	08/	dt	SS	U31	745	=	*Biscay*	9
15/	br	L27	Campbell	-D	7000	+	4-T	*47°45N/01°30E*								10
16/0155	br	TIGRIS	Bone	-Df	250	+	A	*45°44N/03°45W*	16/	fr	-Df	Cimcour	250	+		
19/1505	pl	WILK	Krawczyk	-D	2000	/	3-T	Lister Fjord	09/	da	-D	(Norge) (?)	–	/		11
23/	br	TAKU (?)	Brown	-D		+	-T		23/	nw	-D	Prinsesse Ragnhild	1590	+	N Bodö	12

(1) *Tigris* made a night attack against a supposed U-boat which was later identified as a trawler—probably *Sancte Michael*—and missed *U58*.

(2) *Pionier* was transporting troops, some of whom were rescued.

(3) The Norwegian *Tropic Sea* was a prize of the German AMC *Schiff 36*, was stopped by *Truant* and was scuttled by the prize crew. The crew of the captured British steamer *Haxby* and the Norwegian crew were rescued.

(4) *Tribune* reported a U-boat sunk after sighting debris, but the only two missing German U-boats, *U102* and *U122*, were lost earlier in 6.40.

(5) The claimed German steamer *Heimdal*/2186grt sank on 23.9.40 on a mine.

(6) The Norwegian steamer *Tirranna* was a prize of the German AMC *Schiff 16* and was sunk with three torpedoes.

(7) *Ostmark* was a catapult ship for reconnaissance flying boats.

(8) *Swordfish* assumed that she had sunk one of four *Elbing* class destroyers, *Falke*, *Kondor*, *Greif* and *Wolf*, which were on a minelaying operation.

(9) *U31* was only slightly damaged by gunfire.

(10) The sinking claimed by *L27* could not be verified.

(11) *Wilk* reported three unsuccessful torpedoes fired against a Danish transport which could not be identified.

(12) The loss was at first attributed to a mine.

1	2	3	4	5	6	7	8	9	10	11	12	13	14	15	16	17
OCTOBER 1940 *continued*																
24/	br	SEAWOLF (?)					A		24/0130	dt	AG	WBS5/*Adolf Vinnen	391	+	25m W Stadlandet	1
27/1614	br	SWORDFISH	Cowell	-D	5000	=	-T	49°45/01°20E								2
29/0900	nl	O-24	de Booy	-M		/	-T	Norwegian coast								
NOVEMBER 1940																
02/0230	br	TAKU	Brown	-T	Large	+	-T	46°54N/03°50W	02/	dt	-DT	(Gedania/8923)	–	/	Biscay	3
02/morn	br	TIGRIS	Bone	SS		/	2-T		02/	it	SS	(Veniero)	–	/	*Off Gironde*	4
03/1010	br	STURGEON	Gregory	-D	2000	+	-T	58°59N/10°21E	03/	d	-D	Sigrun	1337	+	59°01N/10°20E	
05/	br	STURGEON	Gregory	-D		/	-T	Lister	05/	nw	-D	(Uly/1200)	–	/		
06/1455	br	STURGEON	Gregory	-D	1300	+	-T	58°34N/05°37E	06/1600	nw	-D	Delfinus	1294	+	Obrestad Lt	
12/2340	br	TIGRIS	Bone	-Df		+	A	45°41N/02°57E	12/	fr	-Sf	Charles Edmond	301	+	60m W Gironde	5
14/							A		14/	fr	-Df		–	/	100m W Rochelle	
25/	br	TALISMAN	Francis	-T		=?	-T	47°37N/03°50W								6
25/1509	br	TALISMAN	Francis	-Df		P	P	47°16N/04°16E	25/	fr	-Df	Le Clipper	40	P	Lorient	6
DECEMBER 1940																
05/1509	br	SUNFISH	Colvin	-D	4000	+	-T	62°03N/05°06E	05/	fi	-D	Oscar Midling	2182	+	Aalesund	7
07/1516	br	SUNFISH	Colvin	-D		=	-T	62°10N/05°05E	07/	nw	-DT	Dixie	1715	=		
10/1120	br	TRIBUNE	Balston	-T		=	-T	Ile de Yeu								8
15/	br	THUNDERBOLT		SS		+	-T	*45°25N/01°22W*	*15/*	it	SS	*Tarantini*	*1031*	+	*Gironde*	9
16/	br	TRIBUNE	Balston	-T		=	-T	46°46N/02°38E	16/	dt	-DT	(Karibisches Meer)	–	/		10
18/0430	br	TUNA	Cavenagh-Mainwaring	SS		=	TA	*45°28N/02°27W*	*18/*	it	SS	*(Brin)*	–	/		9
18/2314	br	TUNA	Cavenagh-Mainwaring	-Tg	250	+	A	45°28N/01°38E	19/0030	fr	-Tg	Chassiron	172	+	Gironde	11

(1) *Adolf Vinnen* was not sunk by destroyers on 15.10.40 but by an unknown submarine. Only *Seawolf* was in the area, but she did not report such an attack.

(2) *Swordfish* attacked a convoy of eight vessels, heard one explosion and saw black smoke.

(3) *Taku* heard a heavy explosion and reported the tanker sunk, but it was probably a premature and *Gedania* was not badly damaged; she was captured on 4.6.41 by HMS *Marsdale* on her next cruise and taken to Gibraltar.

(4) *Veniero* reported a submarine attack, which must have been made by *Tigris*.

(5) *Tigris* reported the vessel sunk by gunfire.

(6) *Talisman* saw the tanker stopped and assumed a hit on an escort. She was sent to capture a tunny fishing vessel, using the prize to observe German U-boat movements. *Le Clipper* operated off Bordeaux and was then taken to Falmouth.

(7) *Oscar Midling* was a neutral Finnish vessel, returning to her home country.

(8) *Tribune* heard explosions and saw the tanker listing.

(9) The sinking of *Tarantini* and the attack on *Brin* may have been a consequence of *Le Clipper*'s reconnaissance. The unsuccessful torpedo attack on *Brin*, returning with *Bianchi* from Ceuta, was followed by a gun action, but the submarines escaped.

(10) *Tribune* claimed a large tanker damaged.

(11) The French vessel was sunk because it was operating from German-held bases.

1	2	3	4	5	6	7	8	9	10	11	12	13	14	15	16	17
DECEMBER 1940 *continued*																
									[18/	dt	-D	Birkenfels/6322]				1
19/	br	TRIBUNE	Balston	-D	5000	/	-T	47°02N/04°14W								2
27/0815	br	TRIDENT	Sladen	-D		/	5-T	Punta Delgada	27/	pa	-D	(Router)	–	/	Punta Delgada	3
JANUARY 1941																
26/	br	CACHALOT	Newton				50M	Biornsund								
30/	br	SUNFISH	Colvin	-T	4000	/	-T	Kristiansand								4
FEBRUARY 1941																
01/1500	br	SEALION	Bryant	-D	4500	=	-T	Off Stadlandet	01/1600	dt	-D	(Convoy)	–	/	62°11N/05°24E	5
02/	br	SUNFISH	Colvin	-D		/	-T	Kristiansand								4
05/1200	br	SEALION	Bryant	-D	1154	+	TA	Stadlandet	05/	nw	-D	Ryfylke	1151	+	Stadlandet	6
11/	br	SNAPPER		–	–	–			11/	dt	PM	(M2, M13, M25)	–	/	47°52N/05°47W	7
12/0611	br	TIGRIS	Bone	-D	1500	+	2-T	43°30N/01°42E	12/	fr	-Df	René Camaleyre	243	+	Biscay	8
15/	br	CACHALOT	Newton	-D			-T	Fro Havet								9
15/	br	CACHALOT	Newton				50M	Vest Fjord								9
19/	br	TIGRIS	Bone	-D		+	-T	Biscay	19/	fr	-D	Jacobsen	523	+	Bayonne	8
19/0245	br	TIGRIS	Bone	-D	3222	+	6-T	44°48N/03°01W	19/	fr	-D	Guilvenec	3273	+	60m W St Nazaire	8
MARCH 1941																
07/	br	PORPOISE	Hopkins	*SS*		/	-T	*57°50N/19°50W*								
20/	br	STURGEON	St Clair-Ford	-D	3000	+	4-T	Obrestad	20/							10

(1) *Birkenfels* was sunk on 18.12.40 off the Schelde by British MTBs, not by the submarines *Tribune* or *Thunderbolt*.

(2) *Tribune* was foiled in her attack by her quarry's very effective dazzle camouflage.

(3) *Trident* stopped the darkened ship but fired torpedoes when she again attempted to enter port.

(4) *Sunfish* missed a tanker and had torpedo failures in an attack on an escorted convoy.

(5) *Sealion* claimed a steamer damaged, but the torpedo detonated on the rocky coast.

(6) *Ryfylke* was sunk by gunfire after a torpedo had missed.

(7) *Snapper* probably attacked the minesweepers and was then sunk by their D/C attack.

(8) The small French vessels were sunk by *Tigris* because they were operating out of German-occupied bases.

(9) No successes reported.

(10) *Sturgeon* claimed to have sunk a Norwegian ship, *Drafn*, of about 3,000t, but according to Norwegian sources the motor tanker *Drafn*/8205 was not in Norwegian waters at the time.

1	2	3	4	5	6	7	8	9	10	11	12	13	14	15	16	17
APRIL 1941																
03/early	br	TIGRIS	Bone	-T	10000	+	TA	100m SW St Nazaire	03/	dt	-DT	Thorn/*Ruth	5486	+	SW St Nazaire	1
18/	br	URGE	Tomkinson	-T	10500	+	1-T	41°36N/08°46W	18/	it	-DT	Franco Martelli	10535	+	46°31N/08°46W	2
18/1756	fr	MINERVE	Sonneville	-D	2000	/	2-T	2m SW Tungenes								
19/1215	fr	MINERVE	Sonneville	-T	6000	+	2-T	58°40N/04°55E	19/1330	dt	APM	(M1101/-DT Tiger)	–	/	58°42N/05°34E	3
25/1137	br	URGE	Tomkinson	-D	3000	/	-T	41°36N/08°46W								
MAY 1941																
23/	br	PANDORA	Linton	SS		/	A									*4*
									[23??	fr	-Df	Notre Dame de Chatelet/488]			45°27N/05°18W	*4*
JUNE 1941																
15/	br	THUNDERBOLT	Crouch	SS		/	8-T	*42°00N/47°00W*	*15/*	dt	SS	(U557)	–	/		*5*
JULY 1941																
05/	br	TIGRIS	Bone	SS		+	6-T	*45°N/04°W*	*05/*	it	SS	*Bianchi*	*1036*	+	*Biscay*	*5*
07/0424	pl	SOKOL	Karnicki	-D	10000	/	4-T	*46°41N/20°30W*								7
07/	br	SEALION	Bryant	-Df		+	A	Off Ushant	07/	fr	-Df	Gustav-Jeanne	39	+	Off Ushant	8
07/	br	SEALION	Bryant	-Df		+	A	Off Ushant	07/	fr	-Df	Gustav-Eugene	120	+	Off Ushant	8
08/	br	SEALION	Bryant	-Df		+	A	Off Ushant	08/	fr	-Df	Christus Regnat	28	+	Off Ushant	8
09/	br	SEALION	Bryant	-Df		+	A	Off Ushant	09/	fr	-Df	St Pierre d'Alcantara	329	+	Off Ushant	8
10/	br	TUNA	Cavenagh-Mainwaring	SS		/	-T	*46°00N/09°40W*								

---

(1) A night attack with torpedoes failed. In a gun action the tanker was heavily damaged and then sunk by another torpedo.

(2) *Franco Martelli* was an Italian blockade-runner coming from Brazil.

(3) *M1101* was escorting the German tanker *Tiger*/3941.

(4) *Pandora* claimed hits in a gun action with an Italian submarine, but the target was not the French vessel, which had already been sunk on 11.5.41 by gunfire from *U43*. The Italian submarine *Otaria* rescued survivors on 23.5.41.

(5) *Thunderbolt* fired first six and then two torpedoes, all of which missed.

(6) The claimed sinking of *Bianchi* by *Severn* on 7.8.41 must be wrong; *Tigris* was probably responsible.

(7) *Sokol* reported launching four torpedoes, which missed, against a large transport.

(8) The French fishing vessels were sunk by Bryant according to an Admiralty Fleet Order which was afterwards cancelled.

1	2	3	4	5	6	7	8	9	10	11	12	13	14	15	16	17
JULY 1941 *continued*																
17/	br	THRASHER	Cowell (?)	-Df		= §	A	S. Sebastian	17/	fr	-Df	Virgo Fidelis	129	=§	S. Sebastian	1
19/	br	TUNA	Cavenagh-Mainwaring	-D	4000	=	6-T	*60m W Gironde*	19/	dt	-MT	(Benno/*Ole Jacob)	–	/	W Gironde	2
19/	br	TUNA	Cavenagh-Mainwaring	DD		=	6-T	*60m W Gironde*								
30/	br	SEAWOLF	Raikes	SS		/	-T	*Off Lorient*	30/1	dt	SS	(U562)	–	/		
AUGUST 1941																
07/night	br	SEVERN	Campbell	SS		+	-T	*34°48N/13°04W*	07/	it	SS		–	/		3
21/1425	fr	RUBIS	Rousselot				19M	58°27N/05°46E								
21/1535	fr	RUBIS	Rousselot	-T	3000	/	-T	58°27N/05°46E	21/							4
21/1535	fr	RUBIS	Rousselot	-D	4000	+	"	58°27N/05°46E	21/	fi	-D	Hogland	4360	+	58°28N/05°47E	4
SEPTEMBER 1941																
02/				-T					02/	dt	-D	Oslebshausen	5074	+	Off Obrestad	
									[10/	dt	APM	M1102/*H. A. W. Müller/460]			58°08N/06°38E	5
21/	fr	MINERVE	Sonneville	-D	1200	/	-T	Bue Fjord								
28/	br	CLYDE	Ingram	SS		/	TA	*Cape Verde*	28/	dt	SS	(U111, U67)	–	/	*Tarafal Bay*	6

(1) *Virgo Fidelis* was beached and became a total loss.

(2) *Tuna*, in a night attack, assumed two hits. The ex Norwegian prize was escorted by *M18*, *M25*, *M27* and *M30*, whose crews heard six detonations.

(3) *Severn* claimed to have sunk *Bianchi*, but the latter must have been lost earlier, probably to a torpedo from *Tigris* on 5.7.41 (q.v.).

(4) The minelaying was interrupted when the first (unsuccessful) attack was made. After completing the minelaying, *Hogland* was sunk by two torpedoes. Five mines were swept on 24.8.41 by the 11th M/S Flotilla.

(5) *M1102* was sunk at 1335 by an RAF airborne torpedo.

(6) Through 'Ultra' the British Admiralty were alerted to a planned replenishment of the German U-boats *U68*, *U111* and *U67* in Tarafal Bay, Cape Verde Islands, and sent *Clyde* to attack. The British torpedoes missed. *U67* rammed *Clyde* lightly and both submarines had to return.

1	2	3	4	5	6	7	8	9	10	11	12	13	14	15	16	17
OCTOBER 1941																
01/	br	SWORDFISH	Langley	DD		+	-T	Cape Barfleur	01/	dt	TB	(4 TB)	–	/		
									[04/	nw	-D	Borgny/3015]			Korsfjord, SW Norway	1
14/									14/1835	dt	APC	UJ1709/*Carl Kämpf (?)	600	+	58°30N/06°07E	1
15/	br	L27	Edmonds	-D		=	3-T	Cherbourg								
29/	fr	MINERVE	Sonneville	-T		/	4-T	Norway	29/	nw	-D	(?)				
NOVEMBER 1941																
19/	br	RORQUAL	Dewhurst				50M	La Rochelle	M	fr	-Df	Coligny	600	+	Off Rochelle	2
26/1530	br	P36	Edmonds	SS		/	-T	47°16N/03°20W								3
DECEMBER 1941																
27/0815	br	TRIDENT	Sladen	-D		/	5TA	Punta Delgada	27/	pa	-D	(Router)	–	/		
JANUARY 1942																
16/1605	fr	RUBIS	Rousselot				32M	43°25N/01°41W								4
FEBRUARY 1942																
../....	br	CLYDE	Ingram	SS		/	2-T	Punta Delgada	../	br	SS	Regent	–	/	Punta Delgada	5
23/0551	br	TRIDENT	Gregory	CA	15700	=	7-T	63°12N/07°00E	23/	dt	CA	Prinz Eugen	14906	=	Lister	6
23/0551	br	TRIDENT	Gregory	CA	12100	?	"	63°12N/07°00E	23/	dt	CA	(Admiral Scheer)	–	/	Lister	6

(1) *Borgny* was not sunk by a submarine as sometimes claimed, but by Norwegian MTBs. *UJ1709* was assumed sunk by an unknown submarine with a torpedo, but is sometimes erroneously claimed by Norwegian submarine *Ula* on 14.10.43. This was possibly also an attack by Norwegian MTBs.

(2) The French trawler *Coligny* was claimed on this minefield.

(3) The track angle was too great.

(4) There were four 8-mine barrages.

(5) *Clyde*, escorting the tanker *Dingledale*, fired two torpedoes at *Regent*, sailing to effect repairs at Punta Delgada. They missed.

(6) *Trident* reported hits on two German cruisers, but only *Prinz Eugen* was struck, in the stern. *Admiral Scheer* was missed.

1	2	3	4	5	6	7	8	9	10	11	12	13	14	15	16	17
MARCH 1942																
									[14/	dt	-D	Nicole Schiaffino/ 4974]			Near Tromsö	1
18/	br	SEAWOLF	Raikes	SS		=	-T	Frohavet								2
21/2003	fr	RUBIS	Rousselot					32M 56°35N/06°18E								3
APRIL 1942																
12/2040	fr	RUBIS	Rousselot					32M 63°06N/06°31E								
18/1400	br	TRIDENT	Hezlet	-D	3000	/	-T	Off Villa								4
20/1400	br	TRIDENT	Hezlet	-D	5368	+	3-T	64°38N/10°49E	20/	dt	-D	Hödur	5368	+	NW Namsos	
MAY 1942																
JUNE 1942																
05/1400	fr	RUBIS	Rousselot					32M 43°37N/01°35W	26.06.M	fr	-Tg	Quand Même	288	+	Vieux Boueau	5
									12.06.M	dt	APM	M4212/*Marie Frans	125	+	43°37N/01°34W	5
									20.09.M	dt	APM	M4448/*Antoine Henriette (?)	77	+	Entrance Bayonne	5
26/	br	UNRIVALLED	Turner, H. B.	SS		/	1-T	65°03N/03°27E								6
JULY 1942																
07/	fr	RUBIS	Rousselot					31M 44°38N/01°24E	10.07.M	dt	APM	M4401/*Imbrien	339	+	44°58N/01°23W	
11/1005	br	UNRIVALLED	Turner, H. B.	SS		/	-T	63°36N/02°20E								7
11/	br	SAHIB	Bromage	SS		/	-T	53°16N/02°E								8

(1) *Nicole Schiaffino* was not sunk by a submarine but grounded near Tromsö and became a total loss.

(2) *Seawolf* fired at long range, heard a detonation and sighted wreckage and oil.

(3) The tug *Talyn*/50, sometimes claimed, was in fact sunk on 21.3.42 near Heligoland.

(4) The torpedoes exploded on the shore.

(5) *M4448* may also have been sunk by an aerial mine. *M4211*/139 (ex *Irena Raphael*), sometimes claimed, was sunk on 24.8.40, salvaged and recommissioned on 5.4.41.

(6) *Unrivalled* was numbered *P45*.

(7) *P45/Unrivalled* unsuccessfully attacked a U-boat with torpedoes and gunfire.

(8) *Sahib* was numbered *P212*.

1	2	3	4	5	6	7	8	9	10	11	12	13	14	15	16	17
AUGUST 1942																
03/2128	br	SARACEN	Lumby	SS		+	6-T	62°48N/00°12W	03/	dt	SS	U335	769	+		1
12/1515	br	STURGEON	Wingfield	-D	3500	+	-T	59°08N/06°25E	12/	dt	-D	Boltenhagen	3335	+	58°08N/06°25E	
12/1610	br	UNSHAKEN	Oxborrow	-D	3000	+	-T	58°37N/05°30E	12/1706	dt	-D	Georg L. M. Russ	2980	+	58°42N/02°08E	2
12/1610	br	UNSHAKEN	Oxborrow	-D	5500	=	"	58°37N/05°30E								2
14/1030	fr	RUBIS	Rousselot				32M	44°40N/01°39W	18.08.M	dt	APC	V406 (Hans Loh)	464	+	45°03N/01°34E	3
									[22.09.M		SS	U600	769	=]	Off Arcachon	3
16/1707	nl	O-21	Van Dulm	SS		/	-T	Holy Loch–Gibraltar	16/	dt	SS	(U254)	–	/		4
SEPTEMBER 1942																
17/									[17/	dt	-D	Karpfanger/4974]			Off Egersund	5
19/1040	fr	RUBIS	Rousselot				15M	69°44N/17°23E								6
OCTOBER 1942																
10/2140	br	SIBYL	Turner, E. J.	-D		/	4-T	Biscay								7
16/1225	fr	JUNON	Querville	-D	4000	/	1-T	61°10N/12°20E	16/	nw	-D	(Norge)	–	/		
18/0815	fr	JUNON	Querville	-D	2000	+	2-T	67°00N/12°46E								8
18/1548	nw	UREDD	Rören	-D	3000	+	2-T	Araldan Island	18/after.	dt	-D	Libau	3713	=§	67°00N/12°46E	9
19/1103	fr	JUNON	Querville	-D	5000	+	2-T	6m S Vestfjord	19/	nw	-D	Nordland	724	+	67°12N/12°57E	10
21/									[21/	dt	-D	Palatia (?)/3979		+]	Nr Lindesnes	11
21/1650	br	GRAPH	Marriott	SS	500	+	-T	44°31N/07°25W	21/	dt	SS	(U333)	–	/		12

(1) *Saracen* was numbered *P247*.

(2) *P54/Unshaken* assumed that she hit two ships.

(3) *U600* was probably damaged on an air-laid acoustic mine.

(4) *O-21* was en route from Holy Loch to Gibraltar.

(5) *Karpfanger* was sunk probably not by an unknown submarine but by air attack.

(6) The Norwegian steamer *Nordland/724*, sometimes claimed, was sunk on 19.10.42 by *Junon* (see Note 10).

(7) *P217/Sibyl* missed with two torpedoes: one ran crooked and one circled.

(8) *Junon* reported one hit and claimed that the vessel was beached.

(9) *Libau/3663* (ex *Kaganovich*) was hit in the engine room and was beached to make the damage waterproof. However, the damage proved to be beyond repair.

(10) *Nordland* is sometimes erroneously credited to *Rubis*.

(11) *Palatia* was probably sunk by an airborne torpedo.

(12) *Graph* claimed a successful attack; *U333* reported torpedoes which missed.

1	2	3	4	5	6	7	8	9	10	11	12	13	14	15	16	17
NOVEMBER 1942																
08/11..	am	HERRING	Johnson	-D	7000	+	4-T	33°34N/07°52W	08/	fr	-D	Ville du Havre	5083	+	Casablanca	1
09/	am	BLACKFISH	Davidson	-D	7000	=	2-T	17°45N/14°50E	08/1259	fr	PS1	(Commandant Bory)	–	/	Nr Dakar	2
20/	nl	KXIV	Geijs	SS		/	-T	Cape Verde								3
22/	nl	KXIV	Geijs	-D		/	-T	Cape Verde	22/	dt	-M	(Blockade-runner) (?)	–	/		3
26/	nl	DOLFIJN	Van Oostrom Soede	SS		/	-T	Biscay	26/	dt	SS					4
DECEMBER 1942																
12/	br	TUNA	Raikes				LM	Bordeaux	../	dt	-D	Alabama	6725	=	Bordeaux	5
							LM	Bordeaux	../	dt	-M	Tannenfels	7840	=	Bordeaux	5
							LM	Bordeaux	../	dt	-M	Dresden	5567	=	Bordeaux	5
							LM	Bordeaux	../	dt	-M	Portland	7132	=	Bordeaux	5
26/2246	am	BARB	Waterman	-T		=	-T	Cape Finisterre	26/	sp	-MT	Campomanes	6276	=	Off Finisterre	6
JANUARY 1943																
04/05..	am	SHAD	MacGregor	APC	600	+	A	43°55N/02°42W	[03/1120	dt	APM	M4242/*Odet/212		=]	St Nazaire	7
04/05..	am	SHAD	MacGregor	-Bg		+	A	43°55N/02°42W								7
09/07..	am	SHAD	MacGregor	-D	800	/	2-T	43°44N/02°28W								

(1) *Ville du Havre* was a Vichy French ship.
(2) *Blackfish* claimed that she had damaged a ship of the *Ango* class/7000grt. The Vichy French sloop, escorting three steamers, reported an exploding torpedo.
(3) The attacks by *KXIV* could not be found in German documents.
(4) The attack by *Dolfijn* remains uncertain.
(5) *Tuna* launched a Royal Marine Commando with canoes at the mouth of the Gironde to paddle upstream and attack German ships with limpet mines. The four ships mentioned, mostly blockade-runners, were damaged; *Sperrbrecher 5* (ex *Schwaneck*) escaped damage when the mine attached to her fell off.
(6) *Barb* is assumed to have hit an Axis vessel.
(7) *M4242* (ex *Odet*) was, according to German sources, sunk by bombs during an Allied air raid on St Nazaire on 3.1.43 but was later raised and repaired.

1	2	3	4	5	6	7	8	9	10	11	12	13	14	15	16	17
JANUARY 1943 *continued*																
17/	nw	UREDD	Rören	AS		=	-T	Aalesund	17/	dt	AS	(*Adolf Lüderitz*)	–	/		1
25/10..	am	SHAD	MacGregor	-D	1200	=	2-T	43°28N/02°59W	25/1030	dt	-D	Nordfels	1214	=	N Bilbao	2
FEBRUARY 1943																
19/1700	am	BLACKFISH	Davidson	APC	1000	+	4-T	43°30N/02°54W	19/1755	dt	APC	V408/*Haltenbank	432	+	43°29N/02°57	3
MARCH 1943																
21/01	am	HERRING	Johnson	*SS*	*500*	*+1*	*2-T*	*44°13N/08°23W*	*[../*	*dt*	*SS*	*U163 (?)]*				4
APRIL 1943																
01/0342	am	SHAD	MacGregor	-D	10000	=	6-T	44°37N/02°18W	01/	it	M	Pietro Orseolo	6344	=	Off Gironde	5
01/0342	am	SHAD	MacGregor	DD		=	6-T	44°37N/02°18W	01/	dt	DD	Z23	2529	=		5
07/2109	br	TUNA	Martin, D. S.	SS		+	5-T	69°38N/05°40W	07/	dt	SS	U644	769	+		
14/	br	TUNA	Martin, D. S.	SS		/	4-T		14/0746	dt	SS	(U302)	–	/	AA 9639	6
									[27/	it	-D	Butterfly/5127]			Off St Nazaire	7
28/even	br	USURPER	Mott	SS		/	-T	Biscay	28/	dr	SS	(U467)	–	/		
MAY 1943																8
30/	br	TUNA	Martin, D. S.	SS		+	8-T	Norway								9
JUNE 1943																
04/	br	TRUCULENT	Alexander	SS		+	-T	64°28N/03°09W	04/	dt	SS	U308	769	+		
10/	br	SEADOG	Pelly	SS		/	-T	Norway								

(1) *Adolf Lüderitz* was sailing from Narvik.

(2) *Nordfels* was slightly damaged by a dud torpedo and returned to Bilbao.

(3) *Blackfish* fired two torpedoes each at two patrol vessels. The second counter-attacked and damaged the submarine.

(4) The attack by *Herring* remains unclear. The missing *U163* was very probably sunk by the Canadian corvette *Prescott*, escorting convoy MKS.9, on 13.3.43 in 45°05´N/15°00´W.

(5) The blockade-runner *Pietro Orseolo*, coming from Japan, was picked up by four German destroyers when one torpedo from *Shad* damaged the ship, which was brought into the Gironde. The destroyer *Z23* was hit by a dud.

(6) *U302* reported an unsuccessful submarine attack with four torpedoes NE of Iceland.

(7) *Butterfly* was sunk by an MTB and not by a submarine.

(8) The oft-reported damage to the German steamer *Bahia Castillo*/8580 on 1.5.43 is a mistake: the ship was damaged on 1.5.40.

(9) *Tuna* reported a success.

1	2	3	4	5	6	7	8	9	10	11	12	13	14	15	16	17
JULY 1943																
02/	br	STUBBORN	Duff	SS		/	6-T	Biscay								1
04/									04/1010	dt	SS	(U586)	–	/	75°39N/17°10E	2
05/	fr	RUBIS	Rousselot				32M	42°21N/01°26W	10.07.M	dt	APM	M4451/*Gauleiter Alfred Meyer	652	+	44°58N/01°10W	3
13/	br	SEANYMPH	Oakley	SS		/	-T	Biscay								4
AUGUST 1943																
05/	fr	RUBIS	Rousselot				32M	47°50N/04°58W								5
22/1147	br	TUNA	Martin, D. S.	SS		/	-T	Biscay								6
27/	br	UNTIRING	Boyd	-Df		+	SA	62°50N/02°10E	27/		nw	-Df	Havbis II	...	+	7
30/1023	fr	RUBIS	Rousselot				32M	43°41N/01°34W								5
SEPTEMBER 1943																
14/	br	UPSTART	Lambert, C. W.	-Df		+		Biscay	14/	fr	-Df	Grotte de Bethlehem	49	+	S Brittany	8
14/	br	UPSTART	Lambert, C. W.	-Df		+		Biscay	14/	fr	-Df	Torpille	46	+	S Brittany	8

(1) *Stubborn* fired at three U-boats escorted by two destroyers.

(2) *U586* reported a submarine attack south of the South Cape of Spitzbergen.

(3) Three mines were swept on 10.7.43. The German steamer *Bordsee*/959 was damaged on 10.7.43 by a mine off La Coubre/Gironde.

(4) *Seanymph* made a snap attack against two incoming U-boats.

(5) There were no successes on the barrages.

(6) *Tuna*'s torpedoes exploded behind the target.

(7) *Untiring* sank the fishing vessel, which was acting in a suspicious manner, and took the crew of seven prisoner.

(8) Both vessels were sunk after the crews had been taken off.

1	2	3	4	5	6	7	8	9	10	11	12	13	14	15	16	17
OCTOBER 1943																
02/	fr	RUBIS	Rousselot				32M	47°44N/04°51W								1
14/	nw	ULA	Sars	APC	600	+	-T	58°20N/00°07E								2
NOVEMBER 1943																
22/1417	nw	ULA	Sars	-D	3500	+	1-T	62°14N/05°14E	22/	nw	-D	Arcturus	1681	+	SW Aalesund	3
22/1417	nw	ULA	Sars	APC	800	+	1-T	62°14N/05°14E								3
24/	nw	ULA	Sars	-D	8000	/	4-T	Bredsund								3
24/	nw	ULA	Sars	-D	4500	=	3-T	62°26N/06°04E	24/	dt	-D	Eisstrom/*Marietje Bohmer	928	+	Aalesund	3
DECEMBER 1943																
18/	br	STUBBORN	Duff	-D		/	-T	Kya Lt								
19/	br	SATYR	Weston	-D		/	-T	Stadlandet	19/1100	nw	-D	(Roald Jarl)	–	/	N Stadlandet	4
26/1157	nl	O-15	Schouwenaar	-D	2500	=	3-T	59°10N/04°55E	26/1248	dt	APC	(UJ....)	–	/	Boknfjord	5
26/1157	nl	O-15	Schouwenaar	-D	2500	=	"	59°10N/04°55E								5
26/1157	nl	O-15	Schouwenaar	-D	2500	=	"	59°10N/04°55E								5
28/	br	SEADOG	Pelly	-D		+	-T	62°13N/05°08E	26/1205	dt	-D	Oldenburg	8537	+	62°13N/05°08E	6
28/	nw	ULA	Sars	-D		/	-T	Skudesnes								

(1) The German auxiliary *UJ1403*/472 (ex *Mecklenburg*) was sunk on 24.10.43 in a collision with the French trawler *Anne Alice* in 47°22´N/05°08´W, and not by a mine as was stated in a court-martial. 14 mines were swept after her loss.

(2) *Ula* also intercepted a Swedish ship, which was released. The claimed *UJ1709*/600 (ex *Carl Kämpf*) was sunk on 14.10.41 (q.v.).

(3) *Ula* first attacked a three-ship convoy, presuming a Norwegian ship and one escort sunk. Two days later she first missed a convoy in a long-range attack, then two hours later sank *Eisstrom*, the former Dutch steamer *Marietje Bohmer*.

(4) *Roald Jarl* reported four torpedoes which missed.

(5) *O-15* reported three hits on three ships. A UJ of the 12th A/S Flotilla reported two torpedoes, which missed, off Boknfjord.

(6) *Oldenburg* was hit by two torpedoes.

1	2	3	4	5	6	7	8	9	10	11	12	13	14	15	16	17
JANUARY 1944																
01/	nw	ULA	Sars	-D		/	-T	Skudesnes	01/0937	dt	-D	(Convoy)	–	/	S Karmsund	1
02/1150	br	SEADOG	Pelly	-D	2000	+	4-T	W Norway	02/1158	dt	APC	(V5308)	–	/	N Stadlandet	2
03/	br	SEADOG	Pelly	-T		/	-T		03/1150	dt	-D	(Convoy)		/	Stadlandet	3
04/	br	SCEPTRE	McIntosh	-D	Small	/	-T		04/	dt	-D	(Convoy)	–	/	Foldafjord	4
04/									04/	dt	APC	(V5717)	–	/	Kristiansand N	5
									[20/	dt	ACM	Skagerrak/1281]			Off Egersund	6
26/1119	br	STUBBORN	Duff	-D	2500	/	4-T	Follafjord	26/1100	dt	-D	(Convoy)	–	/	Namsos	7
FEBRUARY 1944																
03/									03/0928	dt	-D	(Convoy)	–	/	Follafjord	8
05/	br	SATYR	Weston	-D	4500	=?	-T	Off Stadlandet								9
05/	br	SATYR	Weston	-D	5000	+	1-T	Off Stadlandet	05/	dt	-D	Emsland (wreck)	5170	=	Stadlandet	9
07/1030	br	TAKU	Pitt	-D	6000	+	-T	59°07N/05°37E	07/1030	dt	-D	Rheinhausen	6298	+	Skudesnesfjord	
10/	br	SATYR	Weston	-D	2500	/	4-T	Nr Sandy								10
11/1219	br	STUBBORN	Duff	-D	2000	+	6-T	24m WNW Namsos	11/1150	dt	-D	Makki Faulbaums	1907	+	Follafjord	11
11/1219	br	STUBBORN	Duff	-D	3000	+	"	24m WNW Namsos	11/1150	fr	-D	(Cambronne)	–	/	Follafjord	11
11/1219	br	STUBBORN	Duff	-D	3000	=	"	24m WNW Namsos	11/1150	dt	-D	Felix D.	2047	=	Follafjord	11

(1) Three torpedoes, which missed, were reported.

(2) *Seadog* claimed hits on a convoy of three ships and two escorts. It was assumed that *Emsland*/5170grt was one victim, but this ship was struck by an airborne torpedo at 1130 on 20.1.44 west of Stadlandet and beached near Ervik. The wreck was probably torpedoed by *Satyr* on 5.2.44 and bombed on 11.2.44, but this victim is sometimes claimed to be *Eisstrom II*, which could not be identified. *Eisstrom I*, the former Dutch steamer *Marietje Bolmer*/943grt, was sunk on 24.11.43 by the Norwegian submarine *Ula* (q.v.). There is also a claim that *Seadog* sank the gunboat *K2* (ex Dutch) in this attack, but this vessel was heavily damaged on 9.10.44 off Egersund by airborne torpedo and became a wreck. *Seadog*'s attack on 2.1.44 must have been the detonation that *V5308* reported 500 metres aft that day.

(3) A southbound convoy reported torpedoes which missed.

(4) A northbound convoy reported torpedoes which missed.

(5) *V5717* reported a torpedo which missed.

(6) *Skagerrak* (q.v.), sometimes claimed, was sunk in an RAF air attack.

(7) A southbound convoy reported two torpedoes which missed.

(8) A northbound convoy reported five torpedoes which missed.

(9) See Note 2 on this page.

(10) *Satyr* reported the ship with two escorts missed.

(11) *Stubborn* fired six torpedoes and reported hits on three ships. *Cambronne* was assumed to be damaged because of radio intercepts. *Makki Faulbaums* (ex *Rolfs Faulbaums*) was lost and *Felix* damaged from a convoy of seven ships with five escorts and one aircraft.

1	2	3	4	5	6	7	8	9	10	11	12	13	14	15	16	17

FEBRUARY 1944 *continued*

1	2	3	4	5	6	7	8	9	10	11	12	13	14	15	16	17
12/1200	br	TAKU	Pitt	-D	3000	+	4-T	59°34N/05°17E	12/1200	dt	-D	Harm Fritzen	4818	=	Haugesund	1
13/1155	br	STUBBORN	Duff	-D	2000	+	6-T	64°37N/10°25E	13/1146	dt	-D	(Convoy)	–	/	Foldafjord	2
13/1155	br	STUBBORN	Duff	-D	4500	=	"	64°37N/10°25E	13/1146	dt	-D	(Convoy)	–	/		2
13/1710	br	TAKU	Pitt	-D	3000	+	4-T	59°09N/05°24E	13/1710	dt	-D	Hans Bornhofen	2130	+	59°08N/05°24E	3
13/1710	br	TAKU	Pitt	-D	3000	=	"	59°09N/05°24E								3
20/	nw	ULA	Sars	-D		=	4-T	Listafjord	20/1200	dt	AV	(Bussard)	–	/	20m SE Egersund	4
20/	nw	ULA	Sars	-D		=	"	Listafjord								4
24/	fr	RUBIS	Rousselot				32M	401N/130W								5
25/	nw	ULA	Sars	-D	2000	+	-T	Listafjord	25/0845	nw	-D	(Ryfylke/898)	–	/	Off Lister	6

MARCH 1944

1	2	3	4	5	6	7	8	9	10	11	12	13	14	15	16	17
01/	br	SEANYMPH	Oakley	-D	5000	/	4-T	Off Bodö	01/1231	nw	-D	(Jupiter)	–	/	N Mosjoen	7
02/2211	br	VENTURER	Launders	-D	3000	+	1-T	62°10N/05°05E	02/2238	dt	-D	Thor	2526	+	Stadlandet	
03/	br	SEANYMPH	Oakley	D	7000	/	4-T	Off Bodö	03/0940	dt	-D	(Levante)	–	/	Off Bodö	8
06/	br	VENTURER	Launders	-D	6500	=?	4-T	Off Stadlandet								
07/1115	br	SCEPTRE	McIntosh	-D	7850	+	-T	64°32N/10°38E	07/1120	dt	-D	Lippe	8340	=§	Foldafjord	9
07/1115	br	SCEPTRE	McIntosh	-D	3000	=	"	64°32N/10°38E								9
07/1115	br	SCEPTRE	McIntosh	-D	3500	=	"	64°32N/10°38E								9

(1) *Harm Fritzen* was beached, later salvaged and, on 3.5.46, delivered to the USSR.

(2) *Stubborn* reported three hits from six torpedoes fired at two ships; a southbound convoy with five ships, five escorts and two aircraft reported five torpedoes which missed. The submarine was badly damaged by D/Cs from *ND12*, *V5715* and *M151* and had to be towed back to Leith by HMS *Musketeer* and *Scourge*. The claimed Norwegian *Irma*/1392 and *Henry*/634grt were sunk at 1830 by the Norwegian *MTB627* and *MTB632*. The loss of the German steamer *Irma* (ex *Everonika*)/3757 was caused by an accident on 14.3.44 off Frohavet.

(3) *Taku* reported three hits from four torpedoes, but only *Hans Bornhofen* (ex *Magdalena Reith*) was sunk.

(4) *Ula* claimed that she heard two explosions. *Bussard* reported two torpedoes that missed.

(5) The French tug *Bernache*/357 had already been sunk on 9.4.41 (not 23.5.44) in the La Rochelle Canal. She was salvaged after the war.

(6) *Ula* reported two hits; *Ryfylke* reported two torpedoes which missed.

(7) *Jupiter* reported torpedoes which missed.

(8) *Levante* reported four torpedoes missing.

(9) *Sceptre* reported hits on three ships. *Lippe* was damaged and beached but on 8.3.44 broke in two and was a total loss.

1	2	3	4	5	6	7	8	9	10	11	12	13	14	15	16	17
MARCH 1944 *continued*																
12/									12/1727	dt	-D	(*M81*,Convoy)	–	/	64°51N/11°22E	1
13/	br	SCEPTRE	McIntosh	-D	5000	=	-T	Kya Area	13/morn.	dt	-D	(Convoy)	–	/	Follafjord	2
22/1400	br	SYRTIS	Jupp	-D		+	A	66°45N/13°11E	22/1400	nw	-D	Narvik	241	+	66°45N/13°11E	3
24/0838	br	TAKU	Pitt	-T	10000	/	5-T	27m W Namsos	24/0830	dt	-M	(Moshill/5322)	–	/	64°33N/10°37E	4
24/1008	br	SATYR	Weston	-D	991	+	-T	62°16N/05°06E	24/1008	nw	-D	Nordnorge	340	+	Stadlandet	5
24/1312	br	TERRAPIN	Martin, D. S.	-T	8188	+	4-T	58°09N/06°28E	24/1315	dt	-DT	(Wörth/*Omala)	6256	=	S Egersund	6
24/1312	br	TERRAPIN	Martin, D. S.				"	58°09N/06°28E	24/1315	dt	AV	Schwabenland	8186	=	S Egersund	6
25/	fr	RUBIS	Rousselot				32M	41°N/00°W								7
APRIL 1944																
04/0615	nw	ULA	Sars	-T	6000	+	-T	62°15N/05°58E	04/0605	dt	-MT	Ill/*Turicum	7603	=	Stadlandet	8
06/0925	nw	ULA	Sars	-D	2000	+	-T	60°09N/05°07E	06/	dt	-D	Wesergau	1923	=§		9
07/	br	UNSHAKEN	Whitton	-D	7000	+	4-T	58°07N/13°05E	07/0748	dt	-D	Asien	3894	+	Lister	10
08/									08/1215	dt	-D	(Convoy)	–	/	S Obrestad	11
14/	br	X24	Shean	-D	7880	+	LM	Bergen	14/1500	dt	-D	Bärenfels	7569	+	Bergen	12
							LM	Bergen	14/	nw	-D	Krosdol	177	+?	Bergen	12
							LM	Bergen	14/	nw	-D	Rogoland	902	+?	Bergen	12

(1) *M81* heard four explosions of torpedoes that missed.

(2) *Sceptre* reported missing a ship; a convoy reported torpedoes which missed.

(3) *Narvik* (ex *Stabil No 365*) was sunk by gunfire. *Syrtis* was then lost, probably on a German mine.

(4) *Moshill*, in a convoy, reported torpedoes which missed.

(5) *Nordnorge* was claimed to be 991grt.

(6) *Terrapin* fired on a convoy of five ships and five or six escorts and was thought to have hit one ship with two torpedoes and probably damaged a second. *Wörth* was damaged and taken to Flekkefjord, repaired and delivered to Holland on 14.2.46. The flying boat catapult ship *Schwabenland* was damaged, taken to Flekkefjord and beached. She was salvaged and sunk with gas shells in the Skagerrak on 31.12.46.

(7) No results reported. The claimed sinking of the French trawler *Bernache*/352 on a mine laid by the French submarine *Rubis* on 23.5.44 is incorrect: the vessel had been sunk on 9.4.41 off La Rochelle, though she was raised after the war.

(8) *Ill* (ex *Turicum*) continued her voyage at 8kts

(9) *Wesergau* was grounded but became a total loss and was scrapped *in situ*.

(10) *Unshaken* attacked a ship with two escorts, *UJ1105* and *M489*.

(11) A convoy reported torpedoes that missed.

(12) *X24* was towed by *Sceptre*. *Bärenfels* was sunk by a limpet mine. The two small ships were reported to have been alongside, but there is also a claim that they were lost in an air raid.

1	2	3	4	5	6	7	8	9	10	11	12	13	14	15	16	17
APRIL 1944 *continued*																
15/2015	br	VENTURER	Launders	-D	5000	+	-T	58°15N/06°00E	15/2029	dt	-D	Friedrichshafen	1923	+	15m SSE Eger-sund	1
19/0700	nw	ULA	Sars	SS		+	-T	59°08N/05°23E	19/0710	dt	SS	U974	769	+	S Karmsund	
22/0330	nw	ULA	Sars	-D	4000	+	-T	58°07N/06°27E	22/0306	dt	-D	Bahia	4117	+	Lister	
MAY 1944																
17/									17/night	dt	SS	(U965)	–	/	Off Vestfjord	2
18/									18/night	dt	SS	(U...)	–	/	66°45N/10°22E	3
21/0045	br	SCEPTRE	McIntosh	-D		+	-T	43°24N/03°30W	20/	dt	-D	Hochheimer	1762	+	Off Bilbao	4
21/0045	br	SCEPTRE	McIntosh	APC		+	"	43°24N/03°30W								4
21/0045	br	SCEPTRE	McIntosh	APC		+	"	43°24N/03°30W								4
23/1407	br	SCEPTRE	McIntosh	-D		+	-T	Santa Caballo	23/1407	dt	-D	Baldur/*Jacob Christensen	3630	+	Castro Urdial	
JUNE 1944																
15/09..	br	SATYR	Weston	SS		+	6-T	68°01N/05°08E	15/	dt	SS	U987	769	+		5
JULY 1944																
05/	br	VIKING	Bannar-Martin	SS		/	-T	70°N/00°W								6
AUGUST 1944																
08/									08/night	dt	SS	(U482)	–	/	Oslofjord	7
20/1840	br	SATYR	Weston	-D	3000	=	4-T	Skudesnes	20/after.	dt	-D	(Bochum, E. Sauber)	–	/	S Karmsund	8
22/1750	br	SATYR	Weston	-D		+	6-T	Egeröy	22/	dt	-D	(6 ships, 6 escorts)	–	/	Egersund	9
22/1750	br	SATYR	Weston	-D		=	"	Egeröy					–	/	Egersund	9

(1) The convoy comprised three ships, escorted by *UJ1101*, *UJ1102*, *UJ1103* and *UJ1112*.

(2) *U965* reported two torpedoes which missed.

(3) A U-boat reported a torpedo spread which missed.

(4) *Sceptre* reported three hits and assumed that, in addition to *Hocheimer*, she had sunk the escorts *V405* and *V402*, but the latter were scuttled in Bayonne in 8.44.

(5) Two of the torpedoes collided and exploded, but two others hit the U-boat.

(6) The U-boat combed the torpedo tracks.

(7) *U482* reported two torpedoes which missed.

(8) *Satyr* reported one hit, but the torpedo exploded against the shore. The ships were escorted by *V5101*.

(9) *Satyr* reported five explosions; the convoy, with five ships and three escorts, reported six which caused large columns of water. The escorts were *UJ1109*, *M437*, *UJ1709*, *UJ1712*, *R220* and *M5807*.

1	2	3	4	5	6	7	8	9	10	11	12	13	14	15	16	17
SEPTEMBER 1944																
01/1808	br	VIKING	Banner-Martin	-D	3000	=	-T	58°36N/05°39E	01/1808	dt	-D	(3 ships, UJ1113)	–	/	SW Obrestad	1
04/	br	VIKING	Banner-Martin	-DT		/	-T	Egersund	04/1308	dt	-D	(Convoy)	–	/	10m SE Egersund	2
11/1158	br	VENTURER	Launders	-D	3000	+	-T	58°03N/06°34E	11/1225	nw	-D	Vang	678	+	Lister	3
11/1353	br	X24	Westmacott	-Dock			LM	Bergen	11/1353	nw		Floating dock	...	+	Bergen	4
11/1353	br	X24	Westmacott	-D	1820	+	LM	Bergen	11/	nw	-D	Sten	1464	=	Bergen	4
11/1353	br	X24	Westmacott	-D	941	=	LM	Bergen	11/	nw	-D	Kong Oscar II	941	=	Bergen	4
13/1518	br	VENTURER	Launders	-D	1300	+	-T	WNW Egersund	13/after.	nw	-D	(Force/499)	–	/	NW Egersund	5
20/	br	SCEPTRE	McIntosh	-D		/	-T	Skudesnes								6
20/2330	br	SCEPTRE	McIntosh	-D	7000	+	6-T	58°27N/05°51E	20/even.	nw	-D	Vela	1184	+	SW Egersund	6
20/2330	br	SCEPTRE	McIntosh	-D	3000	=	"	58°27N/05°51E	20/2355	dt	PM	M132	685	+	58°23N/05°34E	6
21/									21/	nw	-D	(Karin/750)	–	/	NW Egersund	7
24/	fr	RUBIS	Rousselot				M	58°45N/05°24E	26.09.M	dt	APC	UJ1106/*Grönland	447	+	58°45N/05°24E	8
									27.09.M	dt	-M	Cläre Hugo Stinnes	5295	+	58°45N/05°24E	8
									27.09.M	nw	-D	Knute Nelson	5749	+	58°45N/05°24E	8
									27.09.M	dt	APC	UJ1715/*Lesum	489	+	58°41N/05°31E	8
30/	br	SATYR	Weston	-D		/	-T	Tenholm	30/after.	nw	-D	(Lofoten)	–	/	SW Bodö	9

(1) A convoy reported four torpedoes which missed and four explosions, two of them against the shore.

(2) A convoy reported torpedoes missing.

(3) *Venturer* reported three explosions.

(4) *X24* was towed by *Sceptre* again. The ships were sunk or damaged by limpet mines.

(5) *Force* was missed by three torpedoes and attacked by gunfire, but the submarine had to dive when coastal batteries opened up.

(6) *Sceptre* reported two ships sunk after an unsuccessful attack with six torpedoes. The convoy of two ships was escorted by *M1*, *M132* and *UJ1113*.

(7) *Karin* reported three torpedoes which missed.

(8) The convoy of seven ships and 10 escorts ran into the barrage. The German steamer *Walter/2301*, sometimes claimed, was lost by grounding on 19.10.44 near Stavanger.

(9) *Lofoten* reported torpedoes which missed.

1	2	3	4	5	6	7	8	9	10	11	12	13	14	15	16	17

OCTOBER 1944

1	2	3	4	5	6	7	8	9	10	11	12	13	14	15	16	17
14/1135	br	VIKING	Banner-Martin	-D	2500	+	-T	67°09N/14°09E	14/1135	nw	-D	Standard	1286	+	Saltenfjord	
18/1236	fr	RUBIS	Rousselot				31M	60°44N/04°40E	27.10.M	dt	APC	V5304*/Seehund	320	=	60°55N/000E	1
21/2258	br	SCEPTRE	McIntosh	-D	6000	+	4-T	58°35N/05°30E	20/2258	dt	APC	UJ1111/*F.D.35	510	+	58°37N/05°30E	2

NOVEMBER 1944

1	2	3	4	5	6	7	8	9	10	11	12	13	14	15	16	17
11/	br	VENTURER	Launders	*SS*		+	4-T	*69°17N/16°28E*	*11/*	*dt*	*SS*	*U771*	*769*	+		
24/0443	fr	RUBIS	Rousselot				32M	58°26N/05°49E	24.11.M	nw	-D	Castor	1683	=	Egersund	3

DECEMBER 1944

1	2	3	4	5	6	7	8	9	10	11	12	13	14	15	16	17
16/	nw	UTSIRA	Valvatne	*SS*		+	-T	*Halten*								4
19/	fr	RUBIS	Rousselot				30M	58°51N/05°30E	21.12.M	dt	-D	Weichselland	3654	+	58°50N/05°29E	5
									21.12.M.	dt	APC	UJ1113/*KUJ7	830	+	558°50N/05°32E	5
									21.12.M.	dt	APC	UJ1116/*KUJ11	830	+	558°51N/05°31E	5
									21.12.M.	dt	PR	R402	127	+	558°49N/05°27E	5
									21.12.M	dt	APC	UJ1702/*KUJ16	830	+	58°51N/05°31E	5

JANUARY 1945

1	2	3	4	5	6	7	8	9	10	11	12	13	14	15	16	17
11/	nw	UTSIRA	Valvatne	*SS*		=	-T	*N Vaagsöy*								6
16/0200	nw	UTSIRA	Valvatne	-D	2000	+	4-T	64°36N/14°40E	16/0202	dt	APC	V6408/*Skagerrak	536	+	64°36N/10°40E	
20/	br	VENTURER	Launders	-D	2500	=	4-T	15m NW Namsos								
22/2342	br	VENTURER	Launders	-D	1000	+	1-T	59°06N/05°18E	22/	dt	-D	Stockholm	618	+	NW Stavanger	

(1) *V5304* was damaged and beached, but refloated and repaired.

(2) *Milos*/2207grt, claimed sunk by *Sceptre* on 20.10.44, actually struck a mine and exploded with her load of dynamite. The German steamer *Nordsturm* was damaged when colliding with the sinking wreck. *Sceptre* fired two spreads each of two torpedoes and assumed one transport sunk.

(3) *Castor* was only damaged.

(4) The torpedo detonated prematurely.

(5) The convoy consisted of five ships, one U-boat and six A/S vessels. The circumstances surrounding the loss of *UJ1702* remain unclear.

(6) The torpedoes were again prematures.

1	2	3	4	5	6	7	8	9	10	11	12	13	14	15	16	17
FEBRUARY 1945																
09/1214	br	VENTURER	Launders	*SS*		+	4-T	*60°46N/04°35E*	*09/*	*dt*	*SS*	*U864*	*1366*	+		*1*
12/	br	VENTURER	Launders						*12/*	*dt*	*PM*	*M381*	*543*	+	*63°07N/07°32E*	
MARCH 1945																
19/	br	VENTURER	Launders	-D	1000	+	-T	64°38N/10°36E	19/	dt	-D	Sirius	998	+	15m S Rörvik	2
21/	br	VENTURER	Launders	-D			-T	Norway								
									24/	dt	-D	Priamus	760	+	Kristiansund	3
APRIL 1945																
05/	nw	UTSIRA	Valvatne	-D	1381	+	3-T	Frohavet	05/	nw	-D	Torridal	1381	+	Off Folla	
12/0753	br	TAPIR	Roxburgh	*SS*		+	6-T	*60°44N/04°39E*	*12/*	*dt*	*SS*	*U486*	*769*	+		
									24/	dt	-D	Tübingen	5453	+	N Norway	3
25/	br	VENTURER	Launders	APC		/	-T									4

(1) *Venturer* sank the submerged *U864* in a submerged asdic attack.

(2) *Sirius* sank after receiving two hits.

(3) The losses of *Priamos* and *Tübingen* cannot conclusively be attributed to a submarine.

(4) This last attack against two A/S trawlers was unsuccessful.

III. Baltic

This section lists attacks made by Polish and Soviet submarines in the Baltic Sea (excluding the Skagerrak and Kattegat) during the German–Polish War of 1939, the Soviet–Finnish Winter War of 1939–40 and the German/Finnish–Soviet War of 1941–45. Attacks on neutral vessels are included. The sources used were as follows.

Soviet

'Velikaya Otechestvennaya, Den' za dnem. Iz khroniki boevykh dejstvij VMF v Ijunya 1941–Mae 1945 gg', in *Morskoj sbornik*, 6/1991—5/1995.

Khronika Velikoj Otechestvennoj vojny Sovetskogo Soyuza na Baltijskom morskom teatro. Edited by NKVMF SSSR, Ministerstvo Vooruzhennykh Sil SSSR, Voenno-Morskoe ministerstvo Soyuza SSR/Morskoj generalnyj shtab. Vols 1–8. Moskva: Voenizdat, 1945–50. This material was not accessible before the period of *glasnost*.

Boevaya deyatel'nost' podvodnykh lodok Voenno-Morskogo Flota SSSR v Velikuyu Otechestvennuyu vojnu 1941–45 gg. Edited by G. I. Shchedrin et al. Vol. I: *Podvodnye lodki Baltijskogo flota . . .* Moskva: Voenizdat, 1969. Not accessible before the period of *glasnost*.

Dmitriev, V. I. *Atakujut podvodniki.* Moskva: Voenizdat, 1964.

The several monographs, memoirs, articles and 'epic' stories published prior to 1988 provided some information but have been rendered obsolete by more recent publications and are therefore not mentioned.

Additional information was received via correspondence with the following experts: Professor V. I. Dmitriev, St Petersburg; *Capitaine de Vaisseau* Claude Huan, Paris; I. V. Ustimenko, Mikhailinskii, Belorus; A. Ovcharenko, Kiev, Ukraine; and M. Mozorov, Moscow.

Polish

Correspondence with *Dozent Dr hab.* J. W. Dyskant, Warsaw.

German

Kriegstagebuch der Seekriegsleitung 1939–1945. Edited by Werner Rahn, Gerhard Schreiber and Hansgeorg Maierhöfer. Herford/Hamburg: Mittler & Sohn, Vols 22–63, 1990–96.

For shipping losses on the German side the following sources were used:

Gröner, Erich. *Die deutschen Kriegsschiffe 1815–1945.* Continued and edited by Dieter Jung and Martin Maas. Vols1–8/2 and Index. München/Bonn: Bernard & Graefe, 1982–94.

Dinklage, Ludwig, and Witthöft, H. J. *Die deutsche Handelsflotte 1939–1945.* Vols1–2. Göttingen: Musterschmidt, 1970–71. (Studien und Dokumente zur Geschichte des Zweiten Weltkrieges, Bd.5a/b.)

Schön, Heinz. *Ostsee '45. Menschen, Schiffe, Schicksale.* Stuttgart: Motorbuch Verlag, 1983.

For mine and aircraft attacks:

The RAF in the Maritime War. Vol. V. London: Air Historical Branch (1).

Finnish

Correspondence with Commodore Erik Wihtol, Helsinki.

Swedish

Norges, Sveriges og Danmarks handelsflåter. Tilgang og avgang i 1940–1945. Oslo: Det norske Verita's hovedkontor, 1946

Correspondence with Lieutenant-Colonel Stellan Bojerud, Stockholm.

1	2	3	4	5	6	7	8	9	10	11	12	13	14	15	16	17

SEPTEMBER 1939

1	2	3	4	5	6	7	8	9	10	11	12	13	14	15	16	17
02/1238	pl	SEP	Salamon	*DD*		?	1-T	Central Baltic	02/	dt	DD	*(Friedrich Ihn)*	–	/		1
03/2330	pl	RYS	Grochowski	*SS*		?	2-T	Central Baltic					–	/		1
04/	pl	WILK	Krawczyk				20M	54°31N/18°48E								
07/	pl	RYS	Grochowski				10M	54°42N/19°04E								
09/	pl	ZBIK	Zebrovski				20M	54°46N/18°45E	01.10.M	dt	PM	M85	525	+	*NE Heisternest*	
26/	sj	SC-303				/	-T		26/0600	sj	-D	(Metallist/968)	–	/	Narva Bay	2
28/									28/0200	sj	-D	(Pioner)	–	/	Narva Bay	2

OCTOBER/NOVEMBER 1939: No operations

DECEMBER 1939

1	2	3	4	5	6	7	8	9	10	11	12	13	14	15	16	17
01/	sj	L-1	Mogilevski				20M	Nyhamn								
05/	sj	SC-323	Ivantsov				A	Utö	05/	dt	-D	Oliva	1308	=	Off Utö	3
10/0320	sj	SC-323	Ivantsov	-D	2000	+	A	Utö	10/0430	es	-D	Kassari	379	+	N Dagö	4
10/	sj	SC-322	Poleshchuk	-D	7400	+	1TA	Helsinki	10/	dt	-D	Reinbek	2804	+	59°42N/24°26E	5
10/1602	sj	S-1	Tripolskii	-D	4000	+	A	61°05N/20°51E	10/	dt	-D	Bolheim	3324	+	61°26N/21°04E	
10/1602	sj	S-1	Tripolskii	-D		/	A	Rauma	10/	dt	-D	(Oliva/1308)	–	/	SW Mäntylouto	6
12/	sj	SC-322	Poleshchuk	-D		=	A	Hanko	12/	dt	-D	Helga Böge	2181	=	4m N Revalstein	7
16/	sj	SC-322 (?)	Poleshchuk	-D		=	A	Hanko	16/	dt	-D	Gillhausen	4339	=	S Hanko	8
16/	sj	M-90 (?)	Sidorenko	-D		=?										
17/	sj	S-3 (?)					A		17/	dt	-D	(Pinnau/1209)	–	/	Åland Sea	9
28/2340	sj	SC-311	Vershinin	-D	4000	+	A	Off Vasa	28/0430	dt	-D	(Sigrid/1224)	–	/	Off Vasa	10
29/0400	sj	SC-311	Vershinin	-D		+	TA	Off Vasa	29/0425	fi	-D	Wilpas	775	+	S Norrskär	

(1) Attacks not reported.

(2) The Soviet media claimed that *Metallist* was sunk by an unknown submarine, possibly the Polish *Orzel*, and *Pioner* missed by a torpedo. *Orzel* left Tallinn on 18.9.39 for Great Britain. In fact *Metallist* was sunk on the orders of Party Secretary Zhdanov by the Soviet patrol ship *Tucha* after avoiding torpedoes fired by *SC-303*.

(3) The ship was stopped by three shells but released, having suffered slight damage.

(4) *Kassari* (ex *Ebba Munck*) was sunk by 45mm gunfire.

(5) *SC-322* reported one Finnish transport of 7400t hit after 1min 40sec. This was probably the German *Reinbek*, assumed sunk by a submarine mine on 18.12.39.

(6) *Oliva* was stopped by a shell but released.

(7) *Helga Böge* was struck by four shots and damaged.

(8) *Gillhausen* was slightly damaged by gunfire.

(9) *Pinnau* was attacked with gunfire but escaped undamaged.

(10) *Sigrid* was attacked with gunfire but escaped.

1	2	3	4	5	6	7	8	9	10	11	12	13	14	15	16	17
JANUARY 1940																
05/1529	sj	SC-311	Vershinin	-D	2000	+	A	Off Vasa	05/1532	sw	-D	Fenris	484	+	63°20N/20°13E	1
13/1220	sj	SC-324	Konyayev	-D		+	2-T		13/1140	fi	-D	(Anneberg, Hebe ua)	–	/	60°23N/19°10E	2
FEBRUARY 1940–SEPTEMBER 1940: No operations																
OCTOBER 1940																
23/	sj						TR		23/	fi	-D	Astrid	602	+	Mantyluoto	3
NOVEMBER 1940–MAY 1941: No operations																
JUNE 1941																
24/	sj	M-90 (?)	Tatarinov	-D		/	-T	Abo/Åland								4
25/	sj	S-4 (?)	Abrosimov	-D		?	-T	S Baltic								4
27/	sj	L-3	Grishchenko				20M	55°45N/21°00E	01.10.M	le	-D	Kaija (?)	1876	+	55°08N/21°03E	5
									19.11.M	dt	-D	Henny (?)	764	+	55°43N/21°02E	5
									22.11.M	sw	-MT	Uno (?)	430	+	3m off Klaipeda	5
									26.11.M	dt	-M	Engerau (?)	1142	+	Off Klaipeda	5
27/	sj	S-10	Bakunin	–			-T	Off Pillau	27/0310	dt	APC	(V307/427)	–	/	55°21N/19°35E	6
28/	sj	SC-305	Sereda	SS		/	1-T	Orengrund								7
JULY 1941																
10/1421	sj	S-102	Ivanov, B. V.	DD		?	-T	Kolkasraks								8
12/	sj	S-102	Ivanov, B. V.	LC		?	-T	N Riga								8

(1) *Fenris* was attacked with 73 shells, caught fire and sank.

(2) *SC-324* attacked the convoy of three ships with torpedoes. The escorting Finnish patrol yacht *Aura II*/563 dropped D/Cs but was damaged by them and sank.

(3) *Astrid* was on the way from Mäntyluoto to Kronshtadt when she was rammed by a submarine (probably Soviet) and sank.

(4) Attacks not observed.

(5) The losses caused by this barrage are not clear, because there was also a German defensive mine barrage off Klaipeda. *Henny* and *Engerau* were very close to *L-3*'s position, *Uno* was probably a victim of the German barrage and *Kaija* was possibly lost on the barrage of 19.7.41 (q.v.). The claimed *Pollux*/518 was sunk on 23.11.41 on a British air-laid mine off Rostock; the claimed German motor trawler *Günter*/137 was lost on the German 'Wartburg' barrage.

(6) *V307* (ex *Württemberg*) reported one torpedo which missed, and this can only have been fired by the lost *S-10*.

(7) *SC-305* attacked a Finnish submarine of the *Vesihiisi* type.

(8) The presence of *S-102* in the Gulf of Riga was known from sigint, but there were probably no torpedoes fired, only observations reported.

1	2	3	4	5	6	7	8	9	10	11	12	13	14	15	16	17
JULY 1941 *continued*																
19/	sj	S-11	Sereda	-D	5000	+	1-T	Polanga	19/2327	dt	AM	(Sperrbrecher 11)	–	/	10m NW Polang.	1
19/1330	sj	L-3	Grishchenko				20M	Brüsterort	23.08.M	fi	-D	Cisil (?)	1847	+	Swinemünde–Danzig	2
21/							-T		21/	dt	-T		–	/	Pakerort	3
27/	sj	K-3	Malofeyev				M?	W Bornholm								4
AUGUST 1941																
03/									03/	dt	SS	(U142)	–	/	Irben Strait	5
10/1339	sj	S-4	Abrosimov	-T	15000	+	2-T	Polanga					–	/		6
10/2220	sj	SC-307	Petrov	SS		+	2-T	58°58N/21°24E	10/	dt	SS	U144	314	+	*Stormelö/Dagö*	
13/	sj	KALEV	Nyrov				20M	Cape Uzhava	26.09.M	dt	AS	Mosel I/Frieda (?)	796	+	57°24N/21°33E	7
									07.11.M	dt	-D	Frauenburg/Peet (?)	2111	+	57°26N/21°20E	7

(1) *Sperrbrecher 11/Belgrano*/6095 reported one torpedo which missed. The ship survived the war. *Schiff 11/Hanonia*/1813, also claimed, was at this time undergoing repairs after being damaged through stranding. The claimed war transport *KT11* was commissioned only on 2.4.43.

(2) The claimed *Kaija*/1876 was lost on 1.10.41 on a mine from this barrage or from that laid on 27.6.41 *Cisil* was lost en route from Swinemünde to Danzig, some distance from the mine barrage laid by *L-3*.

(3) A tanker reported one torpedo that missed.

(4) The mining operation by *K-3* had to be cancelled because of technical problems.

(5) One torpedo that missed was reported.

(6) The claim by *S-4* to have sunk *Kaija* is erroneous: she was sunk on 1.10.41 by a mine off Klaipeda (see Note 2 above).

(7) The mining successes can not be precisely confirmed. *Mosel* (not the large transport of 8428t) and *Frauenburg* were sunk by mine close to the entrance of Ventspils, although the mines were laid more to the south, off Uzhava.

1	2	3	4	5	6	7	8	9	10	11	12	13	14	15	16	17
AUGUST 1941 *continued*																
17/	sj	LEMBIT	Poleshchuk				20M W Bornholm		12.11.M	dt	AG	Deutschland (?)	1257	?	W Bornholm	1
									17.11.M	dt	-D	Schwaneck (?)	2194	+	54°07N/14°58E	1
									26.02.M	sw	-D	Starke	2459	=	54°35N/13°45E	1
									30.05.M	dt	-D	Orkan/Baltonia (?)	1905	+	54°11N/14°07E	1
									13.07.M	dt	-D	Käthe O./Ausma (?)	1854	+	54°36N/13°46E	1
19/2230	sj	SC-301	Grachev	-D	8000	+	2-T	Landsort	19/	dt	-D	(Thea Fritzen/288)	–	/		2
7-22 ?	sj	S-5	Bashchenko	-D		/	1-T	Danzig Bay								3
24/1440	sj	SC-301	Grachev	-D	6000	=	1-T	Landsort	24/	sw	-D	(Convoy 3 ships)	–	/		4
SEPTEMBER 1941																
17/	sj	M-97 (?)	Mylnikov	-D		+	-T	Tallinn Roads					–	/		5
26/1505	sj	SC-320	Vishnevskii	-D	4000	+	1-T	55°07N/19°38E					–	/		6
28/	sj	SC-319	Agashin	–			-T	Irben Strait	28/1150	dt	CL	(Leipzig)	–	/	W Svorbe	7
29/	sj	SC-319	Agashin	–			-T	Off Lepaja	29/0855	dt	PM	(M151, M203)	–	/	Steinort	8
OCTOBER 1941																
01/	sj	SC-320	Vishnevskii	-D	1000	/	1-T	Danzig Bay								
13/	sj	SC-320	Vishnevskii	-D	1000	/	1-T	Danzig Bay								

(1) The mine successes cannot be precisely confirmed. The claimed German steamer *Anneliese*/726 was sunk on 3.11.41 off Grosshorst/Kolberg, probably on a German defensive minefield. The claimed Swedish steamer *Vollrath Tham*/5787 was sunk on 10.11.41 off Borkum on a British air-laid mine. The loss of, or damage to, *Deutschland* is not clearly established. *Schwaneck* was lost near Grosshorst/Kolberg, possibly also on a German defensive minefield. *Starke* was damaged and sank after an attempt to beach her failed; raised in 5.43, she was recommissioned on 4.2.46. *Orkan* was sunk, possibly by a British air-laid mine, off Greifswalder Oie. *Käthe O.* may have been sunk on a British air-laid mine or on a mine laid by *Lembit*.

(2) An attack was possibly made on *Thea Fritzen*, but the positions are not known. The claimed Estonian steamer *Liisa*/782 was sunk on 18.8.41 in 59°09′N/22°38′E on a mine laid by the German 2nd MTB flotilla on 24/25.6.41.

(3) *S-5* reported one attack during her patrol, but documents were lost when the submarine was sunk on 28.8.41.

(4) *SC-301* reported a convoy with three transports and a destroyer, and one transport hit; the escorting destroyer reported an unsuccessful attack.

(5) Attack not reported; possibly only observations, and no torpedoes fired.

(6) The claimed German steamer *Mariann*/1991 (ex *Holland*) was sunk on 10.9.41 by a German mine in a defensive field off Kolberg.

(7) During a coastal bombardment the cruiser *Leipzig* observed two torpedoes which missed; they must have been fired by the lost *SC-319*.

(8) The two minesweepers observed one torpedo which missed. *SC-319* was in the area but did not return from this patrol.

1	2	3	4	5	6	7	8	9	10	11	12	13	14	15	16	17
OCTOBER 1941 *continued*																
13/	sj	SC-323	Ivantsov	CL		/	?	N Dagö	*13/*		dt	CL	*(Köln)*		/	*Cape Ristna*	1
15/0641	sj	SC-323	Ivantsov	-D	5000	/	1-T	58°13N/17°32E	15/					–	/		2
15/0900	sj	SC-323	Ivantsov	-D	3000	/	1-T	58°22N/17°35E									
16/2251	sj	SC-323	Ivantsov	-T	17000	+	3-T	57°42N/17°20E	16/2300	dt	-D	Baltenland	3724	+	Västervik	3
17/2138	sj	SC-323	Ivantsov	-D		/	2-T	58°39N/18°10E	17/	dt	-D	*(Paula Faulbaums)*	–	/	Landsort	4
24/0912	sj	M-97	Mylnikov	-D	5000	+	1-T	Nargön	24/0800	dt	-D	(Hohenhörn/3026)	–	/	E Nargön	5
25/1350	sj	M-97	Mylnikov	-D		/	1-T	Off Tallinn									
30/1530	sj	SC-323	Ivantsov	-D	3724	+	1-T	58°04N/17°24E								3
30/ ?	sj	KALEV	Nyrov	–			M	Tallinn Roads	11.06.M	dt	APM	MRS11/Osnabrück	5094	=	N Tallinn	6
NOVEMBER 1941																
03/1905	sj	SC-323	Ivantsov	-D	5000	=	1-T	58°15N/17°30E	03/	dt	-D	(Porto Allegre/6105)	–	/	SW Karlskrona	7
03/	sj	SC-324	Tarkhanshvili	–			-T	Utö area	*03/2240*	dt	PT	*(S...)*	–	/	*SE Russarö*	8
05/	sj	LEMBIT	Matiyasevich				20M	Björkö Sound	13.11.M	fi	APM	T-15 Paukku ?	80	+	Björkö Sound	9
									28.11.M	fi	APM	Porkkala ?	162	=	Koivisto	9
05/1326	sj	SC-323	Ivantsov	-T	12000	+	1-T	57°55N/17°20E	05/	fi	-D	Hertta	343	=	Kalmarsund	10
07/	sj	SC-311	Sidorenko	-D	7000	+	TA	Ölands Rif	07/								11
11/	sj	LEMBIT	Matiyasevich	-D	5800	+	-T	Gulf of Finland						–	/		12
15/	sj	M-98	Bezzubikov	–			-T	N Tallinn	*15/1655*	dt	PT	*(S...)*	–	/	*N Tallinn*	13
15/0443	sj	SC-311	Sidorenko	-D	7000	=	5TA	56°51N/16°53E									14

(1) The attack by *SC-323* was broken off, because it was observed on the German side.

(2) *SC-323* reported that the first torpedo was a surface-runner and that the second ran beneath the target.

(3) *Baltenland* (ex *Tautmila*) sank but was later raised, although she remained a total loss. In some Soviet sources the attack is dated 30.10.41.

(4) The claimed German steamer *Paula Faulbaums*/1885 evaded the attack but grounded near Landsort and became a total loss. There were two attacks, each with one torpedo.

(5) *Hohenhörn* reported one torpedo which missed. Only *M-97* was in the area.

(6) *Kalev* did not report the minelaying before her loss, but her success is probable because *MRS11* was hit by a moored mine and had to be beached, although she was later salvaged and repaired.

(7) The Finnish steamer *Juha*/2733, claimed in this attack, was in fact run aground on 16.11.41 south-west of Karlskrona. *Porto Allegre* reported an unsuccessful attack.

(8) German MTBs reported torpedoes which missed. The lost *SC-324* may have been in the area.

(9) The claimed auxiliary minesweeper *Kuha-3* was damaged by a mine some distance north of the *Lembit* barrage on 3.12.41, *Paukku* was run aground and *Porkkala* was damaged inshore of the barrage and salvaged in 1942, so the mine successes claimed by *Lembit* are very doubtful.

(10) The attack probably hit *Hertta*, which is also said to have been hit on 5.10.41. She was raised and repaired.

(11) The claimed former Estonian (and now Soviet) *Eestirand* was stranded on 21.8.41 at Vrangel Island in the Arctic.

(12) Not reported.

(13) The 10th MTB Flotilla reported two torpedoes which missed. *M-98* was the only submarine in the area.

(14) *SC-311* made five attacks on the same target with two, one, one and one torpedo and 20 × 45mm shells.

1	2	3	4	5	6	7	8	9	10	11	12	13	14	15	16	17
DECEMBER 1941–MAY 1942: No operations																
JUNE 1942																
13/	sj	M-95	Fedorov	-D	2500	/	1-T	Suursaari	13/	sj	-D	(Sauliau, ex lit)	–	/	Off Suursaari	1
15/1151	sj	SC-304	Afanasev, Ja. P.	-D	10000	+	2-T	Porkkala	15/	dt	AM	(Minenräumschiff 12)	–	/	Porkkala	2
16/0145	sj	SC-304	Afanasev, Ja. P.	-D	10000	/	1TA	Porkkala	16/	dt	AM	(Minenräumschiff 12)	–	/	W Porkkala	2
16/1237	sj	SC-320	Vishnevskii	AM	6000	+	2-T	Makiluoto	16/	dt	AM	(Minenräumschiff 12)	–	/	W Porkkala	2
16/	sj	SC-317	Mokhov	–			-T	Swedish coast	16/morn.	fi	-D	Argo	2513	+	59°21N/20°14E	3
16/	sj	SC-317	Mokhov	–			-T	Swedish coast	16/after.	sw	-D	(Ulla/2436)	–	/	Nr Bogskär	3
17/	sj	SC-320	Vishnevskii				5-T		17/0936	dt	ACM	(Kaiser/M1804)	–	/	Cape Ristna	4
19/	sj	SC-317	Mokhov	–			-T	Swedish coast	19/	da	-D	Orion	2405	=	58°08N/18°00E	3
22/	sj	SC-317	Mokhov	–			-T	Swedish coast	22/1214	sw	-D	Ada Gorthon	2399	+	57°09N/18°00E	3
25/	sj	SC-317	Mokhov	–			-T	Swedish coast	25/		-D	Rein (?) Rhein (?)	...	?		3
28/2308	sj	S-4	Abrosimov	-D		/	2-T	30m N Rixhöft	28/2224	dt	-D	(Fritz Schoop/1598)	–	/	25m NE Rixhöft	
JULY 1942																
01/	sj	SC-406	Osipov				-T		01/	sw	-D	(Galeon/1206)	–	/	E Norrbadan	5
01/	sj	SC-406	Osipov				-T		01/	sw	-D	(Mösern Convoy)	–	/	S Landsort	5
04/	sj	SC-317 (?)	Mokhov			–	-T		04/	sw	-S	(Fortuna)	–	/	Smygehuk	6
05/1151	sj	SC-320	Vishnevskii	-D	8000	+	2-T	55°28N/20°58E	05/1101	dt	-D	Anna Katrin Fritzen	676	+	55°30N/21°04E	

(1) Attack not observed.

(2) *Minenräumschiff 12/Nürnberg/5635* reported three submarine attacks with torpedoes which missed. The claimed *Minenräumschiff 11/Osnabrück1/5094* was damaged by a mine on 11.6.42 north of Tallinn and beached; she was later raised and repaired (q.v.).

(3) *SC-317* did not return and report her successes, but these ships must have been attacked by her. Later five ships of 46,000t were attributed to *SC-317*. *Ulla* was unsuccessfully attacked after rescuing survivors from *Argo*. *Orion* was towed to Visby on 22.6.42 by the Swedish APC *Falken*. The claim for *Rein* (possibly the Estonian steamer of 196grt) cannot be confirmed. The German *Rhein* (ex French *Lussac/*1586) sank on 6.8.44 off St Malo.

(4) *Kaiser* reported two attacks with two and three torpedoes which missed.

(5) *Galeon*, in a convoy, reported one torpedo which missed, and the Swedish destroyer *Ehrensköld* dropped D/Cs. It is not clear if the second report concerned the same convoy, which also reported one torpedo which missed.

(6) The Swedish galleasse *Fortuna* reported an unsuccessful submarine attack.

1	2	3	4	5	6	7	8	9	10	11	12	13	14	15	16	17

JULY 1942 *continued*

1	2	3	4	5	6	7	8	9	10	11	12	13	14	15	16	17
05/	sj	SC-320	Vishnevskii					-T	05/1905	dt	-D	(Langsee/998)	–	/	W Nidden	1
06/0829	sj	SC-406	Osipov	-D	8000	+	2-T	Landsort	06/0632	sw	-D	(Convoy)	–	/	Göddan Island	2
07/1428	sj	SC-406	Osipov	-D	6000	+	1-T	Häradsskär	07/				–	/		3
08/								-T	08/	sw	-D	?	–	+	Han Bay	4
08/	sj	SC-317	Mokhov	–				-T	08/0747	dt	-D	Otto Cords	966	+	S Bleckinge	
08/2328	sj	SC-406	Osipov	-S	800	+	1-T	Landsort	08/	dt	-S	Fides/*Madare	545	=	58°36N/17°25E	5
09/	sj	SC-406	Osipov	-D	8000	+	-T	Häradsskär	09/	sw	-D		–	/	E Öland	6
09/1617	sj	S-7	Lisin	-D	7000	/	1-T	E Öland	09/1537	sw	-D	(Noreg/1431)	–	/	Nr Arkö	7
09/1958	sj	S-7	Lisin	-D	7000	+	1-T	29m E Öland	09/1826	sw	-D	Margareta	1272	+	Arkö Sound	7
10/									10/	sw	-D	Hannah	1196	+	Han Bay	8
11/1658	sj	S-7	Lisin	-D	12000	+	2-T	Kalmar Sound	11/1500	sw	-M	Luleå	5611	+	57°45N/17°00E	9
11/1658	sj	S-7	Lisin	-D	8000	+	2-T	Kalmar Sound								
12/0043	sj	SC-303	Travkin	-D	6000	+	2-T	SW Porkkala	12/				–	/		10
12/								-T	12/	sw	-D	(Convoy)	–	/	Häradsskär	11
14/1223	sj	S-7	Lisin	-D		/	1-T	Kalmar Sound	14/	sw	-D	(Convoy)	–	/	Swedish coast	12
14/1438	sj	S-7	Lisin	-D		/	1-T	Kalmar Sound	14/	sw	-D	(Convoy)	–	/	Swedish coast	12

(1) *Langsee* reported an unsuccessful submarine attack.

(2) *SC-406* reported an attack against a convoy with two ships and two escorts and claimed two hits. The escorting Swedish APC *Kaparen* and destroyer *Norrköping* dropped D/Cs.

(3) *SC-406* reported an attack against a convoy with one transport, three sailing vessels and two escorts. There was one hit. No Swedish report.

(4) The German *Sk1* reported the sinking of an unidentified Swedish ship in Han Bay by a submarine but there were no Soviet or Swedish reports.

(5) *Fides* was damaged, but remained afloat thanks to her wooden cargo. The ship was repaired and survived the war.

(6) An attack was made on a Swedish ship but the torpedo missed. Escorts dropped D/Cs.

(7) *S-7* reported an attack on a convoy with nine ships, two escorts and an aircraft. The torpedoes missed. The first attack was possibly directed against the Swedish *Noreg*; the second attack sank *Margareta*.

(8) *Hannah* collided with an submerged object, possibly a submarine and perhaps *SC-317*.

(9) Attack on a convoy with 16 ships, two escorts and one aircraft. D/C attack.

(10) No German or Finnish report.

(11) Convoy reported an unsuccessful attack .

(12) *S-7* reported attacks on two convoys, one with one escorted transport and one with 17 ships, four escorts and an aircraft. The convoy reported one torpedo which missed.

1	2	3	4	5	6	7	8	9	10	11	12	13	14	15	16	17
JULY 1942 *continued*																
16/1329	sj	SC-320	Vishnevskii	-D	8000	+	2-T	Akmenrags	16/1300	dt	-D	(Gudrun/1485)	–	/	3m S Steinort	1
16/									16/1515	dt	-D	(Gudrun/1485)	–	/	4m S Liepaja	1
19/1835	sj	SC-303	Travkin	-D		/	1-T	Utö					–	/		2
20/2135	sj	SC-303	Travkin	-D	12000	+	2-T	Utö	20/2145	dt	-D	Aldebaran	7891	=	59°45N/21°24E	3
22/1313	sj	SC-406	Osipov	-D	7000	+	2-T	Häradsskär	22/	sw	-D	(Bele/1237)	–	/	SE Häradsskär	4
24/	sj	S-7	Lisin	-D		/	-T	Ventspils					–	/		5
24/1758	sj	S-4	Abrosimov	-D		/	2-T	N Pakri					–	/		6
25/1237	sj	SC-406	Osipov	-D	8000	+	2-T	Åland Sea					–	/		7
27/0845	sj	S-7	Lisin	-D		?	2TA	Ventspils	27/0800	dt	-D	Ellen Larsen	1938	=	S Ventspils	8
30/0845	sj	S-7	Lisin	-D	8000	+	2-T	Steinort	30/0750	dt	-D	Käthe	1599	+	56°45N/21°36E	9
AUGUST 1942																
05/1015	sj	S-7	Lisin	-D	1000	+	1TA	Uzhava	05/1030	fi	-D	Pohjanlahti	682	+	57°12N/21°20E	10

(1) *Gudrun* reported two unsuccessful torpedo attacks. The Soviet claim to have sunk the submarine depot ship *Mosel*/8428 is incorrect. This 8428grt freighter was sold to Japan in 1941 and sank as *Taisui Maru* on 1.3.45 on a mine off Shimonoseki. The first submarine tender, *Mosel/Frieda*/350grt, sank on 26.9.41 (q.v.) and the second, *Mosel*/788grt (ex *Karskär*), was only commissioned on 29.1.43.

(2) Attack not observed.

(3) *Aldebaran* was towed into port and repaired.

(4) A Swedish aircraft with a convoy reported a submarine and the Swedish destroyers *Norrköping* and *Karlskrona* and APC *Kaparen* dropped 56 D/Cs.

(5) Attack not observed.

(6) *S-4* reported an unsuccessful attack against a convoy of two ships and two escorts, which was not observed. There is also a doubtful report of an attack north of Rixhöft on 28.7.42.

(7) *SC-406* reported an attack against a convoy of one ship and four escorts but this was not observed.

(8) *S-7* reported one ship damaged. *Ellen Larsen* observed a torpedo, which missed, and was then driven ashore by 2 × 100mm. She was later salvaged.

(9) *S-7* reported two attacks, the second successful.

(10) *S-7* fired one torpedo, which ran ashore, and then attacked with gunfire (380 × 45mm fired).

1	2	3	4	5	6	7	8	9	10	11	12	13	14	15	16	17
AUGUST 1942 *continued*																
14/1117	sj	M-96	Marinesko	-D	7000	+	1-T	Porkkala	14/1030	dt	APG	(SAT 4/*Helene/400)	–	/	SW Porkkala	1
18/1710	sj	L-3	Grishchenko	-D	15000	+	2-T	57°37N/17°00E	18/1515	sw	-D	C. F. Liljevalch	5513	+	57°39N/18°00E 2	
18/1710	sj	L-3	Grishchenko	-D		+	"	57°37N/17°00E					–	/		2
25/1048	sj	SC-309	Kabo	-D	10000	+	2-T	Åland Sea	25/	fi	ACM	(Convoy/Louhi)	–	/	Åland Sea	3
25/1048	sj	SC-309	Kabo	DD		+	"	Åland Sea					–	/		3
25/2153	sj	L-3	Grishchenko				7M	55°08N/13°05E	25.09.M	dt	-M	F. Bohmke/ *Vledderveen	210	+	55°25N/12°50E	4
26/0021	sj	L-3	Grishchenko				4M	55°06N/13°19E	*30.03.M*	*dt*	*SS*	*U416 (?)*	*769*	*=*	*54°55N/14°45E*	4
26/0034	sj	L-3	Grishchenko				9M	55°06N/13°19E								4
26/2356	sj	L-3	Grishchenko	-D	8000	+	4-T	55°13N/14°01E					–	/		5
26/2356	sj	L-3	Grishchenko	-D	7000	+	"	55°13N/14°01E					–	/		5
27/0339	sj	SC-407	Afanasev, V. K.	APC		/	2-T	Baltic Coast	27/0245	dt	APC	(Schiff 47/*W. Huth)	–	/	N Liepaja	6
30/1016	sj	SC-309	Kabo	-D	6000	+	1-T	Åland Sea	30/0830	fi	-D	(Convoy)	–	/	Åland Sea	7
SEPTEMBER 1942																
01/1712	sj	L-3	Grishchenko	DD		+	2-T	55°53N/17°01E					–	/		8
01/1732	sj	L-3	Grishchenko	-D	10000	+	4-T	55°53N/17°01E					–	/		8
01/1732	sj	L-3	Grishchenko	-D		=	"	55°53N/17°01E					–	/		8

(1) The claimed *Helene* (not 2160!) reported an unsuccessful attack; the Finnish steamer *Helen*/1849 was sunk on 16.8.42 in 54°45´N/13°49´E on an air-laid mine.

(2) *L-3* reported two transports sunk, although the second ship was not confirmed.

(3) *SC-309* reported one transport and one escort sunk from a convoy. The Finnish AMC reported torpedoes in a convoy which missed.

(4) The successes due to the mine barrages cannot be clarified precisely. The Norwegian motor ship *Tourcoing*/5798 had already been sunk on 24.8.42 by a mine, very probably British air-laid, off Swinemünde. The German aircraft rescue vessel *Hans Rolshoven*/985 was sunk by a mine on 2.10.42 in 55°01´N/14°44´E, a considerable distance east of *L-3*'s fields. *U416* was sunk by a mine in AO 8381ro, near the south-west tip of Bornholm, again some distance from the *L-3* fields. *U416* was raised and recommissioned on 4.10.43.

(5) *L-3* reported two transports sunk, but there is no German evidence.

(6) *SC-407* reported two attacks each with one torpedo at 0339 and 0348, with no hits. The German Q-ship *Schiff 47*/437 observed two torpedoes which missed and dropped D/Cs.

(7) Westbound convoy with the Finnish steamers *Frej* and *Suomen Pukij* observed a torpedo which missed.

(8) *L-3* made two attacks on a convoy. In the first, one torpedo hit a destroyer; in the second there were two hits, with one transport sunk and one possibly damaged. No German report.

1	2	3	4	5	6	7	8	9	10	11	12	13	14	15	16	17
SEPTEMBER 1942 *continued*																
04/0902	sj	LEMBIT	Matiyasevich	-D	8000	+	2-T	Utö	04/0910	dt	-D	(Convoy)	–	/	15m SW Utö	1
04/1124	sj	SC-309	Kabo	-D	10000	+	2-T	Åland Sea	04/1116	fi	-D	(Convoy)	–	/	Åland Sea	2
11/2253	sj	S-13	Malanchenko	-D	10000	/	1TA	Gulf of Bothnia	11/	fi	-D	(Convoy)	–	/	Simpnäsklubb	3
11/2344	sj	S-13	Malanchenko	-D	10000	+	2-T	Gulf of Bothnia	11/2220	fi	-D	Hera	1379	+	60°56N/19°06E	
12/0348	sj	S-13	Malanchenko	-D	12000	+	2-T	Gulf of Bothnia	12/0000	fi	-D	Jussi H.	2325	+	60°21N/18°00E	4
12/1148	sj	SC-309	Kabo	-D	10000	+	2-T	Åland Sea	12/1115	fi	-D	Bonden	695	+	59°55N/19°54E	
13/1859	sj	LEMBIT	Matiyasevich	-D		/	2-T	Utö	14/	fi	-D	(Convoy)	–	/	Åland Sea	5
14/1207	sj	LEMBIT	Matiyasevich	-D	8000	+	2-T	Nr Utö	14/	dt	-M	Finnland/*Hopeville	5281	=	59°36N/21°12	6
14/1207	sj	LEMBIT	Matiyasevich	-D	5000	+	2-T	Nr Utö					–	/		6
17/2317	sj	S-13	Malanchenko	-D	3000	/	2-T	Gulf of Bothnia					–	/		7
18/0041	sj	S-13	Malanchenko	-D	3000	+	1TA	Gulf of Bothnia	22/	nl	-D	Anna W.	290	=§	62°23N/21°00E	8
27/1430	sj	S-9	Mylnikov	-D	10000	+	1-T	30m W Vasa	27/1428	dt	-DT	Mittelmeer	6370	=	63°06N/21°18E	9
28/1955	sj	S-9	Mylnikov	-T	12000	+	2TA	Off Pori	28/2100	dt	-D	Hörnum/*Holnis	1467	=	15m NW Mantil.	9
28/	sj	SC-308	Kostylev	–												
29/0438	sj	SC-310	Jaroshevich	-D	10000	+	4-T	20m NW Stolpmünde	28/0400	dt	-D	Franz Rudolf	1419	+	Stolpmünde	10

(1) *Lembit* reported one hit and a transport sunk. The German convoy reported one torpedo which missed and ran to ground.

(2) *SC-309* reported an attack against a convoy with seven ships and two escorts, with one transport sunk. The Finnish convoy reported torpedoes which missed.

(3) It is unclear whether the Finnish report is identical with the report by *S-13*. She fired 13 × 100mm.

(4) *S-13* made two attacks, each with one torpedo. The ship was first damaged, then at 0357 sunk.

(5) *Lembit* reported an unsuccessful attack against a convoy. A Finnish convoy also reported an unsuccessful attack, but on 14.09.42; this could possibly have been made by *SC-308*/Kostylev, which did not return, but reported on 20.10.42 that she had sunk three ships of 16,000grt.

(6) *Lembit* reported two hits and two ships sunk but only *Finnland* was damaged and beached (she was later repaired, and recommissioned on 1.7.43).

(7) *S-13* reported two attacks each with one torpedo; both missed. No Finnish report.

(8) *S-13* reported reported one torpedo which missed and a ship sunk with 24 × 100mm shells. This must have been *Anna W.*, which, according to Finnish sources, was lost on 22.09.42 and is sometimes also claimed by *S-9*.

(9) *S-9* reported one transport sunk on 27.09.42 and a tanker twice missed on 28.9.42 and then sunk by 17 × 100mm shells.

(10) Three attacks, with two, one and one torpedo.

1	2	3	4	5	6	7	8	9	10	11	12	13	14	15	16	17
SEPTEMBER 1942 *continued*																
30/0028	sj	SC-310	Jaroshevich	-D		/	4-T	35m NW Stolpmünde	30/0229	dt	-D	(A. Christophersen)	–	/	N Rixhöft	1
30/	sj	S-12	Turayev	*BB*	*13400*	+	-T	*Off Klaipeda*	*30/0930*	dt	PM	*(M..., 24th Flot.)*	–	/	*10m SW Klaipeda*	2
OCTOBER 1942																
02/	sj	SC-308	Kostylev (?)	-D		+	-T	Utö-Hanko	*02/1304*	*fi*	PM	*(Ruotsinsalmi)*	–	/	*Off Hanko*	3
02/1414	sj	SC-307	Momot	-D	15000	+	2-T	Arholm Island	02/	fi	-D	(Wanda/1902)	–	/	Åland Sea	4
02/1414	sj	SC-307	Momot	-D	7000	=	"	Arholm Island	02/	fi	-D	(Wanda/1902)	–	/	Åland Sea	4
03/0957	sj	D-2	Lindenberg	-D	12000	+	2-T	Öland								5
03/1852	sj	SC-310	Jaroshevich	*SS*		/	1-T	*15m N Stiloic*								6
04/0000	sj	S-13	Malanchenko	-D		/	2-T	Off Raumaulf								7
05/0240	sj	S-12	Turayev	-D		/	2-T	Off Liepaja								8
06/0617	sj	S-12	Turayev	-D		/	4TA	Latvian coast	06/0630	dt	APC	(V1707/Viking IV)	–	/	SW Klaipeda	9
07/1104	sj	D-2	Lindenberg	-D		/	1-T	SW Ystad								10
07/	sj	SC-308	Kostylev (?)	-D		+	-T	Utö-Hanko	07/1522	dt	AH	(Rügen/2170)	–	/	10m SW Utö	11
08/2222	sj	D-2	Lindenberg	-D		/	1-T	S Ystad	08/1920	sw	-D	(Gunnar/1258)	–	/	36m N Rügenwald	11
10/	sj	D-2	Lindenberg	-D		/	1-T	Ystad-Bornholm	10/1503	dt	-D	(Timandra/948)	–	/	35m E Bornholm	12
11/0047	sj	D-2	Lindenberg	-D		/	1-T	Smygehuk								13
11/1226	sj	SC-307	Momot	-D	7000	+	2-T	59°58N/19°39E	11/1320	dt	-D	(Hiddensee/Orient)	–	/	57°21N/15°48E	14
13/	sj	SC-308	Kostylev (?)	-D		+	-T	Utö-Hanko	13/	dt	-D	(Hiddensee/Orient/4160)	–	/	Simpnäsklubb	3
14/1039	sj	D-2	Lindenberg	-D		/	1-T	Ystad-Bornholm	14/	dt	-D	(Jacobus Fritzen)	–	/		15
14/1633	sj	D-2	Lindenberg	-D	11000	+	1-T	Off Ystad	14/late	dt	-D	Jacobus Fritzen	4090	+	S Ystad	

(1) *SC-310* reported four single torpedoes fired between 0028 and 0035. *Annelis Christophersen*/1581 observed two misses.

(2) *S-12* reported an attack against a training battleship of the *Schlesien* type. An M-boat of the 24th Flotilla observed a surface-running torpedo.

(3) On 20.10.42 *SC-308* reported three ships of 16,000grt sunk and was lost afterwards. The three attacks on 2, 7 and 13.10.42 were probably made by this boat.

(4) A Finnish A/S hunting group observed two unsuccessful attacks.

(5) *D-2* attacked a convoy with two ships and two escorts and reported one ship sunk. Attack not reported by Swedish sources.

(6) Unsuccessful attack; not observed.

(7) Attack not observed.

(8) Attack not observed.

(9) *S-12* reported four single torpedoes missing; one torpedo, which missed, was observed.

(10) Attack not observed.

(11) One torpedo, which missed, was observed.

(12) This torpedo, which missed, was probably fired by *D-2*.

(13) Attack not observed.

(14) *Hiddensee* and Finnish escort reported one torpedo which missed.

(15) Attack not observed.

1	2	3	4	5	6	7	8	9	10	11	12	13	14	15	16	17
OCTOBER 1942 *continued*																
18/0003	sj	SC-303	Travkin	-D	10000	+	2-T	Norköpping	18/0100	sw	-D	(Convoy)	–	/		1
18/0003	sj	SC-303	Travkin	-D	8000	+	"									1
19/1755	sj	D-2	Lindenberg	-D	12000	+	2-T	55°11N/19°13E	19/1557	sw	-D	(Konung Gustav V)	–	/	10m S Trelleborg	2
19/1755	sj	D-2	Lindenberg	-D	10000	+	"	55°11N/19°13E	19/1711	dt	-D	Deutschland	2972	=	10m S Trelleborg	2
20/1526	sj	SC-303	Travkin	-D	8000	+	2-T	Norköpping								3
21/1536	sj	SC-307	Momot	-D		/	2-T	Åland Sea								4
21/1808	sj	S-12	Turayev	-D	10000	+	2-T	Papensee	21/1710	dt	-D	Sabine Howaldt	5956	=	56°21N/20°55E	5
21/	sj	SC-306	Smoljar (?)	-D		+		Off Utö								6
21/1811	sj	SC-310	Jaroshevich	-D		+	2-T									7
22/late	sj	SC-303	Travkin	TB		/	-T	Gotska Sandö								8
25/	sj	SC-308 (?)	Kostylev	-D		+	-T		25/	dt	-D	(Convoy)		/	Off Utö	9
26/1207	sj	SC-307	Momot	-D	10000	+	2-T	Åland Sea	26/1110	fi	-D	Betty H.	2478	+	59°54N/19°54E	
26/1237	sj	SC-406	Osipov	-D		/	2-T										10
26/2230	sj	SC-406	Osipov	-D	12000	=	4-T	28m W Brüsterort	26/nm	fi	-Df	Mercator	119	+	W Brüsterort	11
27/1435	sj	S-12	Turayev	-D	15000	+	2-T	Steinort	27/	dt	-D	Malgache	6300	=	56°51N/21°00E	12
27/1435	sj	S-12	Turayev	-D	10000	=	"	Steinort	27/	sw	-D	(Gordias/1632)	–	/	56°51N/21°00E	12
28/1608	sj	SC-406	Osipov	-D		/	1-T	Off Stilo	28/1508	dt	-D	(Thyland/243)	–	/	NW Danzig	10
28/	sj	SC-306 (?)	Smoljar			–			28/2306	nl	-D	(Gordias/1632)	–	/	25m W Lyserort	13
28/2319	sj	SC-406	Osipov	-D	8000	+	4-T	54°58N/17°26E	28/2319	sw	-D	Bengt Sture	872	+	15m NW Stilo Lt	14

(1) Attack not observed.

(2) Torpedo, which missed, observed by Swedish ferry *Konung Gustav V*/3150. *Deutschland* reached Trelleborg.

(3) Attack not observed.

(4) Attack not observed.

(5) The claimed *Edith Bosselmann* in fact sank on 9.12.42 on a mine west of Polangen. The ship actually hit was *Sabine Howaldt*.

(6) Attack not observed.

(7) Attack not observed.

(8) Attack not observed.

(9) This may have been another attack by *SC-308*.

(10) These may have been attacks made by *SC-406*. The first-mentioned attack was not observed.

(11) The claimed Finnish steamer *Mercator*/4660 had already been sunk on 1.12.39 by the German *U31* in 42°50´N/04°00´W.

(12) *S-12* reported two salvos against a convoy and observed two damaged and stranded vessels.

(13) This attack may have been made by the missing *SC-306* or by *S-12*.

(14) *Bengt Sture* was attacked at 2319 with two torpedoes and at 2400 with one torpedo, which missed. She sank on 29.10.42 at 0030 as a result of a fourth torpedo. Seven prisoners were taken to Kronshtadt.

1	2	3	4	5	6	7	8	9	10	11	12	13	14	15	16	17
NOVEMBER 1942																
01/	sj	SC-304	Afanasev, Ja. P.	–					01/	fi	APC		–	/	Gulf of Finland	
01/	sj	SC-306	Smoljar	–					01/1345	dt	-D	(Allenstein/939)	–	/	S Utlängan	1
01/1845	sj	SC-406	Osipov	-D	8000	+	1-T	8m N Rixhöft	01/1915	fi	-D	Agnes	2983	+	12m N Rixhöft	
									01/	fi	APC	(Search group)	–	/	Gulf of Finland	1
02/1415	sj	L-3	Grishchenko					10M Off Utö	17.11.M	dt	-D	Hindenburg	7880	+	59°40N/21°20E	2
02/2147	sj	SC-303	Travkin	-D		/	2-T	Off Landsort								3
04/2342	sj	SC-303	Travkin	APC		+	3-T	Landsort								4
04/2342	sj	SC-303	Travkin	-D	15000	+	"	Landsort								4
05/1218	sj	L-3	Grishchenko				7M	Off Klaipeda	09.12.M	dt	-D	Edith Bosselmann	952	+	56°05N/20°05E	5
									05.02.M	dt	-D	Tristan (?)	1701	+	Danzig/Klaipeda	5
									06.02.M	dt	-D	Grundsee (?)	866	+	Danzig/Liepaja	5
06/0007	sj	L-3	Grishchenko	*DD*		/	2-T	*W Klaipeda*								6
06/	sj	SC-306 (?)	Smoljar	–				Pomeranian Bay	06/1030	dt	-D	Elbing IX	467	+	NW Stolpmünde	7
07/	sj	S-12 (?)	Turayev	-D		?	-T									8
10/	sj	SC-311	Sidorenko	-D	7000	=	A									8
11/	sj	M-96	Marinesko	APC		/	1-T	Gulf of Finland								9
12/night	sj	M-96	Marinesko	-D		/	1-T	Gulf of Finland								9
12/	sj	SC-304	Afanasev, Ja. P.	–			1-T		*12/1745*	*fi*	*PM*	*(Ruotsinsalmi)*	–	/	*Gulf of Finland*	10
12/	sj	SC-304	Afanasev, Ja. P	–			1-T		*12/1950*	*fi*	*PM*	*(Ruotsinsalmi)*	–	/	*Gulf of Finland*	10
13/	sj	SC-304	Afanasev, Ja. P.	–			1-T		*13/0227*	*fi*	*PM*	*(Ruotsinsalmi)*	–	/	*Gulf of Finland*	10
13/	sj	SC-304	Afanasev, Ja. P.	–			1-T		*13/0445*	*fi*	*PM*	*(Ruotsinsalmi)*	–	/	*Gulf of Finland*	10

(1) One torpedo, which missed, was observed.

(2) *Hindenburg* was carrying a large number of Soviet POWs, of whom only some were rescued by Finnish ships.

(3) Attack not observed.

(4) Attack not observed. The claimed Swedish *Lidingö*/5895 was sunk on a British air-laid mine in the Fehmarn Belt on this date.

(5) *Edith Bosselmann* was assumed sunk by a torpedo, but as there were no submarines at sea at this time it is more probable that she was lost on a mine laid by *L-3*. *Tristan* was lost without trace between Danzig and Memel and *Grundsee*

was lost between Danzig and Liepaja, possibly on a mine; both ships may have been lost on mines laid by *L-3* en route from Brüsterort to Memel.

(6) Attack not observed.

(7) *Elbing IX* was sunk by an underwater explosion, probably a torpedo. This may have been fired by *SC-306*, which was lost. *Elbing IX* was raised and scrapped.

(8) Attack assumed by Soviet authors; not observed.

(9) *M-96* reported two attacks around midnight on 11/12.11.42.

(10) *Ruotsinsalmi* reported two attacks with one torpedo each, which missed, followed by two attacks on 13.11.42. The last torpedo passed under the ship.

1	2	3	4	5	6	7	8	9	10	11	12	13	14	15	16	17

NOVEMBER 1942 *continued*

1	2	3	4	5	6	7	8	9	10	11	12	13	14	15	16	17
13/1230	sj	L-3	Grishchenko	-D		?	-T	Ventspils								1
13/1300	sj	L-3	Grishchenko				3M	Off Liepaja								2
17/	sj	SC-304	Afanasev, Ja. P.	-D		+	1-T									3
23/									[23/	dt	-D	Maggie/*Phaleron/325	+]		N Stolpmünde	4

DECEMBER 1942

1	2	3	4	5	6	7	8	9	10	11	12	13	14	15	16	17
02/									02/	dt	-D	(Dirschau/762)	–	/		5

JANUARY–APRIL 1943: No operations

MAY 1943

1	2	3	4	5	6	7	8	9	10	11	12	13	14	15	16	17
22/0258	sj	SC-408	Kuzmin	APC		+	-A	Vaindlo Island	22/	fi	PC	(VMV-...)	–	/		6
22/0258	sj	SC-408	Kuzmin	APC		+	-A	Vaindlo Island								6

JUNE–JULY 1943: No operations

AUGUST 1943

1	2	3	4	5	6	7	8	9	10	11	12	13	14	15	16	17
05/	sj	S-12	Bashchenko	APG		+	-T	Tytärsaari								7

SEPTEMBER 1943: No operations

OCTOBER 1943

1	2	3	4	5	6	7	8	9	10	11	12	13	14	15	16	17
04/1851	sj	M-90	Rusin	LC		=	2-T	Khamisher								8
14/0000	sj	M-102	Leskovoj	PM		/	2-T	Narva Bay	14/0022	dt	PM	(M 30)	–	/		9

(1) This submerged acoustic attack was reported by Soviet authors, but others report that the attack was frustrated because of a ramming accident during the approach.

(2) Of the other claimed mine successes by *L-3*, *Wolfram* (not 8648 but 3648grt) was sunk on 10.2.42 off Borkum by an RAF airborne torpedo, *Ostland*/2152grt was stranded on 15.11.42 near Oxelösund and *Marie Ferdinand*/1757grt was stranded on 14.1.43 off Liepaja.

(3) Attack reported by Soviet authors, but not observed.

(4) The loss was attributed to a submarine attack, but, as there were no submarines in the vicinity, an air-laid mine was probably responsible.

(5) *Dirschau* (ex *Tczew*) was not sunk on 2.12.42, as erroneously reported, but on 2.12.44.

(6) *SC-408* was damaged on this day by six Finnish VMV-boats and the minelayer *Riilahti*. The Soviet claim of two sunken A/S patrol vessels is not confirmed by Finnish sources. *SC-408* was damaged again on 24.5.43 and sunk on 26.5.43.

(7) The claimed German gunboat *Ost* (not 1592 but 564grt) in fact sank on 11.7.43 on a Soviet mine in 59°48´N/27°10´E.

(8) *M-90* claimed one hit, but there is no report concerning this attack.

(9) At 0022 on 14.10.43 the minesweeper *M30* reported one surface-running torpedo.

1	2	3	4	5	6	7	8	9	10	11	12	13	14	15	16	17
NOVEMBER 1942–SEPTEMBER 1944: No operations																
																1
OCTOBER 1944																
05/0512	sj	SC-407	Bocharov	-D		/	2-T	Klaipeda	05/0320	dt	-D	(Leda/594)	–	/	56°10N/20°00E	2
05/									05/1300	dt	APG	(SAT18/*Ostsee/336)	–	/		3
																4
06/0404	sj	SC-310	Bogorad	-D	6000	+	2-T	16m W Ventspils								
06/1201	sj	SC-407	Bocharov	-D	9000	=	3-T	44m NW Klaipeda	06/1006	dt	AG	Nordstern/*Minos	1127	+	55°46N/19°45E	4
																5
07/1520	sj	SC-407	Bocharov	-D		/	1-T	Klaipeda								
08/0112	sj	SC-310	Bogorad	APC	600	+	2-T	Uzhava	08/	dt	-Bg	Bagger 3	400	+	57°39N/16°00E	6
08/0125	sj	SC-310	Bogorad	-D	7000	+	3-T	Uzhava	07/2340	dt	-D	RO-24/*Zonnewijk	4499	+	57°24N/21°20E	7
08/1000	sj	D-2	Lindenberg	-D		/	2-T	33m S Hoborg Lt								8
09/0508	sj	S-13	Marinesko	-D	5000	/	3-T	Bay of Danzig	09/	dt	-Df	(Siegfried/563)	–	/		9
09/0510	sj	S-13	Marinesko	-D	5000	/	1-T	Bay of Danzig	09/	dt	-Df	(Siegfried/563)	–	/		9
09/0602	sj	S-13	Marinesko	-D	5000	+	-A	Bay of Danzig	09/0330	dt	-Df	Siegfried	563	=	N Hela	9
									10/0225	*dt*	*LC*	*(F...)*	–	/	*Off Cape Zerel*	10
10/1515	sj	SC-310	Bogorad	-D		/	3-T	Off Ventspils	10/1320	dt	-T	(Hiddensee/643)	–	/	57°21N/21°12E	11

(1) A comparison of the Soviet and German times and positions of these attacks, which is only now possible, has resulted in many corrections being made here to earlier assessments given in Soviet and German publications.

(2) *Leda* reported one premature and one torpedo which missed.

(3) *SAT18* (ex *Ostsee*) reported an unsuccessful attack.

(4) The claimed *Nordstern* (ex *Minos*) was not sunk by *SC-310* off Ventspils but by *SC-407* off Klaipeda; 531 people perished. The ship was raised but scrapped. The German steamer *Neptun*/1594grt, claimed by *SC-407* in its attack on 06.10.44 at 1201, was sunk on 5.10.44 in 54°39′N/12°31′E on a ground mine in the RAF 'Sweet Pea' field.

(5) Attack not reported.

(6) *SC-310* reported one tug or escort sunk. There is an unconfirmed report concerning the loss of a towed barge off Lyserort.

(7) There are some discrepancies about the date, but from the positions and the hour it is clear that *RO-24* was sunk by *SC-310*.

(8) Attack not reported.

(9) *S-13* attacked twice with torpedoes, which *Siegfried* evaded while trying to escape to Gdynia. The ship was then damaged by gunfire and towed to Danzig.

(10) A German group of MFPs reported a torpedo which missed, but there is no report by *SC-310*.

(11) The tanker *Hiddensee* reported two torpedoes which missed.

1	2	3	4	5	6	7	8	9	10	11	12	13	14	15	16	17
OCTOBER 1944 *continued*																
11/	sj	L-3	Konovalov					20M 8.5m NE Arkona	14.11.M	dt	AG	*Alb. Leo Schlageter*	*1634*	=	54°51N/13°35E	1
									20.11.M	dt	B	*T34*	*1294*	+	54°40N/13°29E	1
11/	sj	LEMBIT	Matiyasevich					20M NE Kolberg	23.10.M	dt	-Tg	Pionier 5 (?)	c.100	+	Off Swinemünde	2
									11.M	*dt*	*SS*	*U547 (?)*	*1144*	=	*Off Swinemünde*	2
									24.11.M	dt	APC	Vs302/*Halberstadt?	305	=	54°36N/16°52E	2
									24.11.M	dt	-Df	Spreeufer	216	+	54°27N/15°45E	2
									13.02.M	*dt*	*PM*	*M421 (?)*	*543*	+	*54°25N/15°25E*	2

(1) The assessment of mine successes is generally still difficult, because many successes claimed for Soviet submarines occurred in areas of RAF-laid minefields west of the island of Rügen. In August and September 1944 RAF Bomber Command laid 219 and 83 mines respectively in the 'Geranium 1' and '2' fields north of Usedom and Wollin, 55 and 41 in 'Spinach 1' and '2' north of Rixhöft and Hela, 40 in the 'Privet' fields off Danzig and the Frische Nehrung and 76 and 34 respectively in 'Tangerine 1' and '2' west of Pillau and Brüsterort. The small sailing vessels *Endla*/68grt and *Linnea*, claimed by *L-3*, were sunk by gunfire from the German *U481* on 15.10.44 off Odensholm. The claimed *Vs53*/336grt (ex *Altenburg*) was not lost in 12.44 on a mine laid by *L-3* but on 20.4.45 in 54°35´N/10°53´E in the RAF 'Forget-Me-Not' minefield. The escort vessel *F5*/712—not *TF5* as sometimes reported—was sunk on 29.1.45 in 54°20´N/13°55´E on the RAF 'Geranium 1' field.

(2) *Lembit* laid four banks each of five mines north-east of Kolberg and west of the Stolpebank. The claimed harbour tug *Pionier 5* was missing off Swinemünde from 23.10.44. The claimed German steamer *Schwaneck*/2194grt in fact sank on 17.11.41 off Swinemünde. The damage to *U547* and *Vs302* and the loss of *Spreeufer* and *M421* may possibly have been caused by mines laid by *Lembit*. The claimed sinking of *Berlin*/15,286grt on 31.1.45 and the damage to *Drechtdijk*/9338grt on 16.2.45 were not caused by mines from *Lembit* but by, respectively, three and one RAF air-laid ground mine in the 'Geranium 2' field of 30.1.45 and 16.2.45.

1	2	3	4	5	6	7	8	9	10	11	12	13	14	15	16	17
OCTOBER 1944 *continued*																
12/0423	sj	S-4	Klyushkin	-D	6000	+	2-T	Stolpebank	12/0227	dt	-Df	Taunus	218	+	N Rixhöft	1
12/1401	sj	S-4	Klyushkin	-D	5000	/	2-T	Stolpebank								
12/1430	sj	S-4	Klyushkin	-D	9000	/	2-T	Stilo Lt								
13/0218	sj	LEMBIT	Matiyasevich	-D	5000	/	2-T	45m S Öland								
13/0226	sj	LEMBIT	Matiyasevich	-T	5000	+	2-T	45m S Öland	13/0030	da	-D	Hilma Lau	2414	+	55°20N/15°20E	1
13/0535	sj	S-4	Klyushkin	-T	12000	+	2-T	24m NW Stilo Lt	13/0315	dt	-T	Terra	1533	+	N Leba	1
									13/	dt	-T	(Thalatta/3145)	–	/	N Rixhöft	1
14/0158	sj	SC-310	Bogorad	-D	5000	+	2-T	8m NW Uzhava								2
14/1157	sj	SC-407	Bocharov	-D		/	2-T	12m SW Klaipeda	14/0958	dt	APG	(LAT24/Orion/211)	–	/	55°39N/20°55E	3
15/0050	sj	L-3	Konovalov	-D	5000	+	3-T	10m SE Smygehuk								4
15/0100	sj	LEMBIT	Matiyasevich	APM		/	1-T	45m S Öland								5
15/0105	sj	LEMBIT	Matiyasevich	APM		+	1-T	45m S Öland	15/0227	dt	APM	M3619/Crabeel	150	+	Rixhöft	5
15/2257	sj	SC-318	Loshkarev	*LC*		/	2-T	*12m NW Pappens.*								6
16/0302	sj	S-4	Klyushkin	-D		/	3-T	24m N Stilo Lt								7
16/1644	sj	SC-307	Kalinin, M. S.	-D	8000	+	4-T	Ventspils								8
16/1644	sj	SC-307	Kalinin, M. S.	-D	6000	+	"	Ventspils								8
16/1644	sj	SC-307	Kalinin, M. S.	-T	18000	+	"	Ventspils								8

(1) Published information concerning the sinkings and damage attributable to *S-4* and *Lembit* on 12/14.10.44 should be corrected according to the times of the attacks shown here. *Thalatta* was probably not damaged, because she was delivered to Great Britain on 15.7.45.

(2) *SC-310* claimed the sinking of *Carl Zeiss*/1320grt. This former range-finding training ship was raised after being sunk on a mine on 9.11.42 and was towed, as a wreck, to be sunk as a blockship at Dünamünde. On 13.10.44 there was a leakage, and the ship sank at 0700 on 14.10.44 off Klaipeda.

(3) The gun carrier *LAT24* reported two torpedoes which missed. In the area the ships of the 2nd Task Group reported several sonar contacts, possibly with *SC-407*.

(4) The claimed sinkings and attacks by *L-3* and *Lembit* could not be found in German sources. *M3619/Crabeel and Grabeels* was possibly sunk in the attacks mentioned, but the positions differ. The only report was of an unsuccessful attack against a German U-boat at 1235 in AO 9146.

(5) See Note 4.

(6) Attack not reported.

(7) Attack not reported.

(8) *SC-307* claimed to have sunk one tanker and one transport anchored in the roads off Ventspils, but there is no German report.

1	2	3	4	5	6	7	8	9	10	11	12	13	14	15	16	17
OCTOBER 1944 *continued*																
20/0616	sj	S-4	Klyushkin	-D	8000	+	2-T	19m N Stilo Lt								1
									22/noon	*dt*	*PT*	*(S67)*	–	/	*NW Ventspils*	2
23/late	sj	SC-307	Kalinin, M. S.	-D	3000	+	2-T	Liepaja-Ventspils								3
25/0500	sj	K-56	Popov	?			2-T	13m W Brüsterort								
25/0738	sj	L-3	Konovalov	-D		/	3-T	11m W Memel	25/0520	dt	-D	(Convoy)	–	/	6m NW Klaipeda	4
26/1011	sj	L-3	Konovalov	APC	600	+	2-T	13m W Memel	26/1102	dt	-D	(Convoy)	–	/	6m NW Polangen	5
26/1254	sj	D-2	Lindenberg	-D	5000	+	2-T	8m W Pappensee								6
29/0242	sj	SC-307	Kalinin, M. S.	-D	10000	+	2-T	Akmenrags								7
29/2257	sj	SC-318	Loshkarev	-D	10000	+	2-T	17m S Liepaja	29/2044	dt	-D	(*M256*, convoy)	–	/	56°21N/20°35E	8
									30/2320	dt	-D	(Convoy)	–	/	SW Liepaja	9
NOVEMBER 1944																
01/	sj	SC-318 ?	Loshkarev				3-T		*01/2020*	*dt*	*TB*	*(T3/convoy)*	–	/	*22m SW Liepaja*	10
03/2157	sj	SC-307	Kalinin, M. S.	-D	5000	+	2-T	10m NW Akmenrags	03/2225	dt	AMS	(MRS11, -12, M. Horn)	–	/		11
03/2213	sj	SC-307	Kalinin, M. S.	-D	3000	+	2-T	10m NW Akmenrags								11
04/0010	sj	SC-318	Loshkarev	-D		/	3-T	10m W Bernatu								12
10/0710	sj	SC-309	Vetchinkin	-D	8000	+	3-T	W Ventspils	10/0534	dt	-D	Carl Cords	903	+	57°30N/21°20E	
12/0142	sj	K-52	Travkin	-D	400	/	2-T	25m N Visby								13
12/2110	sj	SC-309	Vetchinkin	-D	4000	+	3-T	16m W Ventspils	*12/1910*	*dt*	*PM*	*(M22)*	–	/	*57°21N/21°00E*	14

(1) Attack not reported.

(2) *S67* reported one torpedo which missed.

(3) Attack not reported.

(4) A German M-boat escorting a convoy reported a torpedo which missed.

(5) A German M-boat escorting a convoy reported a torpedo which missed.

(6) The claimed Norwegian *Nina*/1488grt sank on 27.10.44 in 56°12´N/11°20´E in the RAF 'Silver XIII' minefield.

(7) Attack not reported.

(8) The M-boat *M256*, escorting a convoy, reported two torpedoes which missed. The claimed tanker *Thann*/7412grt (ex *Phobos*) was damaged on 29.12.44 in 54°41´N/12°35´E in the RAF 'Sweet Pea' minefield.

(9) A convoy reported two attacks with two and three torpedoes.

(10) *T3* reported three torpedoes which missed.

(11) The claimed steamer *Skrunda*/2414grt was sunk by Soviet air attack at Liepaja on 30.11.44. At 2225 on 3.11.44 the M-boat *M328*, escorting the ships mentioned, reported a submarine in AO 9322 off Liepaja.

(12) Attack not reported.

(13) Attack not reported.

(14) *M22*, escorting the transports *Cometa* and *Peter Wessel*, reported two torpedoes which missed.

1	2	3	4	5	6	7	8	9	10	11	12	13	14	15	16	17
NOVEMBER 1944 *continued*																
									14/0439	dt		AMX (Ammerland)	–	/	12m SSW Ventspils	1
17/0355	sj	L-21	Mogilevskii	-D	500	/	3-T	40m NW Stilo Lt								2
21/1724	sj	SC-309	Vetchinkin	DD		+	3-T	8m NW Sworbe Lt	21/	dt	DD	(Task group)	–	/		3
23/	sj	L-21	Mogilevskii				17M	54°51N/17°59E	23.11.M	dt	-D	Eichberg	1923	=	54°51N/17°54E	4
									24.11.M	dt	-D	Elie	1837	=	54°50N/17°50E	4
									22.12.M	dt	-D	Eberhard	749	+	N Rixhöft	4
24/0800	sj	L-21	Mogilevskii	-D	7000	+	3-T	18m NW Halskuk	24/1441	sw	-D	Hansa	563	+	58°02N/18°10E	
									[24/	dt	-Df	Spreeufer/218]				5
25/0440	sj	L-21	Mogilevskii			?	2-T	Stolpebank								
27/0625	sj	K-51	Drozdov	APM		/	1-T	NW Stolpebank								6
28/0325	sj	K-51	Drozdov	-D	5000	/	2-T	30m E Bornholm								6
28/0339	sj	K-51	Drozdov	-D	5000	/	1-T	30m E Bornholm								6
28/0519	sj	K-51	Drozdov	-D	5000	+	-A	30m E Bornholm								6
29/1949	sj	K-51	Drozdov	-D	6000	/	3-T	38m NW Kolberg								6
29/2010	sj	K-51	Drozdov	-D	6000	/	1-T	38m NW Kolberg								6
29/2025	sj	K-51	Drozdov	-D	6000	/	2-T	38m NW Kolberg								6
DECEMBER 1944																
01/0743	sj	K-51	Drozdov	-D		/	1-T	36m NW Kolberg								6
01/0802	sj	K-51	Drozdov	-D	8000	+	31A	36m NW Kolberg								6

(1) *Ammerland* reported a torpedo which missed.

(2) Attack not reported.

(3) German 2nd Task Group in the area, but no attack reported.

(4) These three ships are sometimes claimed as mine successes for *Lembit*, but in fact they foundered in *L-21*'s field; the first two were only damaged, the last sank. This minefield was swept by *R256* and vessels of the 2nd Defence Flotilla and the 26th M/S Flotilla on 1 and 4.12.44.

(5) *Spreeufer* was erroneously claimed for *L-3*, but this submarine was at Hanko at the time. The ship must actually have been sunk by a mine laid by *Lembit* (q.v.). *Hansa* was sunk by torpedo from *L-21*, according to her war diary; but there are discrepancies in the reported times (0441, 0520 and 1441) and positions.

(6) *K-51* reported three ships sunk by gunfire, but the vessels could not be identified.

1	2	3	4	5	6	7	8	9	10	11	12	13	14	15	16	17
DECEMBER 1944 *continued*																
03/	sj	LEMBIT	Matiyasevich				20M	Brüsterort	04/1535	dt	-D	Dirschau/Tczew)	762	+	54°47N/17°28E	1
04/1525	sj	SC-407	Bocharov	-D	15000	+	2-T	Putzig Gulf	04/1330	dt	-M	Seeburg	12181	+	54°39N/18°39E	2
04/2259	sj	K-53	Jaroshevich	-D		/	3-T	24m SW Liepaja								3
05/0655	sj	SC-407	Bocharov	-D		/	3-T	9m W Pillau								4
07/0715	sj	SC-309	Vetchinkin	-D	7000	+	3-T	11m NW Uzhava.	07/0515	dt	-D	Nordenham	4592	+	57°24N/22°00E	
10/0124	sj	K-53	Jaroshevich	-D	4000	+	2-T	55°47N/20°32E								5
11/0915	sj	LEMBIT	Matiyasevich	-D	6000	+	2-T	55°12N/19°55E								6
14/2300	sj	S-4	Klyushkin	-D		/	-T	Ventspils								7
14/	sj	S-4	Klyushkin	-D		=	-T	Ventspils								7
									17/1310	dt	SS	(U683)	–	/	N Rixhöft	8
21/0404	sj	SC-310	Bogorad	-D	7000	+	3-T	Off Liepaja								9
22/early	sj	L-21	Mogilevskii	-D		?	A	16m N Brüsterort								
22/	sj	S-4	Klyushkin	-D		?	-A	Bay of Danzig	22/0255	dt	APG	(Convoy, SATs)	–	/	Pillau	
10																
23/0452	sj	D-2	Lindenberg	-D		/	2-T	Irben Strait								11
23/									23/	dt	SS	(U1063)	–	/	*54°51N/19°45E*	12
23/0843	sj	K-56	Popov	-D	8000	+	3-T	54°58N/16°00E	24/0952	dt	AG	(Hansa)	–	/	54°57N/15°15E	13

(1) *Dirschau* was possibly sunk by *Lembit*'s mines, but there is a great difference in the positions. This minefield was swept by *Minenräumschiff 12* and its motor boats on 4.12.44. The claims for *Lembit* included a vessel of 2192grt on 5.12.44 and the transport *Eberhard*/749 on 6.12.44 (q.v.). The claimed *Lütjehörn*/1953grt sank on 4.1.45 in 54°42′N/12°37′E on the RAF 'Sweet Pea II' minefield.

(2) *Seeburg* (ex *Adelaide Star*) is also claimed as a victim of the RAF 'Spinach 1' minefield.

(3) Attack not reported.

(4) Attack not reported.

(5) Attack not reported.

(6) There is no report concerning this attack, but on 12.12.44 *Lembit* claimed the

sinking of the German U-boat *U479* in a collision off Utö. This U-boat went missing off the Finnish Gulf at this time.

(7) Attack not reported.

(8) *U683* reported three torpedoes which missed.

(9) Attack not reported.

(10) A convoy with three gun carriers and four small ships reported a gun attack which scored no hits.

(11) Attack not reported.

(12) *U1063* reported two torpedoes which missed.

(13) The training ship *Hansa* reported one torpedo which missed.

1	2	3	4	5	6	7	8	9	10	11	12	13	14	15	16	17
DECEMBER 1944 *continued*																
25/2217	sj	K-56	Popov	-D		/	3-T	W Stolpebank								1
26/0140	sj	K-56	Popov	-D	10000	+	3-T	55°13N/16°57E	25/2320	dt	-D	Baltenland	3038	=	55°15N/17°05E	1
26/0152	sj	K-56	Popov	-D		/	2-T	55°13N/16°57E								1
									29/1255	*dt*	*DD*	*(Paul Jacobi)*	–	*/*	*54°57N/15°35E*	2
29/2001	sj	D-2	Lindenberg	-D	9000	+	2-T	Irben Strait								3
29/2146	sj	K-56	Popov	-D	6000	+	3-T	55°40N/15°03E	29/1946	sw	-D	Venersborg	1046	+	55°45N/15°30E	
30/0524	sj	SC-310	Bogorad	-D	6000	+	2-T	56°09N/20°26E	31/1940	dt	APC	(V317/*Wega/314)	–	/	N Steinort	4
31/	sj	S-4 (?)	Kyushkin	-T												5
JANUARY 1945																
02/0128	sj	SC-310	Bogorad	-D		/	2-T	Off Liepaja								6
02/0322	sj	K-56	Popov	-D		/	4-T	W Stolpmünde								7
03/0620	sj	D-2	Lindenberg	-D		/	2-T	Off Ventspils								8
07/2334	sj	SC-310	Bogorad	-D	6000	+	3-T	56°11N/20°28E	06/2330	dt	-D	(Convoy)	–	/	Liepaja	9
09/2210	sj	SC-307	Kalinin, M. S.	-D	10000	+	2-T	56°14N/20°28E	09/2045	dt	APC	(V317/*Wega/314)	–	/	W Schwarzort	10
16/1745	sj	SC-407	Bocharov	-D		/	4-T	NW Brüsterort	16/1612	dt	APC	(V1704/*Unitas/341)	–	/	NW Brüsterort	12

(1) There were probably several attacks made against *Baltenland* (ex *Valdona*), which, however, was only damaged.

(2) The destroyer observed one torpedo which missed.

(3) The claimed Norwegian steamer *Nina*/1371 was sunk on a British air-laid mine on 27.12.44 in 56°10´N/11°17´E. No attack reported.

(4) There is a discrepancy in the times of the attack.

(5) The German steamer *Ingeborg*/1538 (ex *Aija*) is sometimes claimed for the lost *S-4*, but this ship was sunk by a mine on 27.5.44 near Domesnäs.

(6) No attack reported.

(7) No attack reported.

(8) No attack reported.

(9) A convoy with three transports and two escorts reported torpedoes which missed.

(10) *V317* reported a sonar contact and dropped D/Cs.

(11) *SC-307* claimed one transport on fire and sunk, but there is no German report.

(12) *V1704* reported two torpedoes which missed.

1	2	3	4	5	6	7	8	9	10	11	12	13	14	15	16	17
JANUARY 1945 *continued*																
16/2146	sj	SC-307	Kalinin, M. S.	-D	6000	+	3-T	56°19N/20°23E	17/	dt	-D	Steinburg (?)	1319	+	Off Liepaja	1
26/	sj	L-3	Konovalov				10M	Ventspils	29.01.M	dt	-D	Henry Lütgens	1141	+	57°20N/21°20E	2
28/2310	sj	K-51	Drozdov	-D	10000	+	4-T	54°26N/16°20E	28/	da	-D	Viborg	2028	+	54°28N/16°23E	
30/2308	sj	S-13	Marinesko	-D	20000	+	3-T	55°08N/17°41E	30/2108	dt	-D	Wilhelm Gustloff	25484	+	55°07N/17°42E	3
									31/	*sw*	*PM*	*(Landsort)*	–	/	*57°28N/17°20E*	4
									31/	dt	-D	(Cap Arkona)	–	/	Central Baltic	5
31/0628	sj	L-3	Konovalov	-D	3000	+	3-T	57°16N/21°07E								6
31/2147	sj	L-3	Konovalov	-D		/	3-T	Off Ventspils								6
31/2212	sj	L-3	Konovalov	-D		/	3-T	Off Ventspils								6
FEBRUARY 1945																
									01/	sw	-D	(Gute in convoy)	–	/	Baltic	7
02/	sj	L-3	Konovalov				10M	N Brüsterort	07.02.M	dt	-AG	Pollux (?)	4191	=§	7m SW Pillau	8
									30.03.M	dt	-D	Jersbek (?)	2804	+	Off Pillau	8
04/1211	sj	L-3	Konovalov	*DD*	+		3-T	55°00N/20°20E	*04/1021*	*dt*	*-TB*	*(T36)*	–	/	*NE Brüsterort*	9
04/1211	sj	L-3	Konovalov	PM	+		"	55°00N/20°20E								9

(1) *SC-307* claimed to have sunk *Henriette Schulte*/1923grt, but this vessel was damaged off Klaipeda and beached near the southern entrance to the harbour. *Steinburg* was assumed to have been hit by a mine off Liepaja and then stranded in a snowstorm, so the attack by *SC-307* was probably directed against this ship.

(2) The claimed *M3138*/*KFK182* was lost on a mine on 23.3.45 off Liepaja.

(3) 5,384 people, most of them refugees, were lost and only 654 could be rescued.

(4) The Swedish minesweeper *Landsort* reported torpedoes which missed.

(5) The transport *Cap Arkona* reported two submarine attacks.

(6) The position for these attacks is not clear. It is possible that the attacks annotated at 5, 6 and 7 are one and the same.

(7) See Note 6.

(8) *Pollux* was claimed to be of 5408 or 518grt, but in fact this vessel was was the icebreaker of 4191grt (5408t). She is also claimed for the RAF 'Tangerine 2' minefield, as was *Jersbek*. *Pollux* was beached, and was salvaged after the war by the Soviet Navy.

(9) *T36* reported torpedoes which missed; *T28* dropped D/Cs.

1	2	3	4	5	6	7	8	9	10	11	12	13	14	15	16	17
FEBRUARY 1945 *continued*																
04/2200	sj	SC-318	Loshkarev	-D	6000	+	3-T	Off Liepaja	04/2145	dt	-MT	Hiddensee	643	+	56°14N/20°23E	1
04/2200	sj	SC-318	Loshkarev	-D	6000	+	"	Off Liepaja								1
06/2205	sj	K-51	Drozdov	-D		/	4-T	55°38N/15°01E								2
06/2324	sj	K-51	Drozdov	-D		/	2-T	55°38N/15°01E								2
10/0250	sj	S-13	Marinesko	CL		+	2-T	*45m N Iershöft*	10/0055	dt	-D	General Steuben	14660	+	55°09N/16°37E	3
12/1828	sj	SC-407	Bocharov	-D	8000	+	4-T	55°27N/19°32E	*12/1615*	*dt*	*PM*	*(TS8)*	–	/	*Brüsterort*	4
12/1828	sj	SC-407	Bocharov	DD		=	"	*55°27N/19°32E*								4
23/0608	sj	SC-309	Vetchinkin	-D	7000	+	3-T	Off Liepaja	23/0435	dt	-D	Göttingen	6267	+	56°18N/20°16	5
24/0106	sj	K-52	Travkin	-D	8000	+	3-T	55°19N/16°42E								6
24/0106	sj	K-52	Travkin	APC		+	"	55°19N/16°42E								6
24/2342	sj	SC-309	Vetchinkin	-D	8000	/	2-T	Off Liepaja								7
26/2315	sj	SC-309	Vetchinkin	-D	8000	/	2-T	Off Liepaja								7
26/2325	sj	SC-309	Vetchinkin	-D	8000	/	2-T	Off Liepaja								7
MARCH 1945																
01/1045	sj	K-52	Travkin	-D	6000	+	3-T	55°08N/16°12E	01/	dt	-D	Bohus	1761	+	N Gdynia (?)	8
04/2207	sj	K-52	Travkin	-D	5000	+	3-T	55°23N/17°38E								9
05/2339	sj	SC-303	Ignatev	-D		/	2-T	Off Liepaja								10
07/	sj	K-52	Travkin	DD		?	3-T	*Stolpebank*								11
07/0219	sj	K-52	Travkin	DD		+	2-T	*55°18N/18°00E*								11
08/0104	sj	K-52	Travkin	-D	4000	+	3-T	55°16N/16°07E								11

(1) There was no second ship hit: the claimed mine destructor ship *Ammerland* (ex *Sandhörn*, ex *August Schulte*/2452) sank on 10.2.45 in 56°26′N/20°30′E following a collision with a patrol vessel.

(2) Attack not reported.

(3) 3,608 people were lost with *General Steuben*, most of them wounded soldiers; only 659 were rescued.

(4) The minesweeper *TS8* reported three torpedoes which missed.

(5) Some 500 people were lost with *Göttingen*. The escorting *M801* dropped a large number of D/Cs.

(6) Attack not reported. The claimed steamer *Erika Fritzen*/4169grt was sunk at 1541 on 26.2.45 on an RAF mine in the 'Sweet Pea 1' field off Warnemünde.

(7) Attack not reported.

(8) Hydroacoustic attack. *Bohus* was the ex *Gerit Fritzen*, but this ship is also claimed as sunk by RAF air attack off Fehmarn.

(9) Attack not reported.

(10) Attack not reported.

(11) Attack not reported.

1	2	3	4	5	6	7	8	9	10	11	12	13	14	15	16	17
MARCH 1945 *continued*																
09/0044	sj	SC-303	Ignatev	-D	7000	+	4-T	Off Liepaja	11/1730	dt	-D	Borbek (?)	6002	+	55°03N/20°45E	1
12/									12/2218	dt	DD	(Z34, T36)	–	/	Grossendorf	2
13/	sj	L-21	Mogilevskii				20M	54°36N/18°52E	14.03.M	dt	TB	T3	839	+	54°39N/18°47E	
									14.03.M	dt	TB	T5	843	+	54°39N/18°47E	
									15.03.M	dt	SS	U367	769	+	54°25N/18°50E	
									10.04.M	dt	DD	Z43	2519	=	Hela	
17/1812	sj	K-53	Jaroshevich	-D	6000	+	3-T	54°30N/15°28E	17/1615	dt	-D	Margarethe Cords	1912	+	54°48N/15°E	
									18/0630	dt	PM	(M801, convoy)	–	/	SE Bornholm	3
18/2305	sj	L-21	Mogilevskii	-D		/	3-T	E Stolpebank								4
18/2332	sj	L-21	Mogilevskii	-D		/	3-T	E Stolpebank								4
23/0630	sj	L-21	Mogilevskii	-T	8000	+	3-T	55°24N/17°00E	23/0435	dt	APC	V2022/E. Colzmann	581	+	55°21N/16°55E	
23/	sj	L-3	Konovalov				10M	54°46N/18°45E	23.03.M	dt	APM	M3138/KFK 182	112	+	Baltic	5
24/	sj	L-3	Konovalov				10M	54°47N/18°50E								
24/0145	sj	L-21	Mogilevskii	-T	8000	+	3-T	55°10N/17°36E	23/	dt	-Tg	Erni/Emil	105	+	55°21N/15°55E	
25/1112	sj	L-21	Mogilevskii	-D	5000	+	3-T	55°11N/17°06E	25/0928	dt	-D	(TS4, convoy)	–	/	N Kolberg	6
27/0044	sj	SC-310	Bogorad	-D	5000	+	3-T	30m SW Liepaja								7
27									27/	dt	CL	(Leipzig)	–	/	Central Baltic	8
30/	sj	LEMBIT	Matiyasevich				20M	54°55N/18°20E	10.04.M	dt	-D	Neuwerk (?)	804	+	Bay of Danzig	9
									25.04.M	dt	APC	Vs343/K300 (?)	112	+	Rixhöft	9

(1) The claim by *SC-303* is for 9.3.45; the German report states that *Borbek* was sunk on 11.3.45, 30m north-east of Hela, by a Soviet torpedo bomber.

(2) The German vessels reported an attack which was repulsed.

(3) *M801* reported one torpedo which missed.

(4) Attack not observed.

(5) The loss position of *M3138* is unknown, the claim by *L-3* uncertain.

(6) The attack was thwarted by *TS4*, which counter-attacked with D/Cs.

(7) Attack not observed.

(8) *Leipzig* reported two submarine attacks evaded.

(9) The claimed sinkings are doubtful. *UJ1108*/460grt (ex *Elbe*) is a misidentification for either *UJ1101* or *UJ1102*, both of which were sunk on 11.4.45 by Soviet aircraft off Hela. *Vs1014*/40grt (ex *Kiel*) was sunk on 18.3.45 in 56°00′N/10°49′E on an RAF mine. *Vs301*/277grt (ex *Karl Bergh*) was sunk on 19.3.45 off Pillau by Soviet aircraft. *Neuwerk* was probably sunk by error by a German S-boat. *Vs343* is possibly correct.

1	2	3	4	5	6	7	8	9	10	11	12	13	14	15	16	17
APRIL 1945																
04/1326	sj	K-56	Popov	CL		+	4-T	*31m NW Stilo Lt*	*04/0440*	dt	*APC*	*(UJ1201)*	–	/	*N Stolpebank*	*1*
10/	sj	SC-310	Bogorad						10/	dt	-D	Ilmenau	1201	+	W Liepaja	2
11/0547	sj	K-56	Popov	APM		/	2-T	55°17N/16°00E								
11/0550	sj	K-56	Popov	APM		+	-A	55°17N/16°00E	11/	sw	-Mf	Ramona	57	+	25m S Utklipp.	
12/0115	sj	SC-310	Bogorad	-D		/	2-T	Off Liepaja								2
14/0113	sj	SC-310	Bogorad	-D	7000	+	3-T	56°23N/20°12E	*13/2218*	dt	*DD*	*(Z34, T36)*	–	/	*Grossendorf*	*2*
17/0048	sj	L-3	Konovalov	-D	12000	+	3-T	55°09N/18°25E	16/2353	dt	-M	Goya	5230	+	55°13N/18°20E	3
									18/1210	dt	APG	(SAT5/Robert Müller 6)	–	/	Off Pillau	4
19/0034	sj	L-3	Konovalov	-D	8000	/	3-T	55°01N/18°25E								4
19/0040	sj	L-3	Konovalov	-D	8000	+	3-T	55°01N/18°25E	18/2341	dt	-Mbt	...	...	+	55°03N/20°45E	4
19/0502	sj	SC-309	Vetchinkin	APM		/	2-T	Off Pillau								5
21/1420	sj	K-52	Travkin	-D	6000	+	3-T	55°17N/17°19E								
21/1922	sj	L-3	Konovalov	-D	8000	+	3-T	55°01N/18°38E	21/noon	dt	-D	(Convoy)	–	/	Off Rixhöft	6
22/0036	sj	SC-310	Bogorad	-D		/	2-T	Off Liepaja	7							
22/2048	sj	K-52	Travkin	-D		/	2-T	Stolpebank	*22/*	dt	*PM*	*(M322)*	–	/	*N Kolberg*	*8*
24/0042	sj	SC-310	Bogorad	-D		/	2-T	Off Liepaja								9
24/0342	sj	SC-309	Vetchinkin	APC		/	2-T	Off Pillau								10

(1) *UJ1201* reported one torpedo which missed.

(2) There are discrepancies in the times of *SC-310*'s attacks. If *Ilmenau* was sunk by *SC-310*, which seems likely, it was probably the 7000grt claim, while the attack against the destroyers was one that missed. The claimed *Cap Guir*/1536grt was in fact sunk on 16.4.45 south of Gotland by a Soviet airborne torpedo.

(3) 6,666 people died aboard *Goya*, only 334 being rescued.

(4) *SAT5/Robert Müller 6*/399 was, according to survivors, attacked on 18.4.45 by Soviet aircraft, receiving two bomb hits and one torpedo and sinking before the time of *L-3*'s attack, but a small motor boat was lost at the stated time.

(5) Attack not reported.

(6) Attack made against a convoy of four ships. A D/C pursuit lasted for six hours.

(7) Attack not reported.

(8) *M322* reported a submarine attacked with D/Cs.

(9) Attack not reported.

(10) Attack not reported.

1	2	3	4	5	6	7	8	9	10	11	12	13	14	15	16	17

APRIL 1945 *continued*

1	2	3	4	5	6	7	8	9	17
25/0017	sj	K-52	Travkin	-D	10000	+	3-T	55°14N/17°53E	1
25/0053	sj	K-52	Travkin	-D		/	3-T	55°14N/17°53E	1
27/0130	sj	K-52	Travkin	-D		/	3-T	55°36N/18°04E	2
27/0148	sj	K-52	Travkin	-D	7000	+	3-T	55°36N/18°04E	2

MAY 1945

06/1751	sj	K-53	Jaroshevich	-D		/	3-T	Stolpebank	3
13/1600	sj	K-53	Jaroshevich	-Df		+	A	Off Utklippan	4
13/1600	sj	K-53	Jaroshevich	-Df		+	A	Off Utklippan	4

(1) *K-52* reported two explosions, but there was no German report.
(2) *K-52* again reported two detonations, but again there was no German report.

(3) No German report.
(4) *K-53* reported two fishing vessels, without crews, found and sunk.

IV. Black Sea

This chapter contains the attacks made by Soviet submarines in the Black Sea on Romanian, Bulgarian, German, Italian and Turkish vessels. The sources used are as follows.

Soviet

'Velikaya Otechestvennaya, Den' za dnem. Iz khroniki boevykh dejstvij VMF v Ijunya 1941–Mae 1945 gg', in *Morskoj sbornik*, 6/1991—5/1995.

Khronika Velikoj Otechestvennoj vojny Sovetskogo Soyuza na Chernom morskom teatro. Edited by NKVMF SSSR, Ministerstvo Vooruzhennykh Sil SSSR, Voenno-Morskoe ministerstvo Soyuza SSR/Morskoj generalnyj shtab. Vols 1–6. Moskva: Voenizdat, 1945–51. This material was not accessible before the period of *glasnost*.

Boevaya deyatel'nost' podvodnykh lodok Voenno-Morskogo Flota SSSR v Velikuyu Otechestvennuyu vojnu 1941–45 gg. Edited by G. I. Shchedrin et al. Vol. III: *Podvodnye lodki Chernomorskogo flota . . .* Moskva: Voenizdat, 1969–70. Not accessible before the period of *glasnost*.

Dmitriev, V. I. *Atakujut podvodniki*. Moskva: Voenizdat, 1964.

The several monographs, memoirs, articles and 'epic' stories published prior to 1988 provided some information but have been rendered obsolete by more recent publications and are therefore not mentioned.

Additional information was received by means of correspondence with the following experts: Professor V. I. Dmitriev, St Petersburg; Rolf Erikson, Phoenix, USA; *Capitaine de Vaisseau* Claude Huan, Paris; and A. Ovcharenko, Kiev, Ukraine

German

Kriegstagebuch der Seekriegsleitung 1939–1945. Edited by Werner Rahn, Gerhard Schreiber and Hansgeorg Maierhöfer. Herford/Hamburg: Mittler & Sohn, Vols 22–63, 1990–96.

Kriegstagebuch Admiral Schwarzes Meer 1941–1945. Original in Bundesarchiv/ Militärarchiv, Freiburg.

For shipping losses on the German side the following sources were used:

Gröner, Erich. *Die deutschen Kriegsschiffe 1815–1945*. Continued and edited by Dieter Jung and Martin Maas. Vols1–8/2 and Index. München/Bonn: Bernard & Graefe, 1982–94.

Dinklage, Ludwig, and Witthöft, H. J. *Die deutsche Handelsflotte 1939–1945*. Vols1–2. Göttingen: Musterschmidt, 1970–71. (Studien und Dokumente zur Geschichte des Zweiten Weltkrieges, Bd.5a/b.)

Romanian/Bulgarian

Details in *Kriegstagebuch Admiral Schwarzes Meer*.

Correspondence with Professor D. Preda, Commission Nat. Roumaine d'Histoire Militaire, Bucharest; and Dr N. Kotev, National Centre for Military History, Sofia,

Turkish

Correspondence with Brigadier-General S. Ercan, Türk Askeri Tarih Komisyonu Genelkurmay ATASE, Ankara; and Bernd Langensiepen, Hamburg.

Jewish Refugee Ships

Rohwer, Jürgen: 'Jüdische Flüchtlingsschiffe im Schwarzen Meer, 1934 bis 1944', in *Das Unrechtsregime*. Edited by Ursula Büttner. Vol. II: *Verfolgung, Exil, Belasteter Neubeginn*. Hamburg: Christians, 1986, pp.197–248.

1	2	3	4	5	6	7	8	9	10	11	12	13	14	15	16	17

JUNE 1941

1	2	3	4	5	6	7	8	9	10	11	12	13	14	15	16	17
26/	sj	SC-206	Karakui	–			1-T	E Constanta	26/0643	sj	DD	(Kharkov)	–	/	44°04N/29°09E	1
26/	sj	SC-206	Karakui	–			2-T	E Constanta	26/0730	sj	DD	(Soobrazitelnyi)	–	/	44°04N/29°14E	1

JULY 1941: No operations

AUGUST 1941

1	2	3	4	5	6	7	8	9	10	11	12	13	14	15	16	17
02/	sj	L-5	Zhdanov				11M	6m SE Mangalia								2
12/	sj	L-4	Polyakov				20M	8m SE Mangalia								3
15/1054	sj	SC-211	Devyatko	-D	8700	+	2-T	42°46N/27°59E	15/0930	ru	-D	Peles	5708	+	N Cape Emine	4
15/1054	sj	SC-211	Devyatko	-T	7000	=	"	42°46N/27°59E	15/0930	it	-T	(Superga/6154)	–	/	N Cape Emine	4
16	sj	L-5	Zhdanov				11M	4.5m E Mangalia								5
16/1425	sj	SC-211	Devyatko	-D	...	/	1-T	N Cape Emine	16/1330	ru	-D	(Ardeal/5695)	–	/	Bulgarian coast	6
19/	sj	L-4	Polyakov				20M	4m E Cape Olinka	29.04.M	dt	LC	F130	155	+	45°52N/30°15E	7
20/1308	sj	M-33	Surov	SS		+	1-T	Constanta	20/1200	ru	SS	(Delfinul)	–	/	4m E Constanta	8
24/	sj	L-4	Polyakov				20M	6m E Cape Olinka								7
28/	sj	L-5	Zhdanov				20M	3m E Mangalia								9

SEPTEMBER 1941

1	2	3	4	5	6	7	8	9	10	11	12	13	14	15	16	17
04/0840	sj	S-33	Alekseyev, B. A.	-D		/	1-T	S Burgas	04/	un	-D	(Cordelia, Szeged)	–	/		10
04/0900	sj	S-33	Alekseyev, B. A.	-D		/	1-T	S Burgas	04/	un	-D	(Cordelia, Szeged)	–	/		10
07/	sj	L-4	Polyakov				20M	Off Varna	15.09.M	bu	-D	Chipka	2304	+	43°17N/28°05E	11
07/1441	sj	S-34	Khmelnitskii	DD		/	1-T	Cape Shabla	07/	ru	PG	(Dumitrescu/315)	–	/	3m E Cape Shabla	12

(1) After the Soviet destroyer leader *Moskva* sank, probably on a mine while evading salvos from the German 'Tirpitz' coastal battery, *Kharkov* and *Soobrazitelnyi* observed torpedo wakes and a submarine breaking surface. The submarine was very probably then sunk by *Soobrazitelnyi*. Since there was no other submarine in the area, it must have been *SC-206*, which went missing at this time.

(2) The minefield was found by Romanian minesweepers on 18.9.41; two mines were swept.

(3) The minefield was not reported.

(4) *SC-211* attacked a convoy with *Peles* and *Superga* under Bulgarian escort. *Peles* was damaged and sank following an explosion on 16.9.41; *Superga* was not hit.

(5) This minefield was reported on 17.8.41; four mines were swept, seven more on 9.9.41 and four more later.

(6) *Ardeal* reported torpedoes which missed, probably in the attack by *SC-211*.

(7) The claimed loss of *FR12* occurred at Kilia Mouth: Cape Olinka or Svyatoi George is at least 30 miles further to the south. Six mines were swept on 11/12.12.41.

(8) *Delfinul* reported a torpedo which missed 4.2m and 125° off the Carol lighthouse off Constanta.

(9) The damage to the Bulgarian freighter *Varna*/2441grt on a mine on 19.9.41 in 42°23´N/27°47´E was possibly caused by one of the German-Romanian defensive flanking barrages off the Bulgarian coast. In September two mines were swept.

(10) Attack not reported.

(11) Following the loss of *Chipka*, German minesweepers swept 19 mines.

(12) *Dumitrescu* reported three torpedoes which missed.

1	2	3	4	5	6	7	8	9	10	11	12	13	14	15	16	17
SEPTEMBER 1941 *continued*																
		?							19.09.M	bu	-D	Rodina (?)	4158	+	42°23N/27°48E	1
13/	sj	L-5	Zhdanov				20M	2m E Cape Galata	10.10.M	ru	ACM	Regele Carol I.	2369	+	Varna	2
18/	sj	L-4	Polyakov				20M	3m E Cape Galata	19.11.M	bu	APM	W-2	...	+	6m E Varna	2
21/0854	sj	M-34	Ilin	-T	5000	+	1-T	Cape Tuzla	21/0800	it	-T	(Superga/6154)	–	/	SE Constanta	3
21/1110	sj	D-5	Savitskii	-T		/	1-T	Cape Shabla	21/1020	it	-T	(Tampico/4958)	–	/	NE Varna	4
23/	sj	M-111	Iosseliani	-D		/	1-T	NW Black Sea	23/	sj	-D	(Transport)	–	/		5
29/	sj	L-5	Zhdanov				20M	4m E Mangalia								6
29/1016	sj	SC-211	Devyatko	-T	7000	+	3-T	Cape Emine	29/0930	it	-T	Superga	6154	=	43°00N/27°53E	7
OCTOBER 1941																
01/									01/1120	dt	-D	(Arkadia/1756)	–	/	Black Sea	8
05/	sj	L-4	Polyakov				20M	6m E Mangalia								6
05/1035	sj	L-4	Polyakov	*DD*		/	2-T	*Mangalia*	*05/1030*	*ru*	*DD*	*(Regina Maria)*	–	/	*Cape Tuzla*	9
									08/1845	dt	AR	(Theresia Wallner)	–	/	SE Bugaz	10
09/1228	sj	SC-215	Apostolov	*PG*		/	1-T	*N Cape Emine*								
15/									*15/*	*ru*	*TB*	*(Sborul)*	–	/	*S Constanta*	*11*
18/1134	sj	SC-210	Zelbst	-T	6875	=	1-T	42°25N/27°40E	18/1045	fr	-T	(Le Progrès)	–	/	Off St Ivan	12
18/1633	sj	M-35	Greshilov	*LC*		+	2TA	*Cape Olinka*	*18/*	*dt*	*LC*	*(SF...)*	–	/	*Ochakov/Kilia*	*13*
20/2207	sj	SC-216	Karbovskii	-D		/	1-T	N Bosporus	20/	un	-D	(Szeged/594)	–	/	N Bosporus	14
									21/	*dt*	*AR*	*(Convoy)*	–	/	*Ilyitchevka*	*15*
24/	sj	L-4	Polyakov				20M	6.5m SE Mangal.								16

(1) *Rodina* is claimed for the minefield laid by *L-5* on 13.09.41, but Cape Galata is near Varna and the position in which the ship sank is further to the south, near Zarewo.

(2) It is unclear whether the auxiliary minelayer *Regele Carol I* was lost on the barrage laid by *L-5* or *L-4*. Bulgarian minesweepers swept 17 mines in the area after *W-2* sank.

(3) *Superga* reported a torpedo which missed.

(4) *Tampico* reported a torpedo which missed.

(5) Soviet transport attacked in error.

(6) No mines found.

(7) *SC-211* attacked a convoy with three ships and two Bulgarian escorts. *Superga* was hit by one torpedo and broke into two on the shore; on 30.9.41 these sections were destroyed by two torpedoes from *SC-211*.

(8) *Arkadia* reported a torpedo which missed.

(9) *Regina Maria* escorted the minelayers *Amiral Murgescu* and *Regele Carol* and observed torpedoes which missed.

(10) *Theresia Wallner* reported one torpedo which missed. *M-60* was in the area but did not report an attack.

(11) No submarine was in the area.

(12) *Le Progrès* reported a torpedo exploding on the shore.

(13) There is a report of an unsuccessful attack off Ochakov at the Kilia Mouth against three tugs and three Siebel ferries. This may have been the attack by *M-35*.

(14) *Szeged* must have been the target but she observed no torpedoes.

(15) A convoy comprising *Theresia Wallner* and three FR-boats, three tugs and seven Siebel ferries reported torpedoes which missed, but there were no submarines in the area at the time.

(16) No mines found.

1	2	3	4	5	6	7	8	9	10	11	12	13	14	15	16	17
OCTOBER 1941 *continued*																
26/	sj	M-35	Greshilov	LC	150	+	110A	Sulina	26/1900	dt	LC	SF25	140	+	Const.–Sulina	1
26/	sj	M-35	Greshilov	LC	150	=	"	Sulina	26/1900	dt	LC	SF36	140	=	Const.–Sulina	1
27/2020	sj	M-35	Greshilov	-D	4500	+	2-T	Sulina	27/1925	dt	APC	(Lola)	–	/	Sulina	2
NOVEMBER 1941																
03/0105	sj	SC-214	Vlasov	-S	350	+	8-A	41°45N/28°16E	03/0015	tu	-S	Kaynakdere	85	+	Igneada	
04/1015	sj	SC-214	Vlasov	-D		/	1-T	Cape Kuruburnu								3
05/2138	sj	SC-214	Vlasov	-T	3336	+	1-T	Cape Kuruburnu	05/2100	it	-T	Torcello	3336	+	42°55N/28°03E	3
06/0846	sj	S-33	Alekseyev, B. A.	DD		/	2-T	Mangalia	06/	ru	DD	(Marasesti)	–	/		4
06/1434	sj	S-33	Alekseyev, B. A.	DD		/	2-T	Mangalia	06/	ru	DD	(Marasesti)	–	/		4
17/	sj	L-6	Bul				20M	Ak Mechet Bay	20.06.M	ru	-Bg	Danubius	550	+	Ak Mechet	5
18/1637	sj	SC-215	Apostolov	-D	1500	+	1-T	42°12N/27°58E	18/1530	tu	-D	Yenice	300	+	1m NW Zarewo	
25/	sj	L-6	Bul				20M	Yarylgach Bay								6
30/	sj	SC-204	Gritsenko	–			A		30/2115	bu	-D	(Zar Ferdinand)...	–	/	Eregli/Burgas	7
DECEMBER 1941																
01/0914	sj	D-4	Izraelyevich	-D		/	3-T	E Cape Kaliakra	01/0812	ru	-M	(Cavarna)	–	/		8
02/1341	sj	SC-209	Kiselyev	-S		/	1-T	Burgas								9
17/									17/0616	ru	DD	(Regele Ferdinand)	–	/	15m SE Bugaz	10
17/	sj	SC-211 (?)	Devyatko (?)						17/	ru	-D	Oituz	2686	=	Cape Emine	11

(1) *SF25* was lost; *SF36* was driven ashore but salvaged.

(2) *Lola* (renamed *Schiff 29* in 1944) observed torpedoes which missed.

(3) The first attack was not observed.

(4) *Marasesti* reported unsuccessful attacks.

(5) Mines observed, but no losses over the ensuing weeks. The mine losses on 24.10.41 (*Theresia Wallner*, the tugs *Brüsterort*/101grt and *Drossel*/175grt and the landing craft *SF16*), on 9.11.41 (the steamer *Ungvar*/1031grt and the motor torpedo boats *Viforul* and *Vijelia*) and on 2.12.41 (the steamers *Cordelia*/1357grt and *Cavarna*/3495grt), sometimes attributed to submarine mines, must have occurred on the Soviet defensive mine barrages E (24.10.41) and S (9.11 and 2.12.41) off Odessa. The loss of *Danubius* is a possibility.

(6) Mines not observed.

(7) The lost *SC-204* was discovered in this area in 1984; its gun had been in action. The convoy observed two torpedoes which missed.

(8) The torpedoes missed and the escorts dropped 34 D/Cs.

(9) The torpedo passed beneath the ship.

(10) *Regele Ferdinand* reported two torpedoes which missed, but *SC-203* had left the area earlier.

(11) No Soviet report, but *SC-211* may have been in the area.

1	2	3	4	5	6	7	8	9	10	11	12	13	14	15	16	17
JANUARY 1942																
01/0007	sj	SC-214	Vlasov	-S	200	+	106A	41°48N/28°15E	01/	tu	-S	Karaltepe (?)	350	+	Igneada	
FEBRUARY 1942																
23/2259	sj	SC-213	Denezhko	-T	300	+	1TA	41°24N/28°54E	23/	tu	-S	Çankaya	164	+	N Bosporus	1
24/1045	sj	SC-213	Denezhko	-D	7000	+	1-T	41°26N/29°10E	24/	pa	-D	Struma	169	+	9m N Bosporus	2
MARCH 1942																
02/1650	sj	SC-213	Denezhko	-D		/	1-T	S Cape Karaburnu								3
03/1158	sj	SC-213	Denezhko	-D		/	1-T	S Cape Karaburnu	04/	tu	-S	(Adana)	–	/	N Bosporus	4
08/	sj	M-36	Komarov, V. N.	-Bg		/	1-T	Yalta	08/1740				–	/	Yalta harbour	5
APRIL 1942: No attacks																
MAY 1942																
02/	sj	A-3 (?)	Tsurikov					Odessa	02/0840	dt	-D	(Arkadia/Salzburg)	–	/	Grün 24/Odessa	6
18/2049	sj	SC-205	Sukhomlinov	-D	1500	+	136A	Karaburnu	18/1910	tu	-D	Duatepe	128	+	Off Tesov	7
18/2102	sj	SC-205	Sukhomlinov	-S	350	+	"	Karaburnu	18/2040							7
									19/	tu	-D	(?)	–	/	Anatoli (?)	8
21/	sj	M-111 (?)	Iosseliani (?)						21/1315	dt	AR	(Uta)	–	/	Cape Burnas	9
									23/0840	dt	PR	(R164)	–	/	Const.-Crimea	10
11/	sj	A-2	Khebyshev	–		/	A	Odessa								
23/0947	sj	SC-205	Sukhomlinov	-D		/	2-T	N Karaburnu	23/	tu	-D	(Safak)	–	/	Off Zarewo	11
23/1009	sj	SC-205	Sukhomlinov	-D	4000	+	2TA	42°08N/27°54E	23/0900	tu	-D	Safak	682	+	Off Zarewo	11

(1) *Çankaya* was the sailing vessel of 164grt, as reported by the German naval attaché, and not the small tanker of 454grt claimed by Soviet sources. The ship was sunk by gunfire.

(2) *Struma* was a Jewish refugee ship. Of the 769 passengers, only one survived.

(3) Attack not observed.

(4) *Adana* reported a possible but unsuccessful torpedo attack on 4.3.42. The only submarine there was *SC-213*.

(5) One torpedo beached in Yalta harbour.

(6) The two steamers reported a torpedo which missed. *A-3* was in the area.

(7) *SC-205* attacked *Duatepe* with gunfire; the ship was beached after 10 hits. *SC-205* reported that a sailing vessel (to date unidentified) came alongside the wreck and was sunk by gunfire also.

(8) *Seekriegsleitung* reported one torpedo which missed, but no submarine was in the area.

(9) *Uta* reported a premature detonation. Only *M-111* was in the area at the time, but she did not report an attack.

(10) *R164* reported two torpedoes which missed and one surface-running torpedo, but no submarine was in the area.

(11) *SC-205* reported one torpedo which missed and one successful attack on *Safak*.

1	2	3	4	5	6	7	8	9	10	11	12	13	14	15	16	17
MAY 1942 *continued*																
29/1023	sj	A-3	Tsurikov	-D	5650	+	2-T	46°33N/30°56E	29/0925	ru	-D	Sulina	3495	+	46°31N/30°52E	
29/	sj	SC-214	Vlasov	-S	100	+	Spr	41°50N/28°14E	29/	tu	-S	Hudarvendigar	c100	+	Off Inada	1
31/	sj	SC-214	Vlasov	-S	100	+	10A	41°55N/28°15E	31/	tu	-S	Mahbubdihan	85	+	Cape Stefanos	1
JUNE 1942																
02/	sj	SC-214	Vlasov	-S	100	+	Spr	41°59N/26°16E	02/	tu	-S		c100	+	Cape Stefanos	1
03/									[03.06.M	dt	LC	F145	155	+]	46°32N/31.15E	2
09/	sj	SC-213 (?)	Denezhko (?)						09/2330	dt	APC	(Delphin 6)	–	/	Off Achtopol	3
11/1512	sj	A-5	Kukuy	-D	5695	=	1-T	46°34N/30°45E	11/1410	ru	-D	Ardeal	5695	=	46°32N/30°56E	4
									11/1710	dt	-Tg	(Romulus)	–	/	46°18N/30°45E	5
20/1918	sj	SC-215	Korshunov	*DD*		/	2-T	*E Cape Olinka*	20/1818	dt	PR	(FR1, FR11)	–	/	44°58N/29°45E	6
JULY 1942																
17/									*17/*	*dt*	*PR*	*(3rd R-Flotilla)*	–	/	*Odessa Bay*	7
AUGUST 1942																
									04/2045	*it*	*PT*	*(MAS 569)*	–	/	*S Kilik Adma*	8
05/0353	sj	SC-205	Sukhomlinov	-D	8000	+	3-T	44°34N/29°28E	05/	dt	-D	(Le Progrès)	–	/		9
06/	sj	L-5	Zhdanov				20M	4m SW Feolent	*17.02.M*	*dt*	*LC*	*F-473*	*155*	+	*1.5m Khersones*	10
07/	sj	M-62	Malyshev, N. I.	*LC*	*350*	+	2-T	*S Sudak*	*07/1050*	*dt*	*LC*	*(F-136 et al)*	–	/		11
07/1728	sj	M-118	Savin	-D		+	2-T	45°09N/30°05E	07/1630	dt	-D	(Convoy)	–	/	N Sulina	12
12/	sj	L-5	Zhdanov				16M	6m SW Feolent								13
									16/1100	dt	-Tg	(Forsch)	–	/	3m S Tuzla	14

(1) The identities of the sailing vessels attacked are unclear. *Hudarvendigar* was one of the vessels lost.

(2) The loss of *F-145* is, in German sources, attributed to a submarine torpedo, but it was actually brought about by a mine from a Soviet defensive barrage. Only *A-3* was in the area at the time, but she reported no attack.

(3) The patrol vessel observed torpedoes which missed, but there was probably no submarine in the area.

(4) *Ardeal* was beached with one hit, but was salvaged and repaired.

(5) The tug reported a detonation on the beach behind the towed convoy ships; *A-5* reported only an unsuccessful attack at 0512.

(6) *FR1* reported one torpedo which missed

(7) A torpedo which missed was reported, but there was no submarine in the area.

(8) *MAS569* reported one torpedo which missed, but the only submarine in the area, *M-62*, attacked on 7.8.42.

(9) *Arkadia*/1756grt is claimed by Soviet sources, but in fact *Le Progrès*, escorted by two Romanian gunboats, must have been the target. *Le Progrès* did not observe the attack.

(10) *F473* may have been a late loss.

(11) *M-62* even reported two MFPs sunk, but *F136* reported two torpedoes passing 10 metres ahead.

(12) One torpedo detonated on the shore; one torpedo missed.

(13) No losses reported.

(14) *Forsch* reported one torpedo which missed. *S-31* was in the area, but no attack was reported.

1	2	3	4	5	6	7	8	9	10	11	12	13	14	15	16	17
AUGUST 1942 *continued*																
17/1347	sj	M-31	Rastochil	-D		+	2-T	46°20N/30°46E	17/1313	dt	-Tg	(Romulus et al)	–	/	46°20N/30°45E	1
19/	sj	L-4	Polyakov				20M	5m SE Sarych								2
23/1838	sj	M-36	Komarov, V. N.	-D	5000	+	2-T	45°49N/30°12E	23/1745	dt	-Tg	Ankara	100	+	45°48N/30°08E	3
22-25	sj	M-33	Surov	APM		+	-T	46°30N/30°54E								4
26/2021	sj	M-113	Stankevich	*SS*		/	*1-T*	*E Cape Burnas*	*26/*	*sj*	*SS*	*(SC-208)*	–	/		5
SEPTEMBER 1942																
05/0508	sj	M-35	Greshilov	-D		/	2-T	E Budaki	05/	ru	-D	(Suceava)	–	/		6
07/2023	sj	SC-207	Panov	*DD*		/	2-T	N Bosporus	07/1935	ru	DD	(Regele Ferdinand)	–	/	*2m NE Bosporus*	7
07/2031	sj	SC-207	Panov	*DD*		+	4-T	N Bosporus	07/	ru	DD	(Marasti)	–	/	*2m NE Bosporus*	7
16/	sj	L-5	Zhdanov				20M	7m ENE Burnas	06.11.M	ru	-Tg	Oitul	95	+	45°47N/30°19E	8
16/	sj	L-4	Polyakov	–		–			16/0505	dt	APC	(Lola)	–	/	44°11N/32°42E	9
19/	sj	L-4	Polyakov				20M	5m SW Cape Burnas								10
20/0255	sj	M-35	Greshilov	-D		/	1-T	E Zhebriyani	20/0200	dt	-Tg	(Tug and barges)	–	/	S Burnas	11
21/1010	sj	M-35	Greshilov	-D	8000	+	1-T	45°54N/30°22E	21/	bu	-D	(Varna, *Naluca*)	–	/		11
21/1302	sj	S-31	Belorukov	-D		/	2-T	S Yalta	21/1200	dt	-D	(Convoy)	–	/	Off Yalta	12
22/1325	sj	S-31	Belorukov	*LC*	350	+	2-T	*S Yalta*	*22/*	*dt*	*LC*	*(Convoy, F359)*	–	/		*13*
25/	sj	M-113	Stankevich	-D		/	2-T	E Portitskoe	25/1630	dt	-D	(Convoy)	–	/	30m NNE Const.	14

(1) *M-31* claimed the tug *Dürenstein*/c300grt sunk, but *Romulus* reported only three torpedoes which missed. In fact *Dürnstein* sank in a storm on 6.1.44 off Odessa.

(2) The claimed *F138* was beached after sustaining damage in an air attack on 14.8.42, hit a German defensive mine while under tow to Sevastopol and was laid up as wreck. German minesweepers swept four mines on 1.2.43.

(3) The ship attacked was the small tug *Ankara*, not the modern freighter of 4768grt, which sank on 18.1.43 off Bizerta on a mine laid by the British submarine *Rorqual* (q.v.).

(4) *M-33* was sunk between 22 and 25.8.42 on a mine in the position stated and is credited with the sinking of a minesweeper, but there was no German report.

(5) Attack probably made in error on *SC-208*.

(6) An attack was not reported, but it must have been on *Suceava* and two gunboats.

(7) The destroyers were picking up the escort of the Italian tankers *Albaro* and *Celeno* at the time, but they evaded a surface-running torpedo and dropped D/Cs.

(8) *Oitul* was probably sunk on this barrage.

(9) *Lola* and the Romanian destroyer *Regele Ferdinand* reported two torpedoes which missed, but *L-4* was attacked with 26 D/Cs and did not fire torpedoes.

(10) No losses reported.

(11) In the first attack two torpedoes, which missed, were reported. The second attack was not observed.

(12) Two torpedoes which missed were reported.

(13) Convoy with six vessels. Attack not observed.

(14) Torpedo which missed reported.

1	2	3	4	5	6	7	8	9	10	11	12	13	14	15	16	17
SEPTEMBER 1942 *continued*																
									27/1620	dt	-Tg	(Towed convoy No 4)	–	/	Ak Mechet	1
28/	sj	M-120	?	APC		/	2-T	SE Sulina	28/*morn.*	ru	TB	(*Naluca*)	–	/	*Ochakov/Kilia*	2
OCTOBER 1942																
01/	sj	M-118	Savin	-D	2300	+	2-T	SE Shagany	01/1415	dt	-D	Salzburg	1742	+	45°54N/30°19E	3
04/	sj	L-23	Fartushnyi				20M	1m NE Feodosiya	*15.06.M*	dt	LC	*F121*	*155*	+	*44°57N/35°26E*	4
04/	sj	L-4	Polyakov				20M	Off Yalta								5
04/	sj	L-24	Apostolov				20M	44°29N/34°10E								5
06/2342	sj	M-31	Rastochil	-Tg	100	+	2-T	45°47N/30°19E	06/2300	ru	-Tg	Mina Daniel	293	+	N Sulina/Burnas	6
07/1342	sj	SC-216	Karbovskii	-Bg		/	2-T	Sulina	07/1530	ru	-D	(Sulina)	–	/	N Sulina	6
07/1423	sj	L-24	Apostolov	-T		=	3-T	41°29N/28°47E	07/1323	it	-T	(Arca/2238)	–	/	41°33N/28°46E	7
10/2044	sj	SC-216	Karbovskii	-D	7150	+	3-T	44°57N/29°46E	10/1950	ru	-D	Carpati	4336	+	45°01N/29°47E	
									12/1905	dt	APC	(D-5, D-6)	–	/	Off Gibrieni	8
14/	sj	SC-213	Isaev	–			1-T		14/	dt	APC	(Xanten)	–	/	44°39N/29°05E	9
14/1343	sj	M-32	Koltypin	DD		+	2-T	*S Cape Burnas*	14/	ru	DD	(*Regele Ferdinand*)	–	/		10
21/1806	sj	M-35	Greshilov	-T	6875	+	2-T	45°08N/29°44E	21/1705	dt	-T	Le Progrès	511	+	45°07N/29°45E	11
24/0433	sj	S-33	Alekseyev, B. A.	-D		/	2-T	N Bosporus	24/	un	-D	(Szeged)	–	/		12
26/0253	sj	SC-207	Panov	-D		/	2-T	S Fidonisi	26/0153	dt	APC	(Xanten)	–	/	Sulina	13
28/	sj	L-5	Zhdanov (?)				20M	10m SSW Burnas								
30/									30/1540	dt	-D	(Convoy)	–	/	Burnas–Bugaz	14

(1) Three torpedoes which missed reported, but no submarine was in the area at the time.

(2) *Naluca* reported two torpedoes which missed.

(3) *Salzburg* was carrying about 2000 POWs, of whom only 34 were rescued.

(4) The claimed *F121* was sunk by a mine in the position stated on 15.6.42 while under tow.

(5) No losses reported.

(6) The dredger reported two torpedoes which missed. The vessel was beached at the entrance but salvaged.

(7) *Arca* was escorted by *R165* and *R166* but only one torpedo, which missed, was seen. *Arca* was sunk on 26.10.42, 9m off Chios (Aegean), by the British submarine *Taku* (q.v.).

(8) Two torpedoes, which missed, were observed.

(9) One torpedo passed 10 metres behind *Xanten*, which dropped 49 D/Cs. *SC-213* was probably sunk.

(10) *M-32* claimed two detonations, but *Regele Ferdinand* evaded the torpedoes and the torpedo boat *Smeul* dropped D/Cs.

(11) Sunk by D/Cs from the German coastal minesweepers *R37* and *R196*.

(12) Attack not observed.

(13) The A/S vessel observed two unsuccessful attacks.

(14) Torpedo seen; D/Cs dropped. *M-31* was in the area but fired both torpedoes on 4.11.42.

1	2	3	4	5	6	7	8	9	10	11	12	13	14	15	16	17
NOVEMBER 1942																
04/1238	sj	M-31	Rastochil	-D		/	2-T	NE Sulina	04/1100	ru	-D	(Bessarabia)	–	/		1
06/	sj	L-23	Fartushnyi				20M	42°17N/27°19E								2
14/1744	sj	L-23	Fartushnyi	-T	2800	+	3-T	41°48N/29°02E	14/1640	dt	-T	Ossag	2793	=	12m NNW Bosporus	
14/									*14/2110*	*dt*	*PR*	*(R35, R36)*	*–*	*/*	*14m S Sulina*	3
19/	sj	L-24	Apostolov				20M	3m SE Cape Kaliakra								4
									25/	dt	APC	(Lola)	–	/	Ochak.–Const.	5
27/1310	sj	M-111	Iosseliani	*LC*	*350*	*+*	*1-T*	*45°43N/30°27E*								6
27/1608	sj	M-111	Iosseliani	-T		=	1-T	45°57N/30°22E	27/1520	dt	APC	(Lola/Xanten)	–	/	44°58N/307E	6
DECEMBER 1942																
08/2200	sj	D-5	Trofimov, I. Ja.	-S	250	+	11A	41°27N/28°37E	08/	tu	-S	Koçiboglu	c100	+	N Bosporus	
									10/	tu	-S		...	+	S Burgas	7
17/1448	sj	M-62	Malyshev, N. I.	-D		+	2-T	45°53N/30°32E	17/	dt	-D	(Durostar, convoy)	–	/		8
?/	sj	L-24 (?)	Apostolov				20M	8m E Kaliakra								9
26/	sj	L-6	Gremyako	*LC*		*/*	*2-T*	*Karkinitski*	25/0505	dt	-D	(Saone, *F176, F341*)	–	/		10
26/1148	sj	M-111	Iosseliani	-D		/	2-T	E Cape Burnas	26/	dt	-D	(Danubius, Tisza)	–	/		11
JANUARY 1943																
07/1555	sj	M-35	Prokofev	-D		+	2-T	45°49N/30°07E	07/1523	bu	-D	(Zar Ferdinand)	–	/	Burnas	12
23/2223	sj	SC-215	Greshilov	-Bg		/	2-T	Tarkhankut								13
24/0105	sj	SC-215	Greshilov	-Bg		/	3-T	Tarkhankut	*23/2330*	*dt*	*LC*	*(F125)*	–	/	*WNW Yevpatoriya*	13
24/	sj	SC-215	Greshilov	-Bg		+	A	Tarkhankut								13

(1) *Bessarabia*, in convoy, observed a submarine conning tower.
(2) Barrage not reported.
(3) *M-35* was in the area, but no attack was reported.
(4) Barrage not reported.
(5) *SC-216* was in the area, but no attack was reported.
(6) First attack not reported. The two A/S vessels reported one torpedo, which missed, in the second attack.
(7) Turkish sailing vessel sunk by gunfire.
(8) *Durostar*, with four escorts, did not observe the attack.

(9) *L-24* was lost between 15 and 29.12.42 off Cape Shabla, probably on a mine, but there was no report of actual minelaying and no losses were reported.
(10) 30 D/Cs dropped.
(11) Convoy, with four escorts, did not observe an attack.
(12) *M-35* claimed one transport sunk; the latter was escorted by three vessels. *Zar Ferdinand*/1994grt reported one torpedo which missed.
(13) *F125* reported two torpedoes which missed. There is no report concerning the sinking of a barge by gunfire.

1	2	3	4	5	6	7	8	9	10	11	12	13	14	15	16	17

FEBRUARY 1943: No operations

MARCH 1943

1	2	3	4	5	6	7	8	9	10	11	12	13	14	15	16	17
08/1752	sj	SC-215	Greshilov	-T		/		3-T Tarkhankut	08/1710	dt	-T	(Wolga-Don)	–	/	SW Tarkhankut	1
11/									11/0905	dt	-Bg	(Moselia)	–	/	Sudak	2
11/1214	sj	M-35	Prokofev	LC		/		2-T Opuk	11/1015	dt	LC	(F170)	–	/	Cape Opuk	2
12/									12/	dt	-T	(Wolga-Don)	–	/		3
13/1109	sj	SC-215	Greshilov	-Bg		/		2-T Tarkhankut	13/0920	un	-M	(Budapest)	–	/	5m W Tarkhankut	4
16/1521	sj	L-23	Fartushnyi	LC		/		3-T Tarkhankut	16/1335	dt	APC	(Lola)	–	/	12m SE Tarkhankut	5
20/	sj	D-4 (?)	Trofimov, I. Ja.	-D		+		-T Tarkhankut	[20/	bu	-D	(Rodina/4158) (?)]	–	/	Tarkhankut	6
22/0754	sj	L-6	Gremyako	-Bg		/		3-T 44°57N/35°51E	22/0610	dt	LC	(F469, F342, F326)	–	/	Cape Chauda	7
25/1803	sj	M-117	Kesayev	-D	2000	+		2-T 44°29N/34°25E								8
26/									26/noon	dt	-D	(Prodromos)	–	/	SW Yevpatoriya	9
27/									27/1355	dt	-D	(Charkov, Suceava)	–	/		9

APRIL 1943

1	2	3	4	5	6	7	8	9	10	11	12	13	14	15	16	17
16/0907	sj	SC-207	Panov	LC		/		2-T Chauda								10
17/	sj	M-35	Prokofev	-D		?	–	65m E Olinka	17/0030	dt	-D	(Arkadia)	–	/		11
									18/0427	dt	SS	(U9)	–	/	90m E Kaliakra	12

(1) *Wolga-Don*/956grt, escorted by two Romanian gunboats, reported three or four torpedoes which missed.

(2) *F170*, escorting, with four other MFPs, the tug *Theben* and the tank barge *Moselia*, reported two torpedoes which missed.

(3) *Wolga-Don* reported a torpedo which missed.

(4) *Budapest*/485grt reported two torpedoes which missed.

(5) The A/S vessel reported two torpedoes which missed.

(6) The claimed *Rodina* had in fact been sunk on 19.9.41 on a mine (q.v.).

(7) Two MFPs from Anapa Convoy No 8 reported 4 torpedoes which missed.

(8) Attack not reported.

(9) The first convoy reported two torpedoes which missed; the second, with two destroyers and three R-boats, reported an attack. *L-23* was in the area but did not report any attack.

(10) Attack not reported.

(11) The attack by *M-35* on *Arkadia*, with two destroyers and three R-boats, was aborted. 12 D/Cs.

(12) *U9* reported evading four torpedoes. No Soviet submarine in the area.

1	2	3	4	5	6	7	8	9	10	11	12	13	14	15	16	17
APRIL 1943 *continued*																
20/0220	sj	S-33	Alekseyev, B. A.	-D	6875	+	3-T	45°01N/31°10E	20/0128	ru	-D	Suceava	6876	+	44°52N/31°22E	
21/1034	sj	M-111	Iosseliani	-Tg		+	1-T	Dvuyakornoe B.	*21/0935*	*dt*	*PT*	*(S...)*	*–*	*/*	*Ivan Baba Hb.*	*1*
23/1005	sj	M-112	Khakhanov	*LC*	*350*	+	2-T	*44°50N/35°12E*	*23/0910*	*dt*	*LC*	*(F406, F301)*	*–*	*/*	*44°N/35°17E*	*2*
									23/1700	*dt*	*LC*	*(F472)*	*–*	*/*	*S Kerch Strait*	*3*
25/0830	sj	M-111	Iosseliani	-D		+	1-T	Sevastopol	25/0800	dt	-Tg	(Woywoda)	–	/	Cape Feolent	4
MAY 1943																
									03/	*dt*	*PR*	*(R164)*	*–*	*/*		*5*
06/1916	sj	M-117	Kesayev	-D	4000	+	1-T	44°24N/33°37E								6
07/1334	sj	M-117	Kesayev	-D	6000	+	1-T	44°38N/34°34E	07/1240	dt	-D	(Dresden)	–	/	SE Crimea	7
07/1410	sj	L-6	Gremyako	-T	2600	=	2-T	45°16N/32°51E	07/1310	dt	-Tg	(Baikal/Amur)	–	/	45°15N/32°52E	8
									09/	dt	-D	(Charkov/6689)	–	/	45°12N/32°42E	9
11/1210	sj	A-3	Tsurikov	*LC*	*350*	+	2-T	*44°22N/34°05E*	*11/1130*	*dt*	*LC*	*(MAL1, MAL2, MAL3)*	*–*	*/*	*Off Yalta*	*10*
12/0730	sj	A-3	Tsurikov	*LC*		+	2-T	*44°51N/35°08E*	*12/*	*sj*	*-D*	Fabritsius (wreck)	?			*11*
16/1121	sj	SC-215	Greshilov	*LC*	*350*	+	2-T	*44°45N/34°56E*	*16/1030*	*dt*	*LC*	*(F170, F316)*	*–*	*/*	*Off Sudak*	*12*
18/	sj	L-23	Fartushnyi				20M	3m NW Khersones								13
18/1326	sj	M-111	Iosseliani	APG	300	/	1-T	44°57N/37°14E								14
18/1619	sj	M-111	Iosseliani	*LC*	*350*	+	*1-T*	*Anapa*	*18/1515*	*dt*	*LC*	*(F470, F373, F326)*	*–*	*/*	*NW Anapa*	*14*

(1) The tug claimed could not be identified. An S-boat at Ivan Baba reported two torpedoes which missed.

(2) The claimed *F127* was delivered to the Romanian Navy in October 1943. The MFPs reported two torpedoes which missed.

(3) MFP reported one torpedo which missed. No submarine was in the area.

(4) The tug, with two MFPs, reported torpedoes which missed.

(5) *R164* reported three torpedoes which missed.

(6) Attack not reported.

(7) *Dresden* reported one torpedo which missed.

(8) The two tugs reported four to six torpedoes which missed.

(9) *Charkov*, with two R-boats and one Romanian gunboat, reported two prematures and one torpedo which missed. *L-6* was in the area but reported no attack

(10) The claimed *F130* had already been sunk, on 29.4.42 on a mine in 45°52´N/ 30°15´E. Three German gun ferries (MAL) reported torpedoes which missed.

(11) The wreck of *Fabritsius* was attacked in error.

(12) The claimed *F241* was never in the Black Sea and was lost off Norway. The MFPs reported two torpedoes passing under the vessels.

(13) From 20 to 22.5.43 fifteen mines were swept.

(14) The first attack was not reported; in the second attack two surface-running torpedoes were observed. The claimed *F367* was sunk on 19.5.43 by air attack at Anapa.

1	2	3	4	5	6	7	8	9	10	11	12	13	14	15	16	17
MAY 1943 *continued*																
20/									20/0205	dt	LC	(F.., F.., F..)	–	/	W Cape Chauda	1
21/1656	sj	M-111	Iosseliani	LC		+	1-T	Anapa	21/1600	dt	LC	(F170)	–	/	3m SE Zhelesny	2
22/0744	sj	M-111	Iosseliani	LC		/	1-T	Anapa								3
22/1103	sj	L-4	Polyakov	LC	350	+	3-T	45°02N/35°58E	22/1013	dt	LC	(F...)	–	/	2m SE Cape Chauda	4
23/0819	sj	L-4	Polyakov	LC	350	+	A	44°40N/34°50E	23/0725	dt	LC	F329	155	=	NE Yalta	5
24/0959	sj	SC-215	Greshilov	-D	5000	+	4-T	44°41N/33°28E	24/0906	it	-T	(Celeno/3741)	–	/	3m N Sevastopol	6
25/0831	sj	M-111	Iosseliani	-D		+	1-T	Anapa								3
25/1235	sj	L-4	Polyakov	LC		/	–	44°46N/35°14E	25/1207	dt	LC	(F170)	–	/	44°52N/35°18E	7
29/									29/1410	dt	LC	(F121)	–	/	44°21N/33°49E	8
29/									29/1440	dt	-Tg	(Netty)	–	/	4m S Sarych	9
29/1843	sj	SC-215	Greshilov	-Tg		/	1-T	44°22N/35°51E	29/1635	dt	-Tg	(Netty)	–	/	6m W Alupka	10
30/1409	sj	M-113	Stankevich	LC		+	2-T	44°23N/33°55E	30/1310	dt	LC	(F301, F304)	–	/	44°22N/33°57E	11
JUNE 1943																
01/1615	sj	D-4	Trofimov, I. Ja.	DD		+	4-T	Crimea	01/1506	ru	DD	(Marasti)	–	/	Crimea	12
01/1922	sj	D-4	Trofimov, I. Ja.	-T	2600	+	2-T	SW Yevpatoriya	01/1905	it	-T	(Celeno/3741)	–	/	45°06N/32°52E	13
									05/1652	dt	LC	(F..)	–	/	5m W Zhelesnyi	14
09/1452	sj	SC-209	Ivanov, V. I.	-D		/	3-T	Tarkhankut	09/1444	dt	-D	(Charkov/Varna)	–	/	Off Yevpatoriya	15

(1) Three MFPs reported two torpedoes which missed. *L-4* was in the area but reported no attack.

(2) *F170,* of Anapa Convoy No 92, reported one torpedo which missed.

(3) Attack not reported. The claimed *F138* was beached after being damaged in an air attack on 14.8.42 and later towed to Sevastopol. She was damaged again on 15.10.42, this time by a German mine, and the wreck was laid up at Sevastopol.

(4) The MFP reported two surface-running torpedoes which detonated at the end of their run.

(5) *F329* was damaged but towed into Feodosiya. See Note 3.

(6) *Celeno* reported three torpedoes which missed. The escorting *R164* was slightly damaged by an end-detonation.

(7) *F170* reported a torpedo fired against a convoy, which missed, but *L-4* had to break off the attack.

(8) *F121* reported a periscope.

(9) The tug *Netty,* in a convoy, reported a torpedo which missed.

(10) *Netty* again reported a torpedo which missed, detonating on the rocks at the coast.

(11) The MFPs reported one torpedo which missed.

(12) Two Romanian destroyers were escorting *Celeno,* with two R-boats and one A/S vessel. *Marasti* was not hit.

(13) *Celeno* observed four torpedoes missing.

(14) An MFP from Anapa Convoy No 105 reported a torpedo which missed, but no submarine was in the area.

(15) The freighters *Charkov* and *Varna* reported three torpedoes which missed.

1	2	3	4	5	6	7	8	9	10	11	12	13	14	15	16	17
JUNE 1943 *continued*																
11/	sj	L-6	Gremyako				20M	2m W Lukull								1
									11/1952	dt	-D	(Swoj Sworme)	–	/	44°30N/34°21E	2
12/1856	sj	SC-209	Ivanov, V. I.	LC		+	2-T	45°13N/32°52E	12/1805	dt	LC	(F304)	–	/	45°15N/33°00E	3
									15/0145	dt	LC	(F418)	–	/	45°15N/32°37E	4
									17/	dt	-D	(Convoy Bansin 10)	–	/	Feodosiya–Taman	5
17/0516	sj	SC-209	Ivanov, V. I.	-D		/	2-T	Tarkhankut								6
20/1134	sj	A-2	Buyanskii	-Bg		+	2-T	44°53N/35°50E	20/1030	dt	LC	(F307)	–	/	44°58N/35°57E	7
									21/0903	dt	LC	(F307, F368)	–	/	45°15N/32°57E	8
21/1542	sj	M-117	Kesayev	LC	350	+	1-T	44°48N/35°11E								9
21/1559	sj	SC-209	Ivanov, V. I.	LC		/	1-T	Tarkhankut	21/	dt		(Convoy)	–	/	Cape Midia	10
									22/2230	dt	LC	(Convoy Bansin 12)	–	/	10m E Chauda	11
23/	sj	A-2 (?)	Buyanskii	?		?	-T		23/2330	dt	LC	(F471)	–	/	Cape Chauda	11
									26/0140	dt	LC	(Convoy Bansin 13)	–	/	43°01N/36°19E	12
									27/0110	dt	LC	(F...)	–	/	S Crimea	13
									27/2330	dt	LC	(F312, F471)	–	/	44°38N/35°54E	14
28/0450	sj	M-111	Iosseliani	LC		/	2-T	Sevastopol								15
									29/0140	dt	LC	F325	155	=	10m S Cape Chauda	16
30/	sj	SC-201	Paramoshkin	-Mb	30	+	A	Tarkhankut	01/	sj		-Mbt MFK-570	10	P	Tarkhankut	17

(1) German minesweepers swept 16 of the mines on 25 and 27.6.43. The loss of the steamer *Charlotte*/1591grt, in 44°54´N/32°28´E, was far to the west of this barrage.

(2) Convoy of seven vessels reported torpedoes which missed. *A-3* was in the area but reported no attack.

(3) *F304* reported one torpedo which missed.

(4) *F418* reported one torpedo which missed. *L-6* and *SC-209* were in the area, but no attack was reported.

(5) The convoy reported one torpedo which missed.

(6) Attack not reported.

(7) *F307*, in a convoy, reported one torpedo which missed.

(8) The two MFPs mentioned dropped 8 D/Cs.

(9) The claimed *F139* was not hit and became US war booty in the Danube in 1945.

(10) There was an unconfirmed report of an submarine attack

(11) *F471*, in convoy 'Bansin 12', reported two torpedoes which missed. There were several additional reports about torpedoes which missed 'Bansin 12', at 2250 and 2330 on 23.6.43 and at 0130 on 24.6.43. Only *A-2* was in the area: this boat could have made only two attacks after its efforts on 20.6.43.

(12) The convoy 'Bansin 13' reported one torpedo which missed.

(13) An MFP in convoy 'Bansin 14' reported two torpedoes which missed.

(14) The two MFPs of convoy 'Bansin 14' reported two torpedoes which missed.

(15) *M-111* reported an attack against a Siebel ferry, but there is no German report.

(16) *F325*, in convoy 'Bansin 14', was hit by a dud and damaged, but there was no submarine in the area.

(17) There was a report about the capture of a former Soviet motor boat off Tarkhankut.

1	2	3	4	5	6	7	8	9	10	11	12	13	14	15	16	17
JULY 1943																
07/0349	sj	SC-201	Paramoshkin	*PR*		/		2-T	*45°05N/32°43E*							1
07/0349	sj	SC-201	Paramoshkin	-D	2700	+		4-T	45°05N/32°43E	07/0336	ru	-D	(Ardeal/Varna)	–	/	45°00N/32°37E	1
13/										13/0305	dt	LC	(Convoy Bansin 23)	–	/	5m S Chauda	2
17/0643	sj	M-111	Iosseliani	-Tg		=		1-T	Feodosiya	17/0545	dt	-M	(Adelheid)	–	/	Cape Chauda	3
18/	sj	L-4	Polyakov					20M	3m S Yevpator.								4
18/1004	sj	M-111	Iosseliani	-Bg	505	+		1-T	44°59N/35°32E	18/	ru	-Bg	Dunarea-1	505	+	Feodosiya	5
22/0602	sj	L-4	Polyakov	-S	100	+		A	Bosporus	22/	tu	-S	Hudayi Bahri	29	+	Off Bosporus	5
22/	sj	L-4 (?)	Polyakov (?)							22/	tu	-M	Tayyari (?)	409	+	Off Bosporus	5
23/	sj	L-4	Polyakov	-S	100	+		A	Bosporus	23/dawn	tu	-S	Gurpinar	c100	+	Off Bosporus	5
										24/0855	dt	-D	(Prodromos)	–	/	44°52N/30°30E	6
25/1647	sj	M-112	Khakhanov	*LC*		+		2-T	*44°31N/34°18E*	25/1550	dt	-D	(Swoj Sworme)	–	/	*44°31N/34°19E*	7
26/	sj	L-23	Fartushnyi					20M	1mW Feodosiya								8
28/1539	sj	S-31	Belorukov	*LC*	350	+		2-T	*45°09N/32°47E*	28/1443	dt	LC	(F...)	–	/	*45°14N/32°50E*	9
AUGUST 1943																	
										03/0059	dt	LC	(F125)	–	/	5m NE Alushta	10
06/1429	sj	SC-216	Karbovskii	-T	7000	+		3-T	41°23N/29°11E	06/1330	dt	-T	Firuz	7327	=	41°19N/29°05E	11

(1) The convoy of three transports, escorted by the destroyers *Marasti* and *Marasesti* and the gunboats *Stihi* and *Ghigulescu*, reported three torpedoes which missed.

(2) 'Bansin 23' reported at 0305 one and at 0454 two torpedoes which missed. The only submarine in the area was *M-111*, but it used its torpedoes on 17/18.7.43.

(3) The motor vessel *Adelheid*, from convoy 'Bansin 25', reported being struck by a torpedo which ran under the ship without causing damage.

(4) From 29 to 31.7.43 German minesweepers swept 16 mines. The claimed German barge *SNR1468*/1200grt? sank on 11.4.44, probably following a TKA attack.

(5) *L-4* reported only two sinkings; *Tayyari* was possibly sunk at another time. *Hudayi Bahri* is also claimed as sunk by *SC-216* on 6.8.43.

(6) *Prodromos*, escorted by the gunboats *Stihi* and *Ghigulescu*, reported one torpedo which missed, but there was no submarine in the area.

(7) A convoy with *Swoy Sworme* and three MFPs reported two torpedoes which missed.

(8) Four mines were swept in 1944.

(9) The claimed *F174* was sunk on 19.1.43 off Dagerort in the Baltic, but an MFP reported one torpedo which missed.

(10) *F125*, with three other MFPs, reported torpedoes which missed.

(11) *Firuz*, escorted by three vessels, was damaged at the bow.

1	2	3	4	5	6	7	8	9	10	11	12	13	14	15	16	17
AUGUST 1943 *continued*																
06/1835	sj	M-35	Prokofev	AM		/	2-T	41°20N/29°01E	06/1820	dt	APC	(Xanten)	–	/	41°17N/29°05E	1
									07/0652	dt	-D	(Prodromos/Kassa)	–	/	32m E Sulina	2
10/2019	sj	D-4	Trofimov, I. Ja.	-D	6688	+	4-T	44°58N/33°08E	10/1935	dt	-D	Boy Feddersen	6689	+	20m WNW Tarkh.	3
									13/0215	dt	-D	(Convoy, *MT2*)	–	/	46°20N/30°39E	4
16/0748	sj	M-51	Golubev	-D		/	–	44°45N/34°53E								5
19/	sj	L-23	Fartushnyi				20M	37m ESE Olinka								6
20/0729	sj	SC-202	Kassatkin	-D		/	3-T	Bosporus								7
20/0847	sj	D-4	Trofimov, I. Ja.	-D	2141	+	2-T	W Tarkhankut	20/0749	bu	-D	Varna	2141	+	45°13N/32°35E	
21/0843	sj	SC-209	Sukhodolskii	-D		/	3-T	Bosporus	21/	un	-D	(Szeged/594)	–	/		8
23/	sj	SC-203 (?)	Nemchinov	–					23/0300	it	SS	(CB-1)	–	/	W Yevpatoriya	9
25/	sj	SC-215	Greshilov	-D		+	-T	Bosporus	25/	tu	-D	Yilmaz	712	+	Off Bosporus	10
26/	sj	SC-215	Greshilov	-D		+	-T	Bosporus	26/	tu	-M	Derviske	100	+	Off Bosporus	10
28/1904	sj	M-111	Iosseliani	-Bg	1500	+	2-T	44°47N/33°26E	28/1810	dt	-Bg	(Hainburg/c400)	–	?	Cape Lukull	11
30/1935	sj	SC-215	Greshilov	-D	1782	+	4-T	41°22N/29°06E	30/1836	dt	-T	Thisbé	1782	+	41°22N/29°08E	12
SEPTEMBER 1943																
10/0854	sj	M-113	Strizhak	-D		/	2-T	Tarkhankut	10/0720	dt	-Tg	(Lübeck)	–	/	45°16N/32°38E	13
16/	sj	L-6	Gremyako				20M	30m E Olinka								14
16/1026	sj	A-2	Buyanskii	*LC*		/	2-T	*44°45N/34°45E*	*16/0935*	*dt*	*LC*	*(F369)*	–	/	*44°46N/34°44E*	*15*
22/0419	sj	S-33	Alekseyev, B. A.	-D	5000	+	3-T	44°38N/31°39E	22/0319	dt	-D	(Burgas)	–	/	5m S Yevpatoriya	16
									24/2128	dt	-Tg	(Lobau/L-1349)	–	/	44°50N/36°08E	17

(1) *Xanten* reported torpedoes which missed in the position where *Firuz* was damaged.

(2) The two escorted vessels reported torpedoes which missed, but there was no submarine in the area.

(3) German sources claim that *Boy Feddersen* (ex *Charkov*) was damaged by an airborne torpedo and sank during the attempt to tow the vessel to Sevastopol after a further torpedo hit 12m south-west of Yevpatoriya.

(4) *MT2* reported one torpedo which missed, but there was probably no submarine in the area.

(5) Attack prevented; seven D/Cs dropped.

(6) No losses known.

(7) Attack not reported.

(8) *Szeged* was missed.

(9) *CB-1* reported torpedoes missing. The lost *SC-203* may have been in the area.

(10) The German *Seekriegsleitung* reported *Yilmaz* already sunk on 27.4.42. *SC-215* was in the area but did not report the attacks.

(11) *Hainburg* was beached after coming under air attack at Ivan Baba on 2.6.43; salved and again damaged on 28.8.43 off the Kerch Strait when she lost her bow, she was later repaired at Linz and sold to Greece. *F581* reported a torpedo which missed.

(12) *Thisbé* was escorted by two destroyers, two A/S vessels and two R-boats and sank after two torpedo hits.

(13) The 'Bodega' convoy reported at 0720 two and at 0758 one torpedo which missed.

(14) No losses reported.

(15) *F369* reported one torpedo which missed.

(16) *Burgas* was not hit.

(17) One torpedo, which missed, was reported. No submarine in the area.

1	2	3	4	5	6	7	8	9	10	11	12	13	14	15	16	17
OCTOBER 1943																
05/1555	sj	M-117	Kesayev	*LC*	350	+	2-T	*44°33N/33°20E*								*1*
08/									08/1430	dt	-D	(Convoy)	–	/	S Crimea	2
10/1451	sj	A-2	Buyanskii	*LC*	350	+	2-T	*44°21N/33°59E*	10/1316	dt	LC	F474	155	+	*44°28N/34°13E*	3
17/0620	sj	S-31	Belorukov	*LC*	350	+	4-T	*44°39N/32°56E*	17/	dt	LC	(F418 ?)	155	=?	*45°31N/32°33E*	4
18/2146	sj	S-31	Belorukov	-D	5000	+	2-T	*44°58N/32°46E*								5
19/0402	sj	SC-202	Leonov	AM		/	3-T	Tarkhankut								5
19/2339	sj	SC-201	Paramoshkin	-D	4000	=	4-T	*45°04N/32°28E*	19/	dt	-D	(Ardeal, Kassa)	–	/		6
									20/	dt	LC	F...	...	+	*Off Yalta*	7
25/1406	sj	M-112	Khakhanov	-Bg	1278	+	2-T	*45°30N/32°37E*	25/1200	dt	-Bg	Tyra-5	1278	=§	*45°31N/32°36E*	8
NOVEMBER 1943																
01/1607	sj	M-35	Prokofev	-Tg		/	1-T	Ak Mechet								9
02/1752	sj	M-35	Prokofev	-Bg	1270	+	1-T	Ak Mechet	02/1600	dt	-Bg	SNR-1293	1270	=§	Ak Mechet Bay	10
03/0905	sj	M-55	Brodskii	*LC*		+	2-T	*Tendra*	03/0700	dt	LC	(F472)	–	/	*Off Yalta*	11
06/2320	sj	M-111	Iosseliani	-D	3000	+	2-T	*45°49N/30°17E*								12
09/									09/0235	dt	LC	(F521, F594)	–	/	*44°58N/33°30E*	13
11/0124	sj	SC-215	Greshilov	-D		/	2-T	Tarkhankut								14
11/0355	sj	SC-215	Greshilov	-D		/	2-T	Tarkhankut								15
12/1357	sj	M-111	Iosseliani	-D	4000	+	2-T	*45°52N/30°20E*	12/1210	dt	-D	Theoderich	3814	=§	*45°54N/30°23E*	16
13/0117	sj	M-117	Kesayev	-D	3500	+	2-T	*45°26N/32°18E*								17

(1) Attack not reported.

(2) The tug *Seefalke* reported one torpedo which missed. *A-2* was in the area, but no attack was reported.

(3) The claim for *F474* by *M-111* is incorrect: the submarine responsible was *A-2*.

(4) *F418* was damaged by three aerial torpedoes and the wreck was towed into Ak Mechet.

(5) Attack not reported.

(6) The convoy was escorted by two destroyers and five R-boats. The attack was not observed.

(7) The *Seekeiegsleitung* reported one MFP or a barge sunk without identifying the vessel. *M-54* was in the area but reported no attack.

(8) *Tyra-5* was missed by two torpedoes but ran aground and became a total loss.

(9) Attack not reported.

(10) *SNR-1293* was not hit but ran aground and became a total loss.

(11) *F472* reported two torpedoes running on to the beach. *M-55* avoided being rammed.

(12) Attack not reported.

(13) Two attacks with one torpedo each, which missed. The claimed *F580* was hit at 1010 on 9.12.43 by a torpedo but was not in the convoy with *F521*, *F594*, *F340* and *F333*.

(14) Attack not reported.

(15) Attack not reported.

(16) *Theoderich* was the former Soviet *Volochayevka*. The ship was damaged, beached and salvaged but sank on a mine 10m west of Ochakov on 22.11.43 while under tow to Odessa.

(17) Attack not reported.

1	2	3	4	5	6	7	8	9	10	11	12	13	14	15	16	17
NOVEMBER 1943 *continued*																
15/0214	sj	SC-215	Greshilov	LC		/	2-T	Tarkhankut	15/0005	dt	-D	(Convoy)	–	/	4mW Tarkhankut	1
15/0631	sj	SC-215	Greshilov	LC	350	+	2-T	45°27N/32°27E	15/0455	dt	LC	F592	155	+	45°25N/32°26E	1
16/1432	sj	SC-215	Greshilov	-D		/	2-T	Tarkhankut	16/1222	dt	-AM	(MT1)	–	/	45°17N/32°55E	2
17/1000	sj	D-4	Trofimov, I. Ja.	-D		?	4-T	NW Yevpatoriya	17/0816	dt	-D	(KT25, Danubius)	–	/	Off Yevpatoriya	3
18/0541	sj	D-4	Trofimov, I. Ja.	-D		?	1-T	NW Yevpatoriya	18/0500	dt	APC	(MT1, Xanten)	–	/	40m SW Tarkhankut	4
23/1000	sj	D-4	Trofimov, I. Ja.	-D	5000	+	4-T	S Yevpatoriya	23/0550	dt	-D	Santa Fé	4627	+	45°05N/33°16E	
23/1037	sj	M-35	Prokofev	APG		+	2-T	Crimea	23/0855	dt	APC	(UJ101, UJ102)	–	/	6m W Ak Mechet	5
									23/2015	dt	-D	(Balkan/3838)	–	/	5m SE Varna	6
25/1907	sj	L-6	Gremjako	-D	6000	+	4-T	45°07N/32°18E	25/1709	dt	-T	Wolga-Don	956	+	45°07N/32°08E	
25/1907	sj	L-6	Gremjako	-D	2000	=	4-T	45°07N/32°18E								
25/2102	sj	M-117	Kesayev	LC	350	+	2-T	45°31N/31°30E	25/	dt	-D	(Convoy Ovid)	–	/		7
29/	sj	D-4 (?)	Trofimov (?)	–			-T	Tarkhankut	29/0005	dt	-D	(Convoy Virgil)	–	/	44°53N/33°15E	8
DECEMBER 1943																
02/0932	sj	M-111	Iosseliani	LC		+	2-T	Sulina (?)	02/0735	dt	-Bg	(Tow-convoy)	–	/	NW Tarkhankut	9
02/1634	sj	SC-209	Ivanov, V. I.	LC	350	+	4-T	45°13N/32°49E	02/1445	dt	LC	F566	155	+	45°11N/32°56E	10
04/0448	sj	SC-201	Paramoshkin	LC		+	4-T	45°18N/31°48E								11
04/1204	sj	SC-209	Sukhodolskii	-D		+	2-T	Tarkhankut	04/	dt	-D	(Convoy)	–	/		12
04/	sj	D-4	Trofimov, I. Ja.	–			2-T		04/1024	dt	APC	(UJ103)	–	/	Tarkhankut	13
05/1615	sj	S-31	Belorukov	LC		/	2-T	Tendra	05/0640	dt	APC	(UJ2312/KFK17)	–	/	L. Qu. 2647	14
09/1206	sj	S-31	Belorukov	LC	350	+	4-T	45°29N/32°18E	09/1010	dt	LC	F580	155	+	45°33N/32°12E	
11/	sj	SC-201	Paramoshkin	-D		?	-T		11/0900	dt	-D	(...)	–	/	Yevpatoriya	15

(1) *F418* or *F592* are claimed, but only *F592* first reported an unsuccessful attack and then sank in the second.

(2) One torpedo, which missed, was reported.

(3) First two torpedoes were fired at the A/S vessel *Rosita*, and then, at 0816, two were fired at *Danubius*. All missed.

(4) The A/S vessel *Xanten* reported a torpedo which missed.

(5) *UJ101/KT39* and *UJ102/KT40* reported torpedoes which missed.

(6) *Balkan* reported torpedoes which missed. No submarine was in the area.

(7) *F592* is claimed for *M-117*, but see *SC-215* above.

(8) Attack possibly made by *D-4*, lost in this area.

(9) The 'Diogenes' convoy reported a torpedo which missed.

(10) *F566* was also claimed, wrongly, for *D-4*.

(11) The claimed attack against an MFP was not reported.

(12) *SC-209* attacked a transport, escorted by one destroyer and three patrol vessels, but was not observed.

(13) *UJ103/KT37* reported two torpedoes which missed. The group with *UJ102*, *UJ103*, *UJ307*, *UJ2305* and *UJ2308* then sank *D-4*.

(14) *UJ2312/KFK17* reported a submarine but no attack.

(15) A German convoy reported a torpedo which missed.

1	2	3	4	5	6	7	8	9	10	11	12	13	14	15	16	17
DECEMBER 1943 *continued*																
16/	sj								16/	tu	-D	Kalkavan	1986	+	Off Karaburnu	1
21/1401	sj	M-35	Prokofev	-D		/	2-T		21/1203	dt	APC	(UJ103/KT37)	–	/	45°15N/32°53E	2
23/2039	sj	M-117	Kesayev	-D	2000	+	2-T	45°17N/31°55E								3
27/1312	sj	M-55	Brodskii	AM		+	2-T	Dvuyakonnyi Bay	27/1115	dt	PT	(S...)	–	/	Ivan Baba	4
27/1912	sj	S-33	Alekseyev, B. A.	-D	4000	+	4-T	45°12N/32°27E	27/1720	dt	APC	(UJ101, UJ106/KT23)	–	/	W Yevpatoriya	5
JANUARY 1944																
05/	sj	L-23 (?)	Fartushnyi					T?	05/2115	dt	-D	(Convoy)	–	/		6
06/0142	sj	S-33	Alekseyev, B. A.	-D	4000	+	4-T	45°07N/32°32E	06/	dt	-D	(Convoy Zenit)	–	/	19m SW Yevpatoriya	7
13/0110	sj	L-23	Fartushnyi	LC		/	5-T	45°36N/31°58E	12/2320	dt	LC	(F372)	–	/	45°14N/32°03E	8
									20/2015	dt	-D	(Saale/G3109)	–	/	Cape Meganon	9
31/0114	sj	M-117	Kesayev	-D	1000	+	2-T	45°25N/32°14E	30/2257				–	/	5m W Ak Mechet	10
FEBRUARY 1944																
									08/0120	dt	LC	(F...)	–	/	24m WNW Ak Mechet	11
10/0250	sj	SC-216	Karbovskii	-D	4000	+	4-T	45°06N/32°06E	10/0050	dt	APC	(UJ106/KT23)	–	/	50m W Yevpatoriya	12
									15/1749	dt	LC	(F...)	–	/	46°34N/31°10E	13
16/							-T		16/0832	dt	APC	(UJ106/KT23)	–	/	Yevpatoriya harb.	14
17/	sj	SC-216	Karbovskii	–			-T		17/1115	dt	APC	(UJ106/KT23)	–	/	18m W Tarkhankut	15
28/2238	sj	M-62	Malyshev, N. I.	LC		/	2-T	SW Tarkhankut								16

(1) No submarine was in the area.

(2) *UJ103* reported two torpedoes which missed. The claim that this attack was made by *S-33* is probably erroneous.

(3) There is no report concerning an attack, only one about a D/C hunt.

(4) An S-boat reported two torpedoes running on to the shore.

(5) The two KT A/S vessels reported two prematures.

(6) There was a report of a probable attack by *Schiff 19*, escorting a convoy of seven transports.

(7) The convoy observed a surfacing submarine and a torpedo track.

(8) MFPs reported a submarine and attacked with D/Cs.

(9) *Saale* reported three torpedoes missing, but no submarine in the area.

(10) An explosion was observed, assumed to be an aircraft crashing. A claimed sinking by *SC-202* of a steamer of 5000–6000grt cannot be verified.

(11) An escorted convoy reported torpedoes missing, but no submarine was in the area.

(12) The claimed *Peter* (ex *Elbe*, ex *PLM.16*) was in fact sunk on 19.2.44 in the Aegean and raised later that year (q.v.). *UJ106* reported one torpedo detonating at the end of its run.

(13) A convoy reported torpedoes which missed, but no submarine was in the area.

(14) *UJ106*, at anchor, reported two torpedo detonations on the shore.

(15) *UJ106* reported a surface-running torpedo before sinking the submarine.

(16) *M-62* is also credited with sinking a steamer of 5000–6000grt south-west of Cape Tarkhankut, but there is no German report.

1	2	3	4	5	6	7	8	9	10	11	12	13	14	15	16	17
MARCH 1944																
14/2140	sj	M-117	Kesayev	-D	3000	+	2-T	W Tarkhankut								1
							2-T		27/0435	dt	-D	(Lola, Totila)	–	/		2
27/0910	sj	SC-215	Greshilov	-D	5000	+	4-T	44°00N/31°00E	27/1155	dt	-D	(Lola, Totila)	–	/	110m E Cape Tuzla	2
									29/1930	dt	LC	(F.../Convoy Rapid)	–	/	18m W Tendra	3
APRIL 1944																
									08/	dt	LC	(F583)	–	/	Off Yevpatoriya	4
13/0913	sj	S-31	Belorukov	-D	3000	+	4-T	43°38N/31°00E	13/0925	ru	-D	(Ardeal)	–	/	43°47N/31°05E	5
14/0934	sj	A-5	Matveyev	LC	350	+	2-T	44°23N/32°56E	14/0855	dt	LC	(F342, etc)	–	/	44°30N/33°00E	6
									15/1108	dt	APC	(UJ103, convoy)	–	/	17m SW Kherson.	7
									15/2340	dt	APC	(UJ106, convoy)	–	/	44°52N/29°45E	8
16/0949	sj	SC-215	Greshilov	-D	1000	/	4-T	45°16N/30°18E	16/0850	dt	APC	(Rosita, convoy)	–	/	44°17N/29°45E	9
16/	sj	L-6 (?)	Gremyako (?)	–			-T		16/1404	un	-D	(Kassa, convoy)	–	/	44°17N/30°15E	9
									17/0045	dt	-D	(Helga, convoy)	–	/		10
17/1155	sj	M-111	Khomyakov	-D	3000	+	2-T	44°30N/30°38E	17/1106	dt	-D	(Helga, convoy)	–	/	44°15N/30°25E	10
18/	sj	L-6 (?)	Gremyako (?)	–			3-T	44°38N/32°13E	18/0708	un	-D	(Kassa, convoy)	–	/		11
18/	sj	L-6 (?)	Gremyako (?)	–			-T		18/1106	ru	-D	(Alba Julia, convoy)	–	/	43°28N/31°32E	11
18/	sj	L-4	Polyakov	-D		?	2-T	43°54N/32°10E	18/2332	ru	-D	(Alba Julia, convoy)	–	/	43°25N/31°28E	11
22/1147	sj	M-62	Malyshev, N. I.	-D	5000	+	2-T	43°51N/31°10E	22/1114	ru	-D	(Ardeal)	–	/	43°42N/31°10E	12
22/1815	sj	M-111	Khomyakov	-D	5000	+	2-T	43°51N/29°52E	22/1815	ru	-D	(Ardeal, convoy)	–	/	43°45N/29°45E	12

(1) Attack not reported.

(2) The convoy, with the two steamers, two A/S vessels and one R-boat, reported first two, then four, torpedoes which missed.

(3) An MFP reported two torpedoes which missed, but no submarine was in the area.

(4) *F583*, in convoy, reported torpedoes which missed. *SC-215* was in the area but reported no attack.

(5) The convoy, with three ships and four escorts, reported three torpedoes which missed.

(6) The convoy, with six MFPs and three KFKs, reported two torpedoes which missed.

(7) The convoy, with *KT25*, *KT26*, *Ossag*, *UJ103* and *R166*, reported a submarine contact but no torpedoes. *M-62* and *A-5* were in area, but no attack was reported.

(8) The convoy, with *UJ106*, reported two torpedoes missing, but no submarine was in the area.

(9) The 'Bambus' convoy, with four steamers and three escorts, was attacked twice: first three torpedoes (probably fired by *L-6*), then two, missed.

(10) Convoy 'Palme', with two steamers and six escorts, reported two unsuccessful torpedo attacks.

(11) The convoy, with two steamers and four escorts, reported first three and then two torpedoes which missed. It is assumed that *L-6* was sunk by the escort at 1232. *Alba Julia* was then damaged by air attack.

(12) *Ardeal*, escorted by *UJ105* and *R166*, reported two submarine attacks with two and one torpedo; both were evaded, and D/Cs were dropped. *M-111* claimed *KFK84*, but in fact this vessel was sunk as *UJ2304* by bombs 80m west of Sevastopol on 3.5.44.

1	2	3	4	5	6	7	8	9	10	11	12	13	14	15	16	17

APRIL 1944 *continued*

23/0849	sj	M-35	Prokofev	-T	1000	+		1-T	44°23N/32°10E	23/0750	dt	APC	(UJ103)		– /	44°22N/32°25E	1
23/1058	sj	A-5	Matveyev	PG	450	+		2-T	44°01N/32°01E	23/1040	dt	APC	(UJ103/Ossag)		– /	44°30N/32°00E	2
26/2313	sj	L-4	Polyakov	-D		/		6-T	43°56N/30°55E	26/2215	dt	-D	(Helga/UJ105)		– /	44°02N/31°05E	3
28/1138	sj	SC-202	Leonov	-D	6000	+		4-T	43°04N/30°16E	28/1041	dt	-DF	(Lola, convoy)		– /	43°52N/30°08E	4
28/1138	sj	SC-202	Leonov	-D	4000	+?		4-T	43°04N/30°16E								

MAY 1944

03/1305	sj	A-5	Matveyev	-D	300	+		2-T	42°35N/38°50E	03/late	dt	-D	(Convoy)		– /		5
03/2334	sj	M-62	Malyshev, N. I.	-D	3000	+		2-T	44°33N/32°12E	03/2333	dt	-Tg	(Junak)		– /	Cape Khersones	6
04/2007	sj	M-111	Khomyakov	-Tg	200	+		2-T	43°54N/32°12E	04/1909	un	-D	(Tisza, convoy)		– /	43°40N/32°08E	7
06/0814	sj	SC-201	Paramoshkin	-T	6000	=		4-T	Kv 1559	06/0712	dt	-D	(KT26)		– /	SW Tarkhankut	8
07/2210	sj	SC-202	Leonov	LC	620	+		2-T	43°45N/30°37E	07/	dt	LC	(F...)		– /	Cape Olinka	9
08/1704	sj	SC-202	Leonov	-Bg	1000	+		2-T	43°55N/30°17E	08/	dt	-Bg	(Elbe-5/c1200)		– /	Sevastopol	10
08/1754	sj	SC-202	Leonov	-Bg		/		1-T	43°54N/30°29E	08/	dt	-Bg	(Vistula)		– /		10
11/0028	sj	M-35	Prokofev	LC	320	+		2-T	43°46N/29°39E	11/	dt	-D	(Convoy Tanne)		– /		11
11/0612	sj	L-4	Polyakov	-T	7000	+		4-T	43°51N/30°11E	11/0513	dt	-T	Friederike	7327	=	43°42N/29°15E	12
11/0829	sj	A-5	Matveyev	LC	350	+		2-T	NW Black Sea								13

(1) *UJ103* reported two torpedoes which missed

(2) *UJ103* again reported two torpedoes which missed. The claimed *Ossag*/2795grt was already damaged and was sunk later by air attack.

(3) The convoy, with two steamers, three MFPs and nine escorts, reported three torpedoes which missed.

(4) Convoy 'Ideal', with three steamers and four escorts, reported three torpedoes which missed.

(5) Convoy 'Richter', with four tugs and nine escorts, reported an attack.

(6) The 'Theben' convoy reported a submarine attack but no hits.

(7) The 'Flieder' convoy, with *Tisza*, *KT25*, *UJ106* and three R-boats, reported torpedoes which missed. The claimed sinkings of *UJ2313/KFK373* and *UJ2314/KFK202* are erroneous: *UJ2313* never reached the Black Sea and became US war booty, while *UJ2314* was sunk on 6.5.44 in an air attack.

(8) Convoy 'Baldur', with *KT26*, *UJ105*, *R163* and *R216*, reported torpedoes which missed. The claimed *KT26* was transferred as *Erpel* to the Aegean at the end of 5.44 and sunk there on 15.9.44 by HMS *Royalist* and *Teazer*.

(9) An MFP from convoy 'Eiche' reported torpedoes which missed.

(10) The claimed *Elbe-5* was from convoy 'Eiche'; the barge was sunk by air attack on 10.5.44. The barge *Vistula* was sunk on 8.5.44 by air attack.

(11) The claimed *KT17/UJ104* was torpedoed by TKAs on 26.4.44 and lost her bow, and the wreck was scuttled on 10.5.44 in Sevastopol.

(12) *Friederike* (ex *Firuz*), from convoy 'Astra', was damaged.

(13) No attack reported.

1	2	3	4	5	6	7	8	9	10	11	12	13	14	15	16	17

MAY 1944 *continued*

1	2	3	4	5	6	7	8	9	10	11	12	13	14	15	16	17
11/1017	sj	SC-201	Paramoshkin	*LC*	350	+	2-T	44°14N/30°58E	*11/noon*	dt	APC	*(UJ105/KT24/* convoy)	–	/	L. Qu .2558	*1*
11/2045	sj	M-62	Malyshev, N. I.	ACM	450	+	2-T	44°13N/32°03E	11/1945	ru	ACM	(Dacia/Convoy Astra)	–	/	W Crimea	2
12/0727	sj	S-33	Alekseyev, B. A.	*LC*	?		A	43°43N/32°00E								3
12/0859	sj	SC-201	Paramoshkin	-D	4500	+	2-T	Kv 1856 Olinka								4
12/0859	sj	SC-201	Paramoshkin	-Tg		+	2-T	Kv 1856 Olinka								4
12/1331	sj	A-5	Matveyev	-D	3000	+	2-T	43°50N/31°50E	12/1200	dt	-D	(Geiserich)	–	/	50m W Sevastopol	4
									12/noon	dt	APC	*(UJ318/KFK195)*	–	/	75m SE Sulina	5
12/1345	sj	A-5	Matveyev	-S	145	+	1-T	43°54N/31°50N	12/1245	dt	-S		...	+		6
12/	sj	S-33	Alekseyev, B. A.	-Bg		+	A	43°43N/32°00E	12/	dt	LC	(Convoy Lobau)	–	/		7
12/2115	sj	SC-201	Paramoshkin	*LC*	350	+	2-T	*Kv 1855*	12/	dt	LC	F568	155	=	*Sevastopol*	8
13/0216	sj	A-5	Matveyev	-S	150	+	1-T	43°54N/31°50E								9
13/1331	sj	A-5	Matveyev	-D	3000	+	2-T	43°50N/31°50E								

JUNE 1944: No operations

JULY 1944

1	2	3	4	5	6	7	8	9	10	11	12	13	14	15	16	17
19/2035	sj	SC-209	Sukhodolskii	-D	6000	=	4-T	41°21N/29°18E	19/2030	tu	-D	(Kanarya/2363)	–	/	700m Bosporus	10
20/1508	sj	SC-209	Sukhodolskii	-S	300	+	1-T	41°43N/28°45E	20/1500	tu	-S	Semsi Bahri	26	+	Off Bosporus	11
26/0650	sj	SC-209	Sukhodolskii	-S	250	+	2-T	Bosporus								
26/0736	sj	SC-209	Sukhodolskii	-S	250	+	1TA	41°32N/28°32E	26/1100	bu	-S	...	c100	=	Off Bosporus	12

(1) Convoy 'Astra', escorted by the gunboat *Dumitrescu* and *UJ105*, reported three torpedoes which missed.

(2) The minelayer *Dacia*, from convoy 'Wolga', reported torpedoes which missed.

(3) The claimed *F130* was probably sunk by air attack at Sevastopol.

(4) The attack by *SC-201* does not tally with German times of attacks. The claimed *Geiserich*/712grt (ex *Neghelli*) was not hit by a submarine torpedo but was damaged in an air attack and towed, on fire, to Constanta, where she was sunk during the afternoon of 12.5.44. There is no report about the sinking of the tug. *Durostor*/1309grt, claimed by *M-62* in convoy 'Artist', was not hit by a submarine torpedo but was also damaged by air attack, as a result of which she sank.

(5) *UJ318* reported a torpedo which missed.

(6) The claimed *Seepferd* had already been sunk, at 1805 on 13.4.44.

(7) The claimed *F130* was sunk by air attack on 12.5.44 at Sevastopol.

(8) The claimed *F568* was only damaged. She reached Constanta, where she sank on 20.8.44.

(9) Attack not reported.

(10) *Kanarya* reported two detonations on the shore.

(11) This sailing vessel was sunk by gunfire after two unsuccessful torpedo attacks. There were seven survivors.

(12) A Bulgarian schooner was damaged by gunfire.

1	2	3	4	5	6	7	8	9	10	11	12	13	14	15	16	17
JULY 1944 *continued*																
28/0841	sj	M-113	Volkov	*LC*		+	*1-T*	*43°37N/29°03E*	*28/0830*	*dt*	*-LC*	*(F...)*	–	*/*	*Sulina/Constanta*	*1*
AUGUST 1944																
05/	sj	SC-215	Strizhak	-Mf	100	+	A	42°03N/28°42E	05/0120	tu	-S	Mefkure	52	+	42°03N/29°08E	2
05/	sj	SC-215	Strizhak	-S	105	+	A	42°03N/28°42E								2
22/1022	sj	M-113	Volkov	-D	2000	+	2-T	Shabla–Mangal.	*22/0550*	*dt*	*-D*	*(KT..)*	–	*/*	*10m SE Constanta*	3
24/1109	sj	SC-215	Strizhak	-D	1500	=	2-T	42°47N/27°55E	24/	tu	-S	Selahettin (?)	96	+	?	4
24/	sj	SC-215	Strizhak	-D	1500	+	A	Burgas								

(1) The convoy, with *UJ117/Schiff 19* and five MFPs, reported two torpedoes which missed.

(2) *Mefkure* was a Jewish refugee ship sailing with two Turkish refugee ships, *Morina* and *Bulbul*, which were not attacked. Apart from *Mefkure*'s Turkish crew, there were only five survivors out of about 320 passengers. *SC-215* assumed she was attacking a German ship with up to 200 armed men and a launch with gunfire, and sank both vessels. The launch must have been the small rescue boat from the ship with the Turkish crew who were saved.

(3) Two KT ships and two minesweepers reported torpedoes, which missed, at 0550 and 1020.

(4) *Selahettin* was a small Turkish sailing vessel chartered by Jewish organisations to bring refugees from Constanta to the Bosporus. The vessel was lost without trace. It is not known whether she had refugees on board or if she was lost empty en route to Constanta. The claimed *UJ107/KT34* was in fact scuttled by her crew on 25/26.8.44 off Cape Kaliakra.

V. Mediterranean

This chapter contains details of attacks by British, French, Dutch, Greek, and Polish submarines in the Mediterranean on Axis and neutral ships. The sources consulted were as follows.

British

Naval Staff History, Second World War. Submarines. Vol. II: Operations in the Mediterranean. London: Historical Section, Admiralty 1955. Not accessible prior to 1990.

Enemy Shipping Losses Assessment Committee (ESLAC), 1941–1946, in the Office of the Senior Officer (Admiral) Submarines. (Extracts provided by Miss J. S. Kay.)

Correspondence with Rear-Admiral Buckley, Naval Historical Section, Admiralty; Gus Britton, HMS *Dolphin*, Gosport; and (especially voluminous exchanges) Miss J. S. Kay, London.

French

Huan, Claude. *Les sous-marins français 1918–1945.*

Correspondence with *Capitaine de Vaisseau* Claude Huan, Paris

Dutch

Bezemer, K. W. L. *Zij vochten op de zeven zeeen. Verrichtingen en avonturen des Koninklijke Marine in de II Wereldoorlog.* Utrecht: De Haan, 1954.

Correspondence with Dr P. C. van Royan, Institute for Maritime History, The Hague.

Greek

Fôka, D. G. *Ekthesis epi ths draseos b. nautikou kata ton polemon 1940–1944.* Tomos A. B., Athens, 1953–54.

Polish

Correspondence with *Dozent Dr habil.* W. Dyskant, Warsaw

Italian

Ufficio Storico della Marina Militare: La Marina Italiana nella Seconda Guerra Mondiale. Rome: 1951–65. Vol. 2: *Navi perdute. Navi Militari* (1951); Vol. 3: *Navi perdute. Navi Mercantili* (1952); Vol. 4: *Le Azioni Navali: 10 Giugno 1940–31 Marzo 1941* (1959); Vol. 5: *Le Azioni Navali: 1 Aprile 1941–8 Settembre 1943* (1960); Vol. 6: *La Difesa del Traffico coll'Africa Settentrionale, 10 Giugno 1940–30 Settembre 1941* (1958); Vol. 7: *La Difesa del Traffico coll'Africa Settentrionale, 1 Ottobre 1941–30 Settembre 1942* (1962); Vol. 8: *La Difesa del Traffico coll'Africa Settentrionale, 1 Ottobre 1942 alle Caduta della Tunisia* (1964); Vol. 9: *La Difesa del Traffico con l'Albania, la Grecia e l'Egeo* (1965).

Letter with corrections and amendments from *Ammiraglio di divisione* Mario Buracchia, Capo, Ufficio Storico della Marina Militare, Rome.

German

Kriegstagebuch der Seekriegsleitung 1939–1945. Edited by Werner Rahn, Gerhard Schreiber and Hansgeorg Maierhöfer. Herford/Hamburg: Mittler & Sohn, Vols 10–66, 1991–96.

Gröner, Erich. *Die deutschen Kriegsschiffe 1815–1945.* Continued and edited by Dieter Jung and Martin Maas. Vols 1–8/2 and Index. München/Bonn: Bernard & Graefe, 1982–94.

Dinklage, Ludwig, and Witthöft, H. J. *Die deutsche Handelsflotte 1939–1945.* Vols 1–2. Göttingen: Musterschmidt, 1970–71. (Studien und Dokumente zur Geschichte des Zweiten Weltkrieges, Bd.5a/b.)

1	2	3	4	5	6	7	8	9	10	11	12	13	14	15	16	17
JUNE 1940																
12/0140	fr	SAPHIR	Roumeas				32M	Cagliari	28.06.M	it	-D	Alicantino	1642	+	Off Cagliari	
13/0815	fr	TURQUOISE	Wacogne				14M	Sottile Pt								1
13/1144	fr	TURQUOISE	Wacogne				16M	Marsala Pt								
13/	fr	PERLE	Bourgeois				32M	Bastia								
13/	br	GRAMPUS	Rowe				50M	Augusta								2
13/	br	GRAMPUS	Rowe	SS		/	-T	Augusta	13/	it	SS	(Bausan)	–	/	Augusta	2
13/	br	GRAMPUS	Rowe				5-T	Augusta	13/	it	TB	(Polluce)	–	/	Augusta	2
13/2321	br	ODIN	Woods, K. MacL.				-T	Taranto	13/2321	it	CA	(Fiume, Gorizia)	–	/	Gulf of Taranto	
14/	br	RORQUAL	Dewhurst				50M	Brindisi	26.06.M	it	-M	Loasso	5968	+	3m T. Preposti	
									25.09.M	it	-D	Rina Croce/*Apuania	569	+	2 5m Brindisi	
15/	br	RORQUAL	Dewhurst	SS		/	-T	Otranto Strait								3
16/1902	br	GRAMPUS	Rowe	-T					16/1902	it	TB	(Circe, Clio)	–	/	Augusta	2
17/	br	PARTHIAN	Rimington	DD		/	-T	Tobruk	17/	it	DD	(Nembo)	–	/	Off Tobruk	4
19/	br	PARTHIAN	Rimington	CA		/	2-T	Tobruk	19/	it	CA	(San Giorgio)	–	/	Tobruk harbour	5
20/1445	br	PARTHIAN	Rimington	SS		+	-T	32°42N/23°49E	20/	it	SS	Diamante	617	+	30m N Tobruk	
JULY 1940																
04/1407	br	PANDORA	Linton	CL	7800	+	-T	Algiers	04/1315	fr	PS	Rigault de Genouilly	1969	+	6m NW Matifou	6
08/0515	br	PHOENIX	Nowell	BB		/	-T	35°40N/18°20E	08/	it	BB	(Giulio Cesare, Conte di Cavour)	–	/	200m E Malta	
16/	br	PHOENIX	Nowell	TB		/	-T	SE Sicily	16/	it	TB	(Albatros)	–	/		7
21/	br	RORQUAL	Dewhurst				50M	32°39N/21°03E	24.07.M	it	-D	Celio	3872	+	10m Tolmeita	
21/	br	RORQUAL	Dewhurst	-D		/	-T	Tolmeita	21/	it	-D	Securitas	5366	=	Off Tobruk	8
27/	br	PARTHIAN	Cayley	-D		/	-T	SE Sicily								9
30/1400	br	OSWALD	Fraser	-DP		=?	-T						–	/		10

(1) The Italian sailing vessel *San Caligero*/57grt, claimed for this barrage, was sunk on 11.6.40 before the mines were laid.

(2) *Grampus* reported her minelaying on 13.6.40 but was sunk on 16.6.40. The attacks listed must have been made by her.

(3) *Rorqual* reported an unsuccessful attack against an Italian submarine

(4) *Parthian* missed a destroyer of the *Nembo* class which evaded the torpedoes.

(5) *Parthian* fired two torpedoes against the old armoured cruiser *San Giorgio* in Tobruk harbour but they exploded in the mud.

(6) *Pandora* reported a cruiser of the *La Galissonnière* class sunk.

(7) *Phoenix* unsuccessfully attacked *Albatros* and was then sunk by her.

(8) *Rorqual* reported an unsuccessful torpedo attack against an Italian steamer. *Securitas* was hit by a dud.

(9) *Parthian* reported an unsuccessful attack against two steamers

(10) *Oswald* heard two explosions but was sunk after this unsuccessful attack by the Italian destroyer *Vivaldi*.

1	2	3	4	5	6	7	8	9	10	11	12	13	14	15	16	17
AUGUST 1940																
14/	br	RORQUAL	Dewhurst				M	Polmetta	14.08.M	it	-D	Leopardi	3298	+	32°39N/21°03E	1
15/2345	br	OSIRIS	Harvey	-D	3000	+	TA	S Adriatic	16/0200	it	-D	Morea	1968	+	50m W Durazzo	2
21/1500	br	RORQUAL	Dewhurst	-D	5000	/	-T	33°08N/22°10E	21/	it	-D	(Verace/1219)	–	/	5m NW Ras Hilal	3
21/1500	br	RORQUAL	Dewhurst	-D	3000	/	"	33°08N/22°10E	21/	it	-D	(Doris Ursino/891)	–	/	5m NW Ras Hilal	3
26/	br	PERSEUS	Bartlett	-D		/	2-T	Off Durazzo	26/	it	-D	(Filippo Grimani/ 3431)	–	/		4
31/1435	br	PARTHIAN	Balston	CA	11870	=?	-T	37°45N/18°30E	31/	it	CL	(Abruzzi, Garibaldi)	–	/	37°45N/18°22E	5
SEPTEMBER 1940																
15/	br	PANDORA	Linton	-D		/	-T	Benghazi								6
22/1830	br	OSIRIS	Harvey	TB	966	+	-T	41°19N/18°34E	21/	it	TB	Palestro	862	+	41°19N/18°34E	
22/	br	TRUANT	Haggard	-D	3000	+	-T	Ischia	22/0940	it	-D	Provvidenza	8459	+	3.5m SE Ischia	
../....	br	TRIAD	Salt	-D		/	-T									
26/	br	TRUANT	Haggard	AE		/	-T	Naples								8
27/	br	TETRARCH	Mills	-D		/	-T	Gulf of Genoa								9
28/		Probably mined							[28/	sp	-D	Monte Moncayo/ 4291+]			8m Cagliari	10
28/	br	PANDORA	Linton	-T	4000	+	-T	Apollonia	28/0930	it	-D	Famiglia	813	+	33°00N/21°38E	
29/	br	OSIRIS (?)	Harvey	-D		+	-T		29/1839	it	-D	Carmen	1434	+	41°17N/19°11E	
30/	br	REGENT	Browne	BB		/	-T	Cape Spartivento	30/	it	BB					11
OCTOBER 1940																
04/	br	RORQUAL	Dewhurst				M	Benghazi								12
04/1000	br	TRITON	Watkins	-D	8000	+	-T	Capo Noli	04/1127	it	-D	Franca Fassio	1858	+	16m E Cape Noli	
04/	br	TETRARCH	Mills	-D		/	-T	Gulf of Genoa								13

(1) First erroneously assigned to *Osiris*.

(2) *Osiris* failed to hit the ship in two torpedo attacks but then sank her by gunfire.

(3) *Rorqual* claimed four hits in an attack against two transports, but the torpedoes missed and the submarine was depth-charged by the Italian torpedo boat *Generale Achille Papa*.

(4) *Perseus* reported an unsuccessful attack.

(5) *Parthian* reported an attack against two *Zara* class cruisers and five *Navigatori* class destroyers, but the torpedoes were prematures.

(6) *Pandora* missed a convoy.

(7) *Triad* made one unsuccessful attack.

(8) *Truant* reported an unsuccessful attack against an ammunition carrier of the *Panigaglia* class; one torpedo was a surface-runner.

(9) *Tetrarch* reported an unsuccessful attack against a supply ship.

(10) *Monte Moncayo* was probably sunk by a mine; there were no Allied or Italian submarine attacks in this area.

(11) *Regent* tried a snap attack against two *Cavour* class battleships but missed.

(12) On 12 October an explosion from the field was heard.

(13) *Tetrarch* reported a second unsuccessful attack.

1	2	3	4	5	6	7	8	9	10	11	12	13	14	15	16	17
OCTOBER 1940 *continued*																
05/morn	br	REGENT	Browne	-S	188	+	R	10m Cape Laki	05/0500	it	-S	Maria Grazia	188	+	41°05N/17°45E	
08/1925	br	TRITON	Watkins	-D	3000	+	-T	Vado Roads	08/	dt	-D	(Spezia/1825)	–	/	Vado Roads	1
09/1630	br	REGENT	Browne	-D	6000	+	-T	41°21N/18°52E	09/1737	it	-D	Antonietta Costa	5900	+	41°17N/19°25E	2
11/	br	REGENT	Browne	-T		/	-T	S Adriatic								2
15/0140	br	TRIAD	Salt	SS		=	TA	38°16N/17°37E	15/0210	it	SS	(Enrico Toti)	–	/	80m E Sidero	3
16/	br	PANDORA	Linton	SS		/	-T	Otranto Strait								4
17/	br	PANDORA	Linton	SS		/	-T	Otranto Strait								4
18/		Probably mine					T/M		[18/	it	-D	Cuma/8260+]			37°02N/14°08E	5
21/	br	PARTHIAN	Rimington	SS		/	R	Cape Colonna								6
NOVEMBER 1940																
02/	br	TETRARCH	Mills	-D		/	-T	Benghazi								7
04/1000	br	TETRARCH	Mills	-D	3000	+	-T	31°35N/19°20E	04/1000	it	-D	Snia-Amba	2532	=§	31°35N/19°20E	8
04/1000	br	TETRARCH	Mills	-D	3000	=	"	31°35N/19°20E								
05/	br	RORQUAL	Dewhurst				M	34°14N/11°56E	27.12.M	it	-D	Caffaro	6476	=	N Tripoli	9
09/	br	RORQUAL	Dewhurst				M	Ras Misurata	05.12.M	it	TB	Calipso	679	+	6m NW Misurata	9
									23.12.M	it	TB	Fratelli Cairoli	649	+	6m NW Misurata	9
28/	gr	PAPANIKOLIS	Iatrides	-D	10000	+	-T	Brindisi								10

(1) *Triton* fired torpedoes against an anchored ship in a river near Savona and claimed to have sunk it.

(2) *Regent* was damaged by D/Cs and later missed a small tanker.

(3) There was a torpedo and gun duel between the two submarines. The Italian claim that the British submarine *Rainbow* was sunk is incorrect.

(4) *Pandora* made two unsuccessful attacks against submarines.

(5) *Cuma* must have been sunk on a mine; there was no submarine attack.

(6) *Parthian* tried unsuccessfully to ram an Italian submarine.

(7) *Tetrarch* reported an unsuccessful attack against a convoy.

(8) *Snia-Amba* was beached but became a total loss.

(9) *Rorqual* laid two mine barrages near Ras Misurata.

(10) On 28 November a convoy with the two large liners *Piemonte* and *Sardegna* reached Brindisi but reported no attack. There is a possibility that the Italian steamer *Chisone*/6168 was attacked by this submarine off Durazzo; 25 D/Cs were dropped.

1	2	3	4	5	6	7	8	9	10	11	12	13	14	15	16	17
DECEMBER 1940																
06/	br	TRITON (?)	Watkins	-D		=	-T		06/0530	it	-D	Olimpia	6040	=	Durazzo–Brindisi	1
/	gr			-S		+	A	Adriatic Sea		it	-D	Adria	364	+	Adriatic Sea	2
08/	br	REGENT	Browne	-D		?	-T	Libyan coast								2
10/		Probably mine							[10/	it	-D	Marangola/5267+]		–	Off Pantellaria	3
11/	br	TRUANT	Haggard	*TB*		+	*-T*		*11/*	it	*TB*	*Alcione*	*679*	=	*35°29N/24°11E*	
13/night	br	TRUANT	Haggard	-D	5500	+	-T	37°59N/16°15E	13/2305	it	-D	Sebastiano Bianchi	1546	+	37°58N/16°15E	
16/night	br	TRUANT	Haggard	-T	9000	+	3-T	E Calabria	16/0235	it	-MT	Bonzo	8177	+	38°28N/16°44E	
19/		Probably mine							[19/	dt	-D	Freienfels/7563+	–		Off Livorno	4
19/		Probably mine							[19/	dt	-D	Geierfels/7605+	–		Off Livorno	4
22/							-T		22/	it	-D	(Convoy Aventino)	–	/	Brindisi-Durazzo	5
22/0135	gr	PAPANIKOLIS	Iatrides	-S		+	A	Adriatic	22/	it	-S	San Giorgio	364	=	Off Brindisi	
22/	gr	PAPANIKOLIS	Iatrides	-S		+	R	Adriatic	22/0610	it	-S	Antonietta	70	+	40°40N/18°40E	
24/	br	REGENT	Browne	-D		?	-T	Libyan coast								2
24/1224	gr	PAPANIKOLIS	Iatrides	-D	20000	+	4-T	4m off Saseno	24/1320	it	-D	Firenze	3952	+	40°34N/19°02E	6
25/	br	OTUS	Favell	*SS*		=?	*-T*	*N of Derna*								7
29/1000	gr	PROTEUS	Hatsikostantis	-D		+	-T		29/1055	it	-DP	Sardegna	11452	+	40°31N/19°02E	
31/	gr	KATSONIS	Spanides	-T	5000	+	TA	10m NW Pt Mend	31/	it	-D	Quinto	531	+	Off Antivari	
31/	br	PARTHIAN	Rimington	-D		/	-T	Cape Spartivento								8

(1) *Triton* did not return and was the only submarine in the area. She was possibly sunk by the escorting Italian torpedo boats *Altair* and *Andromeda* and three MAS-boats.

(2) *Regent* reported three unsuccessful attacks between 8 and 24 December off the Libyan coast. *Adria* and the *Aventino* convoy must have been the targets of Greek submarines.

(3) *Marangola* is sometimes erroneously credited to the French submarine *Narval*, but she was actually lost on 19.12.40 on a Italian mine off Sfax.

(4) *Freienfels* and *Geierfels* were lost on mines; no submarine was in the area.

(5) The convoy, with two steamers and two escorts, reported one torpedo which missed.

(6) *Papanikolis* reported three hits on a convoy of three ships, including a large liner of 22,000grt.

(7) *Otus* reported attacking a *Mameli* class submarine and hearing four explosions.

(8) *Parthian* reported an unsuccessful long-range attack on a convoy.

1	2	3	4	5	6	7	8	9	10	11	12	13	14	15	16	17
JANUARY 1941																
07/2208	br	ROVER	Marsham	-D	7000	=	4-T	32°15N/23°36E	07/	it	-D	(Edda/6106)	–	/	32°13N/23°40E	1
09/	br	PANDORA	Linton	-D	5000	+	-T	39°15N/09°44E	09/0915	it	-D	Palma	2715	+	39°11N/09°40E	
09/	br	PANDORA	Linton	-D	5000	+	-T	39°15N/09°44E	09/0915	it	-D	Valdivagna	5400	+	39°11N/09°40E	
09/	br	PARTHIAN	Rimington	-D	7000	+	4-T	38°28N/16°41E	09/1605	it	-D	Carlo Martinolich	4208	+	38°28N/16°44E	
09/	gr	NEREUS	Rotas	-D	2000	+	-T	Off Brindisi								
09/	gr	TRITON	Zepos	SS		+	-T	*Off Otranto*								
09/2215	br	ROVER	Marsham	-S	400	=	A	32°23N/23°21E								
15/0850	br	REGENT	Browne	-D		+	-T	32°05N/14°11E	14/1400	it	-M	Città di Messina	2472	+	32°59N/14°11E	
22/	br	UNIQUE	Collett	-D		/	1-T	Kerkennah	22/	it	-D	(Esperia)	–	/		2
26/0130	br	UPHOLDER	Wanklyn	-D		/	-T	No 4B Kerkennah								3
									[27/1555	dt	-D	Ingo/3950+]			34°27N/11°48E	4
28/0430	br	UPHOLDER	Wanklyn	-D	8000	+	-T	S Kerkennah	28/morn	dt	-D	Duisburg	7389	=	20m N Tripoli	4
28/	br	RORQUAL	Dewhurst				29M	2m Sansego I.	31.01.M	it	TB	*Francesco Stocco*	670	=	*Off Fiume*	5
28/	br	RORQUAL	Dewhurst				21M	2m off Ancona	27.02.M	it	-D	Ischia	5101	=	Manfredonia	
28/	gr	PAPANICOLIS	Iatrides	-D	10000	+	-T	Off Brindisi			–/					
30/1330	br	UPHOLDER	Wanklyn	-D	5000	+	-T	32°55N/12°41E	30/1700	it	-D	(Motia/Delfin)	–	/	30m N Zavia	6
31/	br	RORQUAL	Dewhurst	-Tg		+	AT	42°50N/16°30E	31/1400	it	AR	Ursus	407	=	Lissa–Curzola	7
31/	br	RORQUAL	Dewhurst	-Bg		=	A	42°50N/16°30E	31/	it	-Bg	GM239	230	=		7

(1) *Rover* reported one premature and three hits against a convoy in a night attack and was counter-attacked and damaged by the Italian torpedo boats *Clio* and *Castore*. This D/C attack was assumed, erroneously, to have sunk the Free French submarine *Narval* (q.v.).

(2) *Unique* missed a convoy with one torpedo which was not observed by the Italians.

(3) *Upholder* reported one unsuccessful attack.

(4) The convoy, with *Ingo*, *Duisburg* and one escort, was first attacked south of Pantellaria at 1700 on 27.1.41, when *Ingo* was sunk, not by *Upholder* as claimed but by FAA Swordfish of 830 NAS, and then on 28.1.41, when *Duisburg* was damaged and towed into Tripoli.

(5) *Francesco Stocco* was damaged by a mine and broke in two parts, which were towed into Fiume on 27.1 and 10.2.41.

(6) *Upholder* claimed hits on the larger of the two ships, but the torpedoes missed and *Upholder* was attacked by the torpedo boat *Aldebaran*.

(7) *Rorqual* attacked the tug *Ursus*, towing the lighter *GM2391*, with torpedoes and then, because of the shallow water, with gunfire. The tug was beached and the barge set alight but the latter was subsequently towed into Dubrovnik.

1	2	3	4	5	6	7	8	9	10	11	12	13	14	15	16	17
FEBRUARY 1941																
									[03/	it	-D	Multedo/1130+]	–	/	Off Benghazi	1
03/0822	br	TRUANT	Haggard	-D	1980	/	3-T	32°18N/19°51E	03/0930	it	-T	(Utilitas/S. Tripcovich)	–	/	Off Benghazi	1
04/1800	br	TRUANT	Haggard	-D		/	3-T	Benghazi	04/	it	-M	(Calino/5186)	–	/	Off Benghazi	1
05/morn	br	UPRIGHT	Norman, E. D.	-D		/	-T	Kerkennah								2
08/	br	URSULA	Mackenzie, A. J.	-D		/	-T	Tunisia								3
08/	br	ROVER	Marsham	-D		/	-T	Calabria								4
09/	br	USK	Ward	-D		/	-T	Tripoli								5
09/	br	TRUANT	Haggard	-D		/	-T	Tripoli								5
09/	br	UTMOST	Cayley	-D		/	-T	Tunisia								6
10/	br	ROVER	Marsham	SS	500	/	-T	*Calabria*								4
11/1415	br	TRUANT	Haggard	-D	4000	=	A	33°36N/12°53E	11/1415	it	-D	(Bainsizza)	–	/	33°32N/12°56E	7
11/1634	br	TRUANT	Haggard	-D	3500	=	3-T	33°46N/12°57E		it	-D	(Bainsizza)	–	/		7
11/1650	br	UNIQUE	Collett	-D		/	-T	Off Tripoli	11/	dt	-M	(Ankara)	–	/	Off Tripoli	8
12/	br	UTMOST	Cayley	-D	8000	+	-T	35°41N/23°01E	12/	it	-M	Manfredo Campiero/ *Mauly	5463	=	Off Tripoli	
14/	br	ROVER	Marsham	-D	6060	+	-T	38°45N/17°25E	14/	it	-T	Cesco	6161	=	SE Cape Rizzuto	
16/										[it	-D	Juventus/4953§]	–	/		9
17/							-T		17/0500	it	-M	(A. Gritti)	–	/	Off Kuriat	
19/	br	UPHOLDER	Wanklyn	-D		/	-T	SE Gulf of Gabès								10
21/1420	br	REGENT	Browne	-D			+	-T	32°41N/12°48E	21/1430	dt	-D	Menes	5609	=	33°41N/12°48E	11
22/1608	br	URSULA	Mackenzie, A. J.	-D	9600	+	-T	35°47N/11°16E	22/1730	it	-D	Sabbia	5788	=	35°47N/11°13E	12

(1) *Truant* made two attacks. In the first, two heavy detonations were heard after 5min 57sec and 7min 57sec; the Italian steamer *Multedo*/1130grt, claimed later, must at this time have been far to the west and was probably sunk in an accident, and the targets were probably the two mentioned ships, in convoy, but they were missed. In the second attack one torpedo detonated after 15sec and the other two after 11min 2sec and 12min 3sec. *Truant* was detected while attacking and was bombed.

(2) *Upright* missed in a night attack.

(3) *Ursula* reported two unsuccessful attacks.

(4) *Rover* reported unsuccessful attacks on an convoy and on a *Perla* class submarine.

(5) *Usk* unsuccessfully attacked a convoy. Three hours later *Truant* reported a large convoy missed.

(6) *Utmost* missed a convoy south of *Ursula*'s attack.

(7) *Truant* reported a gun attack against a convoy but was forced to dive by the escorts. Two hours later the convoy was attacked with torpedoes and a hit was reported, a ship being down by the stern. In fact the attack was unsuccessful.

(8) *Unique* reported two unsuccessful attacks.

(9) *Juventus* was attacked by a Swordfish aircraft and not by the British submarine of that name.

(10) *Upholder* reported torpedoes missing against a three-ship convoy.

(11) *Regent* was depth-charged and damaged by the Italian destroyer *Saetta*.

(12) *Ursula* noted that her victim's decks were awash two hours later, but the ship was towed in. *Ursula* was damaged by D/Cs from the Italian torpedo boat *Montanari*.

1	2	3	4	5	6	7	8	9	10	11	12	13	14	15	16	17
FEBRUARY 1941 *continued*																
22/1700	br	REGENT	Browne	-D		+	-T	Tripoli								1
23/	gr	NEREUS	Rotas	-D	10000	+	-T	40°07N/18°57E								
23/0240	br	UPRIGHT	Norman, E. D.	-D	9600	=?	2-T	34°23N/11°49E	22/even.	it	-D	Silvia Tripcovich	2365	+	60m SE Sfax	1
25/0343	br	UPRIGHT	Norman, E. D.	*CL*	*5008*	+	-T	*34°33N/11°45E*	*25/0340*	*it*	*CL*	*Armando Diaz*	*5321*	*+*	*Off Kerkennah*	
25/0343	br	UPRIGHT	Norman, E. D.	*DD*	*1980*	+?	"	*34°33N/11°45E*								
MARCH 1941																
04 0453	gr	PAPANIKOLIS	Iatrides	-D		+	-T	Off Saseno								
05/1630	br	TRIUMPH	Woods, W. J. W.	-D	2500	+	2-T	37°54N/15°46E	05/	it	-D	Marzanemi	958	+	37°54N/15°46E	
05/1630	br	TRIUMPH	Woods, W. J. W.	-D	2500	+	"	37°54N/15°46E	05/	it	-D	Colomba Lo Faro	897	+	37°54N/15°46E	
08/								-T	08/	it	-D	(Convoy)	–	/	S Trapani	
09/1100	br	UTMOST	Cayley	-D	4000	=	4-T	36°09N/11°07E	09/1005	it	-M	(Attilio Deffenu)	–	/	50m SSW Pantellaria	
09/1100	br	UTMOST	Cayley	-D	3000	+	1-T	36°10N/11°12E	09/1200	it	-D	Capo Vita	5683	+	36°09N/11°07E	
10/	br	UTMOST	Cayley	-D		+	-T									
10/0655	br	UNIQUE	Collet	-D	3000	+	1-T	34°25N/12°40E	10/0655	it	-D	Fenicia	2584	+	34°19N/12°40E	
14?	br	URSULA	Hezlet	-D	9649	+	-T	Libyan coast		it	-D	(Sicilia class) (?)				

(1) *Upright* reported a hit on a petrol tanker; this must have been the missing *Silvia Tripcovich*, which is sometimes erroneously claimed for *Regent*'s attack. The ship is sometimes quoted as the German steamer *Fanny Brunner*/2366, but she survived the war.

1	2	3	4	5	6	7	8	9	10	11	12	13	14	15	16	17
MARCH 1941 *continued*																
16/1243	br	PARTHIAN	Rimington	-D	6000	+	3-T	35°57N/15°40E	16/1243	it	-D	Giovanni Boccaccio	3141	=	Off Palmi	1
16/1243	br	PARTHIAN	Rimington	-T	10000	=	4-T	5°57N/15°40E								
17/							-T		17/	it	-DT	(Labor/510)	–	/	Off Buerat	
19/	br	TRUANT	Haggard	-Bg		=?	-T	Buerat-el-Sun	19/	it	-DT	(Labor/510)	–	/	Buerat-el-Sun	2
20/0900	gr	TRITON	Zepos	-D	4000	+	-T	Off Valona								
20/0900	gr	TRITON	Zepos	TB		/?	-T	*Off Valona*								
20/							-T		20/2000	it	-D	(Costanza)	–	/	Tunisian coast	
23/1028	gr	TRITON	Zepos	-D	6000	+	1-T	40°58N/18°27E	23/1028	it	-D	Carnia	5451	=	30m NE Cape Gallo	
23/1028	gr	TRITON	Zepos	-D	2000	+	3-T	40°58N/18°27E	23/	it	D	(Anna Capano/1216)	–	/	30m NE Cape Gallo	
24/	br	URSULA	Mackenzie, A. J.	-D		/	-T	Cape Bon								3
25/1622	br	RORQUAL	Dewhurst				M	Palermo	26.03.M	it	-D	Verde	1432	+	3m W Trapani	4
									26.03.M	it	-MT	Ticino	1470	+	38°06N/12°31E	4
									28.03.M	*it*	TB	*Generale Antonio Chinotto*	687	+	*4m NE Cape Gallo*	4
26/	br	RORQUAL	Dewhurst	-T	5000	+	-T	Palermo								4
/	gr	TRITON	Zepos	-D	Small	=	A	Adriatic								
28/2200	br	UTMOST	Cayley	-D	6000	+	4-T	35°40N/11°19E	28/0245	dt	-D	Heraklea	1927	=	22m SE Kuriat	
28/2200	br	UTMOST	Cayley	-D	10000	+	″	35°40N/11°19E	28/0245	dt	-D	Ruhr	5954	+	22m SE Kuriat	
30/0257	br	RORQUAL	Dewhurst	-T	4000	+	TA	38°45N/12°20E	30/	it	-DT	Laura Corrado	3645	+	38°45N/12°20E	5
31/	br	RORQUAL	Dewhurst	SS		+	2-T	*38°42N/15°12E*	*31/*	*it*	SS	*Pier Capponi*	786	+	*38°32N/15°15E*	
31/0739	br	UPRIGHT	Norman, E. D.	-D	5000	=	2-T	33°38N/12°40E	31/0845	it	-D	Galilea	8040	=	Off Tripoli	6

(1) *Parthian* claimed two ships hit, but only *Giovanni Boccaccio* was damaged.

(2) *Truant* fired torpedoes at a barge in the harbour at Buerat, but the torpedoes ran under the ship and missed.

(3) *Ursula* missed a convoy.

(4) *Rorqual* reported one torpedo attack after the minelaying sortie which resulted in the sinking of *Ticino*. Italian sources ascribe all losses to the minefield.

(5) *Laura Corrado* was damaged by a torpedo hit and finished off by gunfire.

(6) *Upright* reported a hit on a straggler from a southbound convoy. *Galilea* was never repaired and remained at Tripoli; she was scuttled when the city was evacuated in 1943.

1	2	3	4	5	6	7	8	9	10	11	12	13	14	15	16	17
APRIL 1941																
?	br	TETRARCH	Peacock	-S		/	A	Buerat								1
10/	br	UPHOLDER	Wanklyn	-D		/	-T	Cape Bon								2
10/	br	UPHOLDER	Wanklyn	-D		/	-T	Cape Bon								2
11/	br	UPHOLDER	Wanklyn	-D		/	-T	Cape Bon								3
12/0850	br	TETRARCH	Peacock	-T	8000	+	3-T	30mNW Tripoli	12/1020	it	-DT	Persiano	2474	+	33°29N/13°01E	4
12/	br	URSULA	Mackenzie, A. J.	-D		/	-T	S Cape Bon								
17/1645	br	TRUANT	Haggard	-S	1000	+	A	Apollonia	17/	it	APC	V-62/Vanna	279	+	33° N/22° E	5
17/	br	TRUANT	Haggard	-S		+	A	Apollonia								5
17/	br	TRUANT	Haggard	-D		+	-T		[17/	dt	AK	Samos/2576+]	–		1m W Benghazi	5
21/	br	TRUANT	Haggard	APC		=	A	Tripoli	21/	it	AO	Prometeo	1080	=	Tripoli	6
25/1500	br	UPHOLDER	Wanklyn	-D	5000	+	2-T	34°57N/11°44E	25/	it	-D	Antonietta Lauro	5428	+	2.5m SE Kerkennah	
26/	br	UPHOLDER	Wanklyn	-D		+	S	E Tunisia	26/	dt	-D	Arta	2452	+	Kerkennah	7
27?	br	USK (?)	Darling	–				Cape Bon	[27/M	fr	-D	SNA7/2679+]	2679	+	Cape Bon	8
27/	br	TORBAY	Miers	-D		/	1-T	Cape Ferrato								9
MAY 1941																
01/							-T		01/	dt	-D	(Convoy)	–	/	Off Tripoli	
01/1200	br	UPHOLDER	Wanklyn	-D	6300	+	2-T	34°38N/11°39E	01/1200	dt	-D	Arcturus	2596	+	2m S Kerkennah	10
01/1200	br	UPHOLDER	Wanklyn	-D	7500	=	2-T	34°38N/11°39E	01/1200	dt	-D	Leverkusen	7386	=	2m S Kerkennah	10
01/2100	br	UPHOLDER	Wanklyn	-D		+	-T	E Tunisia	01/2100	dt	-D	Leverkusen	7386	+	4m SE Kerkennah	10

(1) *Tetrarch* fired two torpedoes into the harbour without effect and then attacked with gunfire, but she was forced by coastal batteries to dive.

(2) *Upholder* reported two unsuccessful attacks against a convoy.

(3) *Upholder* missed an independent ship in a night attack.

(4) *Ursula* fired Mk 4 destroyer torpedoes but missed.

(5) *Truant* sank only *Vanna*. The lost Italian tanker *Romagna*/149 was sunk by aircraft off Tripoli. The claimed *Samos* probably sank on an air-laid magnetic mine.

(6) *Truant* fired two torpedoes against the tanker, which missed. The ship was beached but later salvaged.

(7) *Upholder* was sent to finish off a supply ship and a destroyer which had run aground off Kerkennah. *Arta* had already been damaged in a destroyer action on 16.4.41 and was set on fire by *Upholder* after a large number of documents had been taken off.

(8) It is possible that *SNA7* was sunk by the missing *Usk*, but more probably both sank on a recently laid Italian minefield.

(9) *Torbay* missed a medium-sized supply ship.

(10) *Upholder* attacked a five-ship convoy, first sinking *Arcturus* and then damaging *Leverkusen*, which was sunk later with two torpedoes.

1	2	3	4	5	6	7	8	9	10	11	12	13	14	15	16	17
MAY 1941 *continued*																
03/1200	br	TRIUMPH	Woods, W. J. W.	-S	400	+	A	11mW Marsa Br.	03/	it	-M	Tugnin F.	425	+	11m NW M. Brega	1
04/0545	br	UNDAUNTED(?)	Livesay (?)	T?M?					04/0545	it	TB	*Giuseppe la Farina*	635	+	34°55N/11°55E	2
04/	br	TAKU	Nicolay	-Dc		/	-T	Messina Strait								3
06/0735	br	TRUANT	Haggard	-D	7000	+	1-T	1m E Carbonara	06/	it	-D	Bengasi	1716	+	3m SE Cavoli	
06/1400	br	URSULA	McGeogh	-D		/	-T	Tripoli	06/1400	dt	-D	(Brook, T. M. Russ)	–	/	Off Buerat	4
06/1845	br	TAKU	Nicolay	-D	7400	+	2-T	39°11N/15°58E	06/	it	-D	Cagliari	2322	+	39°11N/15°05E	
11/	br	RORQUAL	Dewhurst				M	Gulf of Salonica		it	-D	Genova Perossi (?)	2000	+		5
11/	br	PANDORA	Linton	-T		/	-T	Naples								6
12/	br	RORQUAL	Dewhurst	-S		+	A	Off Lemnos	12/	gr	-S	Aghios Paraskivi	25	+	Off Lemnos	7
12/	br	RORQUAL	Dewhurst	-S		+	A	Off Lemnos								7
14/	br	UNBEATEN	Woodward	-S	1100	+	T	Khoms Roads					–	/		8
14/	br	UNBEATEN	Woodward	-S	800	+	A	Khoms Roads								8
16/	br	UNBEATEN	Woodward	-D		/	-T	Tripoli								9
18/1447	br	TETRARCH	Greenway	-D	5000	+	-T	31°55N/19°54E	18/1500	it	-D	Giovinezza	2362	+	31°55N/19°55E	
19/1240	br	UNBEATEN	Woodward	-D	5000	/	4-T	32°46N/14°06E	19/	it	-D	(Silvio Scaroni/1367)	–	/	Off Tagiura	10
19/									[19/	dt	-D	Preussen/8230=]	–	/	Off Tunisia	11
19/									[19/	it	-M	Panuco/7600=]	–	/	Off Tunisia	11

(1) *Tugnin F.* was boarded and papers and materials were removed.
(2) *Giuseppe la Farina* was lost either on a French mine off Sfax or possibly to an attack by the lost British submarine *Undaunted*.
(3) *Taku* missed a small coaster.
(4) *Ursula* reported missing torpedoes against two ships.
(5) The claimed sinking of *Genova Perossi* cannot be found in Italian records.
(6) *Pandora* missed a small tanker.
(7) *Rorqual* reported a caique and a schooner with German troops on board sunk by gunfire.

(8) *Unbeaten* reported one large schooner sunk by torpedo (later known to be missed) and another damaged by gunfire.
(9) *Unbeaten* reported an unsuccessful attack against two transports and escorts.
(10) *Unbeaten* reported torpedoes hitting the bottom in shallow waters.
(11) *Preussen* and *Panuco* collided and were slightly damaged but continued their voyage. For the attack by *Urge*, see next page.

1	2	3	4	5	6	7	8	9	10	11	12	13	14	15	16	17
MAY 1941 *continued*																
20/1152	br	URGE	Tomkinson	-D	9000	+	4-T	35°46N/11°56E	20/1030	it	-D	(Capo d'Orso/3149)	–	/	35°44N/11°59E	1
20/1152	br	URGE	Tomkinson	-D	7000	=	"	35°46N/11°56E	20/	it	-T	(Superga/6154)	–	/	35°44N/11°59E	1
20/1844	br	UPHOLDER	Wanklyn	-T	4000	+	4-T	37°58N/15°40E	20/	it	-Dt	(Utilitas/5342)	–	/	Cape dell'Armi	1
21/1310	br	URGE	Tomkinson	CL		=	4-T	35°42N/12°24E	21/	it	DD	(Alpino)	–	/		2
23/1229	br	UPHOLDER	Wanklyn	-D	4854	=	3-T	37°56N/15°36E	23/	fr	-DT	Capitaine Damiani	4854	=	35°42N/12°24E	3
24/2045	br	UPHOLDER	Wanklyn	-D	18000	+	1-T	SE Messina	24/2045	it	-D	Conte Rosso	17879	+	10m E Siracus	
28/	br	PERSEUS	Bartlett	-D		/	-T	Gulf of Nauplia									4
30/1925	br	TRIUMPH	Woods, W. J. W.	ACL	3667	=	2-T	Benghazi harbour	30/1930	it	ACL	Ramb III	3667	=	Benghazi harbour	5
30/	br	UTMOST	Cayley	-D		/	-T	Sirte	30/	dt	-D	(T. M. Russ, *Polluce*)	–	/	Sliten	6
30/	br	TORBAY	Miers	-S			+	A	Aegean								7
30/	br	TORBAY	Miers	-S			+	A	Aegean								7
JUNE 1941																
01/0850	br	CLYDE	Ingram	-D	4000	+	1-T	SE Sardinia	01/	it	-D	San Marco	3076	+	5m E Carbonara	
01/	br	CLYDE	Ingram	-D		/	-T	Sardinia									8
01/0745	br	TORBAY	Miers	-S	60	+	5A	Doro Channel	01/	dt	-S	...	...	+		9
02/	br	CLYDE	Ingram	-D		/	-T	Terranova									8
03/	br	UNIQUE	Collett	-D	1000	+	2-T	Lampedusa	03/0800	it	-D	Arsia	736	=	Lampedusa	10
03/	br	TORBAY	Miers	-S			+	A	Mitylene								11
03/1230	br	PARTHIAN	Rimington	-T	8000	=	-T	39°57N/25°38E	03/	it	-MT	Strombo	5232	=	Skaramanka	12
05/1330	br	TRIUMPH	Woods, W. J. W.	-Tg	340	+	A	31°39N/15°39E	05/	it	APG	Valoroso	340	+	31°39N/15°39E	
05/1330	br	TRIUMPH	Woods, W. J. W.	-S	500	+	A	31°39N/15°39E	05/1330	it	-S	Frieda	245	+	31°39N/15°39E	
05/1330	br	TRIUMPH	Woods, W. J. W.	-M	500	+	A	31°39N/15°39E	05/1330	it	-M	Trio Frassinetti	244	+	31°39N/15°39E	

(1) *Urge* reported firing a full salvo, sinking one ship from a southbound convoy and damaging another. However, the claimed *Zeffiro*/5165grt, and probably also *Perseo*/4857grt, in a northbound convoy, were sunk or damaged on the new Italian minefield off Cape Bon. The attack missed *Capo Orso* and *Superga*. *Upholder*, sometimes also credited with *Perseo*, probably attacked *Utilitas*, which reported an unsuccessful torpedo attack.

(2) *Urge* reported a long-range attack against two cruisers and noted two detonations. The destroyer *Alpino*, from the escort, reported torpedoes which missed.

(3) *Upholder* attacked two tankers under the French flag but with Italian names. *Capitaine Damiani* was damaged.

(4) *Perseus* reported an unsuccessful attack against an escorted supply ship.

(5) *Ramb III* was later taken over by the Germans as the minelayer *Kiebitz*. She was scuttled on 1.5.45, salvaged, repaired and recommissioned as the Yugoslav training ship *Galeb*.

(6) It is unclear whether the attack by *Utmost* is the same one reported by *Polluce*.

(7) *Torbay* reported two caiques sunk.

(8) *Clyde* reported an unsuccessful long-range attack against a merchantmen. The next day a small transport was missed because the torpedoes passed under the ship.

(9) *Torbay* sank a caique carrying German troops and stores.

(10) *Arsia* was damaged but repaired.

(11) *Torbay* sank a caique loaded with oil drums.

(12) *Parthian* torpedoed *Strombo*, which was beached but salvaged and arrived, badly damaged, on 5.6.41 at Istanbul.

1	2	3	4	5	6	7	8	9	10	11	12	13	14	15	16	17

JUNE 1941 *continued*

1	2	3	4	5	6	7	8	9	10	11	12	13	14	15	16	17
06/1330	br	TORBAY	Miers	-MT	4000	+	2TA	Cape Helles	07/1415	fr	-MT	Alberta	6131	=§	3m SW C. Hellas	1
07/	br	TAKU	Nicolay	-Tg		=	A	Gharah I.								2
08/	br	CLYDE	Ingram	DD	1700	/	-T	*Naples*								3
08/2000	br	CLYDE	Ingram	-D	2500	+	A	Tyrrhenian Sea	08/	it	-D	Sturla/*Astrid	1195	+	5m Policastro	3
08/	br	TAKU	Nicolay	-D		=?	S	Benghazi harbour								4
08/	br	PARTHIAN	Rimington	-S	500	+	2-T	Mitylene								5
08/	br	PARTHIAN	Rimington	-S	500	+	2-T	Mitylene								5
08/	br	PARTHIAN	Rimington	-Bg		+	2-T	Mitylene								5
09/	br	URGE	Tomkinson	-D		/	-T	NW Lampedusa	09/	dt	-D	(Ingo)	–	/		6
10/0940	br	TORBAY	Miers	-D		/	-T	Dardanelles	10/	it	-DT	(Utilitas/Albaro)	–	/	Dardanelles	7
10/1043	br	TORBAY	Miers	DD		=	3-T	*Dardanelles*	10/	it	-DT	Utilitas	5342	=	Dardanelles	7
10/1208	br	TORBAY	Miers	-D	3300	+	3-T	15m Cape Helles	10/	it	-DT	Giuseppina Ghirardi	3319	+	8m E C. Helles	7
11/0104	br	TORBAY	Miers	-S	40	+	R	15m S Mitylene	11/	gr	-S	...	...	+		8
11/2015	br	TAKU	Nicolay	-D	5500	+	-T	Benghazi	11/	dt	-D	Tilly L. M. Russ	1600	+	Benghazi harbour	9
12/1107	nl	O-24	de Booy	-T	7000	+	-T	43°08N/10°03E	12/	it	-D	Fianona	6660	+	43°08N/10°30E	10
12/1235	br	TORBAY	Miers	-S	120	+	A	39°10N/25°20E	12/	it	-S	Gesu e Maria	238	+	Skyros	
12/2200	br	TAKU	Nicolay	-D	5000	+	1-T	32°27N/18°42E	12/0400	it	-D	Silvio Scaroni	1367	+	32°27N/18°42E	
12/2300	nl	O-24	de Booy	-M	500	+	S	43°45N/09°20E	13/	it	APC	V121/Carloforte	143	+	36m NW Gorgona	
14/	br	CLYDE	Ingram	-S	331	+	A	S Sardinia	14/	it	-S	Giovanni Bottigliere/ *Guglielmo	331	+	20m S Spartivento	

---

(1) *Torbay* first attacked the tanker with two single rounds: the first hit the stern and disabled the rudder and screw, and the second hit and damaged *Alberta*. The ship was boarded and the anchor chain was destroyed by a scuttling charge. When the Turkish tug *Taxiarchis* tried to tow the damaged ship on 9.6.41 *Torbay* fired another torpedo; this missed, but the submarine finished her victim off on 10.6.41 with gunfire and demolition charges.

(2) *Taku* engaged a tug, a lighter and an A/S trawler with gunfire but had to break off the attack.

(3) In the morning *Clyde* missed an *Oriani* class destroyer but in the evening sank *Sturla* with gunfire.

(4) *Taku* sent a shore party which damaged a ship in the harbour.

(5) *Parthian* fired two old torpedoes into the harbour which destroyed two large schooners and a lighter.

(6) *Urge* missed *Ingo*.

(7) *Torbay* missed a convoy with six ships, then hit *Utilitas* with a dud which remained embedded in the hull; then a straggler was successfully attacked. The report citing damage to the Romanian steamer *Alba Julia*/5700 was erroneous.

(8) *Torbay* sank a caique with German troops and stores aboard.

(9) The ammunition cargo aboard *Tilly L. M. Russ* exploded and destroyed or damaged the small vessels *Ninfea, Luigi, Giorgina, Nadia* and *Carolini*.

(10) *O-24* missed *Fianona* with her first salvo because of a surface runner; a second torpedo also missed. The submarine then began a gun action, finally hitting her victim with another torpedo.

1	2	3	4	5	6	7	8	9	10	11	12	13	14	15	16	17
JUNE 1941 *continued*																
16/1335	br	UNBEATEN	Woodward	-D	23000	/	-T	E Sicily	16/	it	-M	(Oceania/Neptunia)	–	/	S Messina Strait	1
17/0650	nl	O-24	de Booy	-T		/	-T	La Spezia								2
20/	br	SEVERN	Campbell	-D		/	-T	Palermo								3
20/	br	TETRARCH	Peacock	-D		/	-T	Lemnos								4
22/1507	br	UNION	Galloway	-D	2800	+	-T	36°11N/12°00E	22/1500	it	-D	Pietro Querini	1004	+	35°17N/12°00E	
22/	br	SEVERN	Campbell	SS	599	=	-T	40°44N/14°20E								5
25/1245	br	PARTHIAN	Rimington	SS	1000	+	-T	33°49N/35°26E	25/	fr	SS	Souffleur	974	+	Off Beirut	
26/2300	br	SEVERN	Campbell	-D	1592	+	-T	40°05N/12°08E	26/	it	-D	Polinnia	1292	+	95m SW Ischia	
26/1235	br	UTMOST	Cayley	-D	6000	+	2-T	38°07N/14°37E	26/	it	-D	Enrico Costa	4080	+	4m Cape Todaro	
27/	br	OSIRIS	Euman	-S		+	A	Tyrrhenian Sea								6
27/0815	br	TRIUMPH	Woods, W. J. W.	SS		+	AT	32°05N/28°47E	27/	it	SS	Salpa	611	+		7
28/	br	OSIRIS	Euman	-S		+	A	Tyrrhenian Sea								6
28/0745	br	SEVERN	Campbell	-D	8000	+	1-T	Gulf of Orosei	28/	it	-D	Ugo Bassi	2900	+	5m NE M. Santo	
29/	br	UTMOST	Cayley	CA		=?										
29/0915	br	URGE	Tomkinson	CA		=	4-T	37°55N/15°35E	29/	it	CA	(Bolzano)	–	/		8
30/0300	nl	O-23	Van Erkel	-D		/	-T	Ligurian Sea								
30/1300	nl	O-23	Van Erkel	-D	8000	+	4-T	43°06N/10°26E	30/	it	-D	Capacitas	5371	+	7m NW S. Vincen	9
30/	br	TORBAY	Miers	-S		+	A	Cape Malea								10
JULY 1941																
02/	br	URGE	Tomkinson	AMC	9000	+	3-T	37°48N/15°21E	02/							11
02/0625	br	TORBAY	Miers	-T	3000	+	6-T	37°41N/24°15E	02/0722	it	-M	Città di Tripoli	2933	+	37°42N/24°16E	12
03/1142	br	UPHOLDER	Wanklyn	-D	5500	+	1-T	37°54N/15°44E	03/	it	-D	Laura Consulich	5867	+	37°55N/15°44E	

(1) *Unbeaten* attacked a large, zig-zagging liner but missed.

(2) *O-24* missed a tanker off La Spezia.

(3) *Severn* missed an escorted ship.

(4) *Tetrarch* missed a *Tarvisio* class vessel.

(5) *Severn* reported firing a torpedo, which missed, at an Italian *Argonauta* class submarine.

(6) *Osiris* reported two caiques sunk in two days.

(7) *Triumph* first engaged *Salpa* with gunfire and then sank her by torpedo.

(8) *Urge* missed a force of two cruisers and four destroyers.

(9) *O-23* achieved three hits.

(10) *Torbay* reported a caique sunk.

(11) *Urge* was assumed to have hit an armed merchant cruiser. The claimed former Norwegian motor tanker *Brarena*/6996grt was sunk on 22.7.41 by Blenheim aircraft off Pantellaria together with the German *Preussen*/8230grt. See 19.5.41.

(12) The steamer *Florida*, mentioned in German sources as damaged, was not in the convoy.

1	2	3	4	5	6	7	8	9	10	11	12	13	14	15	16	17
JULY 1941 *continued*																
?	br	UPRIGHT	Wraith	-D		+	-T									
04/	br	TORBAY	Miers	-S	500	+	A	Doro Channel			dt	-S	...	+		1
04/	br	TORBAY	Miers	-S	500	+	A	Doro Channel			dt	-S	...	+		1
05/1815	br	TORBAY	Miers	SS		+	6-T	37°30N/25°00E	05/1946	it	SS	*Jantina*	611	+	37°21N/15°20E	
06/0800	br	TRIUMPH	Woods, W. J. W.	-D	600	+	A	Ras Tajunes	06/2145	it	-D	Ninfea	607	+	Tajunes/Benghazi	2
06/ "	br	TRIUMPH	Woods, W. J. W.	-Tg		+	A	Ras Tajunes	06/2145	it	-Tg	De Lutti	266	+	2m W Tajunes	2
08/1130	br	TORBAY	Miers	-S	500	+	AS	Aegean	08/1000	dt	-S	LXIV	...	+	E Kythera	3
08/1130	br	TORBAY	Miers	-S		+	A	Cape Maleme	08/1000	dt	-S	LI	...	+	E Kythera	3
09/0220	br	TORBAY	Miers	-S		+	AS	10m N Antikyth.	09/0245	dt	-S	LVI	...	+	E Kythera	3
09/0220	br	TORBAY	Miers	-S		+	AS	10m N Antikyth.	09/0301	dt	-S	LV	...	+	E Kythera	3
09/0536	br	TORBAY	Miers	-S		+	AS	10m N Antikyth.	09/0305	dt	-S	L12	...	=	E Kythera	3
10/1450	br	TORBAY	Miers	-T		+	4-T	37°30N/24°16E	10/	it	-D	Strombo	5232	=	Zea Canal	4
13/0929	br	TAKU	Nicolay	-D	2700	+	1-T	10m Benghazi	13/0930	it	-M	Caldea/*Ogaden	2703	+	10m NW Benghazi	
14/early	br	OSIRIS	Euman	-D		/	TA	Argostoli	14/	it	-D	Capo d'Orso	3149	=	Kephalonia	5
15/1510	br	P33	Whiteway-Wilkinson	-D	8000	+	4-T	36°27N/11°54E	15/1500	it	-M	Barbarigo	*5293	+	36°27N/11°54E	6
15/1750	br	UNBEATEN	Woodward	-S	500	+	A	Marsa Zuag Rd.	15/	it		APM	Nettuno	...	+	Gulf of Sidra	7
15/2000	br	UNBEATEN	Woodward	-S	500	+	A	Marsa Zuag Rd.									7
15/2215	br	TAKU	Nicolay	-S		+	A	Benghazi	15/	it		APM	Vincenzo Padre	270	+	25m ESE Auegia	8
16/1335	br	UNBEATEN	Woodward	-D	Large	=	-T	23m SSW Messina								
17/2100	nl	O-23	Van Erkel	-D	5479	=	-T	S Tyrrhenian Sea	17/1330	it	-D	Maddalena Odero	5479	=		

(1) *Torbay* reported two caiques sunk with troops and stores aboard. They were completely destroyed.

(2) *Ninfea* was sunk by gunfire and *De Lutti* was severely damaged the next day, but the submarine was then forced to withdraw because of damage. *De Lutti* was on fire and sank later.

(3) *Torbay* reported two schooners sunk on 8.7.41 and three on 9.7.41. They had aboard 75 soldiers on leave; there were eight dead. *L12* was only damaged.

(4) *Strombo* was damaged and sank following an explosion in Skaramagna on 22.8.41. *Torbay* was damaged by the escorting Italian torpedo boats *Climene* and *Calatafimi*.

(5) *Osiris* reported two unsuccessful torpedo attacks and hits by gunfire.

(6) *P33* was heavily depth-charged by the escorting Italian torpedo boats *Procione* and *Orsa* and destroyer *Ascari*.

(7) *Unbeaten* reported two schooners each sunk in the two attacks, but it is not clear whether *Vincenzo Padre* was also sunk in these attacks or by *Taku*.

(8) *Taku* intended to attack a tug and a schooner by boarding, but this failed and the submarine then began to attack with gunfire, hitting the tug and a lighter. The schooner was then boarded, papers were captured and the vessel was afterwards sunk by gunfire.

1	2	3	4	5	6	7	8	9	10	11	12	13	14	15	16	17
JULY 1941 *continued*																
20/							-T		20/	dt	-D	(Menes. M. Berendt)	–	/	Sirte	
20/							-T		[20/	it	-MT	Panuco/7600=]	–	/	Off Tripoli	1
20/	br	UNION	Galloway	-D		?	-T	25m SW Pantellaria								2
20/	br	UTMOST	Cayley	-D		/	-T	Ustica								3
20/	br	TETRARCH	Greenway	-D		/	1-T	Aegean								4
21/	br	TAKU	Nicolay	-D		=	S	Benghazi								5
21/	gr	GLAVKOS	Zepos	-S		+	A	Aegean	21/	it	-S	San Nicola	21	+	4m NW Rodi	
21/	br	OLYMPUS	Dymott	-D		?	-T	Naples								6
22/	br	TETRARCH	Greenway	-S		=	A	Karlovassi								7
22/	br	URGE	Tomkinson	-D		/	-T	Palermo								8
22/1650	gr	GLAVKOS	Arslanoglou	-S	40	+	A	Castelorizzo								9
23/	br	OLYMPUS	Dymott	-D	23000	/	4-T	Naples								10
24/1237	br	UPRIGHT	Wraith	Dock		+	2-T	Cape dell'Armi	24/	it	Dock	GO22	–	/		11
24/1418	br	UPHOLDER	Wanklyn	-D	6000	+	1-T	38°08N/12°37E	24/	it	-D	Dandolo	4964	=	2.5m NW Barone	12
25/	br	TETRARCH	Greenway	-D		/	G	Gaidero I.	25/	it	APM	B247/Maria Immacolata	...	+		13
27/1200	br	TETRARCH	Greenway	-S		+	A	5m S Kos	27/	it	-S	Nicita	...	+	Kos	14
28/1951	br	UPHOLDER	Wanklyn	*CL*		+?	*-T*	*38°04N/11°57E*	28/1955	*it*	*CL*	*Giuseppe Garibaldi*	*9050*	*=*	*Marettimo*	
28/2008	br	UTMOST	Cayley	-D	4000	+	1-T	39°28N/15°52E	28/2010	it	-D	Federico C.	1466	+	39°28N/15°52E	

(1) The claimed torpedo damage to *Panuco* was caused by aircraft. The ship was towed to Benghazi.

(2) *Union* was sunk by the escorting Italian torpedo boat *Circe* after an unsuccessful attack on a convoy.

(3) *Utmost* reported an unsuccessful attack on a supply ship.

(4) *Tetrarch* fired a torpedo which missed.

(5) *Taku* sent a landing party into the harbour which attached charges one of the ships there.

(6) *Olympus* carried out a long-range attack against two freighters and one escort, but missed.

(7) *Tetrarch* obtained several shell hits on a number of caiques in the harbour.

(8) *Urge* missed a small convoy.

(9) *Glavkos* reported one caique sunk.

(10) *Olympus* attacked a *Conte Rosso* class liner but three of her torpedoes failed to leave the tubes correctly and the last one missed.

(11) *Upright* missed a large floating dock and was heavily depth-charged. The German steamer *Tirpitz*/7970, sometimes claimed, was sunk by a mine.

(12) *Dandolo* was damaged and later repaired.

(13) *Tetrarch* reported an unsuccessful attack on a German ship.

(14) *Tetrarch* reported a caique sunk with German troops on board.

1	2	3	4	5	6	7	8	9	10	11	12	13	14	15	16	17
JULY 1941 *continued*																
29/1345	nl	O-21	Van Dulm	-D	4000	=	1-T	39°51N/13°46E	29/	it	-D	Monteponi	742	+	10m N C. Comino	1
30/	br	OLYMPUS	Dymott	-D	1500	+	1-T	40°40N/09°50E								1
30/	br	CACHALOT	Newton	-T		=	A	Benghazi	30/0340	it	-D	(Capo d'Orso, *Papa*)	–	/	Sirte	2
31/1340	br	REGENT	Knox	-S	500	+	A	7m NW Benghazi	01/	it	-S	Igea	160	+	7m N Carcura	3
AUGUST 1941																
03/2015	nl	O-21	Van Dulm	-S	500	=	TA	S Sardinia	03/							4
05/06									[05/06	it	-D	Capo Arma]	–	/	Dardanelles	5
06/0632	nl	O-24	de Booy	-D	5000	+	-T	41°47N/12°06E	06/	it	-D	Bombardiere	613	+	5m C. di Fregene	
07/1710	nl	O-24	de Booy	-S		/	-T	Ligurian Sea								
07/2130	nl	O-24	de Booy	-S	1000	+	A	41°23N/12°28E	07/	it	-S	Margherita Madre	296	+	15m Anzio	
12/1250	br	TORBAY	Miers	-T	3000	/	4-T	4m W Benghazi	12/1200	it	-D	(Bosforo, Iseo)	–	/	Off Benghazi	6
12/1020	nl	O-24	de Booy	-SA		/	-T	Ligurian Sea								
14/							-T		14/	it	-D	(Convoy, 5 ships)	–	/	Tunisian coast	
14/	br	TALISMAN	Willmott	*SS*		/	-T		*14/*	br	SS	(*Otus*)	–	/		
15/morn	br	THRASHER	Cowell	-D	4000	/	4-T	Mandri Channel	15/	dt	-M	(Ankara)	–	/	Cape Sunion	7
16/1100	nl	O-23	Van Erkel	-D		=	4-T	39°35N/13°18E								8
16/2100	br	TORBAY	Miers	-S	500	+	S	Benghazi	16/	gr	-S	Evangelista	28	+	Cape Matapan	9
17/	br	P32	Abdy (?)						17/2015	it	-D	(Convoy)	–	/	Off Tripoli	10
18/	br	TETRARCH	Greenway	*TB*	600	/	-T	*Benghazi harbour*	*18/*	*it*	*TB*	(*Calliope*)	–	/	*Benghazi harbour*	*11*
19/0715	br	TETRARCH	Greenway	-D	2000	/	4-T	Off Benghazi	19/2102	it	-D	(Cadamosto)	–	/	Off Benghazi	11
19/1830	br	UNBEATEN	Woodward	-D	12000	/	3-T	15m N Pantellaria	19/	it	-D	(Esperia)	–	/		12

(1) *O-21* probably sank *Monteponi*, which is also claimed for the attack by *Olympus*.

(2) *Cachalot* assumed she had attacked a tanker with gunfire, but the target was actually the Italian torpedo boat *Papa*, which lightly rammed the submarine, damaging her outer hull and forcing the her to scuttle herself.

(3) *Regent* reported sinking *Igea*, which is not in the Italian lists.

(4) *O-21* missed a sailing vessel with torpedoes and then attacked with gunfire.

(5) The submarine attacks against the Italian steamer *Capo Arma*/3172, the German steamer *Salzburg*/1742, the Romanian steamer *Alba Julia*/5700 and the Romanian steamer *Balcic*/3600 are erroneous claims.

(6) *Torbay* missed a small convoy and was heavily depth-charged by the Italian torpedo boat *Partenope*.

(7) *Ankara* was escorted by the Italian torpedo boat *Sirio*.

(8) *O-23* assumed two hits, but missed with Dutch 15,000yd long-range torpedoes.

(9) *Torbay* reported a small schooner sunk by demolition charges.

(10) *P32* was lost on a mine in the area.

(11) *Tetrarch* fired torpedoes into the harbour but they exploded against the boom defence. The next day a convoy was attacked and the Italian torpedo boat *Calliope* twice evaded one torpedo.

(12) *Unbeaten* fired three torpedoes at two large *Esperia* class liners. They missed, and the fourth torpedo did not leave the tube.

AUGUST 1941 *continued*

1	2	3	4	5	6	7	8	9	10	11	12	13	14	15	16	17
20/0927	br	UPHOLDER	Wanklyn	-D	2000	+	-T	6m NW Cape San Vito	20/0935	it	-D	Enotria	852	+	6m NW San Vito	
20/1017	br	UNIQUE	Hezlet	-D	11000	+	-T	33°03N/13°03E	20/1031	it	-D	Esperia	11398	+	11m NW Tripoli	1
20/	br	THRASHER	Cowell	-S	500	+	A	Cape Malea	20/	gr	-S	San Stefano (?)	...	+	Off Andros (?)	
22/1625	br	UPHOLDER	Wanklyn	-D	5500	+	-T	Off C. San Vito	20/1630	it	AK	Lussin	3988	+	2m NW C. San Vito	
23/0615	br	TETRARCH	Greenway	-S	500	+	1-T	12m NW Sirte	23/1200	it	-S	Fratelli Garre	413	+	12m N Sirte	
23/0702	br	TETRARCH	Greenway	-S	500	+	1-T	1m Sirte	23/1200	it	-S	Francesco Garre	399	+	0.5m Sirte	
24/1034	br	UPHOLDER	Wanklyn	CL		=	2-T	38°30N/12°00E	24/	it	CL	*(Luigi di Savoia)*	–	/		2
26/	br	RORQUAL	Napier				M	Zante	..M	it	-D					3
26/0700	br	TRIUMPH	Woods, W. J. W.	CA		=	2-T	*N Messina*	26/	it	CA	*Bolzano*	11600	=	*N Messina*	
26/0700	br	URGE	Tomkinson	-T	8000	/	-T	Marettimo	26/	it	-D	(Pozarica/7751)	–	/	Off Marettimo	4
27/	br	URGE	Tomkinson	-T	5000	=	-T	Marettimo	27/0700	it	-D	Aquitania	4971	=	7m N Trapani	4
27/2346	br	TRIUMPH	Woods, W. J. W.	-S		+	P	Furiano River								5
28/1840	br	RORQUAL	Napier	-D	8000	+	1-T	36°00N/21°31E	28/1840	it	-D	Cilicia	2747	+	36°25N/21°01E	
28/	br	UNBEATEN	Woodward	SS		/	-T	*N Sicily*								6
28/	br	UTMOST	Cayley	-D		/	-T	E Calabria								7
29/night	br	URGE	Tomkinson	-D	23635	=	3-T	Capri	29/	it	-M	(Victoria)	–	/		8
30/1745	br	UNBEATEN	Woodward	-S		+	1-T	Messina Strait	30/1750	it	-S	V51/Alfa	373	+	Augusta Roads	
30/	br	TALISMAN	Willmott	-S	500	+	A	3m N Benghazi	30/	it	APM	San Michele (?)	...	=		9
30/	br	TALISMAN	Willmott	-S	300	+	A	3m N Benghazi	30/	it	APM	Tenacemente (?)	...	=?		9
31/0618	nl	O-21	Van Dulm	SS		/	-T	*Tyrrhenian Sea*				*(Marcello type)*				
31/	br	UPHOLDER	Wanklyn	-D	23000	/	-T	E Tunisia	31/	it	-M	(Oceania/Neptunia)	–	/		10

(1) *Unique* attacked a convoy with the large liners *Oceania*, *Neptunia*, *Marco Polo* and *Esperia*.

(2) *Upholder* fired the last two torpedoes against three cruisers and destroyers but was not able to observe the results.

(3) *Rorqual* reported the sinking of a small Italian steamer on this minefield.

(4) *Urge* first missed a tanker and then damaged *Aquitania*, despite a heavy counter-attack by the Italian torpedo boat *Clio*.

(5) *Triumph* captured and sank a small fishing vessel.

(6) *Unbeaten* missed an Italian *Balilla* class submarine.

(7) *Utmost* missed an escorted vessel.

(8) *Urge* reported the liner *Duilio*/23625 hit in a convoy of three big ships but in fact the torpedo missed *Victoria*/13098.

(9) *Talisman* reported one caique sunk, but the report is doubtful.

(10) *Upholder* unsuccessfully attacked a convoy with the liners *Oceania* and *Neptunia* at long range.

1	2	3	4	5	6	7	8	9	10	11	12	13	14	15	16	17
SEPTEMBER 1941																
03/							-T		[03/	it	-M	Andrea Gritti/6338+]	–	/	37°33N/16°26E	1
03/1430	br	OTUS	Favell	AMC	4000	/	1-T	35°40N/18°07E								
05/0120	nl	O-21	Van Dulm	-D	5919	+	TA	42°48N/09°58E	05/0230	it	-D	Isarco	5738	+	40°12N/13°17E	
05/0745	br	PERSEUS	Nicolay	-D		+	1-T	37°43N/25°57E	05/0750	it	-DT	Maya	3867	=	39°43N/25°57E	2
06/0235	nl	O-24	de Booy	-S	1200	+	TA	43°45N/09°21E	06/0250	it	-Mf	A5 Carla	347	=	Off Spezia	3
06/0428	nl	O-21	Van Dulm	ACL		/	-T	Tyrrhenian Sea								
07/0433	nl	O-21	Van Dulm	ACM		/	-T	Tyrrhenian Sea	07/	it	-D	Ernesto	7271	=	37°08N/11°53E	
07/1500	br	THUNDERBOLT	Crouch	-D	1000	+	1-T	50m W Benghazi	07/0530	it	-D	Sirena	974	+	50m W Benghazi	
08/0729	nl	O-21	Van Dulm	-D		/	-T	Tyrrhenian Sea		it	-D	(Convoy)	–	/		
09/1712	nl	O-24	de Booy	-D	6000	+	1-T	42°47N/09°57E	10/0400	it	-D	Italo Balbo	5114	+	10m W Cape Serre	
10/0230	br	THUNDERBOLT	Crouch	-S	400	+	A	Gulf of Sirte	10/	it	-S	Svan I	388	+	M. el Auegia	
10/1910	br	TORBAY	Miers	-D	3000	+	2-T	Candia harbour	10/	dt	-D	Norburg	2392	=	Candia harbour	4
11/1100	br	THUNDERBOLT	Crouch	-D	2000	+	1-T	31°58N/19°23E	11/1830	dt	-D	Livorno	1829	+	24m NW Benghazi	
13/	br	THUNDERBOLT	Crouch	PM	369	/	1-T	Off Benghazi	13/	it	PM	(Zirona/*Jastreb)	–	/	Benghazi	5
13/0920	br	THRASHER	Mackenzie, H. S.	-D	500	+	4-T	Gulf of Sirte								
14/	br	THUNDERBOLT	Crouch	-D	5000	/	3-T	Benghazi	14/1000	dt	-D	(Tinos)	–	/	30m NW Benghazi	
18/0415	br	UPHOLDER	Wanklyn	-M	19328	+	4-T	33°02N/14°42E	18/0520	it	-MP	Neptunia	19475	+	33°02N/14°42E	6
18/0415	br	UPHOLDER	Wanklyn	-M	19403	=	"	33°02N/14°42E	18/0520	it	-MP	Oceania	19507	=	33°02N/14°42E	6
18/0705	br	URSULA	Hezlet	-M	24469	=	3-T	Off Tripoli	18/0705	it	-MP	(Vulcania/24469)	–	/	33°N/14°E	6
18/0851	br	UPHOLDER	Wanklyn	-M	19403	+	4-T	58m ENE Tripoli	18/0857	it	-MP	Oceania	19507	+	33°N/14°E	6

(1) *Andrea Gritti* was sunk by an airborne torpedo launched by an FAA Swordfish.

(2) *Maya* was beached because she could not be towed.

(3) *O-24* missed the A/A barque with a torpedo and forced her aground by gunfire.

(4) *Norburg* was first torpedoed and beached alongside the pier at Candia harbour, was torpedoed again on 10.11.41 by the Greek submarine *Glavkos* and was finally torpedoed on 24.11.41 by the British submarine *Triumph* (q.v.).

(5) *Thunderbolt* reported an unsuccessful attack against a *Crotone* class minesweeper; this may have been *Zirona*, which was sunk by aircraft in Benghazi in 11.41.

(6) Following 'Ultra' intelligence about a convoy comprising three large liners, *Upholder*, *Upright*, *Unbeaten* and *Ursula* were stationed on the course. *Unbeaten* first reported the convoy and led *Upholder* to her attack. Four torpedoes were fired, one each hitting *Neptunia*, which sank, and *Oceania*, which was stopped and was sunk by another salvo from *Upholder* 5hrs later. Meanwhile *Ursula* had unsuccessfully attacked *Vulcania*.

1	2	3	4	5	6	7	8	9	10	11	12	13	14	15	16	17

SEPTEMBER 1941 *continued*

1	2	3	4	5	6	7	8	9	10	11	12	13	14	15	16	17
18/0800	br	TRIUMPH	Woods, W. J. W.	-T	5900	+	3-T	Off Cape Cimiti	18/	it	-M	Ardor	8960	=	5m Cape Colonne	1
19/1700	br	TORBAY	Miers	-D	2000	/	4-T	Off Gaidoro								
20/									[20/	fr	-D	Monselet/3372+]	–		Off Sfax	2
20/							-T		[20/night	it	-D	Marigola/5996=]	–		Kuriat	2
23/0800	br	TRIUMPH	Woods, W. J. W.	-D	3500	+	1-T	6m NE Sibenik	23/	dt	-D	Luvsee	2373	+	5m W Sibenik	
23/	br	THRASHER	Cowell	-D		/	-T	Benghazi								3
23/	br	TORBAY (?)	Miers (?)	AG		/	-T	Suda–Piraeus	23/	it	AG	(Cyclops)	–	/		4
24/0840	gr	TRITON	Kontoyannis	-D		/	-T	Off Suda								4
24/							-T		24/	it	-D	(Convoy, 3 ships)	–	/	Pantellaria	
24/	br	TRIUMPH	Woods, W. J. W.	-T	5000	=	TA	Off Ortona	24/	it	-D	Poseidone	6613	=	4m Ortona	
24/	br	TRIUMPH	Woods, W. J. W.	AG		+	A	Off Ortona	24/	it	-D	Sidamo	2384	=	Ortona harbour	
24/0228	br	TETRARCH	Greenway	-D		/	-T									
25/	br	THRASHER	Cowell	-D		/	-T	Benghazi	24/	it	-D	Prospero	971	=	Benghazi	5
26/0621	br	TETRARCH	Greenway	-D	5000	+	2-T	10m S Milo	26/0636	it	-D	Città di Bastia	2499	+	36°21N/24°23E	3
27/0910	br	UPRIGHT	Wraith	TB		+	-T	*Messina*	27/	it	TB	*Albatros*	339	+	8m NW C. Rasocol	
27/	br	TETRARCH	Greenway	-D		/	-T	Zea Channel	27/							5
27/	nl	O-21	Van Dulm	-S		+	A	42°N/10°E								
27/1820	br	TETRARCH	Greenway	-S	120	+	A	SW Milos	27/	gr	-S	Panajotis Kramottos	120	+	6m W Ananes I	5
28/2345	br	TETRARCH	Greenway	-D	4000	+	2-T	20m S S. Giorgio	29/0625	dt	AK	Yalova	3751	=	Kythnos (+3.10)	5

OCTOBER 1941

1	2	3	4	5	6	7	8	9	10	11	12	13	14	15	16	17
01/1120	br	TALISMAN	Willmott	-D	4000	/	-T	Zea Channel	01/	it	-D	(Convoy Lauretta)	–	/	Piraeus–Kard.	7
02/0020	br	UTMOST	Cayley	-D	2000	/	1-T	37°53N/12°05E								8
02/0900	br	PERSEUS	Nicolay	-D	3000	+	1-T	10m:W Benghazi	02/0300	dt	-D	Castellon	2086	+	32°30N/19°09E	
02/0900	br	PERSEUS	Nicolay	-D	3000	/	2-T	10mW Benghazi	02/	dt	-D	(Savona)	–	/	32°30N/19°09E	
02/	pl	SOKOL	Karnicki	-D	3000	+	TA	25m N Trapani								

(1) The ship attacked was reported as the tanker *Liri*/5900.

(2) *Monselet* and *Marigola* were attacked on 20.9.41 by RAF aircraft. *Marigola* was again attacked on the shore on 23.10.41 by *Urge* and on 30.10 and 1.11.41 by *Utmost* (q.v.).

(3) *Thrasher* reported making two unsuccessful attacks against convoys, but in the second attack *Prospero* was probably damaged.

(4) The unsuccessful attack on *Cyclops* may have been made either by *Torbay* or, more probably, *Triton*.

(5) *Tetrarch* reported, first, one ship from a convoy sunk, then two torpedoes missing the same convoy two hours later, then sinking a caique with Italian troops on board later in the afternoon. The next day *Yalova* was torpedoed and beached, finally to be destroyed by torpedo from *Talisman* on 3.10.41 (q.v.).

(6) *Proteus* reported two unsuccessful attacks at the end of the month.

(7) *Talisman* reported an unsuccessful attack on a convoy (*Lauretta*, *Arkadia*) and a heavy counter-attack by the torpedo boat *Libra*.

(8) *Utmost* reported an unsuccessful attack on a convoy.

OCTOBER 1941 *continued*

1	2	3	4	5	6	7	8	9	10	11	12	13	14	15	16	17
03/1232	nl	O-21	Van Dulm	-D	4000	+	-T	40°58N/09°59E	03/	fr	-D	Oued Yquem	1369	+	3m Cape Figari	
03/1215	br	TALISMAN	Willmott	-D	4000	+	-T	Hag. Georgios	03/	dt	-D	Yalova (wreck)	3750	+	S. Giorgio I.	1
03/	br	PERSEUS	Nicolay	-D		/	-T	Benghazi								2
04/even.	br	TALISMAN	Willmott	-D	15000	+	1-T	37°45N/24°35E	03/1840	fr	-M	Theophile Gautier	8194	+	37°51N/24°35E	
05/							-T		05/0045	it	-D	(Convoy)	–	/	N Tripoli	
07/1158	br	TALISMAN	Willmott	-D	3000	+	-T	35°45N/24°08E	07/1928	dt	-D	(Salzburg)	–	/	35°31N/26°25E	3
08/1930	br	RORQUAL	Napier			50M		37°22N/23°52E	20.10.M	it	TB	Altair	642	+	3m SW Gaidaro	4
									20.10.M	it	TB	Aldebaran	642	+	Gulf of Athens	4
08/	br	THORN	Norfolk	-D		/	2-T	Tyrrhenian Sea								5
08/	br	THORN	Norfolk	DD		/	2-T	Tyrrhenian Sea								5
10/1904	br	THUNDERBOLT	Crouch	-S	150	+	A	35°31N/26°25E	10/1930	it	-S	Città di Simi	25	+	12m Cape Sidero	6
11/									[11/	it	-D	Zena/5219+]	–	/	34°52N/12°22E	7
13/1735	nl	O-24	de Booy	-T		/	-T	S Tyrrhenian Sea								8
14/1314	br	UNIQUE	Boddington	-D	5500	=	1-T	40°26N/14°20E								9
15/	pl	SOKOL	Karnicki	-D	6000	+	3-T	Gulf of Athens								
15/	pl	SOKOL	Karnicki	-D		=	"	Gulf of Athens								
15/	br	THUNDERBOLT	Crouch	-T		/	-T	Aegean								10
18/0905	br	URSULA	Hezlet	-T	4000	+	-T	35°25N/11°39E	18/1000	it	-T	Beppe	4459	=	85m WNW Tripoli	11
18/0905	br	URSULA	Hezlet	-T	6000	=	"									
18/0800	br	THUNDERBOLT	Crouch	-D		/	-T	Aegean								12
21/							5-T		21/0830	it	DD	(Da Noli, Zeno, ...)	–	/	15m N Benghazi	
21/	br	RORQUAL	Dewhurst				10M	SE Cavioli I.								
22/	br	RORQUAL	Dewhurst				40M	SE Cape Ferrato	09.02.M	it	-D	Salpi	2710	+	2m E Cape Ferrato	13

(1) *Talisman* reported that she hit a beached ship with two torpedoes (see previous page).

(2) *Perseus* reported an unsuccessful attack on a ship bound for Italy.

(3) *Talisman* reported an unsuccessful attack against a convoy.

(4) *Altair* sank while under tow.

(5) *Thorn* reported an unsuccessful attack on an escorted ship and a destroyer, firing two torpedoes at each.

(6) *Thunderbolt* reported only one caique sunk; *Città di Sousse*, also reported, was probably the same vessel.

(7) *Zena* was not sunk by submarine but by an RAF aircraft off Kerkennah.

(8) *O-24* missed an escorted tanker.

(9) *Unique* reported a *Città di Genova* class passenger steamer damaged

(10) *Thunderbolt*'s torpedoes failed to explode when they ran under the big tanker.

(11) *Ursula* fired torpedoes at two targets and heard detonations; FAA aircraft attacked at the same time. *Beppe* was finally sunk a year later by *Unbending* (q.v.).

(12) *Thunderbolt* missed a convoy.

(13) The claim that *Salpi* was sunk by a submarine torpedo is erroneous.

1	2	3	4	5	6	7	8	9	10	11	12	13	14	15	16	17
OCTOBER 1941 *continued*																
22/0750	br	URGE	Tomkinson	-D	1500	+	2-T	35°45N/11°00E								1
22/1830	br	URGE	Tomkinson	-D	4000	+	1-T	35°50N/11°06E	22/1827	it	-D	Marigola	5996	=	Kuriat	1
23/	br	TRIUMPH	Woods, W. J. W.	-S	120	+	A	Gulf of Petali	23/	gr	-S	Panagiotis	120	+	Gulf of Petali	2
23/	br	TRIUMPH	Woods, W. J. W.	-S	120	+	A	Gulf of Petali	23/	gr	-S	Aghia Paraskeva	120	=	Gulf of Petali	2
23/	br	RORQUAL	Napier				M	Cavoli/C. Ferr.								
23/1014	br	TRUANT	Haggard	-D	3500	+	1-T	39°48N/19°06E	23/1018	dt	-D	Virginia S.	3885	+	39°52N/19°00E	3
23/1014	br	TRUANT	Haggard	AMC	8000	=	1-T	39°48N/19°06E	23/	it	AMC	(Arborea/4959)	–	/	39°52N/19°00E	3
24/after.	br	TRUANT	Haggard	-D	3500	+	TA	Off Bari	24/	it	-D	Padenna	1589	=	Off Bari	3
24/	br	TRIUMPH	Woods, W. J. W.	-D		/	-T	Aegean	24/	sp	-D	(Isora/316)	–	/		4
25/	br	TRUSTY	King	-D	5000	+	1-T	38°24N/20°13E								5
25/1318	br	TRIUMPH	Woods, W. J. W.	-D	6000	+	3-T	37°41N/23°53E	25/1330	it	-D	Monrosa	6703	+	37°41N/23°53E	6
27/	br	UNBEATEN	Woodward	SS		/	-T	Augusta		dt	SS					7
28/1010	br	THRASHER	Mackenzie, H. S.	-S	800	+	TA	NE Benghazi	28/1015	it	-S	Esperia	384	+	Sidi Suecher	8
28/1050	pl	SOKOL	Karnicki	ACM	5500	=	4-T	40°42N/13°47E	28/1150	it	ACM	(Città di Palermo)	–	/	Off Naples	
30/2230	br	UTMOST	Cayley	-D	4000	=	A	N Kuriata	30/2232	it	-D	Marigola	5996	=	2.3m S Kuriat	1
31/1655	br	TRUANT	Haggard	-D	5000	+	4-T	S Ortona	31/	it	-MT	Meteor	1685	+	2m Pt Penna	
NOVEMBER 1941																
01/0255	br	UTMOST	Cayley	-D		=	-T	N Kuriat	01/	it	-D	Marigola	5996	=	2m E Kuriat	1

(1) *Urge* reported the Italian steamer *Mario Pompei*/1406 sunk with the second torpedo, but this ship was in fact sunk by an explosion, probably caused by a drifting mine, off Cattaro. *Marigola* was beached after air attacks on 22/23.9.41 and finally destroyed by gunfire from *Utmost* on 30.10/1.11.41.

(2) *Triumph* sank two caiques by gunfire and ramming.

(3) *Truant* first sank *Virginia S.* and claimed later to have torpedoed an escorting armed merchant cruiser which reached port. *Padenna* was first missed by one torpedo and then set ablaze by gunfire, finally being sunk by *Thrasher* on 4.9.42 (q.v.). The Italian steamer *Maria Pompei*/1406 was sunk off Cattaro by a drifting mine.

(4) The Spanish *Isora* was missed.

(5) *Trusty* reported a ship in a convoy sunk, but the claimed *Achille*/2415 was sunk by aircraft on 23.10.41 near Augusta.

(6) *Triumph* was damaged by D/Cs from the Italian destroyer *Sella* and torpedo boats *Libra* and *Sirio*.

(7) *Unbeaten* missed a German U-boat.

(8) *Thrasher* first missed with a torpedo and then sank the vessel by gunfire.

1	2	3	4	5	6	7	8	9	10	11	12	13	14	15	16	17
NOVEMBER 1941 *continued*																
02/0240	pl	SOKOL	Karnicki	-D	3000	+	3TA	38°05N/12°03E	02/0310	it	-D	Balilla	2469	=	38°22N/12°20E	1
02/	br	UTMOST	Cayley		3000		A	38°05N/12°03E	02/	it	-D	Balilla	2469	+	38°30N/12°28E	1
02/	br	THRASHER	Mackenzie, H. S. *CM*		/		-T	*Benghazi*								2
03/	br	URGE	Tomkinson	-D	3000	=	-T	N Kuriat								
03/0407	br	PROTEUS	Nicolay	-T	5000	=	-T	37°53N/24°30E	03/1030	it	-DT	Tampico	4958	=	37°53N/24°30E	3
08/	br	UPHOLDER	Wanklyn	*SS*	*690*	+	*-T*	*36°19N/16°22E*					*–*	/		4
09/0640	br	UPHOLDER	Wanklyn	*DD*	*1450*	+	*-T*	*36°50N/18°10E*	*09/0720*	*it*	*DD*	*Libeccio*	*1615*	+	*37°10N/18°10E*	
09/1107	br	UPHOLDER	Wanklyn	*DD*	*1800*	=	*3-T*	*37°12N/18°33E*	*09/*	*it*	*CA*	*(Trento/Trieste)*	*–*	/		5
09/0225	br	OLYMPUS	Dymott	-D		/	TA	Gulf of Genoa	09/	it	-D	(Mauro Croce/1049)	–	/	Off Cerbere	6
10/0407	br	PROTEUS	Nicolay	-D	3000	+	-T	Off Milos	10/0707	dt	-D	Ithaka	1773	+	2m SW Milos	
10/1730	gr	GLAVKOS	Arslanoglou	-D	3000	=	-T	Iraklion	10/1745	dt	-D	Norburg	2392	=§	Candia/Crete	7
12/	gr	GLAVKOS	Arslanoglou	-S		+	A	N Crete								7
14/	gr	GLAVKOS	Arslanoglou	-S		+	A	N Crete								7
15/1626	nl	O-21	Van Dulm	-D	5524	/	-T	Tyrrhenian Sea	15/	it	-D	(Ninetto G./5335)	–	/		8
16/0745	nl	O-21	Van Dulm	-D	1578	/	-T	Tyrrhenian Sea	16/	it	-D	(Itu/1578)	–	/		8
17/	br	UPRIGHT	Wraith	-D		/	-T	Ionian Sea								9
17/	br	URGE	Tomkinson	-D		/	-T	Ionian Sea								9
18/	br	THORN	Norfolk	-D		/	-T	Aegean								10
19/	pl	SOKOL	Karnicki	*DD*		+?	4-T	*Navarino Bay*	19/	it	DD	Aviere	1690	=	*Navarino*	*11*
20/	br	THORN	Norfolk	-D		/	-T	Aegean								12
21/0739	nl	O-21	Van Dulm	-D		/	-T	Tyrrhenian Sea	21/	it	-D	(Convoy)	–	/		
21/night	pl	SOKOL	Karnicki	-D	3000	=	3-T	36°35N/21°28E	21/	it	-T	Berbera	2093	=	Navarino	13

(1) *Sokol* first missed *Balilla* with a salvo, and, when the ship had been abandoned, missed with the last torpedo and then attacked with gunfire. It is unclear whether *Utmost* participated in this sinking.

(2) *Thrasher* missed a *Cotrone* class minelayer.

(3) *Proteus* damaged *Tampico* and escaped the D/Cs fired by the Italian torpedo boats *Monzambano* and *Castelfidardo*.

(4) *Upholder* heard torpedoes detonating but the Italian submarine was not hit.

(5) *Upholder* missed with three long-range shots against two *Trento* class cruisers but claimed a hit on a destroyer.

(6) *Olympus* attacked *Mauro Croce* by gunfire and torpedoes but scored no hits as the ship escaped towards the shore.

(7) *Norburg* had already been damaged on 10.9.41 by *Torbay* (q.v.) and was again torpedoed on 24.11.41 by *Triumph* (q.v.). *Glavkos* also reported two caiques sunk by gunfire.

(8) *O-21* missed two convoys.

(9) *Upright* and *Urge* both missed the same convoy.

(10) *Thorn* attacked a lighted vessel and missed; it proved to be a Turkish Red Crescent relief ship.

(11) *Sokol* first hit *Aviere*, which was beached. The ship was again torpedoed by *Torbay* on 23.12.41 (q.v.) but raised and repaired, only to be sunk by *Splendid* on 17.12.42 (q.v.).

(12) *Thorn* missed a small convoy.

(13) During the night of 21/22.11.41 *Sokol* attacked a convoy and probably damaged *Berbera*, which was destroyed on 28.11.41 by aircraft at Navarino.

1	2	3	4	5	6	7	8	9	10	11	12	13	14	15	16	17
NOVEMBER 1941 *continued*																
21/2310	br	UTMOST	Cayley	CA	10500	=	-T	37°48N/15°32E	21/2312	it	CA	Trieste	10344	=	SE Messina	1
22/0125							-T		22/0347	it	CL	(Cadorna)	–	/	Brindisi–Benghazi	
22/2245	nl	O-21	Van Dulm	-Mf	300	+	A	41°25N/10°42E	22/	it	-Mf	San Salvatore	92	+	41°25N/10°42E	
23/0205	nl	O-21	Van Dulm	-D		/	-T	Tyrrhenian Sea	23/	it	-D	(Convoy)	–	/		
24/1825	br	TRIUMPH	Woods, W. J. W.	-Tg	1000	+	-T	Iraklion harbour	24/1240	it	-Tg	Hercules	632	+	Iraklion harbour	2
24/1825	br	TRIUMPH	Woods, W. J. W.	-D	3000	=	"		24/	dt	-D	Norburg	2932	=	Iraklion harbour	2
24/0222	nl	O-21	Van Dulm	-S	300	+	A	41°06N/10°02E	24/	it	-S	Unione	216	+		
25/1655	br	THRASHER	Mackenzie, H. S.	-M	5000	+	-T	40°37N/18°27E	25/2100	it	-M	Attilio Deffenu	3510	+	Brindisi	
25/	br	THUNDERBOLT	Crouch	-S	300	+	A	Cape Malea	25/	dt	-S	LVII	...	+	E Kythera	3
27/	br	UPHOLDER	Wanklyn	-T		/	-T	E Tunisia								4
27/	br	TRUSTY	King	-T		/	-T	Argostoli								5
28/0050	nl	O-21	Van Dulm	SS		+	-T	36°24N/03°20E	28/	dt	SS	U95	769	+	N Melilla	6
29/	br	UPROAR	Kershaw	CL		/	-T	39°20N/17°33E	29/	it	CL	(Montecuccoli)	–	/	70m S Taranto	6
DECEMBER 1941																
01/	br	UPHOLDER	Wanklyn	CL		/	-T	E Tunisia								6
01/night	br	REGENT	Knox	-D	2350	=	-T	37°52N/11°52E	01/	it	-D	Enrico	2350	=	Off Trapani	7
02/	br	PERSEUS	Nicolay	-D		/	-T	Ionian Sea								8
04/0830	br	TRUSTY	King	-D		+	-T	Ionian Sea	04/0830	it	-D	Eridano	3586	+	6m S Cape Ducato	9
05/	br	TALISMAN	Willmott	SS		/	-T	Kithera Channel								10

(1) *Utmost* reported a hit on the Italian cruiser *Duca degli Abruzzi*, but in fact *Trieste* was hit.

(2) *Triumph* sank the tug and again torpedoed *Norburg*, already damaged on 10.9.41 by *Torbay* (q.v.) and on 10.11.41 by *Glavkos* (q.v.), but the ship was repaired and taken in late 1942 to the Adriatic.

(3) *Thunderbolt* reported a schooner sunk by gunfire.

(4) *Upholder* unsuccessfully attacked a northbound tanker.

(5) *Trusty* attacked an unescorted tanker, but had a torpedo running in the tube and had to abandon the attack.

(6) *P31/Uproar* reported hits during an attack on three cruisers (*Montecuccoli*, *Duca d'Aosta* and *Attendolo*), but in fact the torpedoes missed. The same force was attacked unsuccessfully by *Upholder* in an asdic-directed engagement.

(7) The damage to *Enrico* was claimed by *Regent*.

(8) *Perseus* made an unsuccessful attack on a ship.

(9) *Trusty* aimed at a destroyer but the circling torpedo hit *Eridano*.

(10) *Talisman* missed a U-boat.

1	2	3	4	5	6	7	8	9	10	11	12	13	14	15	16	17

DECEMBER 1941 *continued*

1	2	3	4	5	6	7	8	9	10	11	12	13	14	15	16	17
06/	br	ULTIMATUM	Harrison	-D	4000	=	2-T	37°56N/15°39E								1
07/	br	TALISMAN	Willmott	DD		/	AT	*Kithera Channel*								2
07/	br	PROTEUS	Francis	-S	300	+	S	Kithera Channel								3
07/0914	br	TRUANT	Haggard	ACL	4000	=	2-T	Suda Bay	07/0920	dt	-D	(Bellona)	–	/	Suda Bay	4
08/night	br	TALISMAN	Willmott	SS		/	3-T	38°00N/20°28E	08/night	it	TB	(Orione)	–	/	36°10n/24°36E	5
09/1430	br	PORPOISE	Pizey	-D	6000	+	-T	5m S Navarino	09/1430	it	-M	Sebastiano Venier	6310	=	Methene	6
11/1330	nl	O-24	de Booy	SS		/	-T	*S Tyrrhenian Sea*	11/	dt	SS					7
11/1430	br	TRUANT	Haggard	-T	8000	+	4-T	35°29N/24°11E	11/1700	it	TB	*Alcione*	679	=§		8
11/1622	br	TALISMAN	Willmott	-D	12000	+	2-T	36°23N/20°33E	11/1625	it	-M	Calitea	4013	+	90m S C. Matapan	9
11/1240	br	TORBAY	Miers	-S	800	+	A	NW Suda	11/	gr	-S	Sofia	...	+		
12/	br	TORBAY	Miers	-D		+	A	NW Suda	12/	gr	-D	PIII	...	+		
12/0130	br	UTMOST	Cayley	-D	5000	=	2-T	39°47N/17°22E	12/	it	-M	(Fabio Filzi ?)	–	/		10
13/0210	br	UPRIGHT	Wraith	-D	7000	+	3-T	40°10N/17°60E	13/0230	it	-M	Fabio Filzi	6836	+	15m S. S. Vito	10
13/0210	br	UPRIGHT	Wraith	-D	7000	+	"	40°10N/17°60E	13/0230	it	-M	Carlo del Greco	6837	+	15m S. S. Vito	10
14/0859	br	URGE	Tomkinson	BB	23600	=	-T	37°53N/15°29E	14/1000	it	BB	*Vittorio Veneto*	41167	=	*Capo dell'Arm*	11
14/1952	br	TALISMAN	Willmott	SS		=	A	34°05N/25°39E	14/	dt	SS	U561	769	=		12
15/	br	TORBAY	Miers	-D	6000	+	2-T	Cape Methene	15/	it	-M	Sebastiano Venier	6318	=	Cape Methene	6
15/	br	TORBAY	Miers	-S	800	+	A	Cape Methene	15/	gr	-S		50	+		13
15/	br	TORBAY	Miers	-S	800	+	A	Cape Methene	15/	gr	-S	Maria (?)	42	+	Patras–Kalam.	13
15/	br	TORBAY	Miers	-S	800	+	A	Cape Methene	15/	gr	-S		15	+		13
16/1640	br	UPROAR	Kershaw	CL		/	-T	*Gulf of Taranto*								14
17/							-T		17/night	it	TB	(Orione)	–	/	W Suda	
22/	br	TORBAY	Miers	-S	800	+	A	Cape Methene	21/	gr	-S		30	+		13

(1) *P34/Ultimatum* reported an unescorted merchant vessel damaged, but the ship was not hit.

(2) *Talisman* missed a destroyer.

(3) *Proteus* reported one caique sunk.

(4) *Truant* claimed a hit on a *Ramb* class merchant cruiser.

(5) *Talisman* assumed she was attacking a submarine, but her objective was in fact the torpedo boat *Orione*. The latter almost rammed *Talisman*, and the next day she did, in error, sink the German submarine *U557* by ramming.

(6) *Sebastiano Venier* had 2000 POWs on board, of which 1800 were saved. The ship was finally sunk on 15.12.41 by *Torbay*.

(7) The U-boat sighted the wakes of the torpedoes and evaded.

(8) *Truant* claimed a hit on a tanker, but in fact the escorting *Alcione* was hit.

(9) *Talisman* reported the ship as a *Virgilio* class liner/11718grt.

(10) *Utmost* attacked the same convoy as *Upright* and reported a hit, but the torpedoes missed.

(11) *Urge* claimed a *Cavour* class battleship.

(12) *Talisman* attacked *U561* with her 4in gun, causing slight damage.

(13) *Torbay* claimed four caiques loaded with captured British ammunition.

(14) *P31/Uproar* attacked a force of three westbound cruisers but missed.

1	2	3	4	5	6	7	8	9	10	11	12	13	14	15	16	17

DECEMBER 1941 *continued*

1	2	3	4	5	6	7	8	9	10	11	12	13	14	15	16	17
									[22/0100	it	-D	Cadamosto/1010+]	–		32°30N/15°01E	1
									[22/0100	dt	-D	Spezia/1825+]	–		32°26N/15°01E	1
23/1900	br	TORBAY	Miers	*DD*		+	-T	*Navarino*	23/	it	DD	*Aviere*	1620	=	*Navarino Bay*	2
28/	br	THORN	Norfolk	-T		=	TA	Cephalonia								3
30/0900	br	PROTEUS	Nicolay	-D	4000	=	2-T	38°07N/20°25E	30/0930	it	-M	Città di Marsala	2480	=	38°35N/20°27E	4
30/1635	br	THORN	Norfolk	-T	6000	+	1-T	38°35N/10°27E	30/1715	dt	-T	Campina	3030	+	Cape Dukato	

JANUARY 1942

1	2	3	4	5	6	7	8	9	10	11	12	13	14	15	16	17
																5
02/1300	br	THUNDERBOLT	Crouch	-D	2000	=	A	Argostoli	02/	it	-D	Anna Capano	1216	=	Off Verdian I	6
03/	br	UPHOLDER	Wanklyn	-D		/	-T	Cape Gallo								7
04/0535	br	UPHOLDER	Wanklyn	-D	5222	+	2-T	38°07N/14°00E	04/	it	-D	Sirio	5223	=	4m NW Cephalon.	8
04/0930	br	THUNDERBOLT	Crouch	-S	32	+	TA	38°07N/22°30E	04/0940	it	APM	R195/*Nuovo San Pietro	32	+	5m SW Cephalon.	
05/0539	br	UPHOLDER	Wanklyn	*SS*		+	*1-T*	*38°22N/15°22E*	*05/0542*	*it*	*SS*	*Ammiraglio St Bon*	*1504*	*+*	*38°02N/15°22E*	
05/0800	br	PROTEUS	Nicolay	-D	8000	+	1-T	38°33N/20°36E	05/0806	it	ACM	Città di Palermo	5413	+	30m W C. Ducato	
05/							-T		05/0800	it	-M	Calino	5186	+	Brindisi–Patrasso	
05/1453	br	UNIQUE	Collett	*BB*	41300	/	-T	40°07N/17°07E	05/	it	BB	(*Littorio/40724*)	–	/		9
07/							-T		07/0915	it	-M	(*Probitas*)	–	/	Tripoli–Trapani	
09/									[09/	it	-D	Venezia Giulia/ 5387+]	–		Pacific	10
10/0400	br	THRASHER	Mackenzie, H. S.	-D	6000	+	1-T	38°59N/19°59E	10/0400	it	-D	Fedora	5016	+	35m SE C. Ducato	
11/	br	PORPOISE	Pizey				M	Cape Drepano	14.01.M	dt	APC	11-V-1/*Palaskos	...	+	Suda Bay	
									15.01.M	it	TB	*Castore*	789	=	*Suda Bay*	
12/1205	br	UNBEATEN	Woodward	*SS*		+	2-T	37°50N/16°00E	12/	dt	SS	*U374*	769	+1	*NE C. Spartivento*	

(1) Both ships were lost on drifting mines from the new field laid by Italian cruisers off Tripoli. *P35/Umbra* did not make her first attack until 17.1.42.

(2) *Aviere* was beached when hit again; she was first hit by *Sokol* on 19.11.41 (q.v.).

(3) *Thorn* reported missing torpedoes but hits with gunfire.

(4) *Città di Marsala* was towed into Argostoli.

(5) The newly operational British submarines of the 'S', 'T' and 'U' classes were in 1942 known only by their 'P' numbers and did not receive their names until 1943. However, their names are quoted here. See index of submarines.

(6) *Thunderbolt* attacked a small steamer with gunfire and observed hits. *Anna Capano* was beached but later repaired.

(7) *Upholder* missed two ships.

(8) *Upholder* had one torpedo running hot in the tube, the other exploding underneath the submarine. In a fresh attack one torpedo hit the ship, but, only damaged, she escaped.

(9) *Unique* attacked a *Littorio* class battleship at long range and heard one heavy explosion, but she had missed after being forced deep by an aircraft.

(10) *Venezia Giulia*, the former Yugoslav steamer *Tomislav*, was sunk as the Japanese *Teian Maru* in 35°00N/140°36E by the US submarine *Pollack*.

1	2	3	4	5	6	7	8	9	10	11	12	13	14	15	16	17
JANUARY 1942 *continued*																
17/0320	br	UMBRA	Maydon	-D	301	+	-T	35°59N/10°46E	17/night	it	AR	Rampino	301	+	Susa–Pantellaria	
18/1730	br	PORPOISE	Pizey	-D	3000	+	1-T	35°38N/24°18E	18/0727	it	-D	Città di Livorno	2471	+	35°42N/24°24E	
19/0906	br	UNBEATEN	Woodward	-T	7000	=	4-T	37°49N/15°52E								1
20/	br	UMBRA	Maydon	-D		/	-T	Kuriat								2
21/	br	UNIQUE	Collett	SS		/	-T	*Gulf of Taranto*								3
22/	br	TORBAY	Miers	CL		/	-T	*Gulf of Taranto*								4
23/							-T		23/morn.	it	-D	(Convoy ships)	–	/	Messina–Tripoli	5
24/0859	br	P36	Edmonds	-D	5000	=	3-T	32°53N/14°15E	24/after.	it	-D	(Convoy 5 ships)	–	/	55m E Tripoli	5
25/1350	br	ULTIMATUM	Harrison	-D	3252	+	-T	37°45N/15°30E	26/0145	it	-D	Dalmatia L.	3352	+	1m S Ranieri	6
28/1200	br	THORN	Norfolk	-D	4000	+	TA	43°30N/15°55E	28/	it	-T	Ninuccia	4583	+	S Sibenik	7
30/1400	br	THORN	Norfolk	SS		+	-T	44°45N/13°56E	30/1410	*it*	SS	*Medusa*	650	+	*S Brioni*	
30/after.	br	THUNDERBOLT	Crouch	-D	3000	/	4-T	Cephalonia	30/after.	it	TB	(Solferino)	–	/	Corfu–Patras.	8
FEBRUARY 1942																
01/1030	br	THUNDERBOLT	Crouch	-D	5000	+	1-T	Off Levkas	01/1046	it	-D	Absirtea	4170	+	37°50N/15°29E	
01/1053	br	URGE	Tomkinson	-D	3500	/	1-T	37°56N/15°42E	01/	it	-D	(Trapani/Rondine)	–	/		9
02/							A		02/	dt	APC	13M3/*Apostolos	...	+	Aegean	
03/1105	br	THUNDERBOLT	Crouch	APC		=	A	Cephalonia	03/	it	APC	Lanciotto Piero	180	=	8m Gheregambe	10
03/1520	br	UMBRA	Maydon	-D	6600	+	2-T	30m E Susa	03/1700	it	-M	Napoli	6140	=§	Mehedia/Tunes	11

(1) *Unbeaten* reported two hits on an escorted tanker.

(2) *P35/Umbra* missed an illuminated six-ship convoy.

(3) *Unique* missed a U-boat.

(4) *Torbay* missed a cruiser/destroyer force at long range.

(5) *P36* missed what were assumed to be three cruisers, but in reality was a convoy. The Italian steamer *Victoria*/13098, sometimes credited, had in fact been sunk earlier in this convoy by FAA Swordfish and Albacore aircraft.

(6) The ship sank on 28.1.42 while under tow.

(7) *Thorn* first missed *Ninuccia* with torpedoes, and a surface engagement was prevented by coastal batteries, but in a second attack the ship was torpedoed and sunk.

(8) *Thunderbolt* missed a two-ship convoy because the torpedo tracks were sighted.

(9) *Urge* missed the two ships close inshore. The torpedo boat *Aretusa* claimed to have sunk the submarine.

(10) *Thunderbolt* damaged the armed trawler with gunfire.

(11) *P35/Umbra* torpedoed the ship, which was beached and then destroyed by FAA aircraft on 11.2.42.

1	2	3	4	5	6	7	8	9	10	11	12	13	14	15	16	17
FEBRUARY 1942 *continued*																
04/	br	UPHOLDER	Norman, C. P.	DD	1916	/	-T	N Sicily								1
05/									05/	dt	-D	(...)	–	/	4m N Trapani	1
05/							-T		05/1345	it	-T	(Rondine)	–	/	Cape San Vito	1
06/	br	THUNDERBOLT	Crouch	SS	500	/	TA	34°26N/23°22E	06/	dt	SS	(U431)	–	/	SW Crete	2
06/	br	UPROAR	Kershaw	-D		/	-T	Tripoli								3
07/	br	UNBEATEN	Martin	-D		/	-T	Kerkennah								4
07/									[07/	sp	-D	Urumea/3520]	. –		Gulf of Genoa	5
08/1740	br	UPHOLDER	Norman, C. P.	-D	2500	+	-T	8m E C. San Vito								6
08/1740	br	UPHOLDER	Norman, C. P.	-D		=	"	8m E C. San Vito	08/	it	-D	Daino	1334	=	Cape Ferrato (?)	6
08/0426	br	PROTEUS	Francis	SS		=	TR	38°41N/15°30E	08/	it	TB	Sagittario	630	=	W Cephalonia	7
12/2100	br	P38	Hemmingway	-D		+	-T	E Tunisia								
12/1530	br	UNA	Martin	-T	8106	+	-T	39°20N/17°25E	12/2315	it	-DT	Lucania	8106	+	39°20N/17°25E	8
12/2100	pl	SOKOL	Karnicki	-S	800	+	AS	15m S Kerkennah	12/2130	it	-S	Giuseppina	392	+	Off Kerkennah	
13/	pl	SOKOL	Karnicki	TB		/	3-T	Gabes Bay								
13/							-T		13/1140	it	-D	(Convoy 4 ships)	–	/	Bari–Durazzo	
13/1315	br	P36	Edmonds	CA	10000	=	4-T	37°42N/38°E	13/	it	CA	(Gorizia)	–	/	S Calabria	9
13/1315	br	P36	Edmonds	CA	10000	=	"	37°42N/38°E	13/	it	CA	(Trento)	–	/	S Calabria	9
14/	br	P36	Edmonds	DD		=	-T	Messina	16/	it	DD	Carabiniere	1715	=	Messina	9
14/2203	br	P38	Hemmingway	-D		+	-T	E Tunisia	15/0131	it	-D	Ariosto	4116	+	12m E Cape Africa	10
16/1155	br	THRASHER	Mackenzie, H. S.	-D	3000	=	-T	Suda Bay	16/	dt	-D	(Arkadia)	–	/	Off Suda Bay	11
23/1149	br	ULTIMATUM	Harrison	-D	9000	/	4-T	32°48N/14°50E	23/1015	it	-D	(Ravello, Unione)	–	/	Off Tripoli	12

(1) *Upholder* missed a *Navigatori* class destroyer. One of the two attacks reported by escorted ships is possibly connected with *Upholder*'s attack.

(2) *Thunderbolt* missed a U-boat with torpedoes and gunfire.

(3) *P31/Uproar* missed a small eastbound vessel.

(4) *Unbeaten* missed an escorted supply ship.

(5) There was no Allied submarine in the area of the reported attack.

(6) *Upholder* reported one ship sunk and another damaged from one convoy, but the claimed *Salpi* was probably lost on a mine laid by *Rorqual* (see 22.10.41).

(7) *Proteus* assumed she was attacking a submarine but met the torpedo boat *Sagittario* head-on. Both the submarine and the torpedo boat were damaged in the collision.

(8) *Lucania* was a safe-conduct ship, detected by the submarine *Tempest*, which let it pass and was then attacked by the torpedo boat *Circe* and sunk.

(9) *P36* missed a force of two cruisers and destroyer escort. The same force was attacked the next day, when the destroyer was damaged. The escorts dropped 225 D/Cs without causing any damage.

(10) *Ariosto* had 294 Allied POWs aboard, of whom 132 were lost. *P38* was sunk by the torpedo boat *Circe* on 23.2.42.

(11) *Thrasher* reported a supply ship damaged off Candia. Lt Roberts and PO Gould defused bombs from a German aircraft which failed to explode and were awarded the VC.

(12) *P34/Ultimatum* missed the convoy with the new ships *Unione*, *Ravello* and *Monginiere*.

1	2	3	4	5	6	7	8	9	10	11	12	13	14	15	16	17
FEBRUARY 1942 *continued*																
26/	br	TURBULENT	Linton	-D		/	-T	Suda Bay								1
27/1906	br	UPHOLDER	Wanklyn	-D	5500	+	-T	32°55N/12°42E	27/1930	it	-D	Tembien	5584	+	24m N Tripoli	2
27/night	br	TORBAY	Miers	-T		/	-T	Cape Dukato								3
27/1437	br	TORBAY	Miers	-D	1000	+	A	15m S Antipaxe	27/	it	-D	Lido	1243	=§		3
27/1445	br	TURBULENT	Linton	-S	60	+	A	Off Nauplia	27/	dt	-S		...	+		4
28/	br	UMBRA	Maydon	-D		/	-T	S Messina								5
MARCH 1942																
01/1900	br	UNBEATEN	Martin, J. D.	-D	6000	+	1-T	35°26N/11°09E	01/1800	fr	-D	PLM20	5417	+	5m E Mehedia	
02/	br	TORBAY	Miers	DD		/	?	*Corfu*								6
02/	br	TURBULENT	Linton	-S	120	+	A	Saloniki Bay	02/	gr	-S	Prodromos	...	+		7
02/	br	TURBULENT	Linton	-S	120	+	A	Saloniki Bay	02/	gr	-S	Aghios Apostolos	...	+		7
02/	br	TURBULENT	Linton	-S	120	+	A	Saloniki Bay	02/	gr	-S	Aghios Yonizov	...	+		7
03/	br	TURBULENT	Linton	-S	120	+	A	Saloniki Bay	03/	gr	-S	Evangelistra	...	+		7
03/	br	TURBULENT	Linton	-S	120	+	A	Saloniki Bay	03/	gr	-S	Aghios Dyonysios	...	+		7
04/	br	TORBAY	Miers	-D		=	-T	Corfu Roads								
05/1330	br	UPROAR	Kershaw	-D	7000	/	1-T	35°18N/12°35E	05/	it	-M	(Marin Sanudo/5081)	–	/		8
05/0530	br	TORBAY	Miers	-D	8000	=	4-T	Corfu harbour	05/	it	-D	Maddalena G.	5212	=§	Corfu	9
05/0530	br	TORBAY	Miers	-D	5000	=	"	Corfu harbour								9
05/0530	br	TORBAY	Miers	DD		=?	"	*Corfu harbour*								9
05/1328	br	UPROAR	Kershaw	-D	7000	+	-T	35°27N/12°12E	05/1331	it	-M	Marin Sanudo	5081	+	10m SW Lampion	8
05/	br	TURBULENT	Linton	-D		/	-T	Doro Channel								10
05/1500	br	THORN	Norfolk	APC	300	+	A	Cephalonia	05/	it	APC	AS91/Ottavia	259	+	2m Cape Alterra	

(1) *Turbulent* unsuccessfully attacked a three-ship convoy.

(2) *Tembien* had 498 POWs aboard, of whom 78 were lost.

(3) *Torbay* missed a tanker at night and later that day hit *Lido*, which was beached and repaired after the war.

(4) *Turbulent* sank a caique carrying German troops by gunfire.

(5) *P35/Umbra* missed a medium-sized ship.

(6) *Torbay* was prevented from attacking by a heavy D/C counter-attack.

(7) *Turbulent* sank three schooners with gunfire and one more on the next day. It is not certain whether the vessels named are *Turbulent*'s victims.

(8) *P31/Uproar* first missed the ship but sank it in a second attack. The submarine was depth-charged by the torpedo boats *Cigno* and *Procione*.

(9) *Torbay* attacked inside the harbour and assumed she had damaged two ships and possibly a destroyer. *Maddalena G.* was not repaired.

(10) *Turbulent* missed a convoy.

1	2	3	4	5	6	7	8	9	10	11	12	13	14	15	16	17
MARCH 1942 *continued*																
10/							-T		10/0930	it	-M	(Monviso/5322)	–	/	Lampione	
12/	br	TURBULENT	Linton	-S	300	+	A	Gulf of Petali								1
13/	br	TURBULENT	Linton	-S	300	+	A	Mykoni	18?	gr	-S	Aghia Traio	...	+	Monemvassia	1
13/1200	br	UNA	Martin, J. D.	-Mf		+	A	Kerkennah	13/1206	it	-Mf	Maria Immacolata	248	+	6m SE Mehedia	
13/							-T		13/1700	dt	-D	(Trapani)	–	/	Tripoli	
14/	br	UNA	Martin, J. D.	-D		/	-T	Kerkennah	14/1730	dt	-D	(Trapani)	–	/		2
14/0645	br	ULTIMATUM	Harrison	*SS*			+	*4-T*	*38°27N/16°37E*	*14/1330*	*it*	*SS*	*Amm. Millo*	*1504*	+	*37°13N/16°45E*	3
16/1706	br	UNBEATEN	Woodward	-D	11000	=	4-T	Cape Buzzano	16/	it	-D	Vettor Pisani	6339	=	Taranto	4
17/									17/	dt	-D	Achaia	1778	+	5m E Pt. Taiura	
17/0600	br	UNBEATEN	Woodward	*SS*	600	+	-T	*37°42N/15°58E*	*17/0620*	*it*	*SS*	*Guglielmotti*	*913*	+	22m C. dell'Armi	
18/1730	br	UPHOLDER	Wanklyn	*SS*		+	-T	*40°45N/17°56E*	*18/1730*	*it*	*SS*	*Tricheco*	*857*	+	Off Brindisi	
19/0900	br	UPHOLDER	Wanklyn	-Mf	200	+	A	Brindisi	19/0900	it	APC	B-14/Maria	22	+	20m S Brindisi	5
19/0900	br	UPHOLDER	Wanklyn	-Mf		=	A	Brindisi								5
23/1736	br	UPHOLDER	Wanklyn	*BB*		/	4-T	*Ionian Sea*								6
28/2250	br	PROTEUS	Nicolay	-DP	8000	+	-T	39°04N/20°05E	28/2325	it	-DP	Galilea	8040	+	39°04N/20°05E	
29/	br	URGE	Tomkinson	Rail			A									
30/0114	br	URGE	Tomkinson	-D	3000	=	TA	N Sicily								7
31/2153	br	PROTEUS	Nicolay	-D	4000	+	1-T	36°54N/21°18E	30/2330	it	-D	Bosforo	3648	+	36°38N/21°15E	

(1) *Turbulent* sank two schooners with gunfire.

(2) *Una* missed the supply ship.

(3) *P34/Ultimatum* achieved two hits.

(4) *Vettor Pisani* was only slightly damaged, probably by a dud torpedo. She was finally damaged beyond repair by aircraft on 28.7.42.

(5) *Upholder* reported one trawler sunk and one damaged.

(6) *Upholder* missed a battleship, which changed course after the torpedoes were fired at 4,000yds.

(7) *Urge* missed with torpedoes and had to break off the surface engagement after three hits because of gunfire from the ship.

1	2	3	4	5	6	7	8	9	10	11	12	13	14	15	16	17
APRIL 1942																
01/0930	br	URGE	Tomkinson	CL	5069	+	-T	11m SW Stromboli	01/0900	it	CL	Bande Nere	5130	+	11m SE Stromboli	
01/	br	UPROAR	Kershaw	-T		/	-T	S Elba								1
01/2013	br	TRUANT	Haggard	-D	7000	+	4-T									
01/2113	br	TRUANT	Haggard	-D	5000	=	"									
02/	br	UPROAR	Kershaw	APC		/	-T	S Elba								1
05/1154	br	UNA	Martin, J. D.	-D	7000	+	-T	37°05N/15°41E	05/1200	it	-D	Ninetto G.	5335	+	12m S C. d'Armi	
07/1430	br	TURBULENT	Linton	-D	1200	+	A	S Cattaro	07/1330	it	-D	Rosa M.	271	+	4m SE C. Platam.	
09/0635	br	THRASHER	Mackenzie	-D	1500	+	1-T	31°49N/19°42E	09/0545	it	-D	Gala	1029	+	25m SW Benghazi	2
09/	br	TURBULENT	Linton	-D	3000	/	-T	Sibenik								3
09/1200	br	TORBAY	Miers	APC		+	A	Prevesa/Corfu	09/1245	it	-S	Avanguardista	34	+	Off Patrasso	
11/1750	br	TORBAY	Miers	-S	200	+	A	NW Corfu	11/1700	it	-S	Gesu Crocifisso	137	+	5m Palerme	
11/1640	br	PROTEUS	Francis	-S		=§	A	NW Corfu	11/	it	-S	Natalina	39	=	5m Palerme	
12/	br	URGE	Tomkinson	-D		/	-T	Lampedusa								4
12/	br	TURBULENT	Linton	SS		/	-T	Fiume								5
13/	br	TURBULENT	Linton	-D		/	-T	Fiume								5
13/0915	br	THRASHER	Mackenzie, H. S.	-D	3500	+	-T	31°42N/19°07E	13/0925	it	-D	Atlas	2297	+	31°26N/18°56E	
13/	br	THRASHER	Mackenzie, H. S.	-Bg		+	A	Benghazi	13/	it	-Tg	Pilo 210	30	+	31°26N/18°56E	6
14/1620	br	UPHOLDER	Wanklyn	-D		/	-T	33° N/14° E	14/	it	-D	(Aprilia)	–	/		7
14/2020	br	TURBULENT	Linton	-S	200	=	A	Sibenik	14/	it	-S	Franco	...	+	Off Sibenik	8
16/1400	br	TURBULENT	Linton	-D	6000	+	-T	40°50N/17°37E	16/1405	it	-D	Delia	5406	+	3m Brindisi	
18/0655	br	UMBRA	Maydon	-D	5000	=	-T	35°05N/11°49E	18/	it	-M	(Nino Bixio/7137)	–	/	40m SW Pantellaria	9

(1) *P31/Uproar* missed a small tanker and the next day an A/S vessel.
(2) *Gala* was assumed by the Italians to have been sunk on a mine.
(3) *Turbulent* reported two unsuccessful attacks.
(4) *Urge* missed a two-ship convoy.
(5) *Turbulent* attacked a *Ballila* class submarine, which evaded, and a steamer, which was missed.

(6) *Thrasher* sank a tug and a lighter trying to salvage the cargo from *Atlas*.
(7) *Upholder* attacked a convoy and was sunk in a counter-attack by the torpedo boat *Pegaso*.
(8) *Turbulent* damaged one of two schooners with gunfire.
(9) *P35/Umbra* reported a northbound ship damaged. *Nino Bixio/7137* was probably missed.

1	2	3	4	5	6	7	8	9	10	11	12	13	14	15	16	17
APRIL 1942 *continued*																
18/0728	br	TORBAY	Miers	-D	1500	+	-T	38°30N/18°10E	18/0728	dt	-D	Bellona	1297	+	38°52N/18°15E	
18/0728	br	TORBAY	Miers	-T		+	A	38°30N/18°10E								
19/1620	br	UMBRA	Maydon	-D	4500	+	-T	34°55N/11°42E	19/1635	it	-D	Assunta de Gregori	4219	+	32°53N/11°23E	
19/1403	br	THRASHER	Mackenzie, H. S. *LC*		=		A	*32°53N/22°23E*	*19/1333*	*dt*	*LC*	*F184*	*155*	=	*2m W Derna*	*1*
19/1236	br	TORBAY	Miers	APC	1400	+	A	35°36N/24°16E	19/1400	dt	APC	13-V-2/*Delpa II	170	+	36°36N/24°15E	2
24/after.	br	UNBROKEN	Mars	-D	4000	=	-T	Genoa								3
25/							A		25/	it	-S	Natalina	39	+	5m W Palermo	
26/dawn	br	UNBROKEN	Mars	-S	200	=	TA	12m Bordighera	26/	it	-S	Vale Formoso II	...	=	Bordighera	4
29/0810	br	URGE	Tomkinson				A		29/0810	it	-S	San Giusto	243	=	Ras Hilal	5
MAY 1942																
02/							-T		02/1030	dt	-D	(Savona)	–	/	W Sirte	
02/	br	PROTEUS	Nicolay	-D	4000	+	-T	38°39N/20°22E	02/	dt	-D	Otto Leonhardt	3680	=	38°41N/20°34E	6
05/	br	PROTEUS	Nicolay	-S	60	+	A	37°08N/21°20E	05/1730	gr	-S	Domenico Evangelista	60		25m NW Navarino	
07/1825	br	THORN	Norfolk	-D		/	4-T	34°34N/17°56E	07/1720	it	-D	(Convoy 2 ships)	–	/	Messina–Benghazi	7
09/	br	UPRIGHT	Wraith	IX		+	A	Cape dell'Armi	09/	it	IX	Floating Dock	...	+		
11/							-T		11/2200	it	-T	(Alberto Fassio/2289)	–	/	Taranto–Tripoli	
14/1801	br	TURBULENT	Linton	-S	500	=§	A	Ras-el-Hilal	14/1700	it	-S	V-32/San Giusto	243	+	10m E Apollonia	8
14/1801	br	TURBULENT	Linton	-S		=§	A	Ras-el-Hilal								8
15/	br	THRASHER	Mackenzie, H. S.	-D		/	-T	S Adriatic								9
16/1447	br	THRASHER	Mackenzie, H. S.	-T	Large	+	-T	Off Bari								9
18/0210	br	TURBULENT	Linton	-D	4000	+	2-T	32°26N/19°16E	18/0112	it	-D	Bolsena	2384	+	32°47N/18°51E	
18/0210	br	TURBULENT	Linton	-D	4000	=	"	32°26N/19°16E								

(1) *Thrasher* attacked an MFP with gunfire but had to break off because of counter-
fire.

(2) *Torbay* reported a small naval auxiliary sunk in a gun duel.

(3) *P42/Unbroken* reported a steamer probably damaged. The ship was not identified.

(4) *Unbroken* attacked the vessel with guns and two torpedoes, which failed, and
when trying to ram identified the ship as a neutral carrying Red Cross supplies for
POWs.

(5) The only submarine in the area might have been the lost *Urge*, which probably
attacked *San Giusto* and three MFPs but was then sunk in a dive-bombing attack
by a CR.42 aircraft.

(6) *Otto Leonhardt* was beached but later used as a training target for frogmen.

(7) *Thorn* fired four torpedoes at a convoy with three ships, but all missed.

(8) *Turbulent* reported two schooners destroyed.

(9) *Thrasher* missed a ship. A second attack on a tanker was also unsuccessful.

1	2	3	4	5	6	7	8	9	10	11	12	13	14	15	16	17
MAY 1942 *continued*																
19/0853	br	THRASHER	Mackenzie, H. S.	-D	3500	+	-T	41°01N/17°16E	19/0800	dt	-D	Penelope	1160	+	3.5m SW Monopoli	
20/							-T		20/0915	it	-D	(Convoy 2 ships)	–	/	Benghazi–Napoli	1
24/							2-T		24/1800	it	-D	(Monviso/Ankara)	–	/	Brindisi–Benghazi	1
26/							?		26/0045	it	-D	(Convoy 2 ships)	–	/	W Benghazi	1
26/							-T		26/0730	it	-M	(Convoy 2 ships)	–	/	Benghazi–Brindisi	1
27/							-T		27/1840	it	-D	(Convoy 3 ships)	–	/	N Benghazi	1
27/							-T		27/1900	it	-D	(Convoy 3 ships)	–	/	N Benghazi	1
29/0310	br	TURBULENT	Linton	-D	4000	+	4-T	70m NW Benghazi	29/0610	it	-D	Capo Arma	3172	+	33°07N/19°28E	
29/0310	br	TURBULENT	Linton	-D	4000	=	"	70m NW Benghazi	29/0330	it	-D	(Anna Maria Gualdi)	–	/	33°07N/19°28E	
29/0310	br	TURBULENT	Linton	*DD*		+	"	*70m NW Benghazi*	*29/0310*	*it*	*DD*	*Pessagno*	*1943*	+	*78m SW Benghazi*	
30/0630	br	PROTEUS	Nicolay	-D	2500	+	-T	34°42N/19°13E	30/0639	it	-D	Bravo/*Junak	1570	+	32°21N/18°54E	
31/0443	br	TAKU	Hopkins	-D	7000	=	-T	33°34N/18°30E	31/0015	it	-D	Gino Allegri	6835	=	32°27N/18°54E	2
31/0541	br	PROTEUS	Nicolay	-D	6000	+	2-T	32°27N/18°54E	31/0445	it	-D	Gino Allegri	6835	+	32°31N/18°36E	2
JUNE 1942																
01/							-T		01/	it	-Tg	Pilo 8	20	+	Tripoli–Benghazi	
02/1250	br	TURBULENT	Linton	*SS*		/	5-T	*32°48N/25°12E*	*02/*	*dt*	*SS*	*(U81)*	–	/		3
02/1309	br	TURBULENT	Linton	*SS*		+	2-T	*32°48N/25°12E*	*02/*	*dt*	*SS*	*(U81)*	–	/		3

(1) It is unclear which submarine or submarines might have made these reported unsuccessful attacks. *Turbulent* was in the area, but she made no reports apart from the attacks mentioned.

(2) *Taku* attacked and probably damaged a large supply ship a short time before *Proteus* attacked; both claimed hits.

(3) *Turbulent* twice missed *U81*, which had, one hour earlier, picked up the crew of the damaged and scuttled *U652*.

1	2	3	4	5	6	7	8	9	10	11	12	13	14	15	16	17
JUNE 1942 *continued*																
08/									08/	it	-D	(Convoy, V. Pisani)	–	/	70m W Trapani	
10/	gr	TRITON	Kontoyannis	-S	20	+	A	Thera								1
11/	gr	TRITON	Kontoyannis	-S	270	+	A	Thera	11/even.	gr	-S	Issodia	...	+	Thera	1
11/	gr	PAPANIKOLIS	Spanides	-S	30	+	A	Maleas								1
12/	gr	PAPANIKOLIS	Spanides	-S	15	+	A	Maleas	12/morn.	gr	-S	Catina	70	+	Cape Maleas	1
12/	gr	PAPANIKOLIS	Spanides	-S	30	+	A	Maleas	12/morn.	gr	-S	Aghia Aikaterini	20	+	Cape Maleas	1
13/	gr	TRITON	Kontoyannis	-S	210	+	A	Kaferea	13/	gr	-S	...	...	+	Off Euboea	1
13/	gr	TRITON	Kontoyannis	-S	150	=	A	Kaferea	13/	gr	-S	...	...	=	Off Euboea	1
13/	gr	PAPANIKOLIS	Spanides	-S	70	+	A	Maleas	13/	gr	-S	...	...	+	Cape Maleas	1
13/	br	UNISON	Halliday	*CL*		=	4-T	38°56N/09°40E	13/2123	it	DD	(Usidomare)	–	/		
14/	gr	PAPANIKOLIS	Spanides	-S	30	+	A	Nauplia	14/	gr	-S	Evangelista	10	+	Off Nauplia	1
15/0645	br	UMBRA	Maydon	*BB*	*41300*	=	4-T	*35°47N/19°03E*	*[15/2339*	*it*	*BB*	*Littorio/41782]*				2
15/1151	br	UMBRA	Maydon	*CA*	*10000*	+	-T	*35°45N/19°04E*	*15/0910*	*it*	*CA*	*Trento*	*10344*	+	*36°10N/18°40E*	2
15/	gr	PAPANIKOLIS	Spanides	-S	30	+	A	Scarpanto								1
15/	gr	PAPANIKOLIS	Spanides	-S	30	+	A	Scarpanto								1
15/	gr	NEREUS	Rallis	-S		+	A	Scarpanto								1
19/	gr	PAPANIKOLIS	Spanides	-D	7000	+	T	Doro Strait	19/	it	AH	Sicilia	9646	=?		1
22/1751	br	THRASHER	Mackenzie, H. S.	-D		/	-T	Libyan coast								3
23/0030	br	TURBULENT	Linton	-D	2500	+	1-T	45m N Sirte								4
23/0133	br	THRASHER	Mackenzie, H. S.	-D	2500	+	-T	31°58N/16°36E	23/0030	it	-D	Sant Antonio/*Anton	1480	+	31°53N/16°35E	3
24/	br	ULTIMATUM	Harrison	*SS*	*500*	+	-T	*34°22N/24°08E*	*24/*	*it*	*SS*	*Zaffiro*	*617*	+		
24/	br	TURBULENT	Linton	-D		+	-T	Sirte	24/1010	it	-D	Regulus	1085	=	4m W Ghemines	4
29/0903	br	THRASHER	Mackenzie, H. S.	*PS*		+	4-T	*33°21N/23°20E*	*29/1120*	*it*	*PS*	*Diana*	*1735*	+	*33°30N/23°30E*	
JULY 1942																
04/	br	THRASHER	Mackenzie, H. S.	*SS*		/	A		04/	it	-M	(Monviso/5322)	–	/		5
04/	br	TURBULENT	Linton	-D		/	-T		04/1030	it	-M	(Nino Bixio)	–	/	Off Benghazi	6
04/	br	TURBULENT	Linton	-D		/	-T		04/1415	dt	-M	(Ankara)	–	/	Off Benghazi	6

(1) *Papanikolis* sank seven, *Triton* four and *Nereus* one caique, and one of them also sank a steamer.

(2) *Littorio* was claimed, but actually she was hit later that day by an aerial torpedo. *Trento* had been damaged in an air attack when she was sunk by *P35/Umbra*.

(3) *Thrasher* attacked a convoy unsuccessfully, but in a second attack she sank *San Antonia* (ex *Anton*).

(4) *Turbulent* reported one small escorted steamer sunk.

(5) *Thrasher* reported unsuccessful torpedo and gun attacks on a U-boat.

(6) *Turbulent* reported a thwarted attack on a three-ship convoy, but both attacks were probably made by her.

1	2	3	4	5	6	7	8	9	10	11	12	13	14	15	16	17
JULY 1942 *continued*																
12/1400	br	SAFARI	Bryant	-S	700	+	A	Sardinia	12/1535	it	-S	Adda	792	+	2.5m M. Santo	1
									16.07.M	tu	SS	*Atilay*	934	+	*Dardanelles*	
15/1000	gr	NEREUS	Rallis	-S		+	A	Scarpanto								2
15/	gr	NEREUS	Rallis	-S		+	A	Scarpanto								2
15/1102	gr	NEREUS	Rallis	-S		+	A	Scarpanto								2
15/	br	SAFARI	Bryant	-D	1500	=	A	Gulf of Orosei	15/	it	-D	Tigrai	1302	=	Gulf of Orosei	1
19/1425	gr	NEREUS	Rallis	-D	6000	/	4-T	Scarpanto	19/	it	AH	(Sicilia/9646)	–	/	Doro Channel	2
24/	br	UNBEATEN	Woodward	-D	6339	+	-T		24/0930	it	-M	Vettor Pisani	6339	=§	38°05N/20°12E	3
26/									26/	it	-D	(Ostia)	–	/	Tobruk/Marsa	
27/	br	P222	Mackenzie, A. J.	-D			P	Cape Palos	27/	fr	-D	(Mitidja)	...	P	Cape Palos	4
28/	br	TRAVELLER	St John	-D	2000	/	-T	Otranto Strait	30/?	it	-D	(Ezilda Croce/1230)	–	/	Bari–Valona	5
30/	br	TRAVELLER	St John	CL	2000	=	6-T	*Off Pola*	31/	it	CL	(Cattaro)	–	/	S Pola	5
AUGUST 1942																
02/1525	br	UNITED	Barlow	-D	2500	+	4-T	Off Linosa								6
03/	br	THORN	Norfolk	-D	6000	+	2-T	Tobruk	03/1525	it	-m	Monviso	5322	+	16m NW Benghazi	7
03/0836	br	TRAVELLER	St John	-D		/	2-T	Sibenik	03/	dt	-D	(Pluto/1156)	–	/	Off Sibenik	5
03/									03/	it	-D	(Petsamo/Pluto)	–	/		
04/	br	PROTEUS	Alexander	-S		+	A	Gulf of Nauplia	04/	gr	-S	...	...	+	E Peloponnes	8
04/	br	PROTEUS	Alexander	-S		+	A	Gulf of Nauplia								8
05/0945	br	TRAVELLER	St John	SS	500	=	TA	42°48N/14°31E								5

(1) *Safari* was numbered *P211*. On 15.7.42 a small steamer was damaged by gunfire, but the action had to be broken off because of return fire.

(2) *Nereus* reported the sinking of three small sailing vessels and an unsuccessful attack on a large supply ship.

(3) *Vettor Pisani* was towed to the area of Argostoli and sunk on 25.7.42 by aircraft.

(4) *P222* was sent to intercept a Vichy ship assumed to have a cargo of cobalt. The ship was intercepted and taken as a prize, but had to be handed over to a Vichy French destroyer.

(5) *Traveller* missed the old cruiser *Cattaro* (ex *Dalmacija*), a steamer, a German U-boat and an Italian submarine. Of 17 torpedoes, five were failures and the others missed.

(6) *P44/United* claimed two hits.

(7) *Thorn* was lost without making a report, probably on 7.8.42 as a result of depth charges from the torpedo boat *Pegaso*. The two other attacks in the area may also have been made by *Thorn* (see next page, Note 4).

(8) *Proteus* reported two caiques sunk.

1	2	3	4	5	6	7	8	9	10	11	12	13	14	15	16	17
AUGUST 1942																
05/	gr	NEREUS (?)	Rallis	-D	1600	+	-T	Off Rhodes	06/	dt	-D	(Wachtfels)	–	/	E Peloponnes	
06/	br	TURBULENT (?)	Linton (?)	DD		+	-T		06/	it	DD	Strale	1206	+	Cape Bon	1
06/	br	PROTEUS	Alexander	-S	80	+	A	Off Rhodes	06/	gr	-S	...	...	+	E Peloponnes	2
06/	br	UNBROKEN	Mars	-D		/	2-T	Capri	06/	it	-D	(Argentina/5085)	–	/		3
06/	br	THORN (?)	Norfolk	–			-T		06/1554	it	-T	(Rondine)	–	/	Off Gaudo	4
07/	br	TRAVELLER	St John	SS		/	3-T	Otranto Strait								5
07/	br	THORN (?)	Norfolk	–			-T		07/	it	-M	(Città di Savona)	–	/		4
07/	br	PROTEUS	Alexander	-S		+	A	Milo								6
07/0730	br	PROTEUS	Alexander	-D	7000	+	1-T	10m NW Milo I.	06/0711	dt	-D	Wachtfels	8465	+	36°55N/24°10E	6
07/0730	br	PROTEUS	Alexander	-D	9000	+	4-T	10m NW Milo I.	07/1014	it	-T	(Rondine/6079)	–	/	Off Cape Spada	6
07/	(Air torpedo)								[07/2345	it	-D	Istria/5416+]			Benghazi–Navar.	
07/	br	PROTEUS	Alexander	-S	200	+	A	36°49N/25°31E	07/1830	gr	-S	Marigoula (?)	267	+	Cape Kyparissi	6
07/	br	PROTEUS	Alexander	-S	200	+	A	36°49N/25°31E								6
08/									08/	it	-D	(Amba Alagi)	–	/	Canarian C.	
08/	br	UNBROKEN	Mars	-D		/	2-T	Capri	08/	it	-D	(Algerino/1370)	–	/		7
08/	br	PROTEUS	Alexander	-S	200	+	A	36°49N/27°31E	08/	gr	-S	Firesia	200	+	S Naxos	6
09/							A		09/			Railway on coast		=	Canarian C.	
10/	br	UTMOST	Langridge	-D	5000	=	4-T	Marettimo	10/1900	it	-D	(Siculo)	–	/	Marettimo	8
12/	br	PORPOISE	Bennington				M	Sollum Bay	22.08.M	it	TB	Generale Antonio Cantore	635	+	Ras el Tin	
12/	br	PORPOISE	Bennington	-D	5000	=	1-T	Ras el Tin	12/0835	it	-D	Ogaden	4553	=	9m NW Ras el Tin	9
12/	br	PORPOISE	Bennington	DD		/	-T	Tobruk								9
12/	br	PORPOISE	Bennington	-D		+	-T	Tobruk	12/	it	-D	Ogaden	4553	+	9m NW Ras el Tin	9
13/0800	br	UNBROKEN	Mars	CA		=	4-T	38°40N/15°00E	13/0813	it	CA	Bolzano	11600	=	38°43N/14°57E	
13/0800	br	UNBROKEN	Mars	CL		=	4-T	38°40N/15°00E	13/0813	it	CL	Attendolo	7405	=	38°43N/14°57E	

(1) This attack was probably not made by *Turbulent* because she only left Beirut on 5.8.42.

(2) *Proteus* reported the sinking of two schooners on 4.8.42 (q.v.),only one of which was reported in German sources. One more caique was sunk on 6.8.42, as also reported in German sources.

(3) *P42/Unbroken* missed *Argentina*.

(4) See Note 7 on the previous page concerning the loss of *Thorn*.

(5) *Traveller* missed an Italian submarine.

(6) *Proteus* reported two large ships sunk on the morning of 7.8.42, but the time for *Wachtfels*' sinking differs; possibly she was hit by *Nereus* (see above). *Rondine* was missed. *Proteus* claimed two more schooners on 7.8.42 and a small caique sunk on 8.8.42.

(7) *P42/Unbroken* missed *Algerino*.

(8) *Utmost* claimed to have damaged the ship, but in fact the latter was unscathed.

(9) After laying her mines, *Porpoise* hit *Ogaden* with one torpedo. The ship had 200 POWs aboard, three of whom were killed. *Porpoise* then missed a destroyer and finally sank *Ogaden*.

1	2	3	4	5	6	7	8	9	10	11	12	13	14	15	16	17
AUGUST 1942 *continued*																
13/night	br	TAKU	Hopkins	-D		/	-T	Benghazi								1
14/	br	TAKU	Hopkins	-D		/	-T	Benghazi	14/1930	dt	-D	(Menes)	–	/	Off Benghazi	1
14/							-T		14/	it	AO	(Stige, *TB Lince*)	–	/	Cape Spada	
15/1928	br	PORPOISE	Bennington	-D	7000	+	-T	34°35N/21°32E	15/1830	it	-D	Lerici	6070	+	34°50N/21°30E	2
16/							-T		16/after.	dt	-D	(Menes)	–	/	Benghazi–Suda	
16/									16/	it	-D	(Sportivo/Bianchi)	–	/	Suda–Tobruk	
16/	br	SAFARI	Bryant	-S	60	=	A	Sardinia	16/	it	-S	Giovannino	158	=	E Sardinia	3
17/1220	br	SAFARI	Bryant	-S	250	+	A	Sardinia	17/1228	it	-S	Ausonia	218	+	11m S Orosei	3
17/1633	br	TURBULENT	Linton	-D	9000	=	4-T	36°35N/21°34E	17/1530	it	-D	Nino Bixio	7137	=	12m SW Navarino	4
17/1633	br	TURBULENT	Linton	-D	9000	/	"	30m S Navarino	17/1530	it	-M	(Sestriere/7992)	–	/	36°36N/21°30E	4
17/	br	UNISON	Halliday	-D	6000	/	-T	Zante	17/	it	-D	(Chisone/6168)	–	/		5
18/0047	br	UNITED	Barlow	-D	7000	+	1-T	50m Pantellaria	18/night	it	-D	Rosolino Pilo	8325	+	50m S Pantellaria	6
18/	br	SAFARI	Bryant	-D		/	-T	Sardinia	18/	it	-D	(Perseo/4857)	–	/		7
18/0925	br	SAFARI	Bryant	-T	10000	+	-T	Cape Carbonera	18/	it	-D	Perseo	4857	+	Cape Carbonara	7
18/	br	SAFARI	Bryant	SS		/	-T	*Sardinia*	*18/*	*it*	SS	(*Bronzo*)	–	/		7
19/	br	TURBULENT	Linton	-D	7000	=	-T	Anti-Kithera	19/	it	-M	Nino Bixio (?)	7137	=		8
19/	br	PORPOISE	Bennington	-D		/	-T	Tobruk	19/0430	it	-D	(Iseo/2366)	–	/	Off Derna	2
21/0343	br	UNISON	Halliday	-D	5000	=	4-T	38°57N/20°24E	19?	it	-T	Pozarica	7751	=	Off Sivota	9
22/									22/	it	LC	(MZ...)	–	/	Gaeta Ischia	
24/							-T		24/morn.	it	-D	(Convoy 2 ships)	–	/	Off Derna	

(1) *Taku* missed a convoy and, during the night of 14/15.8.42, *Menes*.

(2) *Porpoise* was damaged by D/Cs from the torpedo boat *Polluce*. She was badly damaged in the attack on 19.8.42 by the torpedo boat *Lince* and was escorted to Port Said.

(3) *Giovannino* was towed to Arbatax, Sardinia.

(4) *Nino Bixio* had 2000 POWs aboard, 336 of whom were lost. The ship was towed by the destroyer *Saetta* to Navarino, where she was sunk by aircraft on 1.10.42. *Sestriere* was missed.

(5) *P43/Unison*'s torpedoes were seen and evaded by *Chisone*.

(6) *P44/United* sank *Rosolino Pilo*, which had already been damaged by aerial torpedo. The explosion damaged the submarine.

(7) *P211/Safari* sank *Perseo* only in the second attack. Later that day *Bronzo* evaded the torpedoes.

(8) *Turbulent* hit a ship with two torpedoes, but it is unclear whether *Nino Bixio* was hit, towed to Navarino and repaired.

(9) *P43/Unison* torpedoed *Pozarica*, which was beached.

1	2	3	4	5	6	7	8	9	10	11	12	13	14	15	16	17
AUGUST 1942 *continued*																
26/morn.									26/morn.	it	-D	(Ostia/Olympos)	–	/	10m NNE Derna	
27/	br	UMBRA	Maydon	-D	5000	+	1-T	35°39N/23°07E	27/0751	it	-D	Manfredo Campiero	5463	+	35°41N/23°01E	1
27/	br	UMBRA	Maydon	-D		/	-T	W Crete								1
29/							-T		29/0730	it	-D	(Anna Maria Gualdi/ 3289)	–	/	Corinth–Tobruk	
30/	br	RORQUAL	Napier				M	Paxos Islands								2
30/1540	br	RORQUAL	Napier	-T	4000	+	3-T	39°32N/19°53E	30/1415	it	-D	Monstella	5311	=	Ionian Sea	2
SEPTEMBER 1942																
02/	br	UMBRA	Maydon	-D		/	-T									3
04/0355	br	THRASHER	Mackenzie, H. S.	-D	5000	+	-T	32°50N/24°10E	04/0257	it	-D	Padenna	1589	+	32°44N/24°11E	4
05/	br	TRAVELLER	St John	-D		+	1-T	46mNW Derna	05/0135	it	-D	Albachiara	1245	+	24m NNE Rel Tin	
05/2140	br	TRAVELLER	St John	-D		=	4-T	33°17N/21°57E								
07/							A		07/			Coast area		=	Cape Spartivento	
07/0936	br	ULTIMATUM	Harrison	-D	9000	/	4-T	36°17N/21°03E	07/	it	-D	(Luciano Manara)	–	/		5
07/							-T		07/0924	it	-D	(Convoy P)	–	/	Suda–Tobruk	
09/	br	UNBROKEN	Mars	-D		/	-T	Cotrone								6
10/	br	THRASHER	Mackenzie, H. S.	-D		/	-T	Tobruk								7
10/1106	br	UNA	Norman, C. P.	-D	4000	=	-T	35°12N/23°29E	10/morn.	it	-D	(Brioni/1987)	–	/	Tobruk–Pireo	8
12/1710	br	SAHIB	Bromage	-S	200	+	AS	Maddalena	12/	it	-S	Ida S.	24	+	8m SE Maddalena	9
12/	br	SAHIB	Bromage	-S		=	1-T	Buggerru								9

(1) The second attack against a large liner, in the afternoon, missed.
(2) *Rorqual* could lay only some of her mines because 35 became blocked. *Monstella* sank in shallow water and was lost.
(3) *P35/Umbra* missed an escorted ship.
(4) *Padenna* was hit by two torpedoes.
(5) *P34/Ultimatum* fired a salvo and assumed she hit the target, but there was one premature and bomb explosions from an air attack.

(6) *P42/Unbroken* attacked a small convoy without success.
(7) *Thrasher* missed a ship in ballast.
(8) *Una* attacked a motor vessel in bad weather but missed.
(9) *P212/Sahib*, after sinking *Ida S.* by gunfire and demolition charges, fired a torpedo which destroyed some fishing vessels.

1	2	3	4	5	6	7	8	9	10	11	12	13	14	15	16	17
SEPTEMBER 1942 *continued*																
13/	br	UNITED	Barlow	-D	2000	=	-T	Misurata								1
14/	br	SAHIB	Bromage	-S		+	A	W Sardinia								2
15/							-T		15/morn.	it	-T	(A. Fassio/2289)	–	/	Off Derna	
16/	br	TALISMAN	Willmott	-D		?	-T	Marettimo								3
16/	br	SAHIB	Bromage	-S	200	+	A	Cape Argentiera								
17/2100	br	UNITED	Barlow	-D	500	+	TA	W Misurata	16/2000	it	-D	Rostro	333	+	0.5m Sliten	
17/2100	br	UNITED	Barlow	-S	200	+	A		16/2000	it	APC	V-39/Giovanna	158	+	Off Sliten	
17/	br	TAKU	Hopkins	-D		/	-T	Tobruk								4
18/0200	br	TAKU	Hopkins	-D	4000	=	1-T	32°29N/23°34E	18/night	it	-D	(Dora/137 et al)	–	/	35m NW Tobruk	
20/	br	TAKU		-T					20/morn.	it	-M	(Apuania/7949)	–	/	Benghazi	
21/0105	br	UNRUFFLED	Stevens, J. S.	APM	200	+	A	8m NE Mehedia	21/0130	it	APM	N-10/Aquila	305	+	Djerba, Tunisia	5
21/1700	br	UNRUFFLED	Stevens, J. S.	-D	5000	+	1-T	35°36N/11°09E	21/	fr	-D	Liberia/*Cape Corso	3890	+	10m Mehedia	5
22/night	br	UNRUFFLED	Stevens, J. S.	-D	3000	+	TA	35°45N/11°11E	22/0430	it	-D	Leonardo Palomba	1110	+	8m E Kuriat	5
22/night	br	UNRUFFLED	Stevens, J. S.	-D	2000	+	"	35°45N/11°11E								
22/	br	THRASHER	Mackenzie, H. S.	-D	5000	=	-T	Tobruk								
24/		Probably mine							[24/	it	APC	Cypros/1064+]			Zante	
24/1404	gr	NEREUS	Rallis	-D	1500	+	-T	24m C Alupo	24/1410	it	-D	Fiume	662	+	7m SW Rhodes	6

(1) *P44/United* claimed to have damaged a medium-sized ship.

(2) *P212/Sahib* sank a schooner with gunfire.

(3) *Talisman* attacked a convoy and was subsequently sunk, probably on a mine.

(4) *Taku* missed a convoy on 17.9.42 and the next day assumed she damaged one of two ships in the convoy.

(5) *P46/Unruffled* sank the Vichy French ship, which had ignored the warning of running at night. *Leonardo Palomba* was set ablaze by gunfire.

(6) Of the troops on board, 333 were lost and only three survived.

1	2	3	4	5	6	7	8	9	10	11	12	13	14	15	16	17
SEPTEMBER 1942 *continued*																
25/1700	gr	NEREUS	Rallis	-S	80	+	R	Aegean	25/	gr	-S	Simeon	...	+	Aegean	
27/1639	br	UMBRA	Maydon	-D	7000	=	-T	37°04N/20°36E	27/	it	-D	Francesco Barbaro	6345	=		1
27/2240	br	UMBRA	Maydon	-D	7000	+	-T	Cephalonia	27/1642	it	-D	Francesco Barbaro	6345	+	37°15N/19°55E	1
29/							-T		29/1930	dt	-D	(Kreta/1013)	–	/	Off Derna	
30/	br	UNITED	Barlow	-D		/	-T	Cape Spartivento								2
30/	br	SAFARI	Bryant	-D		+	TA	Sibenik	30/	it	-D	Veglia/*Kosovo	896	=	9m SE Korcula	3
OCTOBER 1942																
01/	br	UNITED	Barlow	-D	4000	=	4-T	5m NE Cape Spartivento	01/	it	-D	Ravenna	1148	=	Cape Spartivento	4
02/1107	br	SAFARI	Bryant	-D	900	=§	TA	42°57/17°17E	02/	it	-D	Veglia/*Kosovo	895	=§	9m SE Korcula	
02/									02/night			Rhodes harbour		=	Rhodes harbour	
02/							A		02/	it	AW	Cristiano	...	=	Off Crotone	
02/	br	UNITED	Barlow	-D		/	A	Cape Colonne								5
03/	br	RORQUAL	Bennington				M	Off Tobruk								
03/	br	UNA	Norman, C. P.	-D		/	-T	Lampedusa								6
04/							-T		04/1000	it	-D	(Torquato Gennari)	–	/	NW Palermo	
04/	br	SAFARI	Bryant	-D		/	A		04/	it	-D	(Eneo, Cherson)	–	/	Sebenico	7
05/1121	br	SAFARI	Bryant	-D	600	=§	4-T	43°38N/18°13E	05/	it	-D	Eneo/*Soca	545	=§	Off Split	8
05/							-T		05/	dt	-D	(Ruhr)	–	/	Benghazi	

(1) *P35/Umbra* first damaged *Francesco Barbaro* and then sank her after sustaining a D/C attack. The Italian motor vessel *Unione*/6071 was not hit by a submarine torpedo but by an airborne torpedo.

(2) *P44/United* missed a two-ship convoy.

(3) *P211/Safari* hit *Veglia* with gunfire and torpedo. The ship was beached and, on 12.10.42, salvaged.

(4) *P44/United* attacked *Ravenna*, damaged in an air attack, and hit her with one torpedo, but she was salvaged later.

(5) *P44/United* failed in a gun attack against a small steamer.

(6) *Una* aimed at a small steamer and a tug, but the torpedoes exploded on the rocks.

(7) *P211/Safari* claimed an unsuccessful gunfire and torpedo attack on *Valentino Coda*. The two ships mentioned reported this attack.

(8) *Eneo* was towed to Split and repaired after the war.

1	2	3	4	5	6	7	8	9	10	11	12	13	14	15	16	17
OCTOBER 1942 *continued*																
06/	br	TURBULENT	Linton	-D		/	-T	Benghazi								1
07/	br	TURBULENT	Linton	-D		/	-T	Benghazi								1
08/							T		[08/0044	it	-D	Dandolo/4964+]			60m NE Ras el T.	2
08/0634	br	TURBULENT	Linton	-D	1000	+	A	Ras el Hilal	08/0735	dt	-D	Kreta/*Arkadia	1013	+	10m N Ras Hilal	3
08/1520	br	UNBENDING	Stanley	-Dt	349	+	TA	33°41N/11°44E	08/1635	it	-M	Lupa No 2	379	+	12m NE Djerba	4
08/1729	br	SAFARI	Bryant	-D	1200	+	4-T	43°30N/15°58E	08/	it	-D	(Giuseppe Magliulo)	–	/	S Sebenico	5
09/1520	br	TRAVELLER	St Clair-Ford	-T	6000	=	3-T	35°45N/23°13E	09/	it	-D	(Proserpina/4896)	–	/	W Crete	6
09/1520	br	TRAVELLER	St Clair-Ford	DD		=	"	*35°45N/23°13E*	*08 2100*	*it*	*TB*	*(Ciclone,Castore)*	–	/	*W Crete*	6
09/1900	br	UNBENDING	Stanley	-S	100	+	A	34°08N/11°00	09/	it	-S	Giuseppe Magliulo	846	+	Off Djerba	4
09/2225	br	UNBENDING	Stanley	-D	3000	+	1-T	34°02N/11°05E	09/2330	it	-D	Alga	1851	+	12m N Djerba	
10/1100	br	SAFARI	Bryant	-D	4000	=	4-T	42°32N/18°13E	10/0744	it	-D	(Valentino Coda)	–	/	Gorgona Head	7
10/1123	br	CLYDE	Brookes	SS		=	-T	*34°52N/19°15E*								8
10/1324	br	UNISON	Halliday	-D	8000	+	-T	37°11N/21°26E	10/1450	it	-D	Enrichetta	4652	+	NW Navarino	
10/							-T		10/	it	-D	(Convoy)	–	/	N Hydra/Aegean	
10/	br	UTMOST	Coombe	-D		/	-T	E Sardinia								9
10/							3-T		10/	dt	ACM	(Bulgaria)	–	/	S Cerigotto	
10/	br	UMBRA	Maydon	DD	1900	/	-T	*S Adriatic*								10
11/0900	br	UNRUFFLED	Stevens	-D	2500	+	-T	5m S Capri	11/0935	dt	-D	Una/*St Guillaume	1395	+	4m S Capri	11
12/	br	THRASHER	Mackenzie, H. S.	-S	200	+	A	39°56N/24°17E	12/	gr	-S	...	...	+	Aegean	12
13/	br	THRASHER	Mackenzie, H. S.	-S	200	+	A	40°01N/24°10E								12
13/1733	br	UNRUFFLED	Stevens	-D	1500	+	-T	38°14N/13°14E	13/1744	it	-D	Loreto	1055	+	4m W Cape Gallo	11
13/	br	UTMOST	Coombe	-T	6000	+	3-T	41°01N/09°38E	13/1450	dt	-T	Languste/*Nautilus	2070	+	4m S Cape Figari	

(1) *Turbulent* missed two convoys.

(2) *Dandolo* was sunk by an airborne torpedo.

(3) The attack is also credited to *Utmost*/Coombe.

(4) *P37/Unbending* missed with torpedoes before sinking the ship with gunfire. The next day she sank a trading schooner.

(5) *P211/Safari* reported the 1500t ship damaged.

(6) *Traveller* claimed to have damaged a 6000t tanker and a destroyer.

(7) *P211/Safari* claimed hits on a three-ship convoy.

(8) *Clyde* claimed two hits on an Italian submarine.

(9) *Utmost* missed a mail steamer.

(10) *P35/Umbra* missed a *Navigatori* class destroyer.

(11) *Unruffled* was numbered *P46*. *Loreto* had 400 POWs aboard, 271 of whom were rescued.

(12) *Thrasher* reported two schooners sunk by gunfire and demolition charges.

1	2	3	4	5	6	7	8	9	10	11	12	13	14	15	16	17

OCTOBER 1942 *continued*

1	2	3	4	5	6	7	8	9	10	11	12	13	14	15	16	17
14/	br	UNRUFFLED	Stevens	-S	Med.	+	A	Tyrrhenian Sea								
14/	br	UNRUFFLED	Stevens	-S	Med.	+	A	Tyrrhenian Sea								
17/	br	UNBROKEN	Mars	-D		/	-T	Khoms								1
18/	br	TURBULENT	Linton	-D		+	-T	Ras Hilal								
18/				-T		=	-T	E Calabria								
18/	br	UNA	Norman, C. P.	-T		/	-T	N Catania	18/morn.	it	-MT	(Panuco/7600)	–	/	Napoli–Tripoli	
19/0840	br	UTMOST	Coombe	-D		/	-T	S Pantellaria								2
19/1258	br	UNBENDING	Stanley	-D	6000	+	4-T	35°45N/12°01E	19/1545	it	-D	Beppe	4453	+	28m SW Lampione	2
19/1258	br	UNBENDING	Stanley	*DD*		+	"	*35°52N/12°02E*	*19/1450*	*it*	*DD*	*Da Verazzano*	*1900*	+	*35°12N/12°05E*	2
19/late	br	THRASHER	Mackenzie, H. S.	-Tg	250	+	A	36°43N/26°41E	19/	it	-Tg	Pomo	130	+	Stampalia	
19/1415	br	UNBROKEN	Mars	-D	6000	=	4-T	35°22N/12°15E	19/	it	-D	Titania	5397	=	34°45N/12°31E	2
20/0100	br	UNITED	Barlow	-T	6000	/	4-T	21m W Lampedusa	20/	it	-T	(Petrarca/3329)	–	/	S Pantellaria	2
20/0020	br	SAFARI	Bryant	-T	6000	+	TA	34°45N/12°31E	20/0800	it	-D	Titania	5395	+	34°45N/12°31E	2
20/1418	br	THRASHER	Mackenzie, H. S.	AMC	2000	+	-T	36°26N/27°54E	20/1424	it	-M	Lero	1980	+	6m SW Simi	
22/	br	SAHIB	Bromage	-D	2000	/	-T	Navarino								3
23/0830	br	UMBRA	Maydon	-D	8000	+	2-T	Homs	23/1600	it	-D	Amsterdam	8670	=	Ponte d'Homs	4
23/0830	br	UMBRA	Maydon	-Tg	500	+	4-T	Homs	23/1600	it	-Tg	Pronta	182	+	Ponte d'Homs	4
24/1040	br	TAKU	Pitt	-S	50	+	A	36°23N/27°00E	24/	gr	-S		...	+	60m W Rhodes	5
25/	br	THRASHER	Mackenzie, H. S.	-D		/	-T	Rhodes area								6

(1) *P42/Unbroken* missed a beached ship.

(2) *Utmost* could only make a long-range attack on a convoy comprising one tanker and three transports, reported by air reconnaissance. From the same convoy *P37/Unbending* sank *Beppe* and torpedoed the destroyer, which foundered while under tow by the torpedo boat *Sagittario*. Another attack by *P42/Unbroken* at long range damaged *Titania*. Then *P44/United* damaged *Petrarca*, previously damaged in an air attack. Finally *P211/Safari* sank the damaged *Titania*.

(3) *P212/Sahib* missed a troop transport.

(4) *P35/Umbra* sank the tug *Pronta* while the latter was trying to salvage the damaged *Amsterdam*, which was finally given up on 20.1.43.

(5) *Taku* refrained from sinking a caique because there was no rescue equipment.

(6) *Thrasher* reported an unsuccessful attack against a two-ship convoy.

1	2	3	4	5	6	7	8	9	10	11	12	13	14	15	16	17
OCTOBER 1942 *continued*																
25/	br	TAKU	Pitt	-T	2240	/	-T	Khios	25/even.	it	-T	(Arca/2238)	–	/		1
26/0705	br	THRASHER	Mackenzie, H. S.	-T		/	–	Chalkidike								
									[26/	it	-D	(Tergestea/5890+)]	–		32°02N/24°24E	2
26/0704	br	TAKU	Pitt	-T	2240	+	-T	38°04N/25°27E	26/0705	it	-T	Arca	2238	+	9m S Chios	1
27/even.	br	TAKU	Pitt	-S	500	+	A	Khios	27/	gr	-S	Sifnos	315	=	Kupho	3
27/	br	TAKU (?)	Pitt	-S		+	A	Khios	27/	gr	-S	Lora	121	+	Lemnos	
31/0956	br	TAKU	Pitt	-D	Large	=	4-T	37°30N/24°03E	31/	it	-T	(Cerere)	–	/	Cape Sunion	
NOVEMBER 1942																
05/							-T		05/1000	it	-D	(Convoy 3 ships)	–	/	Napoli–Tripoli	
05/	br	UNISON	Galloway	SS		/	-T	*Stromboli*								4
06/	br	UNRUFFLED	Stevens	SS		/	-T	*Palermo*								4
06/	br	UTMOST	Coombe	SS		/	-T	*S Messina*								4
07/0923	br	UNRUFFLED	Stevens	CL	3500	=	-T	*38°14N/12°41E*	07/0935	it	CL	*Attilio Regolo*	3686	=	*3m SW C. San Vito*	5
08/1549	br	UNITED	Roxburgh	DD		=	-T	*38°15N/12°47E*	08/	it	CL	*(Attilio Regolo)*	–	/		5
08/	br	TAKU	Pitt	AR		/	-T	*Aegean*								6
09/1544	br	SARACEN	Lumby	SS		+	3-T	*38°34N/12°09E*	09/1500	it	SS	*Granito*	630	+		7
10/0625	br	UNA	Norman, C. P.	CL/ DD		=	-T	*37°13N/15°37E*								8
10/0627	br	UTMOST	Coombe	CL		=	-T	*37°16N/15°31E*								8
10/0627	br	UTMOST	Coombe	DD		=	"	*37°16N/15°31E*								8
10/	br	UNA	Norman, C. P.	SS		/	-T	*S Messina*								
11/	br	URSULA	Lakin	SS	500	/	TA	*36°42N/01°46W*	11/	dt	SS	(U73/U561)	–	/		9

(1) *Taku* missed *Arca* on 25.10.42 but sank her on the following morning.

(2) *Tergestea* was sunk by an airborne torpedo.

(3) *Taku* hit a caique on 27.10.42; it was repaired.

(4) *P43/Unison*, *P46/Unruffled* and *Utmost* each missed a U-boat.

(5) *P46/Unruffled* damaged the light cruiser at the bow; *P44/United* missed in an attack on the tow of the damaged cruiser but assumed she scored one hit on an escorting destroyer.

(6) *Taku* missed a naval auxiliary.

(7) *Saracen* was numbered *P247*.

(8) *Una* missed a force of three cruisers and six destroyers at long range; two minutes later *Utmost* missed the same force.

(9) *Ursula* missed *U73* and *U561* and later tried unsuccessfully to attack with gunfire.

1	2	3	4	5	6	7	8	9	10	11	12	13	14	15	16	17

NOVEMBER 1942 *continued*

1	2	3	4	5	6	7	8	9	10	11	12	13	14	15	16	17
11/1627	br	TURBULENT	Linton	-D	4000	+	1-T	39°10N/09°39E	11/	it	-M	Bengasi/*St Philippe/*Almenia	1554	+	32m S Cagliari	
12/	br	UMBRA	Maydon	*BB*		/	-T	*N Messina*								*1*
13/1330	br	SAFARI	Bryant	-S	400	+	A	3m Sousa	13/1400	it	-M	Bice	269	+	3m E Sousa	
13/1655	br	PARTHIAN	St John	-D	4000	+	4-T	N Marettimo	13/	it	-D	(Sivigliano/1270)	–	/	NW Sicily	
13/	br	P48 (?)	Faber				-T		13/1700	it	-D	(Sivigliano/1270)	–	/	Palermo–Bizerta	2
14/	br	P48 (?)	Faber				-T		14/0930	it	-D	(Sivigliano/1270)	–	/	Palermo–Bizerta	2
14/2000	br	SAHIB	Bromage	-D	2019	+	TA	E Tunisia	14/1947	it	-D	Scillin	1579	+	9m Kuriat	3
16/	br	PARTHIAN	St John	-D	10000	=	-T	5m NW Marettimo								
16/							-T		16/0915	it	-DT	(Labor/510, Menes)	–	/	Cape Bon	
16/							-T		16/1000	it	-M	(Narenta, Lago Zuai)	–	/	Cani Island	
16/1600	br	SPLENDID	McGeogh	APC	300	+	AT	43°34N/09°37E	16/1610	it	APC	V-277/San Paolo	209	+	35m SW Spezia	4
16/	br	SPLENDID	McGeogh	*SS*		/	-T	*Naples–Genoa*								5
16/							-T		16/1720	it	-D	(Campania/Rhea)	–	/	Bizerta–Napoli	
16/2220	br	SAFARI	Bryant	-D	2500	+	1-T	30°28N/18°48E	16/2220	dt	-D	Hans Arp	2645	+	Ras el Hilal	
16/	br	SHAKESPEARE	Ainslie	-D	5000	+	2-T	Off Bizerte	16/	dt	-D					6
16/2255	br	UNISON	Halliday	-T	4000	=	-T	N Marettimo	../	it	-T	Abruzzi (?)	680	+	Tripoli–Trapan	7
16/1637	gr	TRITON	Kontoyannis	-D	9000	+	-T	Off Andros	16/	it	-DT	(Celeno/Alba Julia)	–	/		8
17/0800	br	SAFARI	Bryant	LC		+	1-T	Ras Ali	17/	dt	LC	F346	155	+	*Cape Misurata*	9
17/1317	br	UMBRA	Maydon	-D	6000	+	-T	38°21N/15°28E	17/1320	it	-D	Piemonte	15209	=§	N Sicily	10
17/							-T		17/0730	it	-M	(Città di Napoli)	–	/	Cape San Vito	
17/2025	br	SAFARI	Bryant	-S	200		TA	El Brega								9

(1) *P35/Umbra* missed a force of three *Littorio* class battleships.

(2) *P48* returned from her patrol with all torpedoes expended but with no hits.

(3) *Scillin* was transporting 810 British prisoners and 200 Italian troops, of whom 24 and 36 respectively were rescued by the submarine.

(4) The vessel was boarded and documents were seized.

(5) *Splendid* missed two U-boats on 16 and 20.11.42.

(6) *P221/Shakespeare* reported a German transport sunk.

(7) *Abruzzi* was reported missing after leaving Tripoli on 15.11.42; she may have been the victim of *P43/Unison*.

(8) The Greek *Triton* was sunk when attacking a convoy by the German auxiliary *UJ2102* and the destroyer *Hermes*.

(9) *P228/Safari* first fired a torpedo into a landing craft and observed an explosion, then in the evening fired at a schooner, but in this instance the torpedo possibly detonated on the sea bed.

(10) *Piemonte* was beached and salvaged soon afterwards, but she was scuttled when Messina was evacuated.

1	2	3	4	5	6	7	8	9	10	11	12	13	14	15	16	17
NOVEMBER 1942 *continued*																
18/							-T		18/1400	it	-M	(Convoy 2 ships)	–	/	30m Cape San Vito	
18/	br	SAFARI	Bryant	AX		+	A	Ras Ali								1
18/0910	br	SAFARI	Bryant	*LC*		=	A	*10m Ras Ali*								
18/2200	br	PORPOISE	Bennington	-T	10000	+	-T	32°58N/15°38E	19/2140	it	-MT	Giulio Giordani	10534	+	32°58N/15°38E	2
20/	br	SPLENDID	McGeogh	*SS*		/	-T	*Naples–Genoa*								3
20/	br	SAFARI	Bryant	-D		+	-T	Ras Ali/Sirte								4
21/1504	br	SPLENDID	McGeogh	*DD*		=	-T	*40°30N/13°33E*	21/1535	it	DD	Velite	1820	=	*18m SW Ischia*	
21/	br	UNITED	Roxburgh	-S	200	+	A	Buerat Anchorage								
21/1745	br	UNITED	Roxburgh	-S	1000	+	A	Buerat Anchorage	21/	it	-S	Lottoria	...	=	Buerat Anchorage	
22/	br	SAFARI	Bryant	*LC*		+	-T	*Ras Sultan*								4
22/							-T		22/1425	it	-M	(Aspromonte/976)	–	/	Reggio–Bizerta	
22/	br	UNITED	Roxburgh	*SS*		/	-T	*Buerat*								5
23/0544	br	UNITED	Roxburgh	*LC*		=	A	*Buerat area*								6
23/	br	UNRUFFLED	Stevens	*SS*		/	-T	*Buerat*	23/0745	it	SS	(Sciesa)	–	/	*1m Buerat*	5
23/0916	br	PORPOISE	Bennington	AO	739	+	A	Kerkennah	23/1000	it	-D	Fertilia/*Giacoma	739	+	B.7 Kerkennah	
23/1213	br	UTMOST	Coombe	-D	5000	+?	-T	38°31N/12°01E	23/1220	it	AG	(Barletta/223)	–	/	Bizerta–Tunis	8
23/1331	br	SPLENDID	McGeogh	-D	1750	+	A	100m E Cagliar	22/	it	-D	Luigi Favorita	3576	+	W Mediterranean	7
24/	Aerial torpedo								[24/2250	it	-D	Luigi/4283+]	–		40°02N/17°20E	9
25/							-T		25/1200	it	-D	(Convoy 5 ships)	–	/	Aegad. Islands	
25/							-T		25/1350	it	-D	(Convoy 5 ships)	–	/	Aegad. Islands	
27/0047	br	UNA	Norman, C. P.	-D	4000	+	2-T	37°34N/10°33E	27/	dt	-D	(Menes/5609)	–	/		
28/	br	URSULA	Lakin	-D		/	-T	Toulon–Genoa								10
28/	Probably mine								[28/	it	-D	Città di Napoli/ 5418+]			38°13N/12°20E	11

(1) *P211/Safari* sank an unmanned lightship.

(2) The tanker *Giulio Giordani* had been damaged two days previously in an air attack and was on fire, although the blaze had been extinguished when *Porpoise* attacked. The ship was hit by one and then two torpedoes.

(3) *P228/Splendid* missed a U-boat.

(4) *P211/Safari* reported missing a big landing craft with a torpedo and the next day fought a surface action with a Siebel ferry.

(5) *P46/Unruffled* and *P44/United* each missed an Italian supply submarine.

(6) *P44/United* reported a AA barge damaged.

(7) *Luigi Favorita* had been previously damaged by Wellington aircraft.

(8) *Utmost* was lost on 24.11.42.

(9) *Luigi*, sometimes cited as having been sunk by the British submarine *Taurus*, in fact succumbed to an aerial torpedo.

(10) *Ursula* made a several attacks, but the torpedoes ran deep in heavy seas.

(11) *Città di Napoli* probably sank on a mine.

1	2	3	4	5	6	7	8	9	10	11	12	13	14	15	16	17

NOVEMBER 1942 *continued*

1	2	3	4	5	6	7	8	9	10	11	12	13	14	15	16	17
29/2210	br	SERAPH	Jewell	-D	2000	+	4-T	30m W Marettimo	29/	it	-D	(Città di Tunisi)	–	/		
29/2210	br	SERAPH	Jewell	-D		=	"	30m W Marettimo								
29/2210	br	SERAPH	Jewell	-D		=	"	30m W Marettimo								
29/2210	br	SERAPH	Jewell	-D		=	"	30m W Marettimo								

DECEMBER 1942

1	2	3	4	5	6	7	8	9	10	11	12	13	14	15	16	17
01/							-T		[01/0045	it	-M	Tabarca/616+]			W S. di Vado	1
01/2345	gr	PAPANIKOLIS	Roussen	-D	8000	+	4-T	36°15N/27°44E								2
01/	br	URSULA	Lakin	APC	100	+	S	15m S Mele	01/0015	it	APC	V-135/Togo	108	+	13m SE C. Mele	3
									[01/0930	it	AH	Città di Trapani/ 2467+]			11m E Cani	4
02/	br	SERAPH	Jewell	-D	1500	=	4-T	5m Skerki	02/1500	it	-D	Puccini	2422	=	Skerki Bank	5
02/1500	br	UMBRA	Maydon	-D	1100	+	A	35°28N/11°20E	02/1845	it	-D	Sacro Cuore	1097	+	35°27N/11°22E	
02/1800	br	URSULA	Lakin	-D	1854	+	TAS	N Corsica	03/	dt	-D	Saint Marguerite II	1855	+	San Remo	6
03/0830	br	UNRIVALLED	Sprice	-S	75	=	A	37°09N/10°29E								
03/	br	UNRIVALLED	Sprice	TB		=	-T	37°16N/10°22E	03/	it	TB	*Antonio Mosto*	649	=	*Off Tunisia*	7
04/	br	P48	Faber	-D		/	-T	N Tunis	04/0930	dt	-M	(Ankara)	–	/	N Cape Bon	8
04/0930	br	SERAPH	Jewell	-D	5300	/	4-T	37°59N/11°35E	04/1715	dt	-D	(Convoy, Ankara)	–	/	Marettimo	9
05/1515	br	SIBYL	Turner, H. B.	-D	5000	=	4-T	40°23N/14°01E	05/1520	it	-D	(Honestas, Sant' Antioco)	–	/	40°26N/14°06E	10
05/1515	br	SIBYL	Turner, H. B.	-D	5000	=	4-T	40°23N/14°01E								10
06/0146	br	TIGRIS	Colvin	SS	600	+	-T	38°10N/08°35E	06/0156	it	SS	*Porfido*	629	+	*80m NNE Bône*	11

(1) *Tabarca* sank either on a mine or as a result of a marine accident.

(2) *Papanikolis* reported a large steamer torpedoed and sunk in Alimnia Bay.

(3) *Ursula*, with gunfire, forced the A/S vessel *Togo* to beach herself and destroyed the ship with demolition charges after recovering confidential materials.

(4) Although the loss was attributed to *P45/Unrivalled*, *Città di Trapani* must have been sunk on a mine. *Rorqual* only laid mines on 8.12.42. The German steamer *Menes*/5609 on 3.12.42 and the German hospital ship *Graz*/1870 (ex *Ares*) on 5.12.42 must similarly have been lost to mines.

(5) *Seraph* was numbered P219. *Puccini* and the escorting destroyer *Folgore*, sometimes claimed as having been hit by submarine torpedoes, were in fact sunk later that day by surface forces.

(6) *Ursula* sank the ship by torpedo, gunfire and demolition charges.

(7) *P45/Unrivalled* hit the torpedo boat with a torpedo which failed to explode, although the vessel was slightly damaged at the stern.

(8) *P48* reported attacks and returned with all torpedoes expended but had scored no hits.

(9) The attack was probably that reported by *Ankara*.

(10) *P217/Sibyl* claimed one ship sunk and one probably sunk. *Honestas*/4959 and *Sant' Antioco*/5048 were missed.

(11) At the same time *P222* was sunk by the Italian torpedo boat *Fortunale* nearby.

1	2	3	4	5	6	7	8	9	10	11	12	13	14	15	16	17
DECEMBER 1942 *continued*																
07/	br	URSULA	Lakin	APC		+	A	15m S Cape Mele	07/	it	APC	V135/Togo	1C'3	+	Riviera	
08/	br	RORQUAL	Napier				M	Cani Rocks	21.12.M	it	APM	AS-99/Zuri	...	+	La Golette	1
09/0930	br	UMBRA	Maydon	-D	2000	+	-T	36°14N/10°32E	09/1100	dt	-D	Süllberg	1663	+	2m Hammamet	2
10/	br	UMBRA (?)	Maydon	-D	2000	=?	-T	Tunisian coast								2
13/1442	br	UMBRA	Maydon	-D	2875	=	-T	35°54N/10°39E	13/1530	dt	-D	Makedonia	2875	=	1.5m N Sousa	3
14/1114	br	SPLENDID	McGeogh	-D	6000	=	4-T	37°45N/10°39E	14/	it	-D	(Honestas/Castelv)	–	/	N Cap Bon	4
14/1123	br	TAKU	Pitt	-D	5000	+	1-T	37°52N/24°06E	14/1110	it	-D	Delfin	5322	+	4m N Makrosini	
14/	br	TAKU	Pitt	-S		+	A	Aegean								
14/1600	br	SAHIB	Bromage	-D	6000	+	1-T	37°29N/10°46E	14/1400	it	-D	Honestas	4960	+	27m NNW C. Bon	4
14/1600	br	SAHIB	Bromage	-D		+	1-T	37°29N/10°46E								4
14/1623	br	UNRUFFLED	Stevens, J. S.	-D	6000	+	2-T	37°29N/10°46E	14/1430	it	-D	Castelverde	6666	+	27m NNW C. Bon	4
15/1330	br	UNRUFFLED	Stevens, J. S.	-D	4000	+	2-T	37°32N/10°39E	15/1333	it	-D	Sant' Antioco	5050	+	37°37N/10°44E 5	
16/	br	UNSHAKEN (?)	Whitton	?		?	2-T		16/1730	it	-D	(Convoy 2 ships)	–	/	40m N Cape Bon	5
17/	br	RORQUAL	Napier				M	40°46N/13°56E								
17/1111	br	SPLENDID	McGeogh	-D	6000	+	4-T	37°53N/10°05E	17/1115	dt	D	(Ankara)	–	/	38°00N/10°05E	6
17/1111	br	SPLENDID	McGeogh	*DD*		=	"	*37°53N/10°05E*	*17/1115*	*it*	*DD*	*Aviere*	*1620*	*+*	*38°00N/10°05E1*	6
17/1220	br	SARACEN	Lumby	*DD*		=	4-T	*N Bizerta*	*17/1230*	*it*	*DD*	(Camicia Nera)	–	/	*N Cape Blanc*	6
17/1220	br	SARACEN	Lumby	APC	3600	/	"	N Bizerta	17/	dt	-D	(Ankara)	–	/	N Cape Blanc	6
17/	br	P41		-D		+	-T	N Bizerta	17/1230	dt	-M	(Ankara)	–	/	Cape Bon	
17/	br	P41		-D		=	-T	N Bizerta								
18/	br	SAFARI	Bryant	-S	150	+	A	2m S Hammamet	18/1500	it	-S	Eufrasia	49	+	Gulf of Hammamet	
18/even.	br	RORQUAL	Napier	-D	2500	=	4-T	40°53N/13°39E	18/	it	-M	Pietro Foscari	3423	=	SW Gaeta	7
20/	br	UNA	Martin	-D		/	4-T	Kerkennah								8

(1) See Note 5 on previous page.

(2) *Süllberg* exploded. The attack on 10.12.42 is uncertain: it was perhaps made by another submarine.

(3) *Makedonia* was again attacked by FAA aircraft during the night of 14/15.12.42 and became a total loss.

(4) *P228/Splendid* claimed one hit but *Honestas*/4959grt and *Castelverde*/6666grt were later seen being escorted by the torpedo boats *Ardito* and *Fortunale*. *Honestas* was then sunk by *P212/Sahib* while *P46/Unruffled* closed to sink *Castelverde*. *Sant' Antioco,* which did not belong to this convoy, was sunk the next day by *P46/Unruffled*, which was heavily depth-charged by the torpedo boat *Orione*.

(5) *P54/Unshaken* made several unsuccessful attacks, expending all her torpedoes.

(6) *P228/Splendid* was thought to have hit the transport and the destroyer with two torpedoes each but *Ankara* and the escorting destroyer *Camicia Nera* were missed and *Aviere*, repaired after the damage from *Sokol* on 19.11.41 (q.v.), was sunk. *P247/Saracen* attacked the remaining ships from the convoy attacked by *Splendid* and claimed the remaining destroyer damaged, but *Camicia Nera* and *Ankara* evaded the torpedoes.

(7) The Italians assumed that *Pietro Foscari* had struck a mine (see *Rorqual*, 17.12.42), but the ship was more probably hit by a torpedo from *Rorqual*. She was towed into port but was scuttled by the Germans in Genoa in 4.45.

(8) *Una* missed a small steamer with four torpedoes.

1	2	3	4	5	6	7	8	9	10	11	12	13	14	15	16	17
DECEMBER 1942 *continued*																
20/	br	SAHIB	Bromage	-T		=	TA	Cape Bon								1
20/night	br	UNSHAKEN	Whitton	-D	4000	/	A	Off Genoa	20/	fr	-D	(Oasis/1327)	–	/	S coast France	2
20/	br	SAFARI	Bryant	-T	400	+	-T	36°04N/10°30E	20/	it	-D	Constantina	345	=	Sousa	
20/	br	SPLENDID	McGeogh	SS		/	-T	N Bizerta								3
21/1900	br	SAFARI	Bryant	APM	300	+	TA	5m S Hammamet	21/1930	it	APM	Rosina S.	297	+	Trapani–Tripoli	
22/1500	br	TAKU	Pitt	-S	150	+	A	40°13N/23°19E	22/	gr	-S	Niki	150	+	Potidea Channel	4
22/							-T		22/0229	it	-D	(Etruria/2633)	–	/	Marettimo	
23/0820	br	TAKU	Pitt	-S	250	+	A	Port Kumi	23/	gr	-S	Aghios Nikolaos	30	=	Port Kumi	4
23/0820	br	TAKU	Pitt	-S		=	A	Port Kumi	23/	gr	-S	Evangelista	...	=	Port Kumi	4
23/2052	br	SERAPH	Jewell	SS		=	R	57°17N/08°27E	24/	it	SS	(Alagi)	–	/	N Tunisia	5
24/	br	UNSEEN (?)	Crawford				-T		24/1000	it	-M	(Viminale/8657)	–	/	Cape Bon	6
25/	br	UNRIVALLED	Turner, H. B.	-S		/	A	Kerkennah								7
25/	br	SERAPH	Jewell	SS		=?	3-T	Galita I.	25/	it	SS	(Alagi)	–	/		5
25/	br	UNSEEN (?)	Crawford				-T		25/1200	it	-D	(Convoy 2 ships)	–	/	N Tunis	6
26/1300	br	UNBROKEN	Mars	-D	5000	?	-T	40°41N/13°46E	26/	dt	ACM	Westmark/*Djebel Dira	2835	=	Naples	
26/1510	br	UNRIVALLED	Turner, H. B.	-S	450	+	A	35°32N/11°05E	26/1400	it	APM	O-97/Margherita	69	+	4m N Mehedia	
27/0732	br	SAFARI	Bryant	-S	200	+	A	5m E Zuara	27/0700	it	-S	Eleonora Rosa	54	+	10m S Sousa	
28/0600	br	URSULA	Lakin	-D	6000	+	1-T	38°09N/11°54E	28/0600	dt	-D	Gran/*St Odette	4140	+	12m N Marettimo	
29/0950	br	SAFARI	Bryant	-D	1500	+	3-T	34°20N/10°54E	29/0900	it	-D	Torquato Gennari	1012	+	34°20N/10°49E	
29/	br	UNRIVALLED	Turner, H. B.	-D		/	-T	Mahedia								8
29/1754	br	TURBULENT	Linton	-D	4500	+	1-T	39°17N/09°41E	29/1655	it	-D	Marte	5290	+	2m E Cape Ferrato	
30/	br	URSULA	Lakin	-D		/	-T	Cape San Vito								9
31/0617	br	UNRIVALLED	Turner, H. B.	-D	345	+	1-T	35°18N/11°23E	31/0517	it	-D	Maddalena	345	+	S Mehedia	

(1) *P212/Sahib* missed a small coaster with torpedoes and had to break off a gun attack because of approaching aircraft.

(2) See Note 5 on previous page.

(3) *P228/Splendid* missed an Italian submarine.

(4) *Taku* set a caique ablaze with gunfire. Later, in a surface attack on the port of Kumi, hits were observed on caiques and a small merchant ship.

(5) *P219/Seraph* rammed a submerged U-boat, which was probably damaged as a result. In the second attack the impact of a dud was heard.

(6) *P51/Unseen* reported two unsuccessful attacks against convoys.

(7) *P45/Unrivalled* had to break off a surface attack on a schooner because of accurate machine-gun fire.

(8) *P45/Unrivalled* fired a salvo at a southbound ship but missed.

(9) *Ursula* overestimated the distance and was rammed by one of the ships in the convoy she was attacking.

1	2	3	4	5	6	7	8	9	10	11	12	13	14	15	16	17

JANUARY 1943

1	2	3	4	5	6	7	8	9	10	11	12	13	14	15	16	17
03/	br	Chariot XXII	Greenland	CL		+	Ch	Palermo	03/0800	it	-CL	Ulpio Traiano	3362	+	Palermo harbour	1
03/	br	Chariot XVI	Dove	-D		?	Ch	Palermo	03/	it	-D	Viminale	8657	=	Palermo harbour	1
09/1637	br	UMBRA	Maydon	-T	10000	+	1TA	Tunisia	09/1425	nw	-MT	Thorsheimer	9955	=	50m SW Marsala	2
09/2003	br	UMBRA	Maydon	-D	2000	+	3-T	35°57N/11°09E	09/2010	it	-D	Emilio Morandi	1523	+	35°59N/11°22E	3
10/							-T		10/1715	it	-DT	(Saturno/*Massis)	–	/	W Palermo	
10/0700	br	TRIBUNE	Porter	-D	6000	=	2-T	15m San Remo	10/	fr	-D	Dalny	6672	=	San Remo	4
11/0920	br	TURBULENT	Linton	-D	2500	+	TA	39°31N/15°54E	11/1000	it	-M	Vittoria Beraldo	547	+	Cattaro Roads	
11/	br	UMBRA	Maydon	-D		/	1-T	Tunisia								5
11/1702	br	UMBRA	Maydon	-S	100	§	A	36°24N/10°33E	11/1645	it	-M	Nuovo Domenico I.	25	=	Gulf of Hammamet	5
11/1702	br	UMBRA	Maydon	-S	100	§	A	36°24N/10°33E	11/	it	-S	Concetta Falco	152	/		5
11/							-T		11/1110	it	-M	(Convoy 3 ships)	–	/	N Bizerta	
11/	br	SAHIB	Bromage	-D		+	-T	Liguria	11/	fr	-D	San Antonio	6013	+	Liguria	
11/	br	TRIBUNE	(?)	-D		+	-T	50m S Liguria	11/	fr	-D	Dalny	6672	=	C. Cervo, Genova	4
12/	br	UNSHAKEN	Whitton	-T		/	-T	NW Marettimo	12/	it	-T	(Campania/5247)	–	/		
12/	br	UMBRA	Maydon	LC	110	/	1-T	Tunisia								6
14/1305	br	SAHIB	Bromage	-D	2000	+	-T	44°08N/08°18E								
14	br	UMBRA	Maydon	-D		/	A	Tunisia	14/	it	-D	(Pistoia/2448)	–	/	Tunisia	7
15/	gr	PAPANIKOLIS	Roussen	-S		P	P	Milo								8
15/1915	br	SPLENDID	McGeogh	-D	6000	+	1-T	40°37N/13°47E	15/1940	it	-M	Emma	7983	+	40°25N/13°56E	9
16/	br	UNRIVALLED	(?)				A		16/1630	it	-Tg	Genova	91	+	Sousa	

(1) *Chariot XXII* was transported and launched by *Thunderbolt* (Crouch). *Ulpio Traiano* was blown into two; she was under salvage when the evacuation started and was scuttled. The limpet mines attached to the destroyers *Grecale* and *Ciclone* were defused before exploding. *Chariot XVI* was launched by *Trooper* (Wraith). *Viminale* was further damaged while being transferred to Taranto by *P37/ Unbending* on 23.1.43.(q.v.)

(2) *Umbra* is thought to have missed the tanker with one torpedo but then engaged with gunfire. She was sunk by aircraft 20m south-west of Marettimo on 21.2.43.

(3) *Umbra* first missed with two torpedoes and later sank the ship with one more torpedo.

(4) *Tribune* torpedoed *Dalny* on 10.1.43 and the steamer was beached. On 11.1.43 *Tribune* torpedoed the ship again. She was finally destroyed on 4.6.43 by the French submarine *Aréthuse* (q.v.).

(5) *Umbra* missed an escorted ship. She hit two sailing vessels, which were driven ashore; these may have been *Littoria* and *Anna Madre* but were more probably the two vessels cited. The first was only damaged; the second arrived at Bizerta on 23.1.43.

(6) *Umbra* fired one torpedo against a Siebel ferry, but the torpedo ran under the ship.

(7) *Umbra* attacked a ship with gunfire but had to break off because the target answered in kind. It proved to be the Italian steamer *Pistoia*/2448 (ex French *Oued Tiflet*), sunk on 24.1.43 by aerial torpedo.

(8) *Papanikolis* stopped a caique and put a prize crew aboard who took the vessel to Alexandria.

(9) *Splendid* first torpedoed and damaged *Emma*, then missed her, but finished her off at 0835 on 16.1.43.

1	2	3	4	5	6	7	8	9	10	11	12	13	14	15	16	17

JANUARY 1943 *continued*

1	2	3	4	5	6	7	8	9	10	11	12	13	14	15	16	17
17/	br	RORQUAL	Napier				M	Gulf of Tunis	18.01.M	dt	-M	Ankara	4768	+	5m NE Cani I.	
									[22.01.	dt	-D	Ruhr/5955+]			30m NW C. Bon	1
									[30.01.	it	-D	Parma/*Villiers/ 2448+]			Off Tunis	1
									31.01.M	*it*	*TB*	*Prestinari*	*635*	*+*	*18m SE Cani*	
									31.01.M	*it*	*PE*	*Procellaria*	*660*	*+*	*37°20N/10°37E*	
									03.02.M	*it*	*DD*	*Saetta*	*1205*	*+*	*37°35N/10°37E*	
									03.02.M	*it*	*TB*	*Uragano*	*910*	*+*	*37°35N/10°37E*	
17/0845	gr	PAPANIKOLIS	Roussen	-S	220	+	P	3m E Cape Malea	17/	gr	-S	Aghios Stefanos	220	+	Cape Malea	2
17/1006	br	UNSEEN	Crawford	-D	2000	+	3-T	33°51N/11°08E	17/0905	it	-D	Zenobia Martini	1454	+	33°56N/11°06E	
17/1555	br	UNRIVALLED	Turner, H. B.	-Tg	150	+	A	Off Sousa	17/	it	-Tg	Genova No 17	96	=	Off Sousa	3
17/	br	UNITED ?					4-T		17/1700	it	-M	(Ines Corrado/5159)	–	/	Bizerta–Palermo	
17/1727	br	UNITED	Roxburgh	-D	7000	=	-T	38°04N/11°49E	*17/1725*	*it*	*DD*	*Bombardiere*	*1820*	*+*	*38°15N/11°43E*	4
17/							-T		17/2030	it	-D	(Convoy 3 ships)	–	/	Marettimo	
18/1110	br	UNSEEN	Crawford	-D	2000	+	3-T	32°58N/12°10E	18/1020	it	-D	Sportivo	1598	+	33°00N/12°08E	5
18/1430	gr	PAPANIKOLIS	Roussen	-S	100	+	A	25m N Iraklion	18/	gr	-S	Aghios Paraskevi	100	+	N Iraklion	
18/	gr	PAPANIKOLIS	Roussen	-S		+	A	25m N Iraklion								
18/	br	UNSEEN	Crawford	-D		/	-T									5
19/	br	Chariot XIII	Stevens. H. L. H.	-D		=	Ch		19/	it	-D	Giulia	5921	=	Tripoli	6

(1) The German steamer *Ruhr*/5955 and Italian steamer *Parma* (ex *Villiers*), sometimes credited, were in fact sunk by bombs and aerial torpedoes.

(2) *Papanikolis* put a prize crew aboard the caique.

(3) *Genova* beached herself and coastal batteries drove the submarine off.

(4) *United* attacked an escorted merchant ship but hit and sank the destroyer *Bombardiere*.

(5) *Unseen* missed one other ship after the attack on *Sportivo* later that day.

(6) *Chariot XII* or *XIII* was launched by *Thunderbolt* (Crouch), but the principal target, *San Giovanni Batista*, was scuttled just before the attack; *Giulia*, which could not be used as a blockship, was selected instead.

1	2	3	4	5	6	7	8	9	10	11	12	13	14	15	16	17

JANUARY 1943 *continued*

1	2	3	4	5	6	7	8	9	10	11	12	13	14	15	16	17
									[18/	dt	-D	Favor/1323+]	–		15m S Carbonara	1
19/1415	br	SPLENDID	McGeogh	-D	2000	+	-T	39°41N/09°43E	19/1510	it	-D	Commercio	766	+	T. San Giovanni	
19/1415	br	SPLENDID	McGeogh	-D	200	=	A	39°41N/09°43E	19/	it	-D	Violetta	...	?		
19/1415	br	SPLENDID	McGeogh	-S	200	+	A	39°41N/09°43E	19/1415	it	APM	No 107/Cleopatra	72	+	Sardinia	
19/1415	br	SPLENDID	McGeogh	-Tg	400	§	TA	39°41N/09°43E	19/							
19/	br	UNRIVALLED	Turner, H. B.	-D		=	A	Sousse								2
19/1749	br	UNBROKEN	Mars	-D	5000	+	1-T	33°33N/11°20E	19/1745	it	-D	Edda	6107	+	33°45N/11°12E	
20/0315	br	SARACEN	Lumby	-S	200	+	AS	40°14N/14°10E	20/0345	it	APC	V-3/Maria Angeletta	214	+	30m S Capri	
20/1633	br	UNRIVALLED	Turner, H. B.	APM	1500	+	2-T	Mehedia	20/1440	dt	-Df	Grondin	1500	+	L. Mehedia	3
20/1633	br	UNRIVALLED	Turner, H. B.	APM	500	+	"	Mehedia	20/	it	APM	No. 31, No. 36	150	+		3
21/1016	br	UNRIVALLED	Turner, H. B.	-S	140	+	A	5m NE Kuriat	21/1100	it	-S	Margherita	140	+	5m NE Kuriat	3
21/1016	br	UNRIVALLED	Turner, H. B.	-M	200	+	S	5m NE Kuriat	21/1100	it	-M	Ardito	120	+	5m NE Kuriat	3
21/1413	br	TIGRIS	Colvin	-D	4000	+	5-T	40°32N/18°45E	21/1315	it	-M	Città di Genova	5413	+	25m W Saseno	4
21/	br	SAHIB	Bromage	SS		+	-T	41°27N/07°04E	21/	dt	SS	U301	769	+		
22/1050	br	UNRIVALLED	Turner, H. B.	-S	500	=?	A	Kuriat								
22/	br	UNRIVALLED	Turner, H. B.	-S	500		3-T	Tunisian coast								
23/0820	br	UNBENDING	Stanley	-Tg	337	+	-T	37°53N/15°43E	23/	it	-Tg	Luni	337	+	37°52N/15°45E	5
23/0820	br	UNBENDING	Stanley	-D	8500	=	4-T	37°53N/15°43E	23/	it	-M	Viminale	8657	=	38°24N/15°50E	5
23/1054	br	UNRUFFLED	Stevens, J. S.	-S	200	+	TA	4m S Hammamet	23/1030	it	-S	Amabile Carolina	39	+	4m S Hammamet	
23/	br	UNRIVALLED	Turner, H. B.	-D	50	=	A	4m E Sousa	23/1030	it	APM	B.847/Michelino	37	=	4m E Susa	6
23/	br	UNRIVALLED	Turner, H. B.	AG		/	2-T	Sousse								6

(1) The German steamer *Favor*/1323 (ex French *Ste Roseline*) was sunk at 0045 on 18.1.43 15m south of Carbonara by the destroyer *Loyal*.

(2) *Unrivalled* had to break off the attack because of damage to her gun.

(3) *Unrivalled* torpedoed and sank a naval auxiliary with another vessel in tow; the latter beached herself. According to Italian sources, the auxiliary minesweepers *No 31* and *No 36* were lost. *Unrivalled* then attacked two schooners: the larger was sunk and the other set on fire.

(4) *Tigris* first fired four torpedoes, one of which hit, then the ship was finished with a fifth torpedo. There were Greek POWs aboard, 173 of whom were lost.

(5) *Viminale* was damaged by *Chariot XVI* in Palermo harbour on 3.1.43 (q.v.) and was towed to Naples, being attacked while under tow. The submarine was heavily depth-charged by the Italian torpedo boat *Perseo*.

(6) *Michelino* had to be left because of fire from coastal batteries. Later that day a small naval auxiliary was missed with two torpedoes.

1	2	3	4	5	6	7	8	9	10	11	12	13	14	15	16	17
JANUARY 1943 *continued*																
24/	br	TIGRIS	Colvin	-D	2500	/	4-T	Kotor								1
24/	br	RORQUAL	Napier	-D		/	-T	Cape Stilo								
24/	br	UNRIVALLED	Turner, H. B.	-S		+	Sp	Sousa	23/1530	it	-S	Michelino	37	=	4m E Sousa	2
24/	br	TROOPER	Webb	-D		/	-T	Anti-Paxos								3
25/	br	UNRUFFLED	Stevens, J. S.	-S	200	+	A	G. of Hammamet								
25/1403	br	UNRUFFLED	Stevens, J. S.	-T	500	+	-T	Hammamet	25/1300	it	-DT	Teodolinda	361	+	Hammamet Roads	
26/0422	br	UNRUFFLED	Stevens, J. S.	-S	1000	+	A	4m Hammamet	26/0315	it	-M	Redentore/Z-90	46	=§	4m E Hammamet	
26/	br	UNRIVALLED	Turner, H. B.	-S	200	+	A	Off Zuara								
26/	br	SAFARI	Bryant	-D		/	-T	Naples								4
27/0855	br	TURBULENT	Linton	-D	3000	=	4-T	37°46N/11°14E 27/		it	-D	(Noto/3168)	–	/		5
28/	br	UNRUFFLED	Stevens, J. S.	-S		+	A	G. of Hammamet								
29/	br	RORQUAL	Napier	-D		/	-T	Gulf of Squillace								6
30/0944	br	SAFARI	Bryant	-S	200	+	A	39°56N/15°41E	30/	it	-M	Aniello	77	+	Cape Scalea	
30/0944	br	SAFARI	Bryant	-Mf	100	+	A	39°56N/15°41E	30/0955	it	-M	Gemma	67	+	Cape Scalea	
31/1602	br	UNRUFFLED	Stevens, J. S.	-D	2000	+	1-T	3m N Sousa	31/1508	dt	-D	Lisboa	1799	+	5m N Sousa	7
31/	br	TURBULENT	Linton	-D		/	-T	NW Sicily								8
FEBRUARY 1943																
01/1210	br	UNA	Norman, C. P.	-S	250	=	A	36°26N/10°43E								9
01/1210	br	UNA	Norman, C. P.	-S	250	=	A	36°26N/10°43E	9							
01/1211	br	TURBULENT	Linton	-D	5000	+	2-T	38°13N/12°50E	01/	it	-D	Pozzuoli	5345	+	7m NE C. San Vito	
01/	br	TURBULENT	Linton	ACL		/	1-T	38°13N/12°50E	01/	it	ACL	(Ramb class/3667)	–	/		10

(1) *Tigris* fired four torpedoes at an escorted ship but missed.
(2) See Note 6 on previous page.
(3) *Trooper* missed an escorted merchant ship.
(4) *Safari* missed two large escorted steamers.
(5) *Turbulent* attacked two escorted ships with four torpedoes and damaged one of them.
(6) Following an unsuccessful attack on 24.1.43 there was another failure on 29.1.43, this time against two ships with an air escort.

(7) The Italian steamer *Vercelli*/3094 (ex French *Brestois*), sometimes credited to *Unruffled*, was in fact sunk on 30.1.43 by aircraft bombs.
(8) *Turbulent* had to go deep to avoid being rammed by ships in the convoy.
(9) *Una* attacked two large schooners and damaged both before being driven off by gunfire from the shore.
(10) After sinking *Pozzuoli*, *Turbulent* tried to hit an escorting *Ramb* class ACL with a stern torpedo, but this was avoided.

1	2	3	4	5	6	7	8	9	10	11	12	13	14	15	16	17
FEBRUARY 1943 *continued*																
02/							2-T		*02/0515*	*it*	*DD*	*(Mitragliere)*	–	/	*N Tunis*	
02/1438	br	SAFARI	Bryant	-T	2500	+	-T	40°35N/14°29E	02/1450	it	-D	Valsavoia	5733	+	8m E Capri	
02/1438	br	SAFARI	Bryant	-D	700	+	TA	40°35N/14°29E	02/1450	it	-D	Salemi/*Pontet Canet	1176	+	8m E Capri	
04/1733	br	UNSEEN	Crawford	-D	1500	+	2-T	39°16N/17°11E	04/1635	it	-D	Le Tre Marie Sorelle	1086	+	6m S Pt. Alice	1
05/0649	br	TURBULENT	Linton	-D	6000	+	4-T	Off Cefalù	05/0700	it	-T	Utilitas	5342	+	Off Palermo	
07/	br	TORBAY	Clutterbuck	-D		=	A	Spanish coast	*07/*	*sp*	*SS*	*(General Mola/779)*	–	/	*50m Cape Palos*	2
07/	br	UNISON	Daniell	-Bg		/	1-T	Hammamet								3
08/	br	UNISON	Daniell	-S		+	A	Hammamet	08/0930	it	-S	Luigi Verni	58	+	Hammamet	3
08/	br	UNISON	Daniell	-S		+	A	Hammamet	08/0930	it	-S	Carlo P.	64	+	Hammamet	3
08/	br	UNISON	Daniell	-S		+	A	Hammamet	08/0930	it	-S	Angela	56	+	Hammamet	3
08/0625	br	THUNDERBOLT	Crouch	-S	200	=	A	Off Brindisi	08/	it	-S	Maria Grazia Siliato	...	=	12m E Brindisi	
09/1027	br	UNBENDING	Stanley	-D	2500	+	-T	40°56N/17°36E	09/0945	it	-D	Eritrea	2517	+	5m E Monopoli	
09/1100	nl	DOLFIJN	Van Oostrom Soede	*SS*		+	-T	*38°42N/08°52E*	*08/1100*	*it*	*SS*	*Malachite*	*622*	+		
10/1530	br	UNBENDING	Stanley	-DP	1500	=§	2-T	41°57N/19°07E	10/	it	-D	Carlo Margottini/ *Bled	855	=	Adriatic	4
10/1551	br	UNA	Martin	-D	4000	+	1-T	38°52N/16°35E	10/1500	it	-D	Cosala/*Serafin Topic	4294	+	Cape Stilo	
10/	br	UNA	Martin				-T		10/0447	it	-D	Petrarca	3329	=	10m N Cotrone	5
10/	br	THUNDERBOLT	Crouch	-D	1500	/	2-T	Split								6

(1) The ship had been salvaged after being sunk by aircraft on 3.3.42.

(2) *Torbay* sighted a submarine with a steamer and attacked with gunfire. The gun jammed, however, and so the Spanish vessel was hit only once.

(3) *Unison* fired one torpedo which hit the bottom. The next day she attacked three barges with gunfire, sinking two and leaving the third in a sinking condition.

(4) *Unbending* fired two torpedoes which missed and then followed the ship into a bay, where two more torpedoes scored one hit and forced the ship to beach herself, to become a total loss.

(5) *Una* saw the stern of the ship resting on the bottom. She was finally sunk by *Una* on 15.2.43 (q.v.).

(6) *Thunderbolt* missed a ship.

1	2	3	4	5	6	7	8	9	10	11	12	13	14	15	16	17
FEBRUARY 1943 *continued*																
11/0931	br	THUNDERBOLT	Crouch	-D		/	5-T	Split								1
11/even.	br	TORBAY	Clutterbuck	-D	1600	+	-T	Off Sagunt	11/	d	-D	Grete	1563	+	Cape Oropesa	
11/1924	br	UNISON	Daniell	-D	400	+	A	36°26N/10°55E	11/	dt	-D	Lola/*Jaedoer	309	+	Hammamet	2
12/2030	br	SARACEN	Lumby	-Tg	150	+	A	6m S Sardinaux	12/1830	fr	-Tg	Provencale II	124	+	6m S C. Sardinaux	
12/2030	br	SARACEN	Lumby	-Tg	150	+	A	6m S Sardinaux	12/1830	fr	-Tg	Marseillaise V	138	+	6m S C. Sardinaux	
13/	br	THUNDERBOLT	Crouch	APM		+	A	Isola Lungha	13/0900	it	APM	No 112/Mafalda	44	+	3m W Pt Bianca	
14/1311	br	TROOPER	Wraith	-D	6000	=	4-T	39°06N/20°29E								3
15/	br	UNRIVALLED	Turner, H. B.	-Tg		/	3-T	Augusta								4
15/0840	br	SARACEN	Lumby	-T	12000	=?	4-T	Cape Noli/Liguria	15/0842	fr	-Dt	Marguerite Finaly	12309	=	Capo Vado	
15/0840	br	SARACEN	Lumby	LC		=	"	*Cape Noli/Liguria*	*15/0842*	*dt*	LC	*(F134)*	–	/	*Capo Vado*	
15/1745	br	UNA	Martin	-D	4000	+	-T	39°16N/17°08E	15/	it	-D	Petrarca	3329	+	S Pt Alice	5
16/	br	THUNDERBOLT	Crouch	-D		/	-T	Pola								6
16/0932	br	UNRIVALLED	Turner, H. B.	-S	1000	+	3-T	38°18N/16°26E	16/1000	it	-S	Sparviero	498	+	Roccela Ionica	
16/1215	br	UNRIVALLED	Turner, H. B.	-D	6000	=	1-T	38°18N/16°29E	16/1155	it	-D	Pasubio	2216	+	9m S Pt Stilo	
17/1903	br	SPLENDID	McGeogh	-D	5000	+	6-T	38°13N/12°43E	17/1853	it	-D	XXI Aprile	4787	+	3m N C. San Vito	7
17/1903	br	SPLENDID	McGeogh	-D	4000	+	"	38°13N/12°43E	17/1850	dt	-D	(Siena/*Astrée/2147)	–	/	3m N C. San Vito	
18/1130	br	SAHIB	Bromage	-S	150	+	A	38°09N/14°38E	18/1100	it	-S	Francesco Padre	22		19m W C. Orlando	
18/1130	br	SAHIB	Bromage	-S	150	+	A	38°09N/14°38E	18/1100	it	-S	S. Teresa/R.233	20	=	19m W C. Orlando	
18/1415	br	UNRUFFLED	Stevens, J. S.	-S	200	/	3-T	Naboul	18/	it	-S	L'Angelo Raffaelo	75	+	Sousa	8
18/1415	br	UNRUFFLED	Stevens, J. S.	-S	200	?	"	Naboul	18/	it	-S	Micolo lo Porto	80	+	Sousa	8
18/1620	br	THUNDERBOLT	Crouch	PE		=	TA	45°02N/13°35E	18/	it	AMC	San Giorgio	364	=	Off Pola	9

(1) *Thunderbolt* attacked a convoy of two ships with five torpedoes and missed. The Italian steamer *Totonno*/674, sometimes claimed, was in fact sunk on a mine off Smovica Island on 14.2.43.

(2) *Unison* engaged the ship with her gun and started fires; thirty minutes later the ship blew up.

(3) *Trooper* claimed only a possible hit.

(4) *Unrivalled* missed a tug with a lighter first with two and then with a third torpedo.

(5) *Petrarca* had already been damaged by *Una* on 10.2.43 (q.v.) and had been beached as a result of an air attack when she was again attacked by *Una*.

(6) *Thunderbolt* missed a merchant ship with several torpedoes.

(7) *Splendid* fired six torpedoes at two ships, observed two hits and assumed both ships sunk.

(8) *Unruffled* missed two schooners at anchor with three torpedoes, but both were abandoned and became losses owing to weather damage.

(9) *Thunderbolt* missed a corvette with torpedoes but then attacked with gunfire and secured some hits. The ship sank in a bora on 12.2.44.

1	2	3	4	5	6	7	8	9	10	11	12	13	14	15	16	17
FEBRUARY 1943 *continued*																
19/0805	br	THUNDERBOLT	Crouch	-Tg	150	+	A	Off Ortona								1
19/0805	br	THUNDERBOLT	Crouch	-Bg	120	+	A	Off Ortona								1
19/1735	br	SARACEN	Lumby	-S	200	=	A	Cervo Yard								2
19/1735	br	SARACEN	Lumby	-S	200	=	A	Cervo Yard								2
20/0838	br	THUNDERBOLT	Crouch	-S	200	+	A	Off Bari								1
21/0510	br	UNRUFFLED	Stevens, J. S.	-D	2500	+	4-T	36°56N/11°23E	21/0815	dt	-D	Baalbeck	2115	+	18m ESE C. Bon	
21/	br	SAHIB	Bromage	-S		=§	A	N Sicily								3
23/	br	SPLENDID	McGeogh	-T	4000	/	-T									4
24/0624	br	SPLENDID	McGeogh	-T	3000	+	4-T	38°12N/12°47E	24/	dt	-D	(*KT2*, Labor/510)	–	/		5
24/	br	SPLENDID	McGeogh	-T	2000	/	-T			it	-T	(Dalmazia/3252)	–	/		6
25/	br	RORQUAL	Napier				M	S Marettimo								
25/	br	TORBAY	Clutterbuck	APM		=§	A	Off Ajaccio	25/	it	APM	Monte Argentario	80	=	Off Ajaccio	
26/0312	br	TORBAY	Clutterbuck	-D	1327	+	4TS	43°27N/08°08E	26/	fr	-D	Oasis	1327	+	43°27N/08°08E	7
26/	br	TORBAY	Clutterbuck	-D	3561	+	4-T	Off Cannes	26/	sp	-D	Juan de Astigarraga	3561	+	1m W Cape Mele	8
27/	br	TORBAY	Clutterbuck	-D		/	-T	S France								9
27/0130	br	TORBAY	Clutterbuck	APC	200	+	A	43°37N/09°25E	27/0210	it	-S	Baicin/No 276	173	+	36m SW Spezia	
28/1256	br	TORBAY	Clutterbuck	-D	5000	+	3-T	Portofino	28/1320	it	-D	Ischia	5101	+	1m Portofino	10

(1) *Thunderbolt* sank a tug and a dredger with gunfire and next day sank a schooner.
(2) *Saracen* shelled sailing vessels under construction at the yard but was forced to dive by shore batteries.
(3) *Sahib* shelled two schooners and left them wrecked.
(4) *Splendid* reported an unsuccessful attack on a tanker in a glassy sea.
(5) The claimed German tanker *Gerd*/1700 (ex French *Ste Raymond*) was actually sunk on 22.2.43 by aircraft in 37°45´N/11°37´E.
(6) *Dalmazia* was missed by a torpedo from the stern tube.
(7) *Torbay* first made two unsuccessful attacks on *Oasis*, with one and three torpedoes.
(8) *Torbay* sank the Spanish vessel, which was on charter to the Germans.
(9) *Torbay* made unsuccessful attacks on small vessels on 27.2.43.
(10) *Torbay* first missed with one torpedo and then hit with two.

1	2	3	4	5	6	7	8	9	10	11	12	13	14	15	16	17
MARCH 1943																
01/0945	br	TURBULENT	Linton	–			-T	Tyrrhenian Sea	01/0945	it	-D	San Vicenzo	865	+	1m NW Paola	1
01/1310	nl	DOLFIJN	Van Oostrom Soede	SS		/	-T	*Cavoli I.*		it	SS					
02/1501	br	TAURUS	Wingfield	-S	100	+	A	Cape Ferrat	03/	fr	-D	Clairette	...	+	1m Villefranche	
03/1350	br	TORBAY	Clutterbuck	-S		+	A		03/1355	it	-S	Gesu Giuseppe e Maria	64	+	Pt Milazzo	
03/	br	TORBAY	Clutterbuck	-D		/	-T	Maurizio								2
04/	br	UNSEEN	Crawford	-D	2875	+	-T	Off Sousa	04/	dt	-D	Makedonia (wreck)	2875	+	Off Sousa	3
04/	br	UNSEEN	Crawford	IX		+	"	Off Sousa				Crane lighter		+	Off Sousa	3
06/1030	br	TAURUS	Wingfield	-D	3118	+	6-T	Marseilles	06/1100	sp	-D	Bartolo	3120	+	Beauduc/Lion	4
06/	br	UNSEEN	Crawford	-D		/	1-T	Sousa								5
09/	br	THUNDERBOLT	Crouch	-S		+	A									
09/1145	br	SAFARI	Bryant	-S	100	+	A	Cape San Vito	09/1145	it	-S	Stefano M.	69	+	Cape San Vito	
10/1556	br	TROOPER	Wraith	-D	5400	+	-T	Cape Milazzo	10/1625	it	-T	Rosario	5468	+	4m NE Milazzo	
10/1700	br	TAURUS	Wingfield	-D	2000	+	3-T	Marseilles	10/1710	it	-D	Derna	1769	+	Off Sete	
10/1400	br	UNA	Martin				-T									
10/1520	br	UNBENDING	Stanley				-T		10/	it	-D	Margottini	854	=	50m N Durazzo	
11/1129	fr	CASABIANCA	L'Herminier	-D		/	4-T	Bastia	11/	it	-D	(Principessa)				
11/	br	TURBULENT	Linton	–			-T	Bastia	11/1500	it	-D	(Mafalda/459)	–	/	Bastia	7
12/	br	THUNDERBOLT	Crouch	-D	3000	+	-T	N Sicily	12/2219	dt	-D	Esterel	3100	=§	6m E C. San Vito	8

(1) *Turbulent* did not report her attacks and was sunk after 14.3.43, probably on a mine south of Maddalena.

(2) *Torbay* made one more unsuccessful attack and returned with all sixteen torpedoes expended.

(3) *Unseen* attacked a wreck (beached following an attack by *P35/Umbra* on 13.12.42, q.v.) with a crane alongside.

(4) *Taurus* first missed the blacklisted Spanish ship with four torpedoes but two hours later fired two more torpedoes, one of which hit and sank the ship.

(5) *Unseen* fired at a ship inside Sousa harbour, but the torpedo exploded on a breakwater.

(6) *Safari* sank a schooner by gunfire on her way back to Algiers.

(7) *Turbulent* missed *Mafalda* with two torpedoes and was sunk afterwards (see Note 1 above).

(8) *Thunderbolt* was sunk at 0137 on 13.3.43 by the Italian torpedo boat *Libra*. *Esterel* was beached but could not be salvaged before Sicily was evacuated.

1	2	3	4	5	6	7	8	9	10	11	12	13	14	15	16	17
MARCH 1943 *continued*																
13/0936	br	TAURUS	Wingfield	-Tg	150	+	A	16m W Cassis	13/	fr	-Tg	Ghrib	82	+	6m W Cassis	1
13/0936	br	TAURUS	Wingfield	-Bg	100	+	A	16m W Cassis	13/	fr	-Bg	Labillion	...	+	6m W Cassis	1
13/0936	br	TAURUS	Wingfield	-Bg		+	A	16m W Cassis	13/	fr	-Bg	La Bourdette	...	+	6m W Cassis	1
13/0936	br	TAURUS	Wingfield	-Bg		+	A	16m W Cassis	13/							1
13/0936	br	TAURUS	Wingfield	-Ng		+	A	16m W Cassis	13/							1
14/0950	br	SIBYL	Turner, E. J.	-D	2000	+	-T	38°14N/13°13E	14/0950	it	-D	Pegli	1595	+	6m W Cape Gallo	
14/morn.	br	UNBENDING	Stanley	-D	4500	+	4-T	44°00N/14°10E	14/1208	it	-D	Città di Bergamo	2165	+	Cape Spartivento	2
14/morn.	br	UNBENDING	Stanley	-D	4500	+	"	44°00N/14°10E	14/	it	-D	Cosenza/*Ile Rousse	1471	+	3m E Cape Spartivento	2
15/1335	gr	PAPANIKOLIS	Roussen	-S	Large	+	P	Off Rhodes	15/1335	gr	-S	Aghios Dimitrios	220P	/	Rhodes	3
15/2046	br	TROOPER	Wraith	-D	4000	/	4-T	30m S Capri	15/2048	it	-M	(Belluno/*Fort de France/4279)	–	/	30m S Capri	4
16/	gr	PAPANIKOLIS	Roussen	-S	Small	+	AR	Off Rhodes	16/	gr	-S	Aghios Stefanos	...	+	SE Krio	3
16/2030	gr	PAPANIKOLIS	Roussen	-S	Small	+	AR	Off Rhodes	16/	gr	-S	Fiamenta	40	+	SE Krio	3
16/	br	UNSHAKEN	Whitton	SS		/	-T	*Algiers–Malta*								5
17/	br	UNBROKEN	Mars	-D		/	-T	Sousa								6
17/1040	br	SPLENDID	McGeogh	-D	10000	+	-T	6m SW C. S. Vito	17/1058	it	-D	Devoli/*Perun	3006	+	5m WNW Cape San Vito	
17/1211	br	TROOPER	Wraith	-D	4000	+	4-T	45°16N/14°15E	17/1220	it	-D	Forli/*Sebaa	1525	+	45°15N/14°15E	7
17/1211	br	TROOPER	Wraith	-D	4000	+	"	45°16N/14°15E								7
18/0601	gr	PAPANIKOLIS	Roussen	-S	30	+	AR	SE Krio	18/	gr	-S	Rina	30	+	SE Krio	
21/1502	br	SPLENDID	McGeogh	-D	5000	+	-T	38°05N/14°10E	21/1510	it	-T	Giorgio	4887	+	4m ENE Cefal	8
22/1115	br	TRIBUNE	Porter	-T	6500	+	3-T	39°14N/15°59E	22/1115	dt	-Dt	Präsident Herrenschmidt	9103	=	10m NW Cape Suvero	9
23/	br	RORQUAL	Napier				M	Trapani	04.04.M	it	-D	Carbonello	1593	=		10
23/1409	br	UNISON	Daniell	-T	2000	+	4-T	37°57N/16°10E	23/1401	it	-T	Zeila/*Aureola	1835	+	4m C. Spartivento	
23/1525	br	SAHIB	Bromage	-T	2500	+	1-T	S Lipari	24/morn.	it	-D	Tosca	474	+	1m W Cape Calava	

(1) *Taurus* sank a tug and lighters with gunfire.

(2) *Unbending* fired four torpedoes at a convoy and heard three hits.

(3) *Papanikolis* captured a 220t schooner but the vessel was recaptured by the Italians. Two caiques were later sunk by ramming.

(4) *Trooper* missed a northbound convoy in a long-range attack.

(5) *Unshaken* missed a large submarine.

(6) *Unbroken* fired one torpedo at a ship in Sousa harbour but it exploded at the boom.

(7) *Trooper* assumed one and two hits on two ships.

(8) *Giorgio* was under tow at the time.

(9) *Präsident Herrenschmidt* was towed to Naples and sunk there by aircraft on 30.5.43. This ship is sometimes erroneously claimed as the Italian steamer *Ombrina*/6200.

(10) *Carbonello* was probably hit a mine. She was beached and later sunk as a blockship by the Germans.

1	2	3	4	5	6	7	8	9	10	11	12	13	14	15	16	17
MARCH 1943 *continued*																
24/1011	br	UNSEEN	Crawford	-D	3500	=	4-T	37°52N/11°27E	24/1015	it	-M	(Saluzzo/*Tamara)	–	/	W Marettimo	1
27/1545	br	SAHIB	Bromage	-D	5000	=	5-T	Milazzo	27/1535	it	-D	Sidamo	2384	+	Port Milazzo	2
27/1545	br	SAHIB	Bromage	-S	800	=	"	Milazzo								2
28/1038	br	TORBAY	Clutterbuck	-D	2000	+	4-T	39°05N/15°46E	28/1146	fr	-D	Lillois	3680	+	2.5m S C. Scalea	
28/1900	br	PARTHIAN	St John	-S	320	+	AR	39°25N/25°35E	28/	gr	-S	Archangelos	320	+	39°19N/25°18E	
29/0912	nl	DOLFIJN	Van Oostrom Soede	-D	4500	+	3-T	1m SW Carbonara	29/1017	it	-D	Egle	1143	+	Off Cagliari	
29/1415	br	UNRIVALLED	Turner, H. B.	-D	3000	+	3-T	38°05N/13°26E	29/	dt	APC	UJ2201/*Bois Rose	1375	+	Off Picarenzi	3
29/1415	br	UNRIVALLED	Turner, H. B.	-D	6000	+	"	38°05N/13°26E	29/	dt	APC	UJ2204/*Boréal	1188	+	Off Picarenzi	3
29/1900	br	PARTHIAN	St John	-S	140	/	4-T	W Mitylene	29/1700	gr	-S	Angela Mitylene	120	+	W Mitylene	4
30/1110	br	SAHIB	Bromage	-S	150	+	A	Cape Rasocolmo	30/	it	-S	Santa Maria del Salvazione	15	+	8m E Milazzo	5
30/	br	SAHIB	Bromage	-S	150	+	A	Cape Rasocolmo	30/	it	-S	San Vincenzo	29	+	8m E Milazzo	5
30/1515	br	SAHIB	Bromage	-S	150	+	A	Cape Rasocolmo	30/1515	it	-S	Pier della Vigne	69	+	8m E Milazzo	5
30/1515	br	SAHIB	Bromage	-S	150	+	A	Cape Rasocolmo	30							
30/1515	br	SAHIB	Bromage	-S	150	=	A	Cape Rasocolmo	30/	it	-S	Angelina	...	=	8m E Milazzo	5
30/1330	br	TRIBUNE	Porter	-D	6000	+?	4-T	39°37N/13°15E	30/1445	it	-D	(Benevento/5229)	–	/	50m N Ustica	6
30/1300	br	PARTHIAN	St John	12S	140	+	A	Kannavitsa								7
../....	br	SAHIB	Bromage	SS		/	-T	Sicily								8
APRIL 1943																
01/0920	br	UNRIVALLED	Turner, H. B.	-S	300	+	2-T	4m SE C. S. Vito	01/	it	-S	Triglav	231	+	NW Sicily	
01/1006	br	TORBAY	Clutterbuck	-Mf	120	+	A	40°15N/14°54E	01/1200	it	-Mf	Madonna di Porto Salvo	21	+	8m SSE P. Licosa	
01/				T/M?					01/1640	dt	AK	KT13	830	+	37°18N/10°55E	
01/	gr	PAPANIKOLIS	Roussen	-S		+?	A	Cape Malea	01/	gr	-S		...	+		
02/1930	gr	KATSONIS	Laskos	APC	1200	+	4-T	Off Gytheios	02/1930	it	AG	F77/Tergestea	5890	=	Marathonisi	9

(1) *Unseen* reported that she heard one hit.

(2) *Sahib* fired three torpedoes into the harbour, sank *Sidamo* and damaged a coaster and schooners.

(3) *Unrivalled* attacked two vessels outside Palermo with three torpedoes and assumed one sunk and one damaged.

(4) *Parthian* missed an escorted ship.

(5) *Sahib* attacked five schooners with gunfire and sank or damaged them. It is possible that *Trooper* was also attacking.

(6) *Tribune* attacked a southbound ship but could not observe the results because of a heavy D/C attack.

(7) *Parthian* destroyed 12 caiques by ramming between 26.3 and and 5.4.43.

(8) *Sahib* missed a U-boat owing to heavy seas.

(9) *F77* (ex *Tergestea*) was sunk in shallow water though raised soon afterwards.

1	2	3	4	5	6	7	8	9	10	11	12	13	14	15	16	17
APRIL 1943 *continued*																
02/	br	UNSHAKEN	Whitton	-D	4000	+	-T	Hammamet								
03/1128	br	TRIDENT	Newstead	SS		/	6-T	Spezia		dt	SS					1
03/	br	UNBROKEN	Mars	CL	3362	=	-T	37°46N/15°38E	03/	dt	DD	(Hermes/V. Georgios)	–	/	20m S Spartivento	2
03/1300	br	SAFARI	Bryant	APM	350	+	A	Gulf of Orosei	03/1315	it	-D	Nasello	314	+	Gulf of Orosei	
03/1300	br	SAFARI	Bryant	-S	150	+	A	Gulf of Orosei	03/	it	-Mf	San Francisco di Paola	77	+	Gulf of Orosei	
04/1443	br	UNBROKEN	Mars	-T	6000	=	2-T	35°15N/16°30E	04/1640	dt	-DT	Regina	9545	=	Punta Stilo	3
04/	br	UNRIVALLED	Sprice (?)	-D	Small	=		Off Palermo								
05/0920	gr	KATSONIS	Laskos	-D	2357	+	-T	Thermia I.	05/0935	dt	-D	San Isidro/*Labrador	322	+	Kythnos	4
05/0128	br	TRIDENT	Newstead	-D		/	4-T	E Corsica								5
06/1345	br	SAFARI	Bryant	-D	4000	=	3-T	Cagliari	06/1630	it	-D	(Cap Figalo/2811)	–	/	Cagliari harbour	6
07/	br	UNSHAKEN	Whitton	-S		=	A	Naboel								7
08/0712	br	TRIDENT	Newstead	-D		/	4-T	Corsica								8
08/0424	br	UNSHAKEN	Whitton	-D	2000	+	3-T	10m NE Sousa	08/0530	it	-D	Foggia/*Mont St Clair	1227	+	10m NE Sousa	
09/	br	TRIDENT	Newstead	SS		/	2-T	Corsica		it	SS					9
09/1218	br	SAFARI	Bryant	-S	300	+	A	6m W Carbonara	09/1330	it	APM	No 295/Bella Italia	117	+	8m W Cape Carbonara	
10/									[10/	it	-D	San Antonio/6013+?]	–	/	Ligurian coast	10
10/1719	br	SAFARI	Bryant	ACL	5000	+	4-T	10m E Cagliari	10/1820	it	-D	Loredan	1355	+	10m Pt Elia	11
10/1719	br	SAFARI	Bryant	-T	3500	+	"	10m E Cagliari	10/	it	AO	Isonzo	3363	+	12m Pt Elia	11
11/morn.	br	SAFARI	Bryant	-D	3000	+	2-T	Cagliari	11/1820	it	-D	Entella	2691	+	T. Finocchia	11

(1) *Trident* missed an outward-bound German U-boat with six torpedoes, one of which did not leave the tube.

(2) *Unbroken* attacked a *Regolo* class cruiser, assuming one hit, but the victim was the German destroyer *Hermes* (ex *ZG3*, ex *Vasilefs Georgios*).

(3) *Regina* was beached.

(4) *San Isidro* (ex *Labrador*, ex Spanish steamer *Castillo Montes*) was not sunk by *Parthian* but by *Katsonis*.

(5) *Trident* missed a northbound merchant ship.

(6) *Safari* observed two hits from three torpedoes, but the ship entered Cagliari.

(7) *Unshaken* shelled a beached schooner but was driven off by fire from a shore battery.

(8) *Trident* again missed a merchant ship

(9) *Trident* fired two torpedoes at an Italian submarine, which avoided them.

(10) The British submarine *Tribune* is sometimes erroneously credited with the Italian steamer *San Antonio* off the Ligurian coast.

(11) *Safari* fired four torpedoes against a three-ship convoy. Two ships were each hit by two torpedoes and sank, and in the confusion the third beached herself and was hit the next day by two torpedoes.

1	2	3	4	5	6	7	8	9	10	11	12	13	14	15	16	17
APRIL 1943 *continued*																
11/	br	UNRULY	Fyfe	-D		/	2-T	Port Vendres	11/	sp	-D		–	/		1
11/1750	br	TORBAY	Clutterbuck	-S		+	A	Corfu								
11/1554	br	SIBYL	Turner, E. J.	-D	2000	=	4-T	38°19N/13°00E	11/2340	it	-D	(Fabriano/*Mayenne)	–	/	N Sicily	2
12/1415	br	TRIDENT	Newstead	-D	2000	+	2TA	Off Cape Noli								3
12/1445	br	UNRULY	Fyfe	-D	1000	+	-T	42°31N/03°07E	12/1550	dt	-D	St Lucien/*Aalborg	1256	+	Port Vendres	
12/2225	br	ULTOR	Hunt	-D	3000	+	3-T	43°13N/06°52E	12/	fr	-T	(Condé/7202)	–	/	Marseilles/Nice	4
12/2225	br	ULTOR	Hunt	-D	3000	+?	"	43°13N/06°52E	12/	dt	-D	(Nicoline Maersk)	–	/	Marseilles/Nice	4
13/0030	br	TAURUS	Wingfield	-D	2000	+	A	42°19N/09°53E	12/	pt	-D	Santa Irene	520	+	30m SE Bastia	5
14/0751	br	ULTOR	Hunt	-D	2000	+	-T	43°32N/07°12E	14/0852	dt	-D	Penerf	2150	+	15m SSW Nice	
14/0613	br	TRIDENT	Newstead	APC		=	A	43°51N/08°19E	14/	dt	APC	(UJ2202)	–	/		6
14/1420	br	TAURUS	Wingfield	-T	600	+	A	42°16N/09°36E	14/1525	it	-T	Alcione C.	521	+	2m N M. Pruneto	
15/2205	br	TAURUS	Wingfield	-S	1000	+	2-T	41°32N/10°47E	15/2300	it	-S	Luigi	433	+	52m SW Civitavecchia	
17	gr	PAPANIKOLIS	Roussen	-D		+	A	Off Skopoli								
18/0825	br	TORBAY	Clutterbuck	-D	1500	+	2-T	38°58N/18°17E								
18	br	REGENT	Knox	–			-T	5m NE Monopoli	18/1116	it	-T	(Bivona/1646)	–	/	4m SW Cape Gallo	7
18/1236	br	TORBAY	Clutterbuck	APC		+	A	Cape Drepano								
18/1106	br	UNSEEN	Crawford	PE		+	-T	38°16N/13°11E	18/1146	dt	APC	UJ2205/*Le Jacques Coeur	1168	+	38°15N/13°13E	
19/0120	br	UNRIVALLED	Turner, H. B.	-D	2500	+	3-T	38°15N/12°00E	19/0130	dt	-D	Mostaganem	1942	+	38°11N/11°44E	8
									19/0330	it	-D	(Olympos/5216)	–	/	N Akrotiri	9

(1) *Unruly* missed a Spanish ship with two torpedoes.

(2) *Sibyl* attacked an eastbound convoy of three ships and six escorts with four torpedoes, two of which which were claimed to have hit *Fabriano*/2943, but in fact she was sunk by torpedoes from Malta-based aircraft at 2304.

(3) *Trident* reported that she missed a merchant ship off Cape Noli with one torpedo.

(4) *Ultor* fired four torpedoes against two small ships. One sank and one was damaged.

(5) The ship was lit and carried Portuguese neutrality markings, but *Taurus* thought she was attacking a Q-ship. Out of 18 crew members, only one was saved.

(6) *Trident* engaged a small tanker which proved to be an A/S vessel. The latter countered with gunfire and D/Cs after being hit by two shells.

(7) *Regent* was probably responsible for this attack, but there was no report because the submarine was lost that day, probably on a mine.

(8) *KT7*/850, claimed for this attack, was not the target; she was damaged in an air raid. *Mostaganem* was first hit by aircraft bombs.

(9) *Olympos* observed a surfaced submarine which dived.

1	2	3	4	5	6	7	8	9	10	11	12	13	14	15	16	17

APRIL 1943 *continued*

1	2	3	4	5	6	7	8	9	10	11	12	13	14	15	16	17
19/1325	br	SARACEN	Lumby	-D	7600	+	6-T	42°46N/09°46E	19/1512	it	-D	Francesco Crispi	7600	+	18m W Elba	1
19/1325	br	SARACEN	Lumby	-T	3000	+	"	42°46N/09°46E	19/	it	-D	(Tagliamento/5448)	–	/	18m W Elba	1
19/1325	br	SARACEN	Lumby	-D	3616	+	"	Off Bastia								
19/1550	br	UNRIVALLED	Turner, H. B.	-D	3500	+	4-T	38°22N/12°36E	19/1550	it	-D	Bivona/*Socombel	1646	+	20m NW Trapani	2
20/	br	RORQUAL	Napier				M	Trapani								
21/1211	br	UNISON	Daniell	-D	5000	+	4-T	37°48N/11°32E	21/1218	it	-D	Marco Foscarini	6405	+	37°50N/11°30E	3
21/	br	UNISON	Daniell													
21/	br	UNBROKEN	Andrew	SS		/	4-T	*N Sicily*								*4*
21/	br	SPLENDID	McGeogh	DD			1-T	*40°31N/14°16E*	*21/*	dt	DD	(Hermes)	–	/		*5*
22/0102	br	SARACEN	Lumby	-D	6000	+	6-T	42°03N/09°48E	22/0205	it	-D	Tagliamento	5458	+	35m S Pianosa	6
22/	br	SAHIB	Bromage	-Tg		=	A	3m S C. Vaticano	22/day	it	-Tg	Valente/*Michel Venture	286	=	Cape Vaticano	7
22/	br	SAHIB	Bromage	-Bg		=	A	3m S C. Vaticano								7
22/	br	UNBROKEN	Mars	-S	450	+	1-T	38°11N/12°45E	22/1620	it	APM	No 17/Milano	379	+	Cape San Vito	
23/0825	br	SICKLE	Drummond	-D	1049	=	2TA	N Valencia	23/	it	-D	Mauro Croce	1049	=	Sagunto	8
24/0450	br	SAHIB	Bromage	-D		+	-T	5m NW Milazzo	24/0605	it	-D	Galiola	1428	+	5m NW Milazzo	9
26/0300	nl	DOLFIJN	Van Oostrom Soede	SS		/	4-T									
26/1617	br	UNBROKEN	Mars	-D	6000	+?	-T	38°13N/13°26E							Off Palermo	10

(1) *Saracen* attacked a convoy with an AMC and a liner escorted by destroyers. *Bivona*, also claimed, was definitely not hit; she was sunk by *Unrivalled* (q.v.).

(2) *Unrivalled* reported *Bivona* sunk with four torpedo hits.

(3) *Unison* was depth-charged by the Italian torpedo boat *Libra*. The German transport *KT7*, also claimed, was in fact sunk in 38°11′N/11°45′E by the British destroyers *Laforey*, *Loyal* and *Lookout*.

(4) *Unbroken* fired four torpedoes against a U-boat but missed.

(5) *Splendid* was attacked by the German destroyer *Hermes* (ex Greek *Vasilefs Georgios*) and forced to surface but before sinking fired one torpedo which exploded without hitting.

(6) *Saracen* fired two salvos each of three torpedoes; one from each salvo hit.

(7) *Sahib* hit the tug with 45 and the lighter with 25 shells. The tug was set on fire and burnt out.

(8) *Sickle* fired two torpedoes which ran under the ship and then engaged with her gun, scoring 15 hits from 19 rounds. The ship escaped into territorial waters.

(9) *Sahib* was forced to surface as a result of a D/C attack by the Italian corvette *Gabbiano* and had to scuttle herself.

(10) *Unbroken* hit the ship with one of her last three torpedoes. The claimed *Giacomo C./4638* was in fact beached in a USAAF air attack at Palermo though later salvaged.

1	2	3	4	5	6	7	8	9	10	11	12	13	14	15	16	17
APRIL 1943 *continued*																
28/	br	UNSHAKEN	Whitton	*TB*		+	3-T	*37°45N/11°33E*	28/1030	*it*	-TB	*Climene*	640	+	*35m WSW Pt Lib.*	
29/	br	TACTICIAN	Collett	-D	2000	/	3-T	N Bastia		fr	-D					1
29/	br	UNSHAKEN	Whitton	-D		/	4-T	Cape San Vito	30/	fr	-D	(Cape Corse/2444)	–	/	Porticciolo	2
30/	br	RORQUAL	Napier				M	Trapani (?)								
MAY 1943																
02/0902	br	SAFARI	Lakin	-D	450	+	A	Asinara I.	02/	it	-D	Sogliola/No 111	307	+	1m W Asinara	
04/	br	PARTHIAN	St John	-S	50	+	A	10m N Kos	04/0935	it	-S	Despina II	13	+	10m W Kos	
04/1606	br	PARTHIAN	St John	-S		+	A	10m W Kos	04/	it	-S	Spina Secondo	13	+	10m W Kos	
05/1911	br	TACTICIAN	Collett	-S	500	+	A	42°34N/10°45E	05/	it	-S	No 17/Maria Pia	385	+	10m W Grosseto	
05/							-T		[05/2020	it	-S	Sempre Avanti/135+]	–		Trapani–Pantellaria	3
05/2011	br	PARTHIAN	St John	APC		=	A	38°20N/24°46E	05/2015	dt	CM	(Drache/*Zmaj)	–	/	7m NE Doro	4
05/							-T		05/	ru	-D	(Alba Julia/5700)	–	/	7m Can. Doro	4
06/	br	UNRIVALLED	Turner, H. B.	-S		/	-T	Messina	06/	it	-S	(Albina/223)	–	/	Cape Vaticano	5
06/0933	br	SAFARI	Lakin	-Df	300	+	-T	Asinara I.	06/1030	it	-S	Onda	98	+	3m W Plana	
07/	br	UNRIVALLED	Turner, H. B.	-S		+	TA	Cape Vaticano	07/1120	it	-S	Albina	223	=§	Cape Vaticano	5
07/							-T		[07/0700	it	-D	Palomba/3099+]	–		Patrasso–Bari	6
07/	br	PARTHIAN	St John	-S		+	A	Stavros–Naxos	07/	it	-S	Barbara/*Aghia Barbaro	...	+	10m N C. Stavros	
08/0530	gr	PAPANIKOLIS	Roussen	-S	150	+	A	15m N Candia	08/morn.	it	-S	Maria	150	+	N Candia	
08/0915	gr	PAPANIKOLIS	Roussen	-S	250	+	A	30°36N/24°39E	08/0800	it	-S	Vavara	87	+	30m WNW Crete	
08/1958	br	SAFARI	Lakin	-D	2500	+	2-T	Porto Torres	08/	nw	-D	Liv	3070	=	Pt Torres Road	7
08/1958	br	SAFARI	Lakin	-D		+	"	Porto Torres	08/0700	it	-D	Peppino Palomba	2034	+	Santa Maura	

(1) *Tactician* missed a French ship with three torpedoes.

(2) *Unshaken* missed a convoy with four torpedoes.

(3) *Sempre Avanti* was not sunk by a submarine but by air attack or a mine.

(4) *Parthian* attacked an escort but after scoring some hits was forced to dive. *Drache* (ex Yugoslav auxiliary *Zmaj*) was, with the Italian torpedo boat *Castelfidaro*, escorting the Romanian steamer *Alba Julia*, which also reported torpedoes that missed.

(5) *Unrivalled* chased *Albina* on 6.5.43 with torpedoes and again the following day, and then surfaced and sank the vessel with gunfire.

(6) *Palomba* was not sunk by the British submarine *Safari* but, probably, by a mine.

(7) *Safari* fired one torpedo which exploded against a breakwater and a second which hit the ship (which had already been damaged in an air attack).

1	2	3	4	5	6	7	8	9	10	11	12	13	14	15	16	17
MAY 1943 *continued*																
09/1545	br	UNRIVALLED	Turner, H. B.	-D	763	+	2-T	Vulcano I.	09/1607	it	-D	Santa Mariana Salina	763	+	6.5m SE Lipari	
09/	br	UNRIVALLED	Turner, H. B.	-S		/	1-T	Vulcano I.								1
12/1650	br	TRIDENT	Newstead	-D	6000	=	6-T	42°27N/09°53E	12/	it	-D	(Agnani/*Mansour/ 5718)	–	/	SE Corsica	2
13/1800	br	SHAKESPEARE	Ainslie	-S	200	+	A	41°20N/10°26E	13/2100	it	-S	Sant' Anna M.	156	+	41°17N/10°26E	
13/1800	br	SHAKESPEARE	Ainslie	-S	200	?	A	41°17N/10°26E	13/2000	it	-S	Adelina	80	+	41°17N/10°26E	
14/2300	br	TRIDENT	Newstead	-D		/	4-T	43°10N/18°10E	14/	fr	-D	(Cap Corse/2444)	–	/	N Corsica	3
15/1237	br	SICKLE	Drummond	-D	1000	+	4-T	45°25N/07°25E	15/1237	dt	APC	UJ2213/*Heureux	1116	+	43°25N/07°25E	
16/1306	br	UNRULY	Fyfe	AMC	4000	=	3-T	37°35N/15°17E	16/1000	it	-M	Nicolo Tommaseo	4573	=	5m NNE Catania	4
19/1547	br	UNBROKEN	Andrew	-Tg	600	+	2-T	38°45N/16°00E	16/1550	it	-Tg	Enrica	269	+	3m W P. Calabro	
19/1550	br	SPORTSMAN	Gatehouse	-D	2796	+	4-T	43°01N/07°40E	19/1309	fr	-D	Général Bonaparte	2795	+	40m Nice	
19/	br	UNITED	Roxburgh	-Tg		/	2-T	Cape San Vito								5
20/	br	UNBROKEN	Andrew	-Tg		/	2-T	S Eufemia								6
20/2154	br	SICKLE	Drummond	*SS*		/	6-T	*43°00N/06°00E*	*20/*	*dt*	*SS*	*(U431 or U458)*	*–*	*/*	*42°50N/06°00E*	7
21/1512	br	SICKLE	Drummond	*SS*		+	2-T	*42°50N/06°00E*	*21/1643*	*dt*	*SS*	*U303*	*769*	*+*		7
21/1745	br	UNBROKEN	Mars	-D	4000	+	-T	38°34N/15°44E	21/1745	it	-D	Bologna/*Aliki/ *Monaco	5140	+	38°30N/16°E	
21/	br	UNRULY	Fyfe	*SS*		/	*-T*	*Augusta*								8
23/0821	br	ULTOR	Hunt	-Df	500	+	1-T	Off Augusta								
24/0915	pl	DZIK	Romanowski	-T	7000	=	4-T	12m NE Cape Spartivento	24/0800	it	-T	Carnaro	8257	=	16m E Spartivento	9

(1) *Unrivalled* fired her last torpedo, which missed.

(2) *Trident* reported an attack on a *Virgilo* class/12000 liner and thought she heard one hit while diving deep to evade one of her own torpedoes which was circling. *Agnagi* was missed.

(3) *Trident* missed *Cape Corse* because she underestimated the latter's speed.

(4) *Unruly*'s target was probably *Tommaseo*, which was repaired.

(5) *United* missed a tug.

(6) *Unbroken* missed a tug towing dockyard machinery with two torpedoes.

(7) In a first attack *Sickle* missed a U-boat but the next day she sank *U303*.

(8) *Unruly* missed a U-boat in difficult conditions.

(9) *Dzik* heard two hits; the tanker was damaged and set on fire but towed to Messina and repaired.

1	2	3	4	5	6	7	8	9	10	11	12	13	14	15	16	17
MAY 1943 *continued*																
25/	nl	DOLFIJN	Van Oostrom Soede	*PT*		/	-T	*Off Sicily*	25/	it	PC	M9	...	=	Ustica	1
26/1141	br	SPORTSMAN	Gatehouse	-T	7000	=	6-T	42°53N/06°08E	26/	fr	-T	(Marguerite Finaly/ 12309)	–	/	Gulf of Lions	2
27/	br	SERAPH	Jewell	-D		/	3-T	Bonifacio Strait								3
28/1340	br	SPORTSMAN	Gatehouse	-Tg		=	A	Hyres Roads								4
29/1745	gr	KATSONIS	Laskos	-D	1000	+	A	39°12N/23°21E	29/	dt	-D	Rigel/*Turcio di Monte Jurra	552	=	Trikeri Channel	5
30/0438	br	TRESPASSER	Favell	–		/	3-T	Gulf of Lions								6
30/	br	SERAPH	Jewell	-D		/	1-T	E Sardinia								7
31/0443	br	TAKU		-D		+	2-T									7
31/	br	SERAPH	Jewell	-D	3000	/	2-T	E Sardinia								7
JUNE 1943																
02/2013	gr	KATSONIS	Laskos	-D	7000	=	2-T	Karlovassi harbour	02/	it	-D	(Versilia/591)	–	/	Karlovassi	8
03/1332	br	UNRUFFLED	Stevens, J. S.	-T	8000	+	4-T	39°13N/16°01E	03/1523	fr	-T	Henri Desprez	9805	+	70m N Messina	9
03/	br	TAURUS	Wingfield	-S	120	+	A	38°24N/24°14E								
03/	br	TAURUS	Wingfield	-S	60	+	A	38°24N/24°14E								
03/	br	TROOPER	Wraith	-D	3000	/	-T	Off Bari								10
04/1045	fr	ARÉTHUSE	Gouttier	-D	6000	=§	2-T	41°08N/09°32E	04/1045	fr	-D	Dalny	6672	=	Cap Cervo	11

(1) *Dolfijn* grounded near Ustica and damaged a patrol vessel with her gun before making her withdrawal.

(2) *Sportsman* assumed she had hit the tanker with one of four torpedoes, but the ship was damaged by *Saracen* on 15.2.43 (q.v.) and reached Toulon. She was sunk as a blockship at Marseilles in 8.44.

(3) *Seraph* missed a small merchant ship in a convoy.

(4) *Sportsman* attacked a tug and three lighters with gunfire but had to break off after one hit because of counter-fire.

(5) *Rigel* (ex Spanish steamer *Turcio di Monte Jurra*) was damaged in this attack and sunk by *Sickle* on 5.6.44 before this submarine was lost (q.v.).

(6) *Trespasser* fired three torpedoes at a dead whale by mistake.

(7) *Seraph* fired one torpedo at a convoy out of range. The next day two ships were attacked, but one torpedo circled and the other missed.

(8) *Katsonis* fired two torpedoes at an Italian ship in Karlovassi harbour without observing the results.

(9) *Unruffled* scored three hits with four torpedoes, which sank the tanker.

(10) *Trooper* missed a ship, which returned to Bari.

(11) *Dalny* had just been refloated after being beached following torpedo hits by *Tribune* on 10/11.1.43 (q.v.) and was now hit by two torpedoes and beached again.

1	2	3	4	5	6	7	8	9	10	11	12	13	14	15	16	17
JUNE 1943 *continued*																
05/1039	br	UPROAR	Herrick	-T	1500	=?	4-T	39°03N/17°16E								1
06/	br	TAURUS	Wingfield	-S		+	A	Off Skiathos								2
06/	br	TAURUS	Wingfield	-S		+	A	Off Skiathos								2
06/	br	TAURUS	Wingfield	-S		+	A	39°25N/25°43E	06/	gr	-S			...	+	W Mitylene	2
06/	br	TAURUS	Wingfield	-S		+	A	W Mitylene								2
07/	br	SAFARI	Bryant	-D		/	4-T	Maddalena								3
08/1014	br	TRESPASSER	Favell	-T	1000	=	6-T	Off Toulon	08/1350	dt	APC	(UJ6073/Nimet Allah)	–	/	Off Toulon	4
08/	pl	SOKOL	Koziolkowski	-S		/	2-T	E Calabria								5
09/	br	UPROAR	Herrick	-D	2500	/	-T	S Crotone								6
10/1219	br	SAFARI	Bryant	-D	1000	=	3-T	37°57N/09°45E	10/1320	dt	AK	KT12	834	+	4m E Orosei	
10/	br	TAURUS	Wingfield	SS		/	-T	Stampalia								7
10/	br	ULTOR	Hunt	APC	800	/	2-T	S Lipari								8
11/	br	TAURUS	Wingfield	4-S	25	+	A	9m E Piscopi	11/1630	it	-S	Nuova Fortuna	7	+	9m E Piscopi	9
11/	br	TAURUS	Wingfield	3-S	150	+	A	E Piscopi	11/1600	it	-S	San Giovanni	35	+	E Piscopi	9
11/	br	TAURUS	Wingfield	R					11/	gr	-S	San Nicola	14	+	Rhodes–Patmos	9
12/early	br	UNRULY	Fyfe	-D	3000	=	4-T	S Paola								10
12/1220	br	TACTICIAN	Collett	-S	600	+	A	5m NE Bari Lt	12/1236	it	-S	Bice	1459	+	Bari Lt	11
12/	br	TACTICIAN	Collett	APC		=	A	5m NE Bari Lt								11
12/1345	fr	CASABIANCA	L'Herminier	-D		/	4-T	42°40N/09°40E	12/	it	-D	(Capitano Sauro/194)	–	/	Capraia	12
14/0200	br	UNRULY	Fyfe	-D	5000	+	4-T	38°52N/15°27E	14/0200	it	-D	Valentino Coda	4485	+	19m NW Cape Vaticano	

(1) *Uproar* missed a tanker making for Crotone.
(2) *Taurus* reported four sailing patrol vessels sunk.
(3) *Safari* attacked three ships with a destroyer escort after a D/C attack by the escort, but she missed.
(4) *Trespasser* attacked a three-ship convoy and assumed one hit in misty weather, but the torpedo exploded on the coast.
(5) *Sokol* missed a schooner with two torpedoes.
(6) *Uproar* missed a northbound ship at long range.
(7) *Taurus* missed a U-boat.
(8) *Ultor* missed because the attack was observed and evaded.
(9) *Taurus* sank seven caiques ranging from 25 to 150 tons by gunfire.
(10) *Unruly* attacked a southbound ship with a trawler escort and assumed one hit with a torpedo, which, however, did not explode.
(11) In a gun engagement *Tactician* sank a large schooner and damaged an armed boarding vessel.
(12) *Casabianca* made unsuccessful attacks because of faulty torpedoes.

1	2	3	4	5	6	7	8	9	10	11	12	13	14	15	16	17
JUNE 1943 *continued*																
14/1130	br	UNITED	Roxburgh	-D	5000	+	-T	37°54N/15°42E	14/1230	fr	-D	Ste Marguerite/ *Ringulv	5155	+	1m S C. dell'Armi	
14/1130	br	UNITED	Roxburgh	ACL	7000	+	"	Messina								
14/1610	br	TACTICIAN	Collett	-D	7600	+	5-T	40°14N/19°28E	14/1640	it	-D	Rosandra	8035	=§	Preveza–Valona	1
15/	br	RORQUAL	Napier				M	Cape Stilo								
15/1340	br	ULTOR	Hunt	AG	1200	+	3-T	38°25N/15°46E	15/1340	it	APM	No 92/Tullio	137	+	Cape Vaticano	2
15/2015	br	ULTOR	Hunt	*TB*		=	*3-T*	*38°32N/15°47E*	*15/*	*it*	*PE*	*(Euterpe)*	*–*	*l*		
16/1905	br	UNISON	Daniell	-D	3000	+	4-T	7m S C. Molino	16/1908	it	-D	Terni/*Azrou	2988	+	2m N Catania	
16/	br	UNBROKEN	Andrew	-S		/	1-T	Alice Pt								3
16/even.	br	UNBROKEN	Andrew	-DT		/	4-T	N Crotone								3
16/2021	fr	CASABIANCA	L'Herminier	-D	6000	/	2-T	Bastia	16/	fr	-DT	(Champagne/9946)	–	/	Bastia	
17/	pl	DZIK	Romanowski	APM	300	/	3-T	Cape Milazzo								4
17/1940	pl	DZIK	Romanowski	-D	4000	+	3-T	38°40N/15°16E								4
19/									[19/	it	-D	Laurenzo Marcello/1413+]			2m W C. Ducato	5
19/1715	fr	CASABIANCA	L'Herminier	-T	9946	/	3-T	43°05N/09°41E	19/	fr	-DT	(Champagne/9946)	–	/	Bastia	
20/1530	br	UNITED	Roxburgh	-D	4000	+	4-T	37°40N/16°02E	20/1515	it	-D	Olbia	3514	+	37°35N/16°05E	
21/									[21/	it	-D	Salvatore I/715+]	–	/	25m NE C. Figari	6
22/	br	UNSHAKEN	Whitton	-S		+	2-T	Off Augusta	22/1600	it	-S	Giovanni G.	35	+	Off Augusta	
22/1656	br	UNSHAKEN	Whitton	-D	5000	/	4-T	37°03N/15°22E								7
23/1416	br	UNSHAKEN	Whitton	-D	3000	+	2-T	37°10N/15°19E	23/1830	it	-D	Pomo/*Niko Matkovic	1425	+	37°09N/15°15E	
24/0616	br	UNSPARING	Piper	-D	3000	/	4-T	Off C. Antibes	24/	dt	APC	(SG13/Cyrnos)	–	/	Marseilles	
25/	br	PARTHIAN	Pardoe (?)	-D		=	-T	Off Cape Midia	25/	dt	-D	Gerda Toft	1960	=?		8

(1) *Tactician* first fired four torpedoes without observing the results (because of a D/C attack) and later fired a stern shot to finish the beached vessel off.

(2) *Ultor* assumed she had sunk a small cable ship. She later attacked two torpedo boats of the *Climene* and *Orsa* classes and assumed the second damaged.

(3) *Unbroken* missed a stationery schooner with a torpedo which ran under the target. Later in the evening a small tanker was missed.

(4) *Dzik* missed a small auxiliary and later reported two hits on an escorted ship (they

were misses). The submarine was depth-charged by the Italian torpedo boat *Orione*.

(5) *Laurenzo Marcello* was sunk on a mine.

(6) *Salvatore I* was sunk either by air attack or by a mine.

(7) *Unshaken* fired four torpedoes at a merchant ship and three destroyers; all missed.

(8) *Gerda Toft* was possibly hit, but only by a dud.

1	2	3	4	5	6	7	8	9	10	11	12	13	14	15	16	17
JUNE 1943 *continued*																
27/	br	TRIDENT	Newstead	-S	100	+	A	Aegean/Crete								1
27/	br	OSIRIS		-S		+	A	Off Sirena I.	27/day	it	-S	Vittorina	11	+	I Sirina	1
29/	br	SPORTSMAN	Gatehouse	-Sf		+	A	Bordighera								
29/	br	SPORTSMAN	Gatehouse	-Sf		+	A	Bordighera								
29/	br	SPORTSMAN	Gatehouse	-D	2000	+	1-T	NW Spezia	29/1045	it	-D	Bolzaneto	2220	+	3m W P. Mesco	
29/	br	PARTHIAN	Pardoe	-D	3000	/	4-T	35°36N/24°19E								2
JULY 1943																
01/	br	SPORTSMAN	Gatehouse	LC		/	A	*Pt Maurizio*								3
01/							A		01/0700	it	-S	Maria Santissima	23	+	Off Palermo	
02/	br	RORQUAL	Napier				29M	Cape Sepias	07.09.M	dt	-D	PLM24	5391	=§	39°14N/23°19E	
02/	br	TRIDENT	Newstead	3-S		+	A	Off Rhodes	02/	gr	-S		...	+	W Rhodes	4
03/2330	br	TRIDENT	Newstead	-D	3500	+	3-T	37°03N/26°07E	03/2335	it	-D	Vesta	3351	=	W Leros	5
04/	br	TRESPASSER	Favell	-D		/	2-T	Monte Cristo								6
04/	br	TRIDENT (?)	Newstead (?)				A		04/	tu	-M	Sisman	73	+	N Budrum	7
04/	br	TRIDENT	Newstead	-S		+	A	15m S Symi	04/	it	-S	Adalia	165	+	Symi Island	8
04/0708	nl	DOLFIJN	Van Oostrom Soede	-D	7000	+	4-T	42°05N/11°47E	04/0707	it	-D	Sabbia	5788	=	S Civitavecchia	9
04/0911	nl	DOLFIJN	Van Oostrom Soede	-S	50	+	A	15m W Civita-vecchia	04/2115	it	APC	No 50/Adalia	...	+		8
05/early	br	SIBYL	Turner, E. J.	-D		/	4-T	N Bastia								10
06/							3-T		06/1010	dt	-D	(Convoy)	–	/	34m SW Livorno	
06/1010	fr	CASABIANCA	L'Herminier	-T	9946	/	3-T	43°06N/09°33E	06/	fr	-DT	(Champagne/9946)	–	/	Giraglia	
06/1830	br	SARACEN	Lumby	-D	2500	+	-T	S Capreira	06/0900	it	-D	Tripoli	1166	+	15m S Capreira	
07/	br	TRIDENT	Newstead	-D		/	6-T	Doro Channel								11

(1) *Trident* sank a caique. *Vittorina* was probably sunk by *Osiris*.
(2) *Parthian* missed a ship which had an aircraft escort.
(3) *Sportsman* had to break off an engagement with escorted lighters because of ammunition jamming in her gun.
(4) *Trident* sank three caiques by gunfire.
(5) *Trident* assumed one ship sunk from a three-ship convoy, but the vessel reached harbour and was later used by the Germans to block the Corinth Canal.
(6) *Trespasser* fired two torpedoes against two small AMCs but they missed.

(7) *Sisman* was probably another of *Trident*'s victims.
(8) *Adalia* was sunk by *Trident*, the observation craft *No 50/Adalia* by *Dolfijn* as claimed.
(9) *Sabbia* was towed into the port of Civitavecchia but sank there. There is a false report of damage on 5.7.41.
(10) *Sibyl* missed an escorted ship.
(11) *Trident* missed a convoy because of a change of course. On the next day she engaged a German APC with gunfire and was herself attacked with 50 D/Cs.

JULY 1943 *continued*

1	2	3	4	5	6	7	8	9	10	11	12	13	14	15	16	17
07/0930	br	RORQUAL	Napier	-D	7020	+	-T	39°57N/25°50E	07/0807	dt	-D	Wilhelmsburg/*Petrakis Nomikos	7020	+	39°55N/25°50E	
08/0525	br	TAURUS	Wingfield	-D	3000	=	4-T	Pondiko Nisi	08/0430	gr	-D	Konstantinos Louloudis	4697	=	Trikiri Channel	1
08/	br	TAURUS	Wingfield	-S		+	RS	Pondiko Nisi	08/				...	=	70m SSE Salonika	1
08/	br	TAURUS	Wingfield	-S		+	RS	Pondiko Nisi	08/	gr	-S		...	+	N Skyros	1
08/0650	br	TRIDENT	Newstead	APC	150	=	A	Doro Channel	08/0720	dt	APC	GA41/*Tassia Christa	...	=	20m N Doro Ch.	2
08/	br	ULTOR	Hunt	-D	6000	+	1-T	38°18N/15°27E	08/2200	it	-D	Valfiorita	6200	+	38°18N/15°27E	
09/2015	br	TAURUS	Wingfield	4-S		+	2TA	Kastro harbour	09/2015	gr	-S	5 caiques	...	+	Castron/Chios	1
10/	fr	CASABIANCA	L'Herminier	-T	12000	/	-T	Corsica								
11/1125	br	SARACEN	Lumby	-D	2000	+	-T	25m E Corsica	11/	dt	-D	Tell	1349	+	E Corsica	
11/	br	UNRULY	Fyfe	SS		/	4-T	*N Messina*								3
11/							-T		11/	dt	APC	SG13/*Cyrnos	2406	=	83m S Naples	
11/dusk	br	TAURUS	Wingfield	10-S		+	TA	Euboea	12/2000	gr	-S	12 caiques	...	+	Gulf of Salonika	4
11/dusk	br	TAURUS	Wingfield	-Tg		+	TA	Euboea	12/2000	gr	-Tg	Romano	39	+	Gulf of Salonika	4
13/0934	nl	DOLFIJN	Van Oostrom Soede	-S	137	+	A	Lido di Roma	13/2215	it	-S	Stefano Galleano	137	+	Off Ostia	
13/	br	SIMOOM	Milner	-Tg	200	=	4-T	NW Giglio								5
13/	br	TRESPASSER	Favell	APM	242	+	A	25m S Bastia	13/1245	it	APC	V-8/Filippo	242	+	10m NE Alistro	6
13/	br	UNRULY	Fyfe	SS		+	4-T	*38°30N/15°49E*	13/2020	it	-SS	*Acciaio*	630	+	*NE Stromboli*	
14/	br	TRESPASSER	Favell	-D	6000	/	-T	Bastia								6
14/	br	TROOPER	Clarabut	-D	2000	=	TA	S Adriatic								7
14/	br	SIMOOM	Milner	-Tg		=	A	NW Giglio								8
14/1554	br	UNSHAKEN	Whitton	APC	500	+	2-T	37°16N/17°16E	14/1615	it	-Mf	No 265/Cesena	105	+	39°18N/17°16E	

(1) *Taurus* hit the ship with one or more torpedoes but she escaped. Then two caiques were sunk by ramming and demolition charges. On 9.7.43 two torpedoes were fired into Kastro harbour on Lemnos and four caiques were sunk.

(2) *Trident* attacked a German A/S trawler.

(3) *Unruly* missed a southbound German U-boat.

(4) *Taurus* fired one torpedo into the harbour which passed under the pier and then attacked with gunfire. One tug and ten caiques were reported destroyed.

(5) *Simoom* missed one of two escorted ships.

(6) *Trespasser* sank the A/S schooner *Filippo* by gunfire and the next day missed a ship leaving Bastia.

(7) *Trooper* missed the ship with torpedoes and then set it ablaze with gunfire.

(8) *Simoom* attacked a salvage tug with gunfire until A/C forced her to dive.

1	2	3	4	5	6	7	8	9	10	11	12	13	14	15	16	17
JULY 1943 *continued*																
15/							-T		15/morn.	it	-D	(Italia, Argentina)	–	/	12m Cape Ducato	
15/				-S			-T		15/	sp	-S	Liliani	...	+	Cap Cerbère	
16/	br	TACTICIAN	Collett	SS		/	-T	*Brindisi*								1
17/	br	SICKLE	Drummond	-D		/	3-T	Bastia								2
17/	br	SICKLE	Drummond	-S		+	A	Porto Vecchio								3
17/	br	TORBAY	Clutterbuck	-S	127	+	A	SE Giglio	17/1845	it	-S	Pozzallo	127	+	5m W Civitavecchia	
18/	br	SICKLE	Drummond	-S	100	+	A	7m N Gorgona	18/1330	it	APM	No 61/Costante Neri	100	+	7m N Gorgona	
18/	br	SICKLE	Drummond	-S		+	A	7m N Gorgona	18/1330	it	APM	No 164/Rosa Madre	39	+	7m E Gorgona	
18/	br	SAFARI	Lakin	APM		+	A	Cape Comino	18/1410	it	APM	No 47/Amalia	101	+	16m W C. Comino	
18/	br	UNITED	Roxburgh	SS		+	-T	*39°19N/17°30E*	*18/1830*	*it*	SS	*Remo*	*1300*	+	*Pt Alice*	
18/	br	TORBAY	Clutterbuck	-S		+	-T	SE Giglio	18/2215	it	-S	San Girolamo	109	+	20m W F. Grande	
19/	pl	DZIK	Romanowski	SS		/	4-T	*Off Malta*	*19/*	*br*	SS	*(Unshaken)*	–	/		4
19/	br	SICKLE	Drummond	-S		+	A	Pt Vecchio	19/1315	it	APC	No 131/Angiola Maria C.	65	+	33m SW Spezia	3
19/	br	TORBAY	Clutterbuck	-D	5000	/	4-T	SE Giglio								5
19/1200	br	SAFARI	Lakin	APC	1200	+	A	Favone harbour								6
19/1200	br	SAFARI	Lakin	-S		+	A	Favone harbour	19/	it	-S	Margherita	88	=	N Pt Vecchio	6
19/1530	br	SAFARI	Lakin	-Bg	250	+	A	Favone harbour	19/1530	dt	-Bg	Maria	...	+	N Pt Vecchio	6
19/1530	br	SAFARI	Lakin	-Bg	250	+	A	Favone harbour	19/1530	dt	-Bg	Paula	...	+	N Pt Vecchio	6
20/	br	SAFARI	Lakin	APY	1000	+	-T	Corsica	20/1645	it	APY	Silvio Onorato	208	+	Bastia–Maddal	6
21/0848	br	SICKLE	Drummond	AMC	6000	=	4-T	8m WNW Elba	21/1510	it	-D	Oriani	2320	=	18m ENE Bastia	7

(1) In a long-range attack, *Tactician* missed a U-boat entering Brindisi.

(2) *Sickle* missed an escorted convoy.

(3) The schooner was abandoned when the *Sickle*'s periscope was observed and the vessel was boarded and destroyed; documents were captured. It is unclear whether the two vessels with the same name were in fact different ships.

(4) *Dzik* missed a submerged submarine—which was the returning *Unshaken*.

(5) *Torbay* missed an escorted ship.

(6) *Safari* sank one auxiliary and two German barges with gunfire. The next day an A/S yacht was observed and missed with torpedoes but sunk by gunfire.

(7) *Sickle* attacked an AMC with a destroyer escort and reported one hit.

1	2	3	4	5	6	7	8	9	10	11	12	13	14	15	16	17

JULY 1943 *continued*

1	2	3	4	5	6	7	8	9	10	11	12	13	14	15	16	17
21/	br	TEMPLAR	Beckley	SS		/	7-T	W Corsica								1
22/	br	SICKLE	Drummond	-D		/	2-T	Bastia								2
22/0705	br	UNISON	Daniell	-D		/	4-T	N Messina								3
22/0900	br	SAFARI	Lakin	*CM*	*1000*	+	*TA*	*Maddalena*	22/0910	*it*	*CM*	*Durazzo*	*610*	+	*ENE Pt Vecchio*	4
23/	br	UNRIVALLED	Turner, H. B.	-D		/	3-T	N Messina								5
23/	br	UNRIVALLED	Turner, H. B.	*SS*		/	4-T	*N Messina*								5
23/	br	TORBAY	Clutterbuck	-D		+	-T	Spezia	23/1950	it	-D	Aderno/*Ardeola	2609	+	42°04N/11°47E	
24/	br	UNRIVALLED	Turner, H. B.	-S		+	A	38°59N/15°38E	24/morn.	it	-S	Impero	68	+	Off Amantea	6
25/	br	UNRIVALLED	Turner, H. B.	-Tg	80	=	A	1m S C.Vaticano	25/1200	it	-Tg	Iseo	80	+	W Calabria	6
25/	br	UNRIVALLED	Turner, H. B.	-S		+	A	1m S C.Vaticano								6
25/0905	br	SAFARI	Lakin	APC	120	+	2TA	42°42N/10°30E	25/	it		APM	FR70/La Coubre	120	+	W Elba	7

(1) *Templar* attacked a southbound German U-boat first with one, then with four and finally with two torpedoes. All missed.

(2) *Sickle* missed a large ship.

(3) *Unison* missed because the torpedoes were set too deep.

(4) *Durazzo* was driven ashore by gunfire and then torpedoed.

(5) *Unrivalled* missed with torpedoes, surfaced and began a gun engagement, but had to break off because of counter-fire. Later that day a German U-boat was missed.

(6) *Unrivalled* captured documents after this attack. The next day a tug with a schooner was attacked with gunfire and driven ashore.

(7) *Safari* missed an A/S trawler with two torpedoes and then sank her with gunfire.

1	2	3	4	5	6	7	8	9	10	11	12	13	14	15	16	17
JULY 1943 *continued*																
26/	br	SAFARI	Lakin	-D	5000	/	3-T	Piombino								1
26/	br	SAFARI	Lakin	-T	9000	/	3-T	Piombino	26/	fr	-T	(Champagne)	–	/		1
27/	br	UNSPARING	Piper	-D	5000	/	?	N Messina								2
27/1708	br	USURPER	Mott	-D		+	-T	42°04N/08°20E	27/	fr	-D	Château Yquem	2536	+	6m SW Ajaccio	
28/	br	UNRIVALLED	Turner, H. B.	-S		+	A	Cape Vaticano	28/1340	it	-Mf	San Francesco di Paola A.	102	+	Cape Vaticano	3
28/							-T		28/1645	it	-D	(Convoy)	–	/	25m SE Kassandro	
29/0654	br	TROOPER	Clarabut	*SS*		+	-T	*39°48N/18°43E*	*29/0605*	*it*	*SS*	*Pietro Micca*	*1371*	+		
29/morn.	br	SHAKESPEARE	Ainslie	-D	3500		?	Gulf of Gioja								4
AUGUST 1943																
01/	br	UNRUFFLED	Stevens, J. S.	-D		/	1-T	Brindisi	01/1045	it	-D	(Città di Catania/ 3355)	–	/		
02/							-T		02/	dt	APC	SG13/*Cyrnos	2406	=		
03/1058	br	UNRUFFLED	Stevens, J. S.	-D	3500	+	1-T	Brindisi	03/1108	it	-D	Città di Catania	3355	+	40°30N/18°04E	
04/	br	SARACEN	Lumby	-D		+	A	Off Algiers								5
04/	br	UNSEEN	Crawford	*CL*		/	4-T	*Cape Rizzuto*	*04/*	*it*	*CL*	*(Regolo class)*	–	/		6
05/	br	RORQUAL	Napier				21M	Gulf of Salonika								
06/	br	RORQUAL	Napier				29M	SE Lemnos								
06/	br	SHAKESPEARE	Ainslie	*CL*		/	3-T	*NW Ustica*		*it*	*CL*	*(Condottieri class)*	–	/		7
06/2158	br	UPROAR	Herrick	-D	2000	+	-T	41°11N/16°56E	06/2205	it	APC	D-15/Brindisi	1977	+	7m NE Bari	

(1) *Safari* missed an escorted ship and twenty minutes later attacked the tanker, which was also missed.

(2) *Unsparing* had to break off an attack because she was forced to dive by an escort.

(3) *Unrivalled* damaged a large schooner with gunfire; this must have been *San Francesco*.

(4) *Shakespeare* had to go deep to avoid escorts and could not fire.

(5) *Saracen* was asked to sink an Allied ship which was on fire and beached outside Algiers.

(6) *Unseen* missed a *Regolo* class cruiser with two destroyers.

(7) *Shakespeare* attacked two cruisers at long range and missed.

1	2	3	4	5	6	7	8	9	10	11	12	13	14	15	16	17
AUGUST 1943 *continued*																
07/1818	br	RORQUAL	Napier	-D	2500	+	-T	39°50N/25°48E	07/1800	fr	-D	Nantaise	1798	+	38°05N/25°48E	
08/	br	SIMOOM	Milner	-D		/	3-T	Bastia	08/1140	dt	APC	(...)	–	/	E Bastia	1
09/1825	br	SIMOOM	Milner	*DD*		+	6-T	*44°04N/09°32E*	*09/1835*	*it*	*DD*	*Gioberti*	*1685*	+	*5m SW Spezia*	*1*
10/1812	br	UNSHAKEN	Whitton	-D	7000	+	-T	40°44N/18°03E	10/1820	it	AK	Asmara	6860	+	3m E Brindisi	2
15/1050	br	UNRULY	Fyfe	-T		+	4-T	Off Brindisi	15/1050	it	-DT	Cesco	6161	=	Off Brindisi	3
15/2030	pl	DZIK	Romanowski	-D	6000	+	4-T	41°09N/17°25E	15/even.	it	-D	(Città di Spezia/ 2474)	–	/	27m E Bari	3
15/2030	pl	DZIK	Romanowski	-T	5000	+	"	41°09N/17°25E	15/2045	it	-D	Goggiano	1994	=	27m E Bari	3
19/	pl	DZIK	Romanowski	*SS*		/	4-T	*Nr Malta*								
19/							-T		*19/*	*dt*	*AK*	*(KT6)*	–	/	*Otranto Strait*	
20/							-T		20/	dt	-D	(Convoy)	–	/	Off Toulon	
21/	br	UNSEEN	Crawford	-D	Small	/	-T	Bari								4
22/	br	TAURUS	Wingfield	-D		/	?	Cape Helles								5
23/							-T		23/	it	-DT	(Albaro/2104)	–	/	15m W Naples	
23/							-T		23/	it	-D	(Convoy 3 ships)	–	/	6m E Bari	
27/0852	br	UNSEEN	Crawford	-D	1500	+	4-T	41°30N/16°38E	27/0900	it	-D	Rastrello/*Messaryas Nomikos)	1550	+	48m NNW Brindisi	
27/1035	br	UNRUFFLED	Stevens, J. S.	-D	4000	+	4-T	40°30N/16°38E	27/1047	it	-D	Città di Spezia	2474	+	40m E Brindisi	
28/0650	br	SICKLE	Drummond	APC	3000	+	4-T	42°26N/09°50E	28/0705	dt	APC	SG10/*Felix Henri	2526	+	42°24N/09°41E	
28/0730	br	UNSEEN	Crawford	APC	150	+	AS	40°28N/19°11E	28/0730	it	-S	Fabiola	103	+	3m SW Saseno	
28/0815	br	ULTOR	Hunt	*TB*		=	-T	39°24N/17°09E	28/0815	it	-TB	Lince	670	=§	Pt Alice/Tar.	6

(1) *Simoom* first missed a ship off Bastia but the next day attacked the cruisers *Giuseppe Garibaldi* and *Duca d'Aosta* and three destroyers. *Garibaldi* evaded the torpedoes but *Gioberti* was hit and sank.

(2) *Asmara* was beached but capsized the next day.

(3) *Dzik* claimed to have sunk both *Cesco* and *Goggiano*, but the first ship was actually hit by *Unruly*. Both ships were towed in. The torpedoes fired by *Dzik* also narrowly missed the Italian destroyer *Lubiana*.

(4) *Unseen* missed a small escorted ship.

(5) *Taurus* tried to attack a convoy but came too close and collided with the target while going deep.

(6) *Lince* ran aground on 4.8.43 and was in the process of being salvaged when the torpedo from *Ultor* hit her.

1	2	3	4	5	6	7	8	9	10	11	12	13	14	15	16	17
AUGUST 1943 *continued*																
31/1110	br	TORBAY	Clutterbuck	-S	40	+	A	16m W Kos	31/1110	it	-S	Columbo	15	+	15m W Kos	
31/1800	br	UNSPARING	Piper	-D	1300	+	2-T	41°31N/16°57E	31/1759	it	-DT	Flegetone	1162	+	2m E Bari	
SEPTEMBER 1943																
02/0652	br	TORBAY	Clutterbuck	-D	1000	+	4-T	37°11N/25°20E	02/0600	it	-D	Versilia	591	=	37°11N/25°20E	
02/	br	SERAPH	Jewell	-D		/	-T	Corsica								1
03/	br	SERAPH	Jewell	-D		/	-T	Corsica	03/morn.	dt	-D	(Convoy)	–	/	SE Bastia	1
04/	br	UNIVERSAL	Gordon	-T	7000	/	4-T	17m WNW Portofino								2
05/	br	UNRULY	Fyfe	-D	3000	/	-T	Durazzo	05/0715	dt	-D	(...)	–	/	Off Durazzo	
05/1442	br	UNSHAKEN	Whitton	-T	7000	=	4-T	40°36N/18°08E	05/1540	it	-DT	Dora C.	5843	=	9m E Brindisi	
05/	br	TROOPER	Wraith	-S	250	+	A	Skiathos								3
05/	br	TROOPER	Wraith	-Tg		=	A	Skiathos								3
05/	br	TROOPER	Wraith	-S		=	A	Skiathos								3
06/	br	UNIVERSAL	Gordon	-S		+	A	Tino I. Spezia	06/0645	it	-S	Ugo	114	+	33m SW Spezia	
06/	br	UNIVERSAL	Gordon	-S		+	A	Tino I. Spezia	06/0710	it	-M	Tre Sorelle	100	+	41m W Spezia	
06/	br	SPORTSMAN	Gatehouse	-S		+	A	Corsica	06/1840	it	-M	Maria Luisa B.	37	+	Aléria/Corsica	
06/	br	SPORTSMAN	Gatehouse	-S		+	A	Corsica	06/1840	it	-S	Angiolina	41	+	Aléria, Corsica	
07/	gr	KATSONIS	Laskos	-S		+?	A	Trikiri Channel								4
07/	br	SHAKESPEARE	Ainslie	SS		+	6-T	40°07N/14°50E	07/2000	*it*	SS	*Vellela*	689	+	*40°15N/14°30E*	5
07/							-T		[07/	sz	-D	Majola/1788+]	–		Corsica	6
07/							M		[07/	dt	-D	P.L.M.24/5391+]	–		39°22N/23°25E	7
08/1330	br	UNRIVALLED	Turner, H. B.	-D		/	-T	Off Bari								8
09/							M		[09/	it	-D	Ascianghi/610+]	–		Off Piraeus	7

(1) *Seraph* missed an escorted convoy. On 3.9.43 a convoy was again attacked, but one of three torpedoes hit the bottom and exploded.

(2) *Universal* missed a tanker.

(3) *Trooper* sank a schooner by gunfire, set a tug on fire and damaged a second schooner.

(4) There was a report of an attack against an unidentified escort vessel, possibly by *Katsonis*, which was lost on 14.9.43 by being rammed by the German auxiliary *UJ2101* (q.v.).

(5) *Shakespeare* fired six torpedoes against two submarines and sank one.

(6) *Maloja* was sunk in error by Allied air attack.

(7) *PLM24* and *Ascianghi* were sunk on mines, but not on the barrages laid by *Rorqual* on 5/6.8.43 (q.v.).

(8) *Unrivalled* missed a small Italian ship.

1	2	3	4	5	6	7	8	9	10	11	12	13	14	15	16	17
SEPTEMBER 1943 *continued*																
09/	br	UNSHAKEN	Whitton	*SS*		P	P	*Otranto Strait*	*09/*	*it*	*SS*	*Menotti*	*858*	*P*	*Otranto Strait*	1
09/	br	RORQUAL	Napier				M	Trikiri Channel								
09/							-T		*09/*	*dt*	*LC*	*F345*	*155*	*+*	*5m N Terracina*	
10/	br	SERAPH	Jewell	2LC		+	A	Corsica								2
10/	br	SERAPH	Jewell	2-Bg	100	+	A	Corsica								2
10/	br	UNRIVALLED	Turner, H. B.	8-D		P	P	Bari								3
10/	nl	DOLFIJN	Van Oestrom Soede	*SS*		P	P	*E Bastia*	*10/*	*it*	*SS*	*Corridoni*	*833*	*P*		4
10/	br	RORQUAL	Napier				M	N Skiathos								
11/1548	nl	DOLFIJN	Van Oostrom Soede	-D	9000	+	4-T	Nr Corsica	*11/1542*	*it*	*-M*	*Humanitas*	*7980*	*=§*	*Bastia harbour*	5
11/	br	SERAPH	Jewell	AK		/	3-T	Corsica								6
11/	br	SERAPH	Jewell	-D	1400	=	2-T	N Civitavecchia								6
	br	TRESPASSER	Favell	-D		/	-T	SW Aegean								7

(1) Shortly after the announcement of the Italian armistice, *Unshaken* intercepted *Menotti*, boarded her and brought her to Malta.

(2) *Seraph* sank two landing barges and two transport barges of 50 tons each with gunfire.

(3) *Unrivalled*'s CO boarded a trawler outside Bari, entered the port and organised eight merchant ships into a convoy, which he escorted to Malta.

(4) *Dolfijn* met *Corridoni* and ordered her to replenish in Portoferraio and then go to Bone.

(5) *Humanitas* had her stern blown off, was beached and became a total loss.

(6) *Seraph* first attacked a KT ship with two E-boats and missed, then a 1,400-ton ship which, it was assumed, was hit by one torpedo.

(7) *Trespasser* made four unsuccessful attacks during a patrol lasting from 29.8 to 14.9.43.

1	2	3	4	5	6	7	8	9	10	11	12	13	14	15	16	17
SEPTEMBER 1943 *continued*																
12/	br	RORQUAL	Napier				M	Lemnos								
12/	pl	SOKOL	Karnicki	-Mb		+	R	Brindisi	12/	it	-Mb	Meattini	36	+	Pt. Brindisi	
12/	gr	KATSONIS	Laskos	-S		+	P	W Skyros								1
13/1040	nl	DOLFIJN	Van Oostrom Soede	-Bg	250	+	A	44°09N/09°37E	13/	dt	-Bg	...	...	+	Sestri Levante	2
13/1040	nl	DOLFIJN	Van Oostrom Soede	-Bg	250	+	A	44°09N/09°37E	13/	dt	-Bg	...	...	+	Sestri Levante	2
13/	gr	KATSONIS	Laskos	-S		+	P	W Skyros								1
13/	gr	KATSONIS	Laskos	-S		=	A	W Skyros								1
14/	gr	KATSONIS	Laskos	-D	4743	+	-T	Volos	14/	dt	-D	(Sinfra/4743)	–	/	Suda Crete	1
15/1200	nl	DOLFIJN	Van Oostrom Soede	-D		/	-T	Off Corsica	15/	fr	-D	(Dalny/6672)	–	/		3
21/1623	br	UNSEEN	Crawford	-D	2000	+	4-T	43°08N/09°58E	21/1740	dt	ACM	Brandenburg/*Kita	3895	+	Off Capreira	
21/1623	br	UNSEEN	Crawford	-D	2000	+	"	43°08N/09°58E	21/1740	dt	APC	Kreta/*Ile de Beauté	2600	+	43°06N/17°40E	
21/1636	pl	DZIK	Romanowski	-T	6793	+	2-T	Nr Bastia	16/	dt	-T	Nikolaus/*Nicolaou Ourania	6397	+	Bastia	4
21/1636	pl	DZIK	Romanowski	-Tg		+	"	Nr Bastia		dt	-Tg	Kraft	...	+		4
22/	pl	DZIK	Romanowski	*3LC*		+	4-T	*Nr Bastia*								4
22/0917	br	SIBYL	Turner, E. J.	-D	1500	/	4-T	44°11N/09°24E	22/	dt	-D	(Convoy)	–	/	25m E Genova	5
22/0949	br	UPROAR	Herrick	-D	800	+	3-T	42°50N/10°21E	22/	it	-D	Andrea Sgarallino	731	+	Piombino	
22/							-T		22/	it	-M	Rovigno	451	+	Off Valona	

(1) *Katsonis* took two caiques as prizes on 12/13.9.43 and damaged one more. On 14.9.43 she claimed the sinking of *Sinfra* but this vessel was in fact sunk on 19/20.10.43 in an USAAF air attack while transporting 2,664 Italian POWs, of whom only 566 were rescued. *Katsonis* was sunk on 14.9.43 by *UJ2101*.

(2) *Dolfijn* sank two German transport barges with gunfire.

(3) *Dalny* had been previously damaged by the French submarine *Aréthuse* on 4.6.43 (q.v.) and the British submarine *Tribune* on 10/11.1.43 (q.v.), and also by aircraft, and was already a wreck.

(4) *Dzik* fired torpedoes into the harbour at Bastia, and in addition to the two ships mentioned some barges were sunk or damaged. The French steamer *Tiberiade/*2969, sometimes claimed, was in fact hit by aircraft bombs. The next day three Siebel ferries were claimed sunk by surface-running torpedoes.

(5) *Sibyl* missed an escorted ship in ballast.

1	2	3	4	5	6	7	8	9	10	11	12	13	14	15	16	17
SEPTEMBER 1943 *continued*																
23/1623	br	SIBYL	Turner, E. J.	-D	3000	+	-T	44°13N/09°13E	23/	dt	-D	St Nazaire	2910	+	17m NW Spezia	
24/0410	br	ULTOR	Hunt	-T	9946	/	2-T	Bastia	24/0410	dt	-MT	Champagne	9946	=	11m E Bastia	1
24/	pl	DZIK	Romanowski	-T	9946	+	2-T	Nr Bastia	24/1800	dt	-MT	Champagne	9946	=	11m E Bastia	1
24/2210	br	ULTOR	Hunt	-T	9946	=§	4-T	Off Bastia	24/2000	dt	-MT	Champagne	9946	=	Off Bastia	1
25/									25/1033	dt	-D	(...)	–	/	Bastia harbour	
25/morn.	br	ULTOR	Hunt	-T	9946	/	2-T	Off Bastia	25/	dt	LC	SF...	...	?	Bastia	1
27/1805	br	UPROAR	Herrick	-T	9946	+	1-T	Off Bastia	27/1805	dt	-MT	Champagne	9946	+§	Off Bastia	1
27/	br	UPROAR	Herrick	-D	6000	/	3-T	Bastia								1
28/	br	SICKLE	Drummond	-D		/	3-T	Gulf of Genoa								2
28/	br	SPORTSMAN	Gatehouse	-S		+	A	Aléria, Corsica	28/	it	-S	Angiolina	39	+	Aléria, Corsica	3
28/	br	SPORTSMAN	Gatehouse	-S		+	A	Aléria, Corsica	28/	it	-S	Maria Luisa B.	37	+	Aléria, Corsica	3
28/	br	UNSPARING	Piper	-S		+	A	36°27N/23°05E	28/	gr	-S	...	...	+	N Cerigo	4
28/							A		28/noon	gr	-S	...	...	+	Velanidia harbour	
28/	br	UNSEEN	Crawford	-D		/	4-T	Capreira								5
29/							-T		29/	dt	-D	(Convoy)	–	/	E Bastia	
29/	br	SIBYL	Turner, E. J.	*LC*		/	*1-T*	*Bastia*								6
30/	br	ULTIMATUM	Kett	-Bg	500	+	2-T	Toulon								7
30/1526	br	SIBYL	Turner, E. J.	-D	500	+	-T	42°49N/09°40E	30/1700	dt	AG	M7022/*Hummer/ *Auguste Denise	278	+	12m NE Bastia	
30/							-T		[30/	dt	APC	UJ2214/*Clair-voyant/943]	–		Tyrrhenian Sea	8

(1) *Champagne* was first attacked at 0410 on 24.9.43 and this attack is claimed by *Dzik*, but the truth of the claim is uncertain. At 1800 there was another attack, which is not claimed, then at 2000 *Ultor* scored two hits from four torpedoes and the ship had to be beached. On the morning of 25.9.43 *Ultor* fired two more torpedoes: *Champagne* was missed but a Siebel ferry alongside was claimed as sunk. On 27.9.43 *Uproar* finished off *Champagne* with one more hit but later in the day missed a ship with three torpedoes.

(2) *Sickle* missed a coaster.

(3) Both sailing vessels were sunk on 28.9.43 and not on 6.9.43.

(4) *Unsparing* sank a small caique.

(5) *Unseen* missed an escorted ship in bad weather.

(6) *Sibyl* missed a Siebel ferry.

(7) *Ultimatum* attacked a convoy of four barges with seven ex French chasseurs (including *M6041*, *M6043* and *M6047*) and sank one barge.

(8) The attack against the German APC *UJ2214/*Clairvoyant* cannot be confirmed. The vessel was sunk on 24.4.44 (q.v.).

1	2	3	4	5	6	7	8	9	10	11	12	13	14	15	16	17

OCTOBER 1943

1	2	3	4	5	6	7	8	9	10	11	12	13	14	15	16	17
01/	br	UNSHAKEN	Whitton	LC		/	-T	Elba								1
01/							-T		01/	dt	-D	(Convoy)	–	/	E Bastia	
01/	br	SICKLE	Drummond	APC		/	3-T	Gulf of Genoa	02/	dt	APC	(UJ2210)	–	/	Porto Ferraio	2
02/	br	UNSHAKEN	Whitton	-D		/	2-T	Elba								1
02/dark	br	UNSHAKEN	Whitton	LC		=	A	Elba								1
03/	br	UNRUFFLED	Stevens, J. S.	-D		/	-T	Bastia	03/	dt	PR	(R212)	–	/	Off Bastia	3
03/							3-T		03/	dt	APC	(UJ2208)	–	/	SE Rapallo	
03/1340	br	UNSHAKEN	Whitton	-D	3000	=	3-T	Pt. Longone Elba	03/	it	-D	(Nina/2212)	–	/	Elba I.	1
									04.10.M	it	-D	Sigliano	...	=	10m S Pola	
04/0758	pl	SOKOL	Koziolkowski	-D	6000	+	2-T	Pola/Adriatic	04/							4
04/	pl	SOKOL	Koziolkowski	-D		/	2-T	Pola	04/	it	-D	(Sansego)	–	/	38m SE Pola	4
05/	br	UNRUFFLED	Stevens, J. S.	-D		/	-T	Gorgona								5
05/		Probably not submarine mine					M		[05/0845	dt	ACM	Pommern/2955+]	–		1.5m S San Remo	
07/0600	br	UNRULY	Piper	LC		=	-TA	Amorgos	[07/0450	dt	-D	Olympos/852+]	–		Stampalia	6
07/	br	UNSHAKEN	Whitton	-D		/	3-T	Corsica								7
07/0710	pl	SOKOL	Koziolkowski	-D	4600	+	3-T	Pola/Adriatic	07/0740	it	-D	Eridania	7095	+	Cape Promontore	
07/0710	pl	SOKOL	Koziolkowski	-D		+	"	Pola/Adriatic								
07/	pl	SOKOL	Koziolkowski	-D		/	1-T	Off Pola	07/1445	it	-D	(Sansego)	–	/	Cape Promontore	8
07/1600	pl	SOKOL	Koziolkowski	-D	1500	=	A	Pola	07/	it	-D	(Ugliano)	–	/	Zara–Pola	8
07/							-T?		[07/even.	it	AH	Gradisca/13870=?]	–		Patras harbour	9

(1) *Unshaken* missed F-lighters in two attacks and the next day missed a coaster at long range. After dark F-lighters were attacked with machine-gun fire. On 3.10.43 a torpedo was fired into the harbour, damaging a ship and the jetty.

(2) *Sickle* fired two torpedoes at a UJ boat but these were evaded.

(3) *Unruffled* missed a ship in ballast entering Bastia.

(4) *Sokol* reported one ship sunk, but *Dea Macelli*/3080, sometimes claimed, was sunk by Yugoslav partisans. *Sokol* attacked also a southbound ship and missed, one torpedo circling.

(5) *Unruffled* missed a convoy.

(6) *Unruly* attacked a convoy with *Olympos*, five MFPs and *UJ2111* with an infantry battalion aboard en route for Coos; she missed with torpedoes but hit some MFPs later with gunfire. *Olympos* was sunk later by British surface forces.

(7) *Unshaken* missed an escorted tanker.

(8) *Sokol* missed with torpedoes and then attacked with gunfire, scoring several hits.

(9) The hospital ship *Gradisca* was preparing for an exchange of Allied and German badly injured casualties when two explosions erupted near the stern. There was only minor damage, however, and the ship left on 15.10.43 for Oran.

1	2	3	4	5	6	7	8	9	10	11	12	13	14	15	16	17

OCTOBER 1943 *continued*

1	2	3	4	5	6	7	8	9	10	11	12	13	14	15	16	17
08/	br	UNRIVALLED	Turner, H. B.	-D		/	3-T	SW Aegean	08/*morn.*	dt	CM	(*Drache*/Bulgaria)	–	/	*Piraeus-Kos*	1
08/	nr	UNSPARING	Piper	-S		P	P	Aegean								2
08/1706	br	UNRULY	Fyfe	-D	1500	+	4-T	36°43N/25°49E	08/1523	dt	ACM	Bulgaria	1108	+	36°46N/25°51E	3
11/	br	UNRULY	Fyfe	-D	920	+	-T	Argostoli								
13/	br	TROOPER (?)	Wraith	–			-T		13/2140	dt	-D	(Marguerite/*Maria Amalia*)	747	+	38°05N/21°02E	4
									[13/	dt	AO	M7023/*Languste/ *Nautilus*/2027]	–	/	4m SW C. Figari	5
14/0900	nl	DOLFIJN	Van Oostrom Soede	-Dc		/	A	Nr Toulon	14/0955	fr	-S	...	...	=	6m Cape Tropez	
14/0900	nl	DOLFIJN	Van Oostrom Soede	-Dc		/	A	Nr Toulon								
14/after.	br	TROOPER (?)	Wraith				A		14/aft.	dt	APC	(2 GK...)	–	/	Kasos Passage	6
15/0603	br	UNTIRING	Boyd	SS		/	4-T	*Toulon*	15/	dt	SS	(U616)	–	/		7
15/	br	TORBAY	Clutterbuck	-S	50	+	A	E Leros	15/1340	gr	-S	...	...	+	Pezonda Bay	8
15/	br	TORBAY	Clutterbuck	-D	749	+	-T	Naxos–Kos	15/	it	-D	Tarquinia	749	+		
16/1300	br	TORBAY	Clutterbuck	-D	1000	+	4-T	36°59N/26°11E	16/1101	dt	-D	Kari/*Ste Colette	1925	+	36°59N/26°10E	9
16/	br	TORBAY	Clutterbuck	-D	1855	=	-T	Kos–Leros	16/	dt	-D	Trapani	1855	=		
18/							-T		18/1550	dt	-D	E. H. Fisser	5145	+	6m Dubrovnik	
19/	br	UNTIRING	Boyd	LC		/	2-T	*Gulf of Frejus*								10
19/	br	ULTOR	Hunt	-D	3500	+	2-T	Civitavecchia	19/1212	dt	-D	Aversa/*Kakoulima	3723	+	Off Rapallo	
19/	br	UNSPARING	Piper	PR			-T		19/	dt	-PR	R40	110	+	*Aegean*	
21/	br	UNTIRING	Boyd	-D		/	2-T	NW Spezia							Cape Sicié	11
22/	br	UNSEEN	Crawford	LC		+	4-T	*Off Imperia*	22/	dt	LC	F541	155	+	*Off Imperia*	12
22/	br	UNSEEN	Crawford	LC		=	4-T									12
24/	br	ULTOR	Hunt	-D		/	-T	Gulf of Genoa	24/0752	dt	AK	(Convoy, *KT.*.)	–	/	Off Genoa	

(1) *Unrivalled* missed a small merchant ship carrying troops

(2) *Unsparing* towed an abandoned caique to Beirut.

(3) *Bulgaria* and *Drache* had laid the minefield in which the British submarine *Trooper* sank on 15.10.43, and three destroyers were hit.

(4) *Marguerite* (ex Spanish steamer *Maria Amelia*) was sunk, possibly by the lost *Trooper* or on a mine; 350 out of 900 passengers were rescued.

(5) *Languste* was the former Italian motor tanker *Nautilus*. She could not, as claimed, have been sunk by the British submarine *Utmost* because the latter had already been lost one year earlier.

(6) *Trooper* may have made this attack before being lost.

(7) *Untiring* missed the U-boat, which observed the attack and evaded.

(8) *Torbay* sank a Greek caique and was depth-charged by the Q-ship *GA45*.

(9) Of the 500 troops on board, 320 were rescued.

(10) *Untiring* missed two large landing barges.

(11) *Untiring* missed a merchant ship at close range.

(12) *Unseen* attacked two F-lighters with three torpedoes and scored two hits on one of them; the fourth torpedo damaged the other lighter, which had been beached.

1	2	3	4	5	6	7	8	9	10	11	12	13	14	15	16	17
OCTOBER 1943 *continued*																
25/	br	SURF	Lambert. D.	-D		/	A	Amorgos	25/0545	dt	APC	GA54/Chlaros	...	=	5m E Amorgos	
26/	br	SHAKESPEARE	Ainslie	-S		+	A	38°06N/25°22E	26/2030	gr	-S	Aghios Konstantinos	...	+	23m NE Andros	1
27/1219	br	ULTIMATUM	Kett	-D	3000	=?	4-T	Cape Sicié								2
27/	br	SERAPH	Jewell	-S		+	A	Naxos–Mykoni								3
27/	br	SERAPH	Jewell	APC		/	2-T	Naxos–Mykoni								3
29/	br	UNSPARING	Piper	-D	3000	+	4-T	36°33N/25°54E	29/0056	dt	-D	Ingeborg G./*Ste Martine	1160	+	W Stampalia	
29/0812	br	UNSPARING	Piper	*PR*	60	+	1-T	*W Stampalia*	29/0812	dt	APC	GA.../*AS49/*Nioi	60	+	W Stampalia	
29/	br	SURF	Lambert. D.	-D		/	5-T	Mykoni harbour	29/0830	dt	APC	(Hunting group)	–	/	S Amorgos	4
29/							-T		29/after.	dt	-D	(Gerda Toft)	–	/	Panormos Bay	
30/	br	ULTIMATUM	Kett	*SS*		+	3-T	*43°04N/05°57E*	*30/*	*dt*	*SS*	*(U73)*	–	+		
31/1515	br	UNSPARING	Piper	-S		=	A	36°44N/25°48E								5
../	br	UNRULY	Fyfe	-S		=	A	Aegean								6
NOVEMBER 1943																
02/	br	UPSTART	Chapman	-D		/	-T	Toulon	02/	fr	-D	(Medjerda/4578)	–	/	Off Toulon	7
02/							-T		[02/	dt	APC	UJ2206/*Saint Martin Legasse	1179	+]	Off San Stefano	8
03/	br	SHAKESPEARE	Ainslie	-S	100	+	A	Off Kos								
05/2330	br	SERAPH	Jewell	-S	150	+	A	Kaso Strait	05/	dt	-S	Aghios Miltiades	150	+	Kaso Strait	9
06/	br	SERAPH	Jewell	-S		+	1-T	Scarpanto	06/	dt	-S	Narkyssos	...	+	Pegadia Bay	9
07/							-T?		07/	dt	-D	Diana	1190	=	40m SE Pola	
07/	br	SIMOOM (?)	Milner (?)				-T		07/	dt	APC	UJ2145/*Eleni S.	110	+	Aegean	10
09/							-T		09/	dt	-Tg	Z16/*Sicam 42	52	+	Saseno harbour	
10/	br	SIMOOM (?)	Milner (?)				-T		10/	it	-D	Trapani	1855	+	Aegean	10

(1) *Shakespeare* sank a large two-masted caique with gunfire.

(2) *Ultimatum* heard one detonation, but the victim was not, as sometimes claimed, the Red Cross ship *Padua*/665.

(3) *Seraph* sank a caique and then attacked two A/S vessels with torpedoes, which missed.

(4) *Surf* fired two torpedoes into the harbour without observing any results. Three hours later three more torpedoes were fired, without result.

(5) *Unsparing* had to break off an attack on a caique.

(6) *Unruly* attacked a caique with gunfire on an unspecified date after 27.10.43.

(7) *Upstart* made two unsuccessful attacks on merchant ships.

(8) *UJ2206* was not sunk by a submarine but by the US *PT212*.

(9) *Seraph* took 14 German prisoners from this ship. The next day she fired one torpedo into the harbour and the vessel blew up.

(10) The attacks may have been made by the British submarine *Simoom*, which was lost on 19.11.43, possibly to a torpedo fired by *U565* off Coos.

1	2	3	4	5	6	7	8	9	10	11	12	13	14	15	16	17

NOVEMBER 1943 *continued*

1	2	3	4	5	6	7	8	9	10	11	12	13	14	15	16	17
11/	pl	SOKOL	Koziolkowski	-S	140	+	1TA	Aegean	11/	it	-S	Argentina	64	+	Amorgos	1
12/	br	UNSEEN	Crawford	-T	4000	/	4-T	Toulon								2
15/	br	SPORTSMAN	Gatehouse	-S	100	+	A	Naxos–Mykoni	15/	gr	-S	....		...	+	Naxos area	3
15/	br	SIMOOM (?)	Milner (?)	–			A		15/2030	gr	-S	Trias		...	+	Mudros Mytilene	4
17/	pl	DZIK	Klopotowski	-S		+	A	Monemvasia								5
18/	br	SICKLE	Drummond	-S	80	+	A	Leros								6
18/	br	SPORTSMAN	Gatehouse	*TB*		/	-T	*Naxos–Mykoni*								*3*
18/	pl	SOKOL	Koziolkowski	-S	20	+	A	Santorin								7
19/0730	pl	SOKOL	Koziolkowski	-S	200	+	2-T	San Nicolo I.	19/0808	gr	-S		–	/	Siteia Bay	7
19/	pl	SOKOL	Koziolkowski	-S	200	+	3-T	San Nicolo I.	19/1400	gr	-S	...		...	+	Siteia, Crete	7
19/	pl	SOKOL	Koziolkowski	-S	200	+	"		19/1400	gr	-S	...		...	+	Siteia, Crete	7
19/	pl	SOKOL	Koziolkowski	*PT*		+	"		19/1400	dt	APC	Möve		...	+	Siteia, Crete	7
19/	br	UNSEEN	Crawford	-D	3000	/	-T	Toulon								8
19/	br	UNIVERSAL	Gordon	-D		/	4-T	Cannes–Toulon								9
19/							-T		[19/	ru	-D	Balcic/3600=]	–		Dardanelles (?)	10
19/1545	br	SICKLE	Drummond	-D	3500	+	3-T	Monemvasia	19/1654	it	-D	Giovanni Bocaccio	3141	+	Monemvassia	
19/2411	br	SIBYL	Turner, E. J.	4-S	250	+	A	Saloniki								11

(1) *Sokol* attacked first with her gun, then fired a torpedo which caused the crew to abandon ship, which was then boarded and sunk by demolition charges.

(2) *Unseen* made an unsuccessful attack against a tanker.

(3) *Sportsman* sank a 100-ton caique on 15.11.43 and on 18.11.43 missed a destroyer in moonlight.

(4) The lost *Simoom* may have been responsible for these attacks (see Note 10, previous page).

(5) *Dzik* sank a caique with gunfire.

(6) *Sickle* sank a caique with gunfire and took a German prisoner.

(7) On 18.11.43 *Sokol* sank a caique with gunfire; on 19.11.43 first a gun attack was made, then two torpedoes were fired which destroyed the vessel, which had troops on board. The third caique was attacked by torpedo; this missed, but it blew up another small vessel. Later an E-boat was sunk with another torpedo.

(8) *Unseen* missed a ship in difficult light and weather conditions.

(9) *Universal* missed a large merchant ship in bad weather.

(10) *Balcic* has sometimes been credited to *Simoom*, but the latter was lost in the Aegean while *Balcic* was, on 10.11.43, at Split.

(11) Between 18 and 21.11.43 *Sibyl* sank four caiques, having taken off the Greek crews.

1	2	3	4	5	6	7	8	9	10	11	12	13	14	15	16	17
NOVEMBER 1943 *continued*																
21/	br	TORBAY	Clutterbuck	-S	50	+	A	39°30N/24°10E								1
22/	br	UNIVERSAL	Gordon	-Bg		+	3-T	Cannes–Toulon								2
22/1540	br	TORBAY	Clutterbuck	IX	15000	+	7-T	39°24N/23°24E	19/	dt	AX	(Floating dock)				1
							M		23/	sp	-D	Alma	253	+	Naxos	
23/1415	fr	PROTÉE	Garreau	-D	2000	=	-T	Cape Camarat	23/	dt	AN	(NTII/997)	–	/	St Tropez	
23/							A		23/	gr	-S	Panagia Chios	...	+	17m Skopelos	
25/	br	SICKLE	Drummond	-S		+	A	37°22N/24°15E								3
25/	br	SICKLE	Drummond	-S		+	A	37°22N/24°15E								3
26/							-T		26/	tu	-M	Issani Huda	...	+	Off Smyrna	
26/	br	TORBAY	Clutterbuck	-D		/	3-T	Lemnos–Tenedos	26/0954	dt	-D	(Salomea/751)	–	/	Off Lemnos	4
27/0704	br	TORBAY	Clutterbuck	-D	2609	+	2-T	Karlovassi	27/0700	dt	-D	Palma/*Polcevera	2609	+	Karlovassi	4
DECEMBER 1943																
01/	br	UNSPARING	Piper													
02/	br	UNRULY	Fyfe	-S	50	+	58A	S Levitha	02/0610	gr	-S	...	...	+	8m S Levitha	5
03/							-T		03/	dt	-D	Menes	5609	+	Off Crete	
03/	br	SHAKESPEARE	Ainslie	-S	100	+	A	Kos								6
05/	br	UNRULY	Fyfe	-S		/	2-T	Mykonos								7
06/0820	br	UPROAR	Herrick	-DP	6000	+	3-T	Toulon	06/0820	dt	-DP	Virgilio/*Dubrovnik	11718	=§	NE St Tropez	8
07/1130	fr	CURIE	Sonneville	LC		?	1-T	Camarat	07/	dt	LC	(F518/220)	–	/	Camarat	
07/	fr	ORPHÉE	Dupont	-Tg		=	3-T	43°02N/06°01E	07/1440	fr	-Tg	Faron	348	+	Off Toulon	

(1) On 21.11.43 *Torbay* sank a caique and on 2311.43 fired first five torpedoes at a floating dock and two tugs, which missed, and later two more, which hit the dock.

(2) *Universal* sank a large motor barge with one hit.

(3) *Sickle* sank two caiques.

(4) On 26.11.43 *Torbay* missed a small merchant ship and on 27.11.43 hit *Palma* with her last two torpedoes. Some 1,100 Germans and 'loyal' Italians perished.

(5) *Unruly* achieved 12 hits from 58 rounds.

(6) *Shakespeare* sank a caique with gunfire.

(7) *Unruly* fired at two caiques but the torpedoes exploded on the rocks.

(8) *Virgilio* became a total loss as a result of this attack.

1	2	3	4	5	6	7	8	9	10	11	12	13	14	15	16	17
DECEMBER 1943 *continued*																
07/even.	br	UNRULY	Fyfe	-D		/	2-T	Vathi, Samos	07/	dt	-D	(Leda)	–	/		1
08/	br	SURF	Lambert, D.	-D		/	4-T	Mykoni Channel	08/0923	dt	-D	(Leda)	–	/	NE Stenopas	2
09/1915	br	SURF	Lambert, D.	-D		+	5-T	1m S Lemnos	09/1810	dt	-D	Sonja/*SNA9	2719	+	Off Kythnos	3
11/	br	UPROAR	Herrick	-D	7800	/	-T	Cannes–Monaco	11/0500	dt	-D	(Convoy)	–	/	S Cannes	4
11/	pl	SOKOL	Koziolkowski	-D	4500	+	4-T	Nr Lemnos	11/	gr	-D	(Xanthippe/4000)	–	/	Lemnos	5
12/	pl	SOKOL	Koziolkowski	-S		+	A	Nr Lemnos	12/2100	gr	-S	Nicolaos Pi. 790	...	+	Nr Lemnos	6
12/	pl	SOKOL	Koziolkowski	-S		+	A	Nr Lemnos	12/2100	gr	-S	Nicolaos Sy. 436	...	+	Nr Lemnos	6
12/	pl	SOKOL	Koziolkowski	-S		+	A	Nr Lemnos	12/2100	gr	-S	Nicolaos Sy. 262	...	+	Nr Lemnos	6
12/	pl	SOKOL	Koziolkowski	-S		+	A	Nr Lemnos	12/2100	gr	-S	Aghios Eleimon Sy. 274	...	+	Nr Lemnos	6
13/	br	UNRULY	Fyfe	-D		/	2-T	Samos	*13/*	dt	CM	(Drache)	–	/		7
14/	br	UNTIRING	Boyd	-D	1000	+	1-T	Monaco	14/	dt	AN	Netztender 44/ *Prudente	396	+	Monaco harbour	
16/	pl	SOKOL	Koziolkowski	-S	20	+	P	E Mudros	16/	gr	-S	...	...	P		8
17/0700	pl	SOKOL	Koziolkowski	-D	4000	=	4-T	Nr Lemnos	17/	dt	-D	(Balkan/3838)	–	/	C. Irene/Lemnos	9
17/	br	UNTIRING	Boyd	-D	500	+	-T	Toulon	17/	dt	-Tg	Faron	...	+	Off Toulon	10
17/	br	UNTIRING	Boyd	-D	500	+	-T	Toulon	10							
17/noon							2-T	S Savona	17/noon	fr	-Bg	2 pinnaces	...	=	S Savona	

(1) *Unruly* missed a ship with two escorts.

(2) *Surf* unsuccessfully attacked *Leda*, which had 5,000 Italian prisoners on board; *TA16* dropped 24 D/Cs.

(3) *Surf* fired four torpedoes, one failing to run and three missing; then the stern shot hit and sank the ship.

(4) *Uproar* made a submerged attack by moonlight but missed.

(5) *Sokol* made a snap attack under the watchkeeping officer Sub-Lt Fritz but the detonation heard was probably caused by a bomb dropped by an escorting aircraft. Greek prisoners reported the ship sunk as the Greek *Xanthippe*, but this is not confirmed by German records.

(6) *Sokol* sank four sailing vessels with gunfire and took six Greeks prisoner. A fifth caique escaped.

(7) *Unruly* missed a merchant ship with two destroyers and two E-boats.

(8) From this caique *Sokol* took six Greeks and seven Germans prisoner. The Greeks were transferred from the captured caique to a Turkish vessel, then the caique was sunk.

(9) The hits reported were probably bombs dropped by escorting aircraft.

(10) *Untiring* sank two coasters laden with ammunition.

1	2	3	4	5	6	7	8	9	10	11	12	13	14	15	16	17
DECEMBER 1943 *continued*																
18/	br	ULTOR	Hunt	-Bg	250	+	2-T	French Riviera								1
18/1130	br	UNIVERSAL	Gordon	-D	5000	+	4-T	44°15N/09°20E	18/1120	dt	-D	La Foce	2497	+	44°15N/09°18E	
19/							3-T		19/0622	dt	LC	(F...)	–	/	N Elba	
19	br	SPORTSMAN	Gatehouse	-S		+	S	S Lemnos	19/	gr	-S		...	+		2
19/1430	fr	CURIE	Sonneville	LC		+	1-T	Camarat	19/	dt	LC	(F518/220)	–	/		
20/	br	SICKLE	Drummond	LC		+	4TA	Karlovasi	20/1850	dt	LC	(F...)	–	/	Samos/Piraeus	3
21/	b	SPORTSMAN	Gatehouse	-S		+	A	S Lemnos	21/0855	gr	-S	Spiridon Sy. 283	...	=	S Lemnos	
22/1530	fr	CASABIANCA	Bellet	APC		+	4-T	43°06N/05°51E	22/1550	dt	APC	UJ6076/*Volontaire)	916	+	2m S Cape Sicié	
23/	br	SPORTSMAN	Gatehouse	-D	3840	+	-T	39°44N/25°16E	23/1030	dt	-D	Balkan	3838	+	Off Mudros	
23/							-T		23/1320	dt	LC	(F...)	–	/	Sestri Levante	
24/							2-T		24/1130	dt	LC	(F...)	–	/	Cape Camarat	
25/	br	TORBAY	Clutterbuck	-S	80	=	A	Cape Stavros	25/1505	gr	-S	...	...	?	NNW Iraklion	4
26/	br	SICKLE	Drummond	-S		+	A	E Mykonos	26/	gr	-S	...	...	+		5
26/	br	SICKLE	Drummond	-S		+	A	E Mykonos	26/	gr	-S	...	...	+		5
27/									27/	dt	-D	Estella (?)	...	?	Sestri Levante	
28/	br	UPROAR	Herrick	-D	3000	/	4-T	Genoa	28/	fr	-D	(Chisone)	–	/		6
28/0902	fr	CASABIANCA	Bellet	-D	4000	=	4-T	43°12N/06°42E	28/0948	fr	-D	Chisone	6168	=	CJ 1448/Toulon	6
28/							-T		[28/	dt	APM	M7009/*Marylou	18	+]	Civitavecchia	7

(1) *Ultor* sank a French canal barge with one hit.

(2) *Sportsman* took four Greeks prisoner.

(3) *Sickle* fired four torpedoes at an F-lighter and a caique. One premature affected the other torpedoes, which missed.

(4) *Torbay* had to dive because of counter-battery fire.

(5) *Sickle* sank two caiques with gunfire, having taken off the crews.

(6) *Uproar* missed a ship with a destroyer and UJ escort. The ship was sunk a short time later by *Casabianca*, which was heavily depth-charged by *UJ2210*.

(7) *M7009* was actually sunk in an air attack.

1	2	3	4	5	6	7	8	9	10	11	12	13	14	15	16	17
JANUARY 1944																
03/0507	br	UPROAR	Herrick	-D		/	4-T	French Riviera									1
06/							-T		06/	dt	-Bg	(.../F...)	–	/	Sestri Levante	
06/1135	br	UNTIRING	Boyd	*LC*		+	3-T	*44°13N/09°29E*	*06/noon*	*dt*	*LC*	*F296*	*155*	+	*Rapallo*	2
07/0749	pl	DZIK	Romanowski	-D	5600	+	4-T	39°42N/26°02E	07/	dt	-DT	(Brunhilde/*Bacchus/ 1810)	–	/	S Tenedos	3
08/2330	pl	DZIK	Romanowski	3-S	200	+	A	39°37N/25°43E	08/	dt	-S	Elleni	200	+	Mytilene area	3
08/	br	UNRULY	Fyfe	-S	100	+	A	Cape Doro								4
08/0030	br	SIBYL	Turner, E. J.	-S	30	+	A	Cape Baba	08/	gr	-S	Taxiachos	32	+	N Mitylene	5
09/	br	SIBYL	Turner, E. J.	-S	200	+	A	Cape Baba	09/night	dt	-Mb	...	...	+	Baba Burnu	5
09/							-T		[09/	it	-Mf	Ivagete I/61+]	–		Off Genoa	6
09/	pl	DZIK	Romanowski	-S	30	+	A	38°25N/25°21E								
10/							-T		10/night	it	-D	(Mediceo/5083)	–	/	Trieste–Venezia	
11/	br	UNRULY	Fyfe	-S	100	+	A	Vitali Bay	11/	gr	-S	...	...	+	Off Andros	4
11/	br	UNRULY	Fyfe	-S	40	+	A	Panormus harbour								4
11/	br	UNRULY	Fyfe	-S	100	+	A	37°39N/25°05E								4
11/	br	UNRULY	Fyfe	-S	40	+	A	37°39N/25°05E								4
12/									[12/	fr	-D	Capitaine Luigi/ 3176+]	–		Off Marseilles	7
12/	pl	SOKOL	Koziolkowski	-S	40	+	A	36°30N/24°44E	12/	gr	-S	No 53	...	+		
15/0300	br	UNRULY	Fyfe	-S	20	+	A	37°38N/24°54E	15/0300	gr	-S	Aghios Giorgios/ Pi997		+	N Syra	4
15/1605	br	UNSPARING	Piper	-S		+	A	Port Plati	15/1500	gr	-S	...	...	+	Off Lemnos	
15/1605	br	UNSPARING	Piper	-S		+	A	Port Plati	15/1500	gr	-S	...	...	+	Off Lemnos	
15/1605	br	UNSPARING	Piper	3S		=	A	Port Plati	15/1500	gr	-S	...	...	=	Off Lemnos	
20/							-T		20/0030	dt	APM	...	–	/	Gulf of Genoa	
21/	br	UPSTART	Chapman	-T		/	4-T	Cape Camarat								8
22/							-T		22/	dt	-D	(Convoy)	–	/	SW Cape Camarat	

(1) *Uproar* heard two detonations, but these were D/Cs.
(2) *Untiring* sank an F-lighter.
(3) *Dzik* heard explosions, but the German tanker was unaware of the attack. The Greek crew and 10 Germans were taken prisoner from *Elleni*.
(4) *Unruly* sank six caiques.

(5) *Sibyl* sank two caiques, having taken the Greek crews prisoner.
(6) *Ivagete I* was sunk by an Allied MTB or a mine.
(7) *Capitaine Luigi* sank on a German mine.
(8) *Upstart* missed a large tanker.

1	2	3	4	5	6	7	8	9	10	11	12	13	14	15	16	17
JANUARY 1944 *continued*																
26/0252	br	TORBAY	Clutterbuck	-D		/	5-T	S Amorgos	26/	dt	-D	(Leda)	–	/		1
26/0357	nl	DOLFIJN	Van Oostrom Soede	-D		/	–	S Amorgos	26/	dt	TB	(TA14/Turbine)	–	/		*1*
30/0944	br	UNTIRING	Boyd	-D	7000	/	4-T	43°08N/06°45E								2
30/0944	br	UNTIRING	Boyd	-D	3500	/	"	43°08N/06°45E								2
31/0818	nl	DOLFIJN	Van Oostrom Soede	-D		/	3-T	Aegean Sea	31/0730	dt	-D	(Oria)	–	/	W Stampalia	3
31/1128	br	UNTIRING	Boyd	-D	500	+	4-T	43°24N/06°54E	31/1130	dt	-Bg	Jean Suzon/FP.352	...	+	SE C. Drammont	4
31/1128	br	UNTIRING	Boyd	-D	500	+	"	43°24N/06°54E	31/1130	dt	-Bg	St Antoine/FP.358	...	+	SE C. Drammont	4
31/	br	TORBAY	Clutterbuck	-S			Sp	SE Lemnos	31/2030	gr	-S	...	...	+	S Lemnos	
FEBRUARY 1944																
04/0700	nl	DOLFIJN	Van Oostrom Soede	-S		/	-T	Aegean Sea		it						5
08/	br	SIBYL	Beale	-D		/	2-T	34°40N/25°00E	08/	dt	-T	(Centaur)	–	/		6
08/0324	br	ULTOR	Hunt	-D	4000	+	4-T	Toulon/Cannes	08/	dt	ACM	(Niedersachsen)	–	/	E St Raphael	7
08/0830	br	SPORTSMAN	Gatehouse	-D	4975	+	4-T	35°35N/24°09E	08/0634	dt	-D	Petrella/*Capo Pino/ Aveyron	4785	=	35°34N/24°18E	8
08/1215	br	SPORTSMAN	Gatehouse		4975		1-T	35°35N/24°09E	08/	dt		Petrella/*Capo Pino/ Aveyron	4785	+	35°34N/24°18E	8
08/	gr	PIPINOS	Rallis	-D	2500	/	-T	Off Suda Bay	08/	dt	-D	(Pomona/2198)	–		Suda Bay	9
10/							-T		10/0230	dt	LC	(F...)	–	/	*Off Arbo mouth*	

(1) *Torbay* missed *Leda*, with two T-boats and two R-boats as escort, by underestimating the speed. The subsequent attack by *Dolfijn* on the same target was prevented by *TA14*.

(2) *Untiring* missed two ships in convoy.

(3) All three torpedoes exploded at the ends of their runs.

(4) *Untiring* sank two coasters which were escorted by four vessels.

(5) *Dolfijn* had to abandon the attack because of return fire.

(6) *Sibyl* first missed with two torpedoes, and two other attacks were frustrated by escorts.

(7) *Ultor* heard an explosion, as did *Uproar* nearby, but the German auxiliary minelayer *Niedersachsen* and the steamer *Chisone* were probably missed.

(8) *Sportsman* noticed the letters 'POW' on the ship's side, indicating that there were Italian prisoners-of-war on board, but fired and and hit the ship with two torpedoes. At 1215 the *coup de grâce* was delivered and the ship was sunk, taking with her all but 691 men out of 165 Germans and 3173 Italian POWs.

(9) *Pipinos* missed *Pomona*, which was sunk by aircraft.

1	2	3	4	5	6	7	8	9	10	11	12	13	14	15	16	17
FEBRUARY 1944 *continued*																
15/1522	br	ULTOR	Hunt	-S	50	+	A	S St Raphael	15/	dt	-S	Paule	27	+	NE Hyeres	
15/1706	br	UPSTART	Chapman	-D	3000	+	3-T	43°03N/05°54E	15/1708	dt	ACM	Niedersachsen/ *Acqui/*Guyane	1794	+	43°03N/06°02E	
18/	br	UPSTART	Chapman	SS		/	4-T	Toulon								1
19/0311	br	UNSPARING	Piper	-T		=	1-T	39°31N/23°18E	19/	dt	-D	Peter/*Sifnos	3754	=	39°33N/23°22E	2
22/	br	UNSPARING	Piper	-S		+	A	Off Volos	22/	gr	-S	Evangelistria	...	+		
23/							-T		23/	dt	-Tg	(...)	–	/	W Rhône mouth	
23/									[23/	dt	-D	Lisa/*Livenza/ 5343+]	–		Nr Candia	3
24/	br	UNSPARING	Piper	-S		+	A	Gulf of Salonika								
25/	br	UNSPARING	Piper	-S		+	A	39°55N/24°00E	25/	gr	-S	...	...	+	Chalkidike	4
25/	br	UNSPARING	Piper	-S		+	A	39°55N/24°00E								4
									[25/	gr	-D	Isis/*Isora/316+]	–		3m SW Navarino	5
27/0420	br	UNIVERSAL	Gordon	-T	7000	=	4-T	Cape Camarat	25/0420	dt	-D	Casteriane	6600	=§	E St Tropez	6
29/1440	br	UPROAR	Hunt	-D	3000	+	4-T	43°02N/05°19E	29/1450	it	-D	Chietti/*Artesien	3152	+	Off Cape Cepet	
MARCH 1944																
02/1353	fr	ORPHÉE	Dupont	-D		/	1-T	Barcelona	02/1353	sp	-D	(Virgen de Montserrat/106)	–	/	Off Barcelona	
07/	nl	DOLFIJN	Van Oostrom Soede	-S		+	A	Off Milos								
08/0126	gr	PIPINOS	Rallis	-D		/	3-T	Gulf of Salonika	08/0030	dt	-D	(Burgas)	–	/	Aegean	7
13/	br	ULTOR	Hunt	LC	350	+	1-T	36°41N/23°03E								
14/	nl	DOLFIJN	Van Oostrom Soede	APC		/	3-T	Kaso Strait								8

(1) *Upstart* missed a U-boat leaving Toulon with three torpedoes and missed her again three hours later with the last torpedo when the submarine returned.

(2) *Unsparing* damaged *Peter*, which was escorted by *Drache* and *R195*; the ship was beached. *Peter* was destroyed in Suda Bay on 4.3.44 by air attack, not by the Greek submarine *Pipinos* as is sometimes claimed.

(3) *Lisa* (ex Italian steamer *Livenza*) was sunk by aircraft, not by submarine.

(4) *Unsparing* sank two caiques.

(5) *Isis*/316 (ex *Isora*) was sunk by aircraft.

(6) *Universal* heard a hit. The tanker was towed by the escorts *UJ221*.. and *SG15* to Toulon.

(7) *Pipinos* missed the minelayer *Drache* and the transport *Burgas*.

(8) *Dolfijn* attacked two APMs with three torpedoes but missed.

1	2	3	4	5	6	7	8	9	10	11	12	13	14	15	16	17

MARCH 1944 *continued*

1	2	3	4	5	6	7	8	9	10	11	12	13	14	15	16	17
19/	br	UNSWERVING	Tattersall	-D	2000	/	4-T	Monemvasia	19/0740	dt	-D	(Gertrud/Gerda Toft)	–	/	Cape Maleas	1
20/0545	br	UNSWERVING	Tattersall	-S	70	+	A	35°57N/24°02E	20/0545	gr	-S	...	...	+	30m NNW Rethimnon	
20/							A		20/	dt	APC	GPi 223/Agia	...	+	10m N Akotiri Paraskevi	
21/							2-T		21/0430	dt	APC	(G...)	–	/	Mudros Bay	
26/0500	br	UNSWERVING	Tattersall	-D	2000	/	4-T	35°40N/24°20E	26/0959	dt	-D	(Gertrud/Gerda Toft)	–	/	35°33N/24°18E	1
26/1445	br	UPROAR	Herrick	-T	5000	=	A	Oneglia harbour	26/	dt	-T	Matara/*General Gassouin	5011	=	Oneglia harbour	2
26/							A		26/	tu	-S	...	...	+	Iskenderun	
26/							?		26/	dt	APC	GL58/*Evros	...	+	N Chios	
28/1015	fr	CURIE	Chailley	-D		+	4-T	Cape Cepet	28/1015	dt	APC	UJ6073/Nimet Allah	1710	+§	Off Toulon	
28/2227	br	SPORTSMAN	Gatehouse	-Dc	450	=	1-T	Monemvassia	28/2130	dt	-Dc	MT3/Vienna	425	+	Monemvassia	
28/	br	SPORTSMAN	Gatehouse	APC	40	+	A	Aegean	28/2147	dt	APC	(UJ2147)	–	/	Monemvassia	
30/							-T		[30/	tu	-D	Kron/3359+]	–		N Rhodes	3
30/	br	UPROAR	Herrick	*SS*		/	4-T	*Off Toulon*	*30/0920*	*dt*	*SS*	*(U466)*	–	/	*Off Toulon*	4
31/	br	SPORTSMAN	Gatehouse	-M	200	+	-T	Monemvassia	31/2145	dt	-S	Grauer Ort	212	+	Cape Maleas	

APRIL 1944

1	2	3	4	5	6	7	8	9	10	11	12	13	14	15	16	17
02/	fr	CURIE	Chailley	-Mb		/	A	Cape Camarat	02/1158	dt	AH	(Seenotboot 583)	–	/	Cape St Tropez	
02/	br	UPSTART	Chapman	*LC*		/	4-T	*Cape d'Antibes*								5
03/	br	ULTOR	Hunt	-S	80	+	A	Kyporissi Pt	03/	dt	-S	...	...	+	Kythera	6
03/	br	ULTOR	Hunt	-S	80	=	A	Anti Kythera	03/	dt	-S	...	...	+	Kythera	6
03/	br	ULTOR	Hunt	-S	30	+	A	Pt S. Nikolo, Kythera	03/	dt	-S	...	...	+	Kythera	6
03/	br	ULTOR	Hunt	-S	60	+	A	Pt S. Nikolo, Kythera	03/	dt	-Mbt	...	–	+	Kythera	6

(1) Two torpedoes passed under *TA16/Castelfidardo*. *Gertrud* (ex *Gerda Toft*) was again missed on 26.3.44. *TA17/San Martino* then dropped D/Cs.

(2) *Uproar* reported 16 shell hits.

(3) *Kron* must have been sunk on a mine since there were no Allied or German submarines in the area.

(4) *Uproar* reported no hits.

(5) *Upstart* reported missing a convoy of MFPs with four escorts.

(6) *Ultor* sank three caiques and destroyed one more on the stocks.

1	2	3	4	5	6	7	8	9	10	11	12	13	14	15	16	17
APRIL 1944 *continued*																
04/	br	ULTOR	Hunt	-S	40	+	A	36°49N/23°17E								
05/	br	ULTIMATUM	Kett	-S	40	+	A	Off Suda Bay	05/0745	dt	-S	...	...	+	Suda Bay	
06/	br	ULTOR	Hunt	-S	50	+	A	Kyporissi Pt								
06/	br	ULTOR	Hunt	-S	40	+	A	37°01N/23°09E								
06/	br	ULTOR	Hunt	-S		+	A	37°01N/23°09E								
07/							-T		07/night	dt	-D	(Convoy)	–	/	30m S Spezia	
07/	br	ULTOR	Hunt	-S	200	+	-T	36°40N/23°02E	07/1045	dt	-S	...	...	+	Monemvassia	
10/	br	ULTIMATUM	Kett	-S	40	+	A	Off Suda Bay								
10/	br	ULTIMATUM	Kett	-S	50	+	A	Anti Kythera								
11/0130	br	UNTIRING	Boyd	-D	5000	+	2-T	43°22N/07°00E	10/0134	dt	APM	M6022/*Enseigne	136	+	15m S Cannes	
12/	br	UNTIRING	Boyd	-D	2500	+	4-T	SW Cannes	12/	dt	-D	Cerere	1198	+?		1
12/1420	br	UNTIRING	Boyd	-D	1500	+	2-T	43°25N/06°51E	12/1555	dt	-D	Diana/*Maid of Samos	1190	+	5m S Oneglia	2
12/1625	br	UNSPARING	Piper	-D	2000	=?	4-T	W Rhodes	12/	dt	-D	(Anita)	–	/	SW Kos	3
13/0800	gr	PIPINOS	Rallis	-S		+	R	20m N Suda Bay	13/0830	gr	-S	Taxiarchos	585	+	30m NW Milos	4
14/1032	nl	DOLFIJN	Van Oostrom Soede	APC		/	-T	Aegean Sea	14/morn.	dt	APC	(G....)	–	/	17m N Monemvassia	
15/							-T		15/night	dt	-D	(Convoy)	–	/	E Genoa	
16/0018	br	UNRULY	Fyfe	-D	2000	=?	4-T	Doro Channel	16/morn.	dt	-D	(Brunhilde/*Bacchus)	–	/	25m N Lemnos	5
17/							-T		17/00..	dt	-D	(Convoy)	–	/	20m N Steno Passage	
17/	br	UNRULY	Fyfe	*DD*		=	-T	*Aegean*	17/	dt	-D	(Brunhilde/*Bacchus)	–	/	Doro Passage	5
17/0530	nl	DOLFIJN	Van Oostrom Soede	-S	129	+	A	SW Milos	17/	gr	-S	Hydrea	129	+		
17/1520	nl	DOLFIJN	Van Oostrom Soede	-S	75	+	A	SW Milos	17/	gr	-S	Aghios Georgios Theonie (?)	75	+		
18/							-T		18/2245	dt	APC	(UJ2211, UJ2223)	–	/	S Rapallo	

(1) *Untiring* heard two hits.

(2) *Untiring* reported one hit.

(3) *Unsparing* heard three explosions but there was no hit. The escorting *TA19* was narrowly missed.

(4) *Pipinos* sank a small caique between 13 and 21.4.44.

(5) *Unruly* heard detonations, but they were of D/Cs from *TA19*, which was again narrowly missed.

1	2	3	4	5	6	7	8	9	10	11	12	13	14	15	16	17
APRIL 1944 *continued*																
19/	br	UNRULY	Fyfe	-S	30	+	A	Gulf of Izmir								1
19/	br	UNRULY	Fyfe	-S	30	+	Sp	Gulf of Izmir								1
21/	br	UNRULY	Fyfe	-S	30	+	Spr	N Chios	21/	gr	-S	...	...	+	Chios	2
21/							A		21/	gr	-S	...	...	+	Chios	
23/							A		23/even.	dt	-D	(...)	–	/	Oneglia harbour	
24/	br	UNTIRING	Boyd	APC		+	-T									
24/2127	fr	CASABIANCA	Bellet	-D		=	A	Imperia	24/2127	dt	Dc	(...)	–	/	Imperia	
27/1901	br	UNTIRING	Boyd	APC	1000	+	3-T	42°48N/05°52E	27/even.	dt	APC	UJ6075/*Clairvoyant	943	+	43°01N/05°58E	
28/1634	br	SPORTSMAN	Gatehouse	-D	5830	+	2-T	39°26N/25°07E	28/1638	dt	-D	Lüneburg/*Luxem- bourg	5809	+	4m N Iraklion	3
MAY 1944																
01/0440	br	UNTIRING	Boyd	-D	2000	+	4-T	Port Vendres	01/0945	dt	-D	Siena/*Astrée	2147	+	Port Vendres	
01/dusk	br	ULTIMATUM	Kett	-S		+	A	SE Cape Matapan								
02/1858	br	UPSTART	Chapman	-D	4000	/	2-T	Nice harbour	02/	dt	APC	(FNi-07)	–	/	Nice harbour	4
02/	br	ULTIMATUM	Kett	-S	200	+	A	Gulf of Kalamata								5
02/	br	ULTIMATUM	Kett	-S	100	+	A	Gulf of Kalamata								5
02/	br	ULTIMATUM	Kett	-S		§	A	Gulf of Kalamata								5
02/	br	ULTIMATUM	Kett	4-S		§	A	SW Pt Kalamata								

(1) *Unruly* sank two caiques.

(2) *Unruly* reported a caique flying the Red Cross flag, but carrying German supplies, sunk by demolition charges.

(3) *Lüneburg* was escorted by three T-boats, one R-boat, five A/S vessels and aircraft. Two torpedoes hit.

(4) *Upstart* fired two torpedoes, which missed, at a ship behind the breakwater.

(5) *Ultimatum* bombarded the harbour at Kalamata, sinking two caiques, destroying five on the slips and damaging one other.

1	2	3	4	5	6	7	8	9	10	11	12	13	14	15	16	17
MAY 1944 *continued*																
02/noon	br	SPORTSMAN	Gatehouse	-D	–	–		Anaes Island	02/	dt	-D	(Gertrud/Susanne)	–	/	Piraeus–Crete	1
03/	br	UNSWERVING	Tattersall	-D	–	–		Hydra–Melos	03/	dt	-D	(Gertrud/Susanne)	–	/		1
03/	br	ULTIMATUM	Kett	-S	650	§	A	Koroni/Kalam.								
03/	br	UPSTART	Chapman	*PR*		/	*1-T*	*Ile Ste Honorat*									2
03/	br	UNSWERVING	Tattersall	-S	25	+	A	Gulf of Nauplia								3
03/	br	UNSWERVING	Tattersall	-S	45	+	A	Gulf of Nauplia								3
04/							A	Cannes harbour								
05/	br	UNSWERVING	Tattersall	-S	25	+	A								Gulf of Nauplia	3
05/	br	UNSWERVING	Tattersall	-S		+	A	Gulf of Nauplia								3
05/	br	UNSWERVING	Tattersall	-S		+	A	Gulf of Nauplia								3
08/	br	SICKLE	Drummond	-S	50	+	A	Doro Channel								4
08/	br	SICKLE	Drummond	-S	40	+	S	Doro Channel								4
08/	br	SICKLE	Drummond	-S	20	+	R	Doro Channel								4
08/	nl	DOLFIJN	Van Oostrom Soede	-S		+	A	30m WNW Lettino, Crete								
08/	nl	DOLFIJN	Van Oostrom Soede	-S		+	A	30m WNW Lettino, Crete								
09/2050	fr	LA SULTANE	Javouhey	APC		=	3-T	2m SW C. Ferrat	09/2056	dt		APC	(UJ6070/M6027)	–	/	Villefranche	
11/	br	ULTOR	Hunt	-D	800	+	2-T	Cape Hyères									5
12/	br	SICKLE	Drummond	-S	200	+	A	Standia I.								E Iraklion	6
12/	br	VAMPIRE	Taylor	-S		+	R	Monemvassia									7
12/1933	fr	CURIE	Chailley	-Df		=	A	La Ciotat	12/1933	fr	-Df	(...)		–	/	3m SSE Ciotat	8
12/2052	fr	LA SULTANE	Javouhey	APC	800	=	3-T	2m E Cape Gros	12/2052	dt		APM	(M6020/M6027)	–	/	Cape Antibes	
13/	br	SICKLE	Drummond	-S	200	+	-A	36°00N/25°00E	13/night	dt	-S	...	...	=	N Rethymon	
15/1703	br	ULTOR	Hunt	-Mc	80	= §	A	Briande. Bay	15/after.	fr	-Df	...	...	=	Cape Camarat	
15/							A		15/even.	dt	-S	...	...	+	Off Nysiros	

(1) *Sportsman* tried to attack a convoy with two ships and four escorts but was forced deep before firing. The same convoy was unsuccessfully attacked by *Unswerving*.

(2) *Upstart* missed an R-boat.

(3) *Unswerving* sank two caiques on 3.5.44 and three on 5.5.44.

(4) *Sickle* sank three caiques with gunfire and demolition charges and by ramming.

(5) *Ultor* reported a KT ship sunk with one torpedo hit.

(6) *Sickle* sank a caique at night with radar-controlled gunfire.

(7) *Vampire* sank a small caique by ramming.

(8) *Curie* had to break off the action when her gun jammed. Two hits were observed.

1	2	3	4	5	6	7	8	9	10	11	12	13	14	15	16	17
MAY 1944 *continued*																
17/2104	fr	CURIE	Chailley	-Tg		=	-T	Port Vendres	17/2104	dt	-Tg	(FVe01/Provence/32)	–	/	Port Vendres	1
19/	br	UNSPARING	Piper	-S		+	A	Kamara Bay, Kos								
19/	br	UNSPARING	Piper	-S		+	A	Kamara Bay, Kos								
19/	br	UNSPARING	Piper	-S		=	A	Kamara Bay, Kos								
19/	br	UNSPARING	Piper	-S		=	A	Kamara Bay, Kos								
21/1826	br	UPSTART	Chapman	-D	2954	+	4-T	Port Vendres	21/1830	dt	-D	Tolentino/*Saumur	4898	+	0.5m E Vendres	
22/1247	br	UNIVERSAL	Gordon	PG		+	2-T	*Off Ciotat*	22/	fr	PG	*Ysere*	576	+?	*Le Ciotat harbour*	
23/	br	UNIVERSAL	Gordon	APC		+	2-T	Off Ciotat	23/2346	dt	PE	SG15/Rageot de la Touche	647	+	*Tyrrhenian Sea*	2
25/									[25/	sp	-D	Jose Illueca/648+]	–		Off Port Vendres	3
28/	br	UPSTART	Chapman	PR		/	1-T	*Port Vendres*								4
28/	gr	PIPINOS	Rallis	-D		/	4-T	SW Aegean	28/	sw	-D	(Relief ship)	–	/		5
30/	br	UNRULY	Fyfe	-S		+	S	N of Suda								
30/0657	br	ULTOR	Hunt	ARS	1000	=	4-T	49°10N/06°41E	30/0720	dt	AN	(Netztender 38)	–	/	4m Cape Camarat	6
30/0657	br	ULTOR	Hunt	PR		+	1-T	*49°10N/06°41E*								6
30/0657	br	ULTOR	Hunt	-Bg	400	+	1-T	49°10N/06°41E	30/0720	dt	-Bg	Vinotra III	...	+	4m Cape Camarat	6
31/	br	ULTOR	Hunt	APM	150	+	A	Verte Isle	*31/2220*	dt	LC	(F800)	–	/	*NW La Ciotat*	7
31/	br	ULTOR	Hunt	APM	150	/	A	Verte Isle	*31/2220*	dt	LC	(F814)	–	/	*NW La Ciotat*	7
31/2245	br	ULTOR	Hunt	APM		+	A	Off Cassis	31/	dt	APM	FCi01	...	+	Off Cassis	
JUNE 1944																
01/	br	VOX	Michell	DD		/	4-T	*Off Candia*								8
02/0834	br	ULTOR	Hunt	-D	5000	+	3-T	N Port Vendres	02/0905	dt	APC	SG11/Alice Robert	2588	+	42°30N/09°07E	
04/	br	SICKLE	Drummond	APC		=?	A	Mitylene	04/	dt	APC	(GA75, GA91)	–	/		9
06/1130	br	SICKLE	Drummond	-D	550	+	3-T	38°00N/24°35E	06/1142	dt	-D	Reaumur/*Rigel	549	+	38°24N/24°35E	10
08/							A		08/after.	dt	-S	3 sailing vessels	...	+	N Skopelos	

(1) *Curie* missed a trawler ahead.

(2) *Universal* attacked a beached *Elan* class escort.

(3) The Spanish steamer *Jose Illueca* must have been lost on a mine since no submarine was in the area.

(4) *Upstart* fired at an R-boat which was hove-to, and missed.

(5) *Pipinos* attacked a Swedish relief ship against the sun but, fortunately, missed.

(6) *Ultor* attacked a convoy of eight craft and sank first a salvage vessel with one of four torpedoes and then, with one torpedo, an R-boat alongside a lighter.

(7) *Ultor* attacked two minesweepers with gunfire, blowing up the first one. In fact, two MFPs were missed.

(8) *Vox* missed a destroyer and was attacked with D/Cs.

(9) *Sickle* had a gun duel with the two German patrol vessels. One crew member was washed overboard when *Sickle* dived and was picked up by the Germans.

(10) *Reaumur* was the former Spanish steamer *Rigel*, damaged on 29.5.43 by the Greek submarine *Katsonis* (q.v.). The missing *Sickle* possibly made one other attack.

1	2	3	4	5	6	7	8	9	10	11	12	13	14	15	16	17

JUNE 1944 *continued*

1	2	3	4	5	6	7	8	9	10	11	12	13	14	15	16	17
09/0158	fr	CASABIANCA	Bellet	-Tg	500	?	1TA	43°03N/34°30E	09/0145	dt	APC	(UJ6079/*KT 41*/700)	–	/	E Ile du Levant	
09/0301	br	VIVID	Varley	-D	1545	+	4-T	35°40N/25°11E	09/0313	dt	-D	Tanais	1545	+	35°35N/25°11E	
09/	br	SICKLE	Drummond	-D	1500	/	-T	Off Lemnos	09/	dt	-D	(Lola/309)	–	/	W Lemnos	1
09/1306	br	UNTIRING	Boyd	*PE*	660	/	4-T	*43°03N/05°43E*	09/after.	dt	APC	(UJ6073/Nimeth Allah)	–	/	Off Toulon	2
10/1132	br	UNTIRING	Boyd	APC	800	+	3-T	43°08N/05°36E	10/1132	dt	APC	UJ6078/La Havraise	398	+	La Ciotat	
11/							-T		11/	dt	APC	(V7004)	–	/	Off Monaco	
12/	br	SICKLE	Drummond	-D		?		Steno Pass	12/1200	dt	-D	(Convoy)	–	?	Steno Pass	3
14/	br	VIVID	Varley	-D		/	-T	SW Kos	14/	dt	-D	(Anita)	–	/		
14/							A		14/0645	dt	-S	...	...	+	S Mytilene	
15/							-T		[15/	it	-D	Rapido/5363+]	–		S Grado	4
17/	br	UNSWERVING	Tattersall	-S		+	2-T	Anti Kythera	17/1325	dt	-D	(Convoy)	–	/	Anti Kythera	5
17/	br	UNSWERVING	Tattersall	-S		+	2-T	Anti Kythera								
17/	br	UNSWERVING	Tattersall	*LC*		/	*-T*	*Anti Kythera*								
17/	br	UNIVERSAL	Gordon	-D	3823	+	-T	Off Cassis	17/	it	-D	Canosa/*Sampiero Corsa	3823	+	Off Cassis	
18/	br	ULTOR	Hunt	-Tg		/	1-T	Off Nice								6
20/0751	br	ULTOR	Hunt	*LC*		+	*2-T*	*43°30N/07°20E*	20/	dt	-Tg	Cebre	...	+	S Cannes	7
21/	br	UNSPARING	Piper	APC		+	4-T	Cape Malea	21/1652	dt	APC	UJ2106/Tenedos	460	+	Monemvassia	8
21/	br	UNSPARING	Piper	*LC*		+	*2-T*		*21/1652*	*dt*	*LC*	*SF284*	*110*	+	*Monemvassia*	8
21/	br	UNSPARING	Piper	-Bg		+	-T	Cape Malea	21/	dt	-Bg	Sybille/*Cassion	...	+		
21/	fr	CURIE	Chailley						21/2148	dt	-Bg	(Phare-Flak Abt. 983)	–	/	Port Vendres	

(1) *Sickle* reported an unsuccessful attack.

(2) *Untiring* had a premature explosion of a firing pistol.

(3) *Sickle* made a signal about a convoy and was lost after this report, probably on a mine. The German convoy was escorted by three TA-boats and two R-boats, which reported a trail of oil but no attack by a submarine.

(4) *Rapido* was lost in an air attack or on a mine, but not to a submarine torpedo.

(5) *Unswerving* attacked a group of caiques and two APCs in Patamos Bay and observed heavy explosions. However, all the torpedoes detonated on the rocks.

(6) *Ultor* attacked a tug with an R-boat in tow but was observed and had to break off.

(7) *Ultor* hit a lighter with two torpedoes.

(8) *Unsparing* fired four torpedoes at a steamer and an APC, sinking *UJ2106*, then two single torpedoes were fired against *SF284*, which was picking up survivors.

1	2	3	4	5	6	7	8	9	10	11	12	13	14	15	16	17
JUNE 1944 *continued*																
21/	br	UNIVERSAL	Gordon	APC	250	+	-T	Rion Isle/Toul	21/2224	dt	APC	FMa06	...	+	S Marseille	1
22/0630	br	UNIVERSAL	Gordon	-D	12000	=	4-T	Off Cassis	22/1611	dt	-D	President Dal Piaz	4929	+	Off Cassis	2
22/0630	br	UNIVERSAL	Gordon	-D	6003	+	"	Off Cassis	22/1611	dt	-D	Canosa/*Sampiero Corso/P.8	3823	+	Off Cassis	2
23/	it			*CA*	*11000*	=	LM	*La Spezia*	*23/*	*it*	*CA*	*Bolzano*	*11600*	=§	*La Spezia Roads*	*3*
23/	br	UPSTART	Chapman	*PR*		/	4-T	*Oneglia*								*4*
23/							3-T	Nice	23/1200	dt	APC	(F....)	–	/	Cap Bonet	
23/							"	Nice	23/1200	dt	APC	(F....)	–	/	Cap Bonet	
23/0330	br	VAMPIRE	Taylor	-S		+	AS	Kandeliusa	23/	gr	-S	Abba, KA1610	50	+	Anti Kythera	
23/0330	br	VAMPIRE	Taylor	-S		+	A	Kandeliusa								
23/0330	br	VAMPIRE	Taylor	-S		+	A	Kandeliusa								
23/	br	UNSWERVING	Tattersall	APC		+	A	Skiathos	23/0330	dt	APC	GN61	...	+	Skiathos Passage	5
23/	br	UNSWERVING	Tattersall	APC		+	A	Skiathos	23/	dt	APC	GN62	...	+	Skiathos Passage	5
24/	br	VAMPIRE	Taylor	-S	100	=	A	Mandraki								6
24/	br	VAMPIRE	Taylor	-S	200	=§	A	Mandraki								
24/	br	VAMPIRE	Taylor	-S	40	=	A	Mandraki								
24/	br	VAMPIRE	Taylor	-S	40	=	A	Mandraki								
24/	br	VAMPIRE	Taylor	-S	40	=	A	Mandraki								
27/0504	br	ULTOR	Hunt	-D	3000	+	4-T	43°38N/07°19E	27/0426	dt	-DT	Felix 1/*Cap Blanc	3316	+	Off Nice	7
27/0831	br	ULTOR	Hunt	-D	7000	+	2-T	43°34N/07°15E	27/1000	fr	-DT	Tempo 3/*Pallas	5259	+	Off Nice	7
30/	br	VIGOROUS	Ogle	-S		/	A	N Aegean	*30/morn.*	*dt*	*LC*	*(SGF...)*	–	/	*Chalkidike*	
JULY 1944																
03/0114	br	ULTIMATUM	Kett	APC		=	2-T	Off Toulon	03/	dt	APC	(UJ6073/*Nimet Allah)	–	/	Off Toulon	8
03/	br	UNIVERSAL	Gordon	APC		+	-T	Off Cannes								

(1) *Universal* blew up an A/S yacht with one torpedo.

(2) Both ships were sunk while being prepared for scuttling as blockships at Cassis. *Sampiero Corso* was salvaged in 11/12.45.

(3) The Italian destroyer *Grecale* and the British *MTB74* launched three Italian and two British *Maiali*/chariots which penetrated Spezia Roads and attached limpet mines to *Bolzano*.

(4) *Upstart* attacked an R-boat towing another one, but missed.

(5) *Unswerving* sank two German A/S caiques with gunfire and picked up seven crew members.

(6) On 23.6.44 *Vampire* sank three caiques with gunfire and demolition charges and on 24.6.44 bombarded a large caique, which was beached. One more was hit on the stocks and three others damaged.

(7) *Ultor* first obtained two hits on a 3000grt motor vessel, and in the second attack both torpedoes hit the target. More than 100 D/Cs were dropped by the escort.

(8) *Ultimatum* fired at a destroyer and a UJ and assumed one hit on the latter but it was a premature.

1	2	3	4	5	6	7	8	9	10	11	12	13	14	15	16	17
JULY 1944 *continued*																
03/0140	br	UNRULY	Fyfe	-D	860	=	3-T	Mykonos	03/	dt	-D	(Erpel/Pelikan)	–	/	NE Mykonos	1
03/	br	VOX	Michell	-S	30	+	A	Monemvassia	03/	dt	-S	...	...	+	Monemvassia	
03/	br	VOX	Michell	-S	50	+	A	Monemvassia	03/	dt	-S	...	...	+	Monemvassia	
03/even.	br	UNRULY	Fyfe	-D	800	+	3-T	SW Nikaria	03/1836	dt	-D	(KT-ship)	...	+	Monemvassia	
04/2145	br	VOX	Michell	-S	150	+	3-T	S Santorin	04/	dt	-S	Kal. 14	150	+	Santorin	
10/	br	UNTIRING	Boyd	APC		/	-T	Port Vendres	10/	dt	APC	(V...)	–	/	Off Cannes	2
10/0900	br	VOX	Michell	-D	1200	+	3-T	37°40N/25°00E	10/0957	dt	-D	Anita/*Maria e Jesú/*Arezzo	1165	+	Andros–Tinos	3
11/0422	br	UNRULY	Fyfe	AK	830	=	4-T	S Kos	11/night	dt	-D	(Pelikan)	–	/	W Kos	4
13/0008	fr	*CURIE*	*Chailley*	*LC*		/	*2-T*	*Cape Cepet*	*13/0008*	*dt*	*LC*	*(F812 et al)*	*–*	*/*	*Cape Cepet*	
13/0405	fr	*CURIE*	*Chailley*	*LC*		/	*2-T*	*Cape Cepet*	*13/0405*	*dt*	*LC*	*(F940 et al)*	*–*	*/*	*Cape Cepet*	
13/2144	fr	*CURIE*	*Chailley*	-D		/	4-T	Cape Cepet	13/2144	it	-D	(Pascoli/4139)	–	/	Cape Cepet	
14/1000	br	VIVID	Varley	-D	550	+	2-T	Livadia Bay	14/1030	dt	-D	Susanne/*San Juan	553	+	Livadia Bay	
14/1631	br	UNIVERSAL	Gordon	-S	350	+	TA	Port Vendres	15/1715	sp	-S	Sevillina	...	=	Port Vendres	5
16/	fr	ARCHIMÈDE	Bailleux	-D		/	4-T	Cape Camarat	16/0258	it	-D	(Giorgio/797/SG21/ *Amiral Sénès)	–	/	Cape Camarat	
18/	br	UNSPARING	Piper	-S		/	A	N Suda Bay								6
19/	br	VIVID	Varley	-S	80	+	A	Santorin	18/1930	gr	-Df	...	...	+	NW Dia	
19/	br	VAMPIRE	Taylor	-D	830	/	4-T	Off Milos	19/2300	dt	-D	(Pelikan/TA19)	–	/	Anti Milos	

(1) *Unruly* fired three torpedoes at a KT-ship and assumed one hit.
(2) *Untiring* fired on overlapping A/S vessels, but missed.
(3) *Anita* was damaged and beached, but rolled off and sank in deep water.
(4) *Unruly* attacked *Pelikan* for the second time and assumed one hit, but the attack was not observed by the Germans.

(5) *Universal* attacked a Spanish schooner with three torpedoes and gunfire. The vessel was abandoned, but the submarine was forced to dive by coastal batteries. The schooner continued and was attacked again with two torpedoes and sunk.
(6) *Unsparing* had to break off the attack on two caiques when starshell illuminated the submarine.

1	2	3	4	5	6	7	8	9	10	11	12	13	14	15	16	17
JULY 1944 *continued*																
20/0449	br	UNSWERVING	Tattersall	-D	830	=	3-T	N Suda Bay	20/morn.	dt	-D	(Pelikan/*TA19*)	–	/	Suda Bay	1
21/	br	VIVID	Varley	-S	100	+	A	Santorin	21/	dt	-Tg	...	...	+	Monemvassia	2
21/0043	br	ULTOR	Hunt	-D	500	+	2-T	SW C. Camarat	21/night	dt	APC	UJ2211/Hardy	916	+	6m W Genova	3
22/	br	VIVID	Varley	APC		+	4-T	Suda Bay	22/noon	dt	APC	(GA71/Pétrel VI)	–	/	N Suda Bay	4
26/2330	br	VIRTUE	Cairns	-D		/	4-T	Off Suda Bay	26/	gr	-S	(Doxa)	–	/	Suda Bay	5
27/0100	br	VIGOROUS	Ogle	-S	300	+	A	W Milos	27/0130	gr	-S	Doxa	504	+	18m S Milos	5
27 0130	br	ULTIMATUM	Kett	*LC*		+	4-T	*43°03N/05°34E*	26/noon	dt	LC	F811	168	+	*43°03N/05°34E*	
27 0130	br	ULTIMATUM	Kett	*LC*		=	"	*43°03N/05°34E*									
28/0136	br	UPSTART	Chapman	-D	4000	+	4-T	SE Cap Cepet		it	-D	(Pascoli)	–	/		6
28/	br						-T		28/1620	dt	PR	(R34)	–	/	N Crete	
29/0619	br	VIRTUE	Cairns	-S	80	/	A3T	E Ananes	29/	dt	-S	(...)	–	/	13m SSW Milos	7
30/dawn	br	VIRTUE	Cairns	-D		/	1-T	E Ananes	30/	dt	-D	(Dresden/120)	–	/		7
AUGUST 1944																
01/	br	VOX	Michell	-S	25	+	A	S Santorin								
03/2209	fr	CURIE	Chailley	-D	3000	=	4-T	La Ciotat	03/2213	dt	-D	(Pascoli/4139)	–	/	La Ciotat	8
03/late	br	VOX	Michell	APC		/	2-T	S Santorin									9
04/0200	br	VOX	Michell	*PR*		+	*3-T*	*N Heraklion*	04/0215	dt	APC	GK61/*Pétrel 8	75	+	N Crete	9
04/0215	br	VOX	Michell	-S		+	A	35°52N/28°15E	04/0215	dt	-S	Thetis	...	+	N Crete	9
04/0215	br	VOX	Michell	-S	25	+	A	35°52N/28°15E	04/0215	dt	-S	SA83	...	+	N Crete	9
04/	br	UNIVERSAL	Gordon	APM		+	-T	S France	04/	dt	APM	*Petrel	80	+		

(1) *Unswerving* heard detonations at the end of the torpedoes' runs.

(2) *Vivid* attacked a convoy of four caiques in company with one APC and sank the largest caique.

(3) *Ultor* assumed a coaster sunk, but the victim was in fact an A/S vessel.

(4) *Vivid* assumed one hit but the torpedoes missed.

(5) *Doxa* was first missed by *Virtue* and then sunk by *Vigorous*.

(6) *Upstart* reported two explosions but they were prematures.

(7) *Virtue* first attacked a 80-ton caique with gunfire but the vessel escaped. The submarine then fired torpedoes at other ships, but these missed.

(8) The reported explosion was a premature.

(9) *Vox* attacked a convoy of three caiques and one R-boat, first sinking the latter by torpedo and then surfacing and attacking the caiques with gunfire. One caique was sunk and a second damaged and later sunk.

1	2	3	4	5	6	7	8	9	10	11	12	13	14	15	16	17
AUGUST 1944 *continued*																
07/	br	UNSWERVING	Tattersall	-S		=	A	Aegean								
08/	br	UNIVERSAL	Gordon	APC		=	1-T	Hyères								1
09/	br	VOX	Michell	-Dc		=	A	Off Candia								
09/1705	gr	PIPINOS	Loundras	*TB*		+	4-T	*Karlovassi*	*09/1702*	*dt*	*TB*	*TA19/Calatafimi*	*863*	+	*37°45N/26°59E1*	2
09/1914	gr	PIPINOS	Loundras	-D	800	+	4-T	Karlovassi	09/	dt	-D	(Orion/700)	–	/	Karlovassi harbour	2
09/1914	gr	PIPINOS	Loundras	-Bg	250	+	"	Karlovassi								
09/1914	gr	PIPINOS	Loundras	-Bg	500	+	"	Karlovassi								
10/0100	br	VOX	Michell	APC		/	1-T	Off Santorin	10/morn.	dt	-D	(Convoy)	–	/	Off Heraklion	3
10/	br	VOX	Michell	-S		=	2TA	Off Santorin								3
10/	br	UNSWERVING	Tattersall	-D	1500	+	4-T	Milos	10/	dt	-D	(Toni/*Thalia/638)	–	/	Off Milos	4
11/0115	br	VIVID	Varley	-T	100	=	TA	36°01N/24°05E	11/	dt	-D	(Toni/638)	–	/	Milos–Suda	5
11/								-T	11/	it	-D	Giuseppe Dormio	1008	+	Pola–Fiume	
16/0815	br	VIRTUE	Cairns	-S	20	+	AR	9m S Milos								6
16/0815	br	VIRTUE	Cairns	-S	25	+	AR	9m S Milos								6
16/0815	br	VIRTUE	Cairns	-S	20	+	AR	9m S Milos								6
17/								A	17/night	dt	-S	(...)	–	/	Athens Gulf	
18/								M	[18/	it	-D	Numidia/5339+]	–		Off Parenzo	7
19/	br	VIRTUE	Cairns	-S		+	A	W Milos	19/1900	dt	-S	...	...	+	S Milos	6
21/	br	VIRTUE	Cairns	-S	20	+	A	Cape Spada	21/0730	dt	-S	...	...	+	W Cape Spatha	6
21/	br	VIRTUE	Cairns	-S		+	A	Cape Spada	21/1645	dt	-S	...	...	+	N Cape Spatha	6
	br	VIGOROUS		-S		+	A	Aegean								
	br	VIGOROUS		-S		+	A	Aegean								
25/1006	br	VAMPIRE	Taylor	-S	50	+	A	37°34N/25°30E								8
25/1215	br	VAMPIRE	Taylor	-S	60	+	A	Mykonos								8
25/1215	br	VAMPIRE	Taylor	-S	30	+	A	Mykonos								8

(1) This was the 1,289th and last torpedo fired by a submarine of the 10th Flotilla.

(2) *Pipinos* waited off Karlovassi for *TA19/Calatafimi* for eight hours and sank her when she left harbour. Between 1914 and 1928 she fired four torpedoes at *Orion* behind the breakwater, but the ship suffered only splinter damage.

(3) *Vox* saw the first torpedo run beneath the target and the other two miss. She surfaced, and the caique was slightly damaged by gunfire.

(4) *Unswerving* had one premature and three torpedoes detonating at the end of their runs.

(5) *Vivid* engaged with gunfire and inflicted some damage before being forced to dive by an R-boat.

(6) *Virtue* sank altogether six caiques of 150grt, three by ramming and three with gunfire.

(7) *Numidia* was lost on a mine, not to a submarine torpedo.

(8) *Vampire* sank three caiques with gunfire.

1	2	3	4	5	6	7	8	9	10	11	12	13	14	15	16	17
AUGUST 1944 *continued*																
31/							-T		31/0225	dt	APC	(UJ2171/KFK)	–	/	E Dia Isle	
31/0400	br	VOX	Michell	-D	830	/	4-T	NE Candia								1
31/1148	br	VOX	Michell	-S	25	+	A	35°29N/25°11E								
31/	gr	PIPINOS	Loundras	-Bg		=	-T	Karlovassi								
31/	gr	PIPINOS	Loundras	-Bg		=	-T	Karlovassi								
SEPTEMBER 1944																
01/	br	VOX	Michell	-D	830	/	4-T	W Cape Stavros								2
03/0619	br	VIGOROUS	Ogle	-S		+	3-T	Poximadi I.	03/	dt	-S		...	+		3
03/0619	br	VIGOROUS	Ogle	-S		+	"	Poximadi I.								3
03/	gr	PIPINOS	Loundras	-Dc		+	3-T	Iraklion	03/0615	dt	-Dc	...	...	+	Heraklion	
06/							-T		06/night	dt	AH	(Seenotboot ...)	–	/	Mirabella/Crete	
06/	gr	PIPINOS	Loundras	-D	830	=	4-T	Off Candia	06/0426	dt	APC	(UJ2171/KFK)	–	/	N Cape Stavros	4
07/	gr	PIPINOS	Loundras	-S	200	/	1-T	Off Candia								5
09/							-T		09/	dt	PR	(R.., G...)	–	/	Suda Bay	
10/1540	br	VIVID	Varley	-D		/	4-T	Skiathos								6
12/	br	VIRTUE	Cairns	APC		/	3-T	NW Psathura	12/2335	dt	-D	(Convoy)	–	/	Tira–Heraklion	7
13/							?		13/	it	-D	Thalia	638	+	Santorin	
13/0600	br	VIRTUE	Cairns	AK	830	=	3-T	Skiathos Channel	13/0854	dt	AN	(Piräus/670)	–	/	Milos	8
14/							A		14/0018	dt	-D	(Convoy)	–	/	Santorin–Heraklion	
14/							-T		14/06..	dt	APC	GK06	...	+	35m N Heraklion	
15/	br	VORACIOUS	Challis	APC		/	3-T	Skopelos Channel	15/2110	dt	APC	(UJ2110)	–	/	5m N Skopelos	

(1) *Vox* missed a KT-ship.
(2) *Vox*'s torpedoes were evaded.
(3) *Vigorous* attacked a convoy comprising caiques and a R-boat and sank one caique.
(4) *Pipinos* assumed a hit, but air reconnaissance reported the ship undamaged in port.
(5) *Pipinos* was hit in the conning tower by gunfire from the caique.
(6) *Vivid* missed an escorted ship.
(7) *Virtue* missed an A/S trawler.
(8) *Virtue* heard an explosion but this must have been a premature.

1	2	3	4	5	6	7	8	9	10	11	12	13	14	15	16	17
SEPTEMBER 1944 *continued*																
17/	br	VORACIOUS	Challis	-D		/	4-T	Skopelos Channel								1
21/2354	br	VOX	Michell	-D	200	=	A	37°29N/25°46E								2
21/2354	br	VOX	Michell	APC		=	A	37°29N/25°46E								2
22/							-T		22/night	dt	APC	(G...)	–	/	SW Ikaria	
22/1356	br	VAMPIRE	Varley	-D	3000	+	4-T	5m N Skiathos	22/1258	dt	-D	Peter/*PLM16	3754	+	Volos Gulf	3
23/0918	br	VAMPIRE	Varley	APC		/	4-T	N Skiathos	23/night	dt	APC	(UJ2102)	–	/	Cape Sunion	3
24/1817	br	VISIGOTH	Haddow	-S	Large	=	A	Strati harbour								4
24/1817	br	VISIGOTH	Haddow	-S	Large	=	A	Strati harbour								
24/2022	br	VOX	Michell	-S	80	+	A	39°44N/23°30E								
24/2212	br	VIGOROUS	Ogle	-S	80	+	A	SE Cape Drepano	24/	dt	-S	...	...	+	E Cassandra	
25/1917	br	VOX	Michell	-S	80	+	A	39°34N/23°04E	25/	gr	-S	Vol	54	+	Cassandra	
25/1922	br	VISIGOTH	Haddow	-S		/	4-T	Mudros								4
26/2320	br	VIGOROUS	Ogle	-D	1500	+	4-T	SE Saloniki	26/even.	dt	-D	Salomea	751	=	S Cassandra	
27/2200	br	VIGOROUS	Ogle	*LC*		+	2-T	*Cassandra Gulf*	27/	*dt*	*LC*	*SF121*	*110*	+	*Cassandra*	
27/2200	br	VIGOROUS	Ogle	-D		+	"	Cassandra Gulf	27/	dt	-D	Salomea	750	+		
28/2314	br	VOX	Michell	-Bg	500	+	3-T	39°28N/23°11E								
29/0430	br	VOX	Michell	-Bg		/	3-T									5
29/	br	VIGOROUS	Ogle	-Bg		/	2-T	N Skiathos								6
OCTOBER 1944																
01/	br	VISIGOTH	Haddow	-Bg		/	3-T	Off Nikaria								7
02/	br	UNSWERVING	Tattersall	-D			3-T	Cape Cassandra	02/1033	dt	ACM	(Zeus)	–	/	6m SSE Cassandra	8

(1) *Voracious* missed a merchant ship, the torpedoes running under the target.

(2) *Vox* damaged a coaster and a caique with gunfire.

(3) *Vampire* first hit *Peter* with two torpedoes and sank her; on 23.9.44 *UJ2102* evaded the torpedoes and attacked with D/Cs.

(4) *Visigoth* attacked several caiques in Strati harbour and damaged some of them. The next day a convoy with two caiques and three APMs was missed.

(5) *Vox* fired four torpedoes at a Danubian barge but they exploded prematurely.

(6) *Vigorous* missed a large escorted barge.

(7) *Visigoth* missed an escorted lighter.

(8) *Zeus* was being escorted by *TA37/Gladio* on a minelaying sortie.

1	2	3	4	5	6	7	8	9	10	11	12	13	14	15	16	17

OCTOBER 1944 *continued*

1	2	3	4	5	6	7	8	9	10	11	12	13	14	15	16	17
02/2104	fr	CURIE	Chailley	-D	2500	+	4-T	39°20N/23°20E	02/1904	dt	-D	Zar Ferdinand	1994	+	19m NW Skiathos	1
03/0113	br	UNSWERVING	Tattersall	-DT	1810	+	3-T	10mE C. Sepias	03/0118	dt	-DT	Berta/*Brunhild/ *Bacchus	1810	+	4m S Cassandra	1
03/2055	fr	CURIE	Chailley	APC	125	+	3-T	Skiathos	03/2055	dt	APC	GM03/*11V3/*Netz- tenderXII/*Salamis	125	+	Skiathos	
04/							-T		04/	dt	LC	SF191	220	+	8m N Skiathos	
04/1447	br	UNTIRING	Boyd	*DD*		/	4-T	*Cape Cassandra*	04/	dt	-TB	(TA18/Solferino)	–	/		
05/	br	UNTIRING	Boyd	-S	80	+	A	Cape Cassandra								2
05/1100	br	UNTIRING	Boyd	-D 2		/	4-T	Cape Cassandra	05/	dt	-D	(Burgas)	–	/		
07/1609	br	UNTIRING	Boyd	*LC*		=	A	*W Lemnos*								2
08/	gr	MATROZOS	Massouridis	-D		/	A	W Chios	08/	dt	-D	(Achilles)	–	/		
08/	br	VIVID	Varley	-D		+	-T	NW Chios	08/	dt	-D	Achilles	1150	+		3
08/	br	VIVID	Varley	-S		+	A	NW Chios	08/	dt	-Tg	Horst	210	+	Aegean	3
08/	br	VIVID	Varley	-S		+	A	NW Chios	08/	dt	-Tg	Paul	...	+		3
09/1100	br	VIRTUE	Cairns	-S	35	+	A	35°25N/24°57E	09/	gr	-S	Aghios Matthaios	35	+	Aegean	4
10/0710	br	VIRTUE	Cairns	-S	50	+	A	35°32N/25°03E	10/	gr	-S	Aghia Anna	50	+	Aegean	4
10/0930	br	VIRTUE	Cairns	-S	150	+	A	35°31N/25°12E	10/	gr	-S	Sophia	150	+	Aegean	4
11/1258	br	VIRTUE	Cairns	-T	200	+	A	S Cape Dhia								4
11/1258	br	VIRTUE	Cairns	-S	40	+	A	S Cape Dhia								4
11/1258	br	VIRTUE	Cairns	-Mb	20	+	A	S Cape Dhia								4
28/	br	VAMPIRE	Taylor	AH		P	P	Saloniki	28/	dt	AH	Gradisca	13870	P		5

(1) The convoy with the two ships was escorted by *TA18/Solferino*, *UJ2102*, *UJ2144* and two patrol vessels.

(2) *Untiring* first sank a caique with gunfire and hours later missed a merchant ship, misidentified as *Burgas*, which evaded the torpedoes. The escorting *UJ2102* also evaded the torpedoes and erroneously claimed the submarine sunk. On 7.10.44 a lighter picking up survivors from vessels sunk by aircraft was missed.

(3) *Vivid* first sank the concrete transport *Achilles* by torpedo and then the two tugs, identified as caiques, were scuttled.

(4) *Virtue* sank four caiques and a water tanker.

(5) *Gradisca* was suspected of carrying German soldiers purporting to be wounded and was escorted to Chios.

VI. Pacific

This chapter details the attacks made on Japanese vessels by Soviet submarines in August 1945 in the Sea of Japan and the Sea of Okhotsk. The information provided in the Soviet and Japanese sources differs, but the data that follow are likely to be correct. Sources for this section are as follows:

Soviet

'Velikaya Otechestvennaya. Den' za dnem. Iz khroniki boevykh dejstvij VMF v August i Septembr 1945 gg'. *Morskoj sbornik*, 8/9/1995.

Boevaya deyatel'nost' podvodnykh lodok Voenno-Morskogo Flota SSSR v Velikuyu Otechestvennuyu vojnu 1941–1945 gg. Edited by G. I. Shchedrin et al. Vol. III: *Glava 10: Boevaya Dejetel'nost' podvodnykh lodok Tikhookeanskogo flota*. Moscow: Voenizdat, 1969/70. Not accessible prior to the period of *glasnost*.

Bozhenko, .V. 'Podvodniki Tikhookeantsy v boyakh s protivinkom (1941–1945 gg.)'. *Tajny podvodnoj vojny*. Moskva, 1995, pp.13–35.

Strelbitskii, K. B., *August 1945: Sovetsko-japonske vojna na more*. Tsena Pobedy. Lvov, 1996.

Japanese

Kôseisho Engokyoku, *Sônan Kansen Meibo* (list of shipping disasters in World War II), pp.192–3.

Karafuto Shsenshi (The War's End. History of Sakhalin). Tokyo, pp. 335–45.

Correspondence with Captain Prof. Kawano, Teruaki, Tokyo; the National Institute for Defense Studies, Tokyo; and Rolf Erikson, Phoenix, USA.

1	2	3	4	5	6	7	8	9	10	11	12	13	14	15	16	17
AUGUST 1945																
09/1147	sj	L-17	Kislov	AM		/	–	E Seishin								1
12/1526	sj	SC-119	Kalashnikov	-D		/	–	W Maoka								2
13/1012	sj	SC-119	Kalashnikov	-D	1500	/	3-T	W Maoka					–	/		3
13/1152	sj	SC-119	Kalashnikov	AM		/	1-T	W Maoka					–	/		4
15/14..	sj	SC-127	Melnikov	-D		/	–	41°10N/135°00E								5
19/1155	sj	SC-122	Kuznetsov	*SS*		/	–	*E Seishin*								6
21/1615	sj	SC-126	Morozov	-Mbt		+		50A	Sea of Japan							7
22/0511	sj	L-12	Shchelgantsev	-D	4000	/	3-T	40m Rumon/ Hokkaido	22/0422	jp	AG	Ogasawara Maru	1403	+	43°50N/141°13E	8
22/0518	sj	L-12	Shchelgantsev	-D	10000	+	3-T	6m S Rumon/ Hokkaido	22/0455	jp	AG	Shinkô Maru 2	2577	=	44°15N/141°26E	9
22/0957	sj	L-13	(?)	-D		?	-T	Off Abashiri/	22/....	jp	-D	Daito Maru 49	...	+	44°05N/144°28E	10
22/1142	sj	L-12	Shchelgantsev	-D	5950	+	3-T	Rumon/Hokkaido	22/1020	jp	-D	Taito Maru	887	+	44°04N/141°27E	9
22/2058	sj	L-12	Shchelgantsev	-D		/	–	Rumon/Hokkaido								11
22/2200	sj	L-19	Kononenko	-D	8000	+	-T	Cape Nashi/ Hokkaido	22/	jp	-D	Tetsugo Maru	...	=	W Laperouse Strait	12
23/	sj	L-19	Kononenko	–			-T	N Hokkaido	23/	jp	PE	*Kaibokan 75 (?)*	745	+	*Wakkanai, N Hokkaido*	12
24/	sj	S-52	Fomenko	APC		/	–	Rumon/Hokkaido								13

(1) Attack prevented by air attack.

(2) Attack on a group of vessels prevented, 12 D/Cs dropped.

(3) Attack missed target.

(4) Torpedo missed target; 12 D/Cs dropped.

(5) Attack on a group of vessels prevented.

(6) Attack on submarine not completed.

(7) Motorboat sunk by 50 × 45mm shells.

(8) First attack with three torpedoes assumed unsuccessful, but the Communications Department submarine cable ship *Ogasawara Maru* was probably sunk. Five D/Cs were dropped.

(9) In the first attack the Navy Special Service ship was only damaged and arrived at 0900 in Rumon harbour. In the second attack the transport *Taito Maru* was sunk; 553 men perished.

(10) *Daito Maru 49* was lost in *L-13*'s area of operations.

(11) Attack prevented.

(12) According to Soviet sources, *Tetsugo Maru* (not identified) was damaged. This must have been in the attack made by *L-19*, lost on a mine in the Laperouse Strait. The Japanese corvette *Kaibokan 75*, missing since leaving Wakkanai harbour, Hokkaido, on 23.8.45, may also have been a victim of *L-19*, but her loss to a mine is a possibility.

(13) No Japanese report.

Index of Submarines

Index of Commanding Officers

Note: Entries are arranged according to family name, with initals of forenames. Nationality and rank are given in parentheses, the British equivalents being as follows:

Abbreviation		Rank	Equivalent
am	LtCdr	Lieutenant-Commander	Lieutenant-Commander
am	Cdr	Commander	Commander
br	SL	Sub-Lieutenant	Sub-Lieutenant
br	Lt	Lieutenant	Lieutenant
br	LtCdr	Lieutenant-Commander	Lieutenant-Commander
br	Cdr	Commander	Commander
fr	EV	Enseigne de vaisseau de 1ère classe	Lieutenant
fr	LV	Lieutenant de vaisseau	Lieutenant-Commander
fr	CC	Capitaine de corvette	Commander
fr	CF	Capitaine de frégate	Commander
gr	LtCdr	Plotarchis	Lieutenant-Commander
gr	Cdr	Antiploiarchos	Commander
nl	Lt	Luitenant ter Zee der 2de klass	Lieutenant
nl	LtCdr	Luitenant ter Zee der 1ste klass	Lieutenant-Commander
nl	Cdr	Kapitein-Luitenant ter Zee	Commander
nw	Lt		Lieutenant
nw	LtCdr		Lieutenant-Commander
pl	LtCdr		Lieutenant-Commander
pl	Cdr		Commander
sj	SL	Starshi-Leitenant	Lieutenant
sj	KL	Kapitan-Leitenant	Lieutenant-Commander
sj	K3R	Kapitan 3. ranga	Commander
sj	K2R	Kapitan 2. ranga	Commander
sj	K1R	Lapitan 1. ranga	Captain

Index of Ships Attacked

Names of warships appear in *italics*